The publisher gratefully acknowledges
the generous contribution to this book provided by
the Samuel H. Kress Foundation
and by the Art Book Endowment Fund
of the Associates of the University of California Press,
which is supported by a major gift from
the Ahmanson Foundation.

PORTRAYED ON THE HEART

PORTRAYED ON THE HEART

Narrative Effect in Pictorial Lives
of Saints from the Tenth through the
Thirteenth Century

CYNTHIA HAHN

UNIVERSITY OF CALIFORNIA PRESS
BERKELEY   LOS ANGELES   LONDON

University of California Press
Berkeley and Los Angeles, California

University of California Press, Ltd.
London, England

© 2001 by the Regents of the University of California

Library of Congress Cataloging-in-Publication Data

Hahn, Cynthia J. (Cynthia Jean)
   Portrayed on the heart : narrative effect in pictorial lives of saints
from the tenth through the thirteenth century / Cynthia Hahn.
      p.   cm.
   "Ahmanson-Murphy fine arts imprint."
   Includes bibliographical references and index.
   ISBN 0-520-22320-9 (cloth : alk. paper)
      1. Christian hagiography.   2. Christian saints in art.
   3. Illumination of books and manuscripts, Medieval.
   4. Christian art and symbolism—Medieval, 500–1500.   I. Title.
   BX4662 .H34   2001
   760'.044863—dc21   2001027319

Manufactured in Canada

10   09   08   07   06   05   04   03   02   01
10   9   8   7   6   5   4   3   2   1

The paper used in this publication meets the minimum requirements
of ANSI/NISO Z39.48-1992 (R 1997) *(Permanence of Paper)*.♾

For Rick, Ted, and Meara

It is better to copy the examples of the saints in the heart than to carry bones in bags, to have gospel teachings in one's mind than to carry them round one's neck written on scraps of parchment.

—Alcuin, letter no. 290

CONTENTS

PREFACE

This book is the product of many years of thinking about, looking at, and writing about Lives of saints. When I first began this project as a dissertation twenty years ago, the study of saints' Lives remained very much the domain of religious scholars and hagiographic specialists. In the time since, a torrent of studies of more general interest has been produced and published, including a book of my own. Although I have obviously benefited from this scholarly abundance, the core of what I write here is based on questions about hagiographic narrative that I first posed in those early years. My hope is that this study offers a coherent and sustained response to those "first" questions.

One consistent concern has been to understand how saints were perceived in their time, to understand how narratives worked on their audiences—even to ask why anyone took the trouble in the first place. After all, the decision to illustrate a book would not have been entered into lightly: it entailed a great deal of effort and thought, and, I think, usually can be assumed to have had a serious purpose. So, in this study, I do not linger on lost models nor do I often assume that "scribal" error explains unusual results. I take the books as I find them.

But "taking them as I find them" extends as a principle beyond the question of manuscripts as objects. It also applies to the texts of the Lives and even to the saints themselves. In this study, I am not concerned with whether events that are told in saints' Lives ever happened, whether they happened in the order in which they are told or with the detail with which they are related. In fact, I do not consider whether the saints that will be discussed ever lived (and indeed, Margaret of Antioch has been swept from the Canon by the Catholic Church for lack of such evidence). With these principles in mind, I have turned to the Lives themselves, which have proved remarkably rich, complex, subtle, and self-reflexive when considered as objects in and of themselves. It has truly been a stimulating and enjoyable experience to spend time among them.

Along the way, I have also had the privilege of sharing ideas and friendship with many other scholars; foremost among these have been my students. In fact, in writing this book I have kept graduate students very much in mind as a primary audience. The "project" has inspired many seminars and paper topics as I have used my teaching to further my understanding of issues encountered in the research. The first paper was Christine Sauer's senior thesis on All Saints' imagery in my first year of teaching, later published in *Kloster Fulda*. One of the more recent was Jane Chung's dissertation on the Paris manuscript of Guillaume de Saint-Pathus's Life of St. Louis. Other students who have contributed ideas in papers and classes include David Areford, Carla Funk, Anne Heath, Kimberley Kelly, Areli Marina, and Steve Wagner. At the University of Michigan I gave a seminar on "the saints' book" to see how it would go over with a fresh audience. The experience was tremendously rewarding; for their contributions I thank Linda Bangert, Lisa Bessette, Jane Chung, Rebecca Garber, Michele McNulty, Martin Walsh, and John Wickstrom—the last two, visiting colleagues from departments of theater and history, respectively.

Among mentors and fellow scholars, Sandra Hindman must be singled out for her suggestion—indeed, her *insistence*—that I write this book. Thomas Head has taken a preeminent place as a continuing intellectual companion who has challenged me, corrected me, inspired me, and also just been a good friend. The loosely and informally constituted pictorial hagiography study group has also been an inspiration: Barbara Abou-el-Haj, Magdalena Carrasco, Marilyn Schmitt, and Rosemary Argent Svoboda. (Our informal archive at the Getty Center was facilitated by Fran Terpak.)

Other art historians who served as readers, inspirations, and sounding boards have included Jonathan Alexander, Karen Bearor, Brigitte Buettner, Robert Deshman, Jack Freiberg, Paula Gerson, Anne Hedeman, Henry Maguire, Jim Marrow, Elizabeth McLachlan, Larry Nees, Barbara Shailor, Pamela Sheingorn, Dorothy Verkerk, and, of course, my dissertation adviser, Herb Kessler, who has always been both generous and demanding.

Historians have also listened to my ideas, encouraged, and helped. I must mention Peter Brown, John Coakley, Giles Constable, Patrick Geary, Antonia Gransden, Warren Hollister, Susan Ridyard, Sally Vaughn, and last but surely not least, my colleague Ralph Turner. Students of medieval literature who have encouraged me to trespass upon their domain include Susan Bielstein, Renate Blumenfeld-Kosinski, Kathryn Gravdal, Pat Hermann, Lori Walters, and above all Gene Vance, who has always been an inspiration.

A number of institutions have been essential in the production of this book. Foremost are the keepers and libraries that hold the manuscripts: François Avril at the Bibliothèque nationale in Paris, Bernard Meehan at Trinity College Library, Dublin, Roger Wieck at the Morgan Library, Godfrey Waller at the Cambridge University Library, and Janet Backhouse at the British Library all were very gracious with their help. Frauke Steenbock made my work in the Berlin Kupferstichkabinett a special delight. I also thank the Bibliothèque royale in Brussels, the Bodleian Library, the Burgerbibliothek in Bern, the Hannover Niedersächsische Landesbibliothek, the Preußischer Staatsbibliothek in Berlin, the Vatican Library, and the Municipal Libraries in Poitiers, Saint-Omer, Saint-Quentin, Tours, Troyes, and Valenciennes for their hospitality.

Grants from the Fulbright Foundation, the National Endowment for the Humanities, Florida State University, and Dumbarton Oaks were invaluable for research in Europe as well as time to catch up on all those new hagiography books. The Department of Art History at Rutgers University gave me a place to work during the sabbatical year that I spent writing. Again, my sincerest thanks to all of these people and institutions.

Of course, finally, my biggest debt is due to my husband, Richard, and my children, Ted and Meara. They sustained me through it all.

INTRODUCTION

In the eleventh-century manuscript of the Life of Liudger of Werden, the saint is introduced as a child in a miniature that shows him busy at a remarkable task (fig. 1). Rejecting the games of other children, he is making books, writing in them, and studying them. When asked how he has learned these skills, he answers simply, "God taught me."[1] Although the miniature underscores the continuity of Liudger's activity under the blessing and guiding hand of God, it also depicts a seemingly momentary gesture: the child makes a gift of one of his books to an enthroned female figure.

In recounting this incident, the saint's written *vita,* or Life, mentions only the presence of a nurse. However, this royally dressed woman with two attendants, seen against a gold ground within a grand building, is no mere servant: she is the saint's holy mother, mentioned earlier in the Life and here depicted as Ecclesia, the Church personified.[2] The miniature reverses modern expectations. This is not a child eagerly showing his mother what he has made, but rather the infant saint, occupied with learning and serving the Church. He is *puer senex,* the "old" or wise child.

The learned child is a saintly common-place (*lieu commun*), or *topos,* ultimately tracing its origin to the account of the Christ child who taught the elders of the Temple, doing his "Father's business" (Luke 2:42–52). Like the Christ child, the future bishop Liudger here precociously inaugurates his vocation, a life of learning, authority, and service to his "mother," the Church. However, Liudger does not merely study books; he also makes them. Furthermore, rather than copies of the works of spiritual or classical authorities, the books he is making are his own, and they are shown to be worthy gifts to the Church. In short, this miniature characterizes Liudger as born into a life of texts and text-making. Given that Liudger is

Figure 1. Liudger makes books, *Life of Liudger of Münster,* Werden, c. 1100.
Berlin, Staatsbibliothek, Cod. lat. theol. fol. 323, fol. 4v. (Staatsbibliothek
zu Berlin, Preußischer Kulturbesitz)

not known for writing theological treatises or other scholarly texts, surely what he
"writes" can only be the text of his own saintly Life.

This remarkable image of saintly text-making has significance beyond its place
in one saint's Life. The infant saint's activity is a richly evocative metaphor for the
medieval production of holy Lives, intimating their qualities of imputed self-fash-
ioning and of insistent intertextuality. We find this suggestive metaphor recurring
throughout the Middle Ages in a number of revealing contexts.

In the living of a holy life, saints were said to actively follow the "books" of other
saints and that of Christ. Numerous examples tell of saints reading the texts of other
saints' Lives in order to imitate them. As in Liudger's case, the intertextual force
of the metaphor becomes even more striking when the physical qualities of books
themselves come into play. One writer of the twelfth century describes a holy
woman seeking pious inspiration by inspecting "the impress of the letters" of a Life.[3]

Most dramatically, rather than codices, the books of the saints were even figured as "written" bodies. The fourth-century poet Prudentius, citing a form of writing familiar in his time, compares the bloody wounds pricking the skin of a martyr to the stylus pricks marked into a wax diptych.[4] A thirteenth-century example is most vivid of all: "[He was author of] the book . . . because He suffered of His own will. The small and black letters of it were written on the parchment as it were of His own body, the red letters and capitals by the piercing of the nails . . . parchment [that had] been polished beforehand by many a blow, . . . and lined with the reed."[5] This last book is, of course, required reading for all saints: it is the book of salvation written by Christ.

Finally, the dedication poem for a collection of illustrated saints' Lives includes pictures in the metaphor. The tenth-century Byzantine writer describes the book's illuminations and text as an image of the court of heaven. The poem is addressed expressly to those who see and emphatically implicates the sense of sight:

> Beholders, duly contemplate here the most exquisite of works, containing the best deeds, a most beautiful work of God, astonishing to the mind, a work which, with reason, fills the whole creation with joy . . . a book truly like unto another Heaven, stretched out from sheets of leather provided by nature. This book contains beautiful images like stars, . . . eager mediators before the Lord at the time of Judgement, and providers of ineffable glory and the Kingdom of God.[6]

I know of no Western example in which illustrations are part of the book metaphor, but this poet's version properly highlights the importance of visual elements. Like the literary practice of *ekphrasis,* the metaphor of "Life as book" insists upon visual perception as part of the textual imagination. Thus, as writer and artist of his or her own Life, the saint reads and sees other Lives and the Life of Christ and, in finding grace, reproduces those texts on his own body, on her own skin.

The metaphor of the Life as book underscores several issues essential to this study. Foremost is the general and specific importance of the visual in the intertextual creation of saints' Lives. The visual is demonstrably effective: Augustine heard the story of Anthony and converted, and Margaret read the stories of virgin saints and imitated them; in the same manner, Asterios of Amaseia was moved by the painted acts of martyrs.[7] More specifically, visual details "read" in the Lives of saints can expand understanding. In Liudger's Life, the elements of the illustration—a pictured hand of God and Ecclesia—decisively amplify the significance of the text. The divine hand blesses and controls the "scribal" copying of Christ's Life into that of the saint, producing a fitting narrative that will ultimately find its place in the service of the Church.

Finally, the miniature of the child Liudger introduces a number of other points that will be important throughout this study: the alien and extraordinary nature of saintly miracle; the figurative, metaphorical, or perhaps even typological quality of saintly action; questions of narrative versions and narrative production (the many books); and the ways in which saints fulfill expectations of saintly types.

Considered from a different perspective, Liudger's efforts at text-making are an equally apt metaphor for more contemporary labors. Today the Lives of saints are again associated with a prodigious making of books; scholars and students have turned their attention to reading and writing about the Lives with exemplary fervor.[8] Moreover, in an intriguing coincidence of terminology, the work of contemporary critical reading of saints' Lives is called by the same term—hagiography—as is that of the original writing of the texts in the Middle Ages. Even if they often work against the grain of the texts they read, today's hagiographers do in some sense continue to "make books" of the saints.

The present book is thus one of many, but I hope has its own valuable perspective. Although reading against the text—finding substance in subtexts and erasures—has been a fruitful modern approach to hagiography, in the main I take a different tack. There is still much of interest to learn from reading *with* the texts. The narratives, their strategies, and their constructions, especially as expressed in images, remain relatively unexplored.[9] One particular aspect of hagiography that has received scant attention is the question of the audience's effect on and in saints' Lives. Some consideration has been given to the issue of who read particular Lives, but little has been said about how audiences shaped the Lives they read, or, more precisely, how hagiographers took account of audience concerns and reactions in their works. Speaking as part of the audience created by the text, Evelyn Birge Vitz writes perceptively:

> Our desire does more than merely frame and echo the desires expressed within the story being told: it is the very condition of the existence of this text; without us this saint's life—this hagiographical text—would not exist. . . . The process by which a saint and a hagiographical work came into existence required three subjects: God, the saint, and the people.[10]

The audience's desires have yet to be thoroughly explored in textual studies; they have virtually gone unmentioned in art history.[11]

This absence is problematic, given that an act of reception stands at the very origin of pictorial hagiography.[12] With few exceptions,[13] artists or patrons of illustrated saints' Lives read or heard texts before they conceived of pictorial representations of saints. Furthermore, the saints they considered were often those of the most ancient and venerable cults. For example, the manuscript Life of Liudger illustrated a text that was already some two centuries old. Rather than considering new saints and new texts that might better represent contemporary cultural expectations, pictorial hagiographers for the most part "updated" older saints for present use.[14] In this way, illustrated saints' Lives constitute an ideal opportunity for the study of text and image. They provide an almost archaeological layering of successive "receptions" of sanctity. Text begat image begat text, in an endless succession of narrative production.

The chapters that follow bear witness to this fluid interpenetration of reading, hearing, and viewing in saints' Lives. From the tenth through the thirteenth century, no other textual genre seems to have been as important to such a wide audience and yet so flexible and responsive to that audience. The images that were created in the literal midst of these texts share a similar fluidity in generating meaning and response.

To understand how meaning and response are evoked, we must view saints' Lives as products of a genre that is concomitantly literary and artistic. Hagiographic narratives produce effects in large part by means of generic expectations, but the genre is neither monolithic nor simple. From the early Middle Ages, hagiography comprised a number of subgenres or types. Indeed, any collection of hagiographic materials not organized by feast day (as were, for example, legendaries), was organized according to *types* of saints.[15] In one particularly clear schema—the prologue to the *Vita s. Martini Vertavensis*—Letaldus of Micy, an eleventh-century monk of Fleury, defines several types of saints by how they teach about God: "The patriarchs and prophets looked to the future, the apostles taught what they knew directly, the martyrs spoke through their blood and the confessors continue to express *virtus* equivalent to that of the martyrs, although in different circumstances."[16] Letaldus rationalizes the medieval tendency to classify the saints by linking their positions to knowledge informed by time: the prophets knew the future, as the apostles knew Christ, giving both tremendous prestige but a certain remoteness. The martyrs spoke with their blood, a physical sign that might and often does endure as a relic, giving an immediacy to their testimony. Finally, although they were not martyred, it is the confessors who sustain the tradition into the present. Clearly, for Letaldus, saintly type is essential to understanding the powers of the saints.

Perhaps the most familiar example of the categorization of types is the Litany, a part of the liturgy in which the Christian asks that each of a series of saints "Pray for me."[17] By the ordering and grouping of names, the Litany classifies these saints into categories—usually those of patriarchs, prophets, apostles, martyrs, virgins, and confessors.

The classes of saints were also rendered visually—in images such as the All Saints' illustration in the Göttingen Sacramentary or the death of St. Omer in his *vita*. The Göttingen miniature illustrates the Feast of All Saints on the first of November with a hierarchy of saints, arranged in the choirs of the court of heaven (fig. 2).[18] For the tenth-century artist of the sacramentary, as for Letaldus, the patriarchs, prophets, and apostles are distant in time and space. They assume the anonymity of a crowd, clustered around the Lamb of God, along with the angels and Mary. The saintly types of more contemporary concern take up the lower ranks. In the second row, next to the figure of Ecclesia (who holds a cup to catch Christ's blood) are the virgins; to the left are the martyrs. Beneath them, an entire row of confessors is divided into monks on the right, and lay figures and bishops on the left. Some of the saints make gestures that we might interpret as the prayers of intercession for which the Litany pleads.

In the eleventh-century miniature of the death of St. Omer, the classes of saints are labeled with phrases from a hymn to the saint: archangels, prophets, apostles, martyrs, confessors, and virgins (fig. 3).[19] The choirs of saints welcome their new member to heaven. Both the Saint-Omer and Göttingen miniatures meticulously represent the saintly ranks, emphasizing how important any saint's specific place in the heavenly hierarchy was to a medieval audience.

The texts and the illustrations of the Lives of individual saints attest to an awareness of these classificatory systems and to their importance. Plainly, viewers were familiar with types and expected to experience the individual saint's Life in terms of its form and strictures.[20] At the same time, the types are largely ideal: they represent a set of expectations to which few saints conform entirely. Moreover, most of the narratives we will investigate are mixtures of more than one type, and not all types can be represented in this study because not all types found pictorial representation.[21] Thus, although study of the saints is generally framed here in terms of their types, divergences from type are equally important to the discussion of how hagiography was received by its audiences.

Reception is a primary concern of this study, but a wide range of other issues pertaining to historical conditions and pictorial production are also important, es-

Figure 2. All Saints' Feast, *Göttingen Sacramentary,* Fulda, late tenth century. Göttingen, Niedersächsische Staats- und Universitätsbibliothek, Cod. theol. 231, fol. 111r.

pecially because they directly affect reception. An introductory chapter reviews the findings of research conducted on these issues[22] and sketches the historical circumstances surrounding pictorial hagiography—primarily in manuscripts produced in the Western medieval world.

A practical reason to consider manuscripts derives, of course, from the poor survival rate of other arts of the Church and the appearance of stained glass narratives only at the very end of the history I am tracing.[23] Saints' Lives in frescoes were obviously more public than manuscripts, but the daunting task of reconstructing fragmentary remains (which must precede interpretation) looms large. Manuscripts, by contrast, preserve their narratives in relatively complete form, and they survive together with their relatively undisturbed "context." Not only do we usually know something of the monastery or the workshop that produced them, but manuscripts also preserve abundant evidence between their own covers. Through the observable details of their assembly, the inclusion of ancillary texts, and even the presence of marginal notations that indicate direct use, manuscripts offer a

Figure 3. The death and ascension of St. Omer, *Life of Omer (Audomarus),* for the canons of St. Omer, third quarter of the eleventh century. Bibliothèque de l'Agglomération de Saint-Omer, MS 698, fol. 26r.

wealth of information about their manufacture and function (for representative details, see the appendix). The "book" thus is more than a metaphor; in the form of surviving medieval manuscripts, books provide a relatively clear perspective into hagiographic reception of the past.

Given the potential richness of manuscripts, a discussion of historical contexts in chapter 1 is important to understanding how Lives were received by their audiences.[24] On the one hand, successive adjustments and versions of saints' Lives may reflect both general trends in hagiographic fashion and specific historic circumstances. On the other hand, historical context allows us to recognize that a narrative may aim to coerce the way it is received; many Lives grow out of a specific ideology or even attempt to impose a point of view on a particular audience under unique political circumstances.[25] Barbara Abou-el-Haj has examined hagiographic material (including many of the manuscripts considered here) from the perspective of ideological coercion.[26] While such a reading is thought provoking, except perhaps to the degree that sanctity itself represents power, only a few scenes can be interpreted as having precise political ends.[27] Although very important, the political and the historical take a subsidiary role in this study, which focuses on issues surrounding the narrative construction of sanctity.

Chapter 2 turns directly to issues of reading and viewing saints' Lives, analyzing the peculiarities of hagiographic narrative and the special qualities of pictorial hagiographic narrative.[28] The chapters that follow loosely track the saintly types of the Litany. Chapter 3 considers the narrative characteristics of martyr stories—the foundation narratives of hagiography. Chapter 4 continues within the martyr type, which takes masculinity as the norm, to examine the problematically gendered form of the martyr, the virgin saint. Chapters 5 through 8 treat the narrative permutations effected to create a picture of sanctity for holy confessors—bishops, monks and abbots, kings and queens. Because these types of saints do not suffer martyrdom, miraculous proof of sanctity is much more at issue, and narrative proof of sanctity is also problematized. Chapter 9 considers the end of the monastic tradition of hagiography and changes that occur in thirteenth-century narrative Lives. The epilogue assesses other recent theories of narrative, especially pertaining to stained glass, and contrasts these to the way that hagiographic narratives, genre, and types have been seen to work.

A series of questions that have hovered over this study since its inception has done much to structure what follows. First, the simple question: Why were illustrated saints' Lives produced in such great numbers between the tenth and the thirteenth century? Why were they illustrated at all, given the trouble and expense of such illustration? To whom did the saints' Lives appeal? If the illiterate were meant to use them, how did they? How could the common Christian take inspiration from saints—such remote, perfect beings? Did the Lives indeed edify (as their authors claimed)? Finally, the question that dogs all modern considerations of hagiography: Why are saints' Lives so much alike? In answer to the last: they are and they aren't, as we will presently see.

1

THE HISTORICAL SETTING

The Production of Saints' Lives

ॐ

[Saints] are the living splinters of heaven.
—Sheri Holman, *A Stolen Tongue*

A BRIEF SKETCH of the historical contexts of reading, hearing, and looking at hagiography between the sixth and the thirteenth century will serve here as a prologue to our own efforts as readers and viewers. An overview of textual sources indicates important commonalities.[1]

Throughout the Middle Ages, many readers would have begun their reading in the Lives of the saints with either of two familiar hagiographic collections, written contemporaneously in the late sixth century.[2] Apparently without knowledge of each other, Gregory I the Great (c. 540–604; pope from 590), and Gregory, bishop of Tours (538–93), each wrote collections of saints' Lives.[3] Gregory of Tours's *Glory of the Martyrs, Life of the Fathers,* and *Glory of the Confessors,* written between c. 585 and 590, were part of an ambitious project to educate his congregation.[4] Gregory the Great's *Dialogues,* written in 593–94, most likely at the request of members of the papal *curia,*[5] similarly treats many types of saints and considers various issues of cult and miracle.

In addition to these founding documents of early medieval hagiography, certain other texts, as widely read sources of hagiographic information, warrant particular attention: prologues to various *vitae* of renowned saints; a sermon by Victricius of Rouen delivered in 396 to celebrate the reception of relics he received from Ambrose, bishop of Milan; and, of course, the works of Augustine (bishop of Hippo, 354–430), especially his sermons and the *City of God.*[6]

Gregory the Great and Augustine remained remarkably influential throughout the Middle Ages concerning questions of hagiographic doctrine.[7] Similarly, the works of Gregory of Tours endured as a lively compendium of hagiographic stories and an essentially unparalleled resource until equally wide-ranging works by such writers as Caesarius of Heisterbach (1220–35) came onto the scene.[8] Perhaps one reason the older sources were valued for so long is that hagiography remained largely a matter of cult, and cult was concerned with practice rather than doctrine. Although cult practice changed dramatically between the sixth and the thirteenth century, the theological underpinnings and spiritual goals of hagiography generally seem to have developed at a slower pace. Later writers, such as Abbot Guibert of Nogent in *On the Relics of the Saints* (early twelfth century)[9] and the scholar Bernard of Angers in *The Book of Miracles of St. Faith* (eleventh century),[10] tended to focus on issues of practice while maintaining without question the theological principles that had been established centuries before.[11] One of the major issues addressed by both authors was not sanctity itself but how sanctity could be verified—distinguishing the true saint or relic from the false. Indeed, canonization and the authority to determine sanctity became central issues in hagiographic cult during the later Middle Ages.[12]

Because we will be considering "looking" as well as reading and hearing, it is essential to take into account documents concerning the cult of images along with those of the cult of saints. Here again, doctrinal sources are few and early, primarily found in the letters of Pope Gregory.[13] Like the cult of saints, the cult of images is an aspect of medieval religion more readily characterized by evidence of practice than by doctrine. In fact, because of a lack of doctrinal evidence, both cults have been taken as manifestations of so-called popular religion. However, throughout the Middle Ages the cult of saints and the cult of images were enthusiastically accepted and promoted by the Church as tools to stir up or increase devotion.[14] Recent studies have examined both as sophisticated tools of religious practice used by all segments of society.[15] Rather than manifestations of "popular religion" (whatever that term means for the Middle Ages), images and hagiography were clearly controlled by the Church with the intention of minimizing abuse and misunderstanding and encouraging clarity of expression. In discussing the cult of images and the cult of saints, medieval and modern scholars alike shift readily between text and image.[16] For that reason, I refer generally to narrative rather than distinguish between written text and pictorial narrative.

The commentaries of Gregory the Great and of John of Damascus (eighth century), and even the *Libri Carolini* (late eighth century),[17] works to which art historians have repeatedly turned to define the status of early medieval art, classify pictorial narratives with texts as means to teach the doctrines of the Church. Invariably, the Lives of saints are specifically mentioned or alluded to in these texts.[18] In the works of Agnellus of Ravenna (ninth century), Basil of Caesarea (fourth century), and John of Ephesus (sixth century), we even find hagiographic images standing for texts.[19] Ultimately, the reason for this easy equivalence, as John of Damascus makes clear, is that nonscriptural texts and manufactured images rank quite low as potential likenesses of the divine. Nevertheless, these forms persisted because they served specific functions. As the ever-practical Pope Gregory insists, images can teach the illiterate, elevating their audience to a new plane of understanding. Images had the power to move their audience, whether literate or illiterate, and ultimately to effect conversion.[20] This conversion, whether from paganism to Christianity or from passive to active belief, is one of the primary functions of saints' Lives. Even the most literate cleric (such as Peter the Deacon in Gregory's *Dialogues*) could use them to exchange moral laxity for the heat of devotional ardor or for Gregory's ultimate goal, the "tears of compunction."

TERMS OF HAGIOGRAPHIC STUDY: THE DOSSIER AND ITS ELEMENTS

The saint's "dossier," in current usage, comprises the various documents that pertain to and support his or her sanctity. Given the multiplicity and fluidity of "versions" of any saint's story, however, these documents might equally well contradict or negate one another.

The first element of the dossier is the saint's *vita,* or Life—the document of foremost concern to the student of hagiography. It can be a text of a few pages, or it can fill a substantial tome.[21] Although I refer to the constructed "Life" of a saint (as distinct from his or her lived "life") as singular, the Life of a particular saint may in fact exist in several versions,[22] a result of the renewal of literary (as well as pictorial) style in different periods, the addition of miracles, or even free translations into other languages. Lives may also vary so substantially that a saint represented in an early Christian account may be all but unrecognizable in his or her own fourteenth-century legend and pictures.[23] Nevertheless, for the study of sanctity, no single version is to be preferred; each to some degree documents the religious experience and expression of its time.

The written Life is a prerequisite for the ecclesiastical cult or liturgical celebration of the saint; without it (the Church argues) one cannot be sure of the saint's worthiness for veneration. Popular cults often arise in its absence, but no cult was or is sanctioned by the Church without a *vita*. Indeed, a sufficiently persuasive *vita* became one of the main elements of canonization.

Although in its most basic meaning, canonization is simply the acceptance of a saint into the calendar of the Church, it is a complex process and has been the impetus for some of the most significant studies in the field of modern hagiography.[24] The term may have originated in the early Church to designate the inclusion of a saint in the Canon of the Mass, that is, the official calendar of saints' feasts.[25] In the early Church, however, canonization was not a formal procedure. The closest thing to a canonization was the solemn liturgical celebration of a translation, or relocation, of a saint's body by a bishop.[26] Often such translations might bring the body from a cemetery or other common place of burial into a specially built church dedicated to the saint. The text written to describe the event and the miracles that often surrounded it are analogously called the translation, or *translatio*, another sort of text that is part of the dossier.[27] Formal canonization as a privilege of the pope only began in the tenth century with St. Udalrich. By the thirteenth century, it had become a fully judicial proceeding.

The process of canonization has never been formulaically based on a specific number of miracles—not surprising, given the equivocal nature of those supernatural events—but miracle books, too, became an element of the dossier.[28] Just as the notion of the miracle is difficult to define for today's scientific and skeptical world, it was equally hard to pinpoint in the Middle Ages. Miracles, or events much like them, could be effected by demons as well as by saints, and almost anything could be considered a miracle, from the untimely stumbling of a horse to the resurrection of the dead. Augustine emphasized that miracles were necessary for faith.[29] Gregory the Great in the *Dialogues* focused on the *admiratio,* the astonishment, that the miracle produced, forcing sluggish minds out of habitual ways into recognition of the eternal presence of the divine in the world.[30] The narrative context of the event and the beliefs of the audience involved—even their political loyalties—were all important in the assessment of the miraculous: much depended on how the story was recounted by its narrator and received by its audience. Even when "scientific" evidence came to play a part in papal canonization procedures, parallels to the Old and New Testament and other hagiographic accounts were essential to the acceptance of a miracle. Furthermore, miracles, however implausible, gained validity if preceded by a prayer, a vision, or a devotional act.[31] They could even be considered "heavenly sacraments."[32] More important than these qualities to the assessment of any miracle's significance, however, is the theological dictum that miracles do not make the saint; they only reveal the holy. Pope Gregory is careful to note that it is virtue alone, not miracles, that defines sanctity.[33] Similarly, at the end of the twelfth century, Pope Innocent III confirmed that virtues stand before miracles.[34] Nonetheless, it is a common narrative assumption in saints' Lives and their images that God usually draws attention to a saintly example through miracles.

Medieval saints were celebrated not only in written or pictorial memorials but also in physical remains, especially the relics of their bodies. Veneration of relics occurred first and foremost in the carefully manipulated atmosphere of the saint's shrine or memorial tomb, where the body could be displayed (in whole or in part).[35] In either case, as Victricius of Rouen asserts in the *De laude sanctorum,* "even the smallest relics and particles of dust share the virtue of the whole."[36] That virtue consists largely in a real connection between earth and heaven: the saint resides in the earthly body at the same time that he or she dwells in heaven. Thus saints, in the form of their relics, can serve as intercessors between the supplicant and God; they are mediators, whose own prayers are empowered by their virtue or suffering.[37]

Relics can be celebrated not only as part or whole of the body but also in the form of objects that the saint touched or used in life—what are known today as second-degree relics. Relics of the Virgin Mary, who was assumed bodily into heaven, are necessarily of the latter sort, and Chartres, for example, holds the Virgin's tunic as its most precious relic. One other category of object, termed third-degree relics, was seen to acquire sanctity through contact with relics of the first and second categories. For example, to avoid dismembering the holy body of St. Peter and to satisfy frequent requests for the revered saint's relics, the clerics at Rome lowered little pieces of linen cloth into the saint's sarcophagus to touch the relics. These *brandea* were perceived to be demonstrably heavier as a result of their saturation with the saint's *virtus,* or power, and were distributed as relics in their own right.[38]

It became custom and finally law to place relics in each consecrated altar.[39] Because relics were difficult to identify without an established tradition (always at risk of disruption during the early Middle Ages), it also became customary to identify the bone or fragment with a little slip of parchment (called an *authentic*) attached to it. In a sense, reliquaries—decorated repositories for saints' relics—are authentics made literally glorious. One twelfth-century authority described "[relics] enclosed . . . in a costly shell of gold" as "visible evidence descending to this age to provide fresh testimony."[40] If the gorgeous containers could portray something of the life and significance of the saint, all the better.[41] A few such narrative reliquaries will take a prominent place in our study.

Liturgical material in both textual and performed manifestations is also an important part of the dossier. It surrounds, or even creates, the most visible (and, often, audible) manifestation of the cult of the saints. For example, the appearance of the name in the *Litany* (the list of saints enlisted to intercede on behalf of the supplicant) constitutes the first evidence of the cult of a saint.[42] These lists have a distinctive hierarchical order: although the saints make up a community or court in heaven, they are not all equal in stature.[43]

A second form of evidence of the liturgical cult is the short *vita,* or epitome, contained in the martyrology. These epitomes, of about a paragraph's length, give the saint's type, geographic origin, and date of death.[44] Litanies and martyrologies provide one means of spreading—and thus tracing the spread of—a saint's cult.

The incidence of a saint's name in the liturgical calendar indicates that the Mass was celebrated in the name of the saint on a certain date in the locale from which the calendar originated. This can be powerful evidence of a local cult, provided the saint is not a universal martyr (that is, included in the Roman Canon).[45]

If the saint receives the full degree of recognition from the Church, one or more days will be dedicated to his or her memory and an *office* will survive. Such an office contains readings for each of the canonical hours at which monks pray. The office will often also include notations of music, hymns sung to the saint, and sermons delivered on the saint's feast day.[46] Special liturgical celebrations at the saint's place of patronage—usually his or her burial spot—may include feasts for the anniversaries of the translation, or other relic-related events, notably the invention or elevation. The *invention,* or *inventio,* celebrated the discovery (usually through a dream or vision) of previously unknown relics.[47] The *elevation,* or *elevatio,* of relics involved raising the relics from a grave to the altar, implying increased honor and dignity.

Other physical evidence of the cult might include the dedication of numerous churches or chapels, ex-votos left by pilgrims and suppliants, and, of course, pictorial records of the saint's appearance and acts.[48] Like other elements of a hagiographic dossier, all were important in the construction of a saint's Life.

PICTORIAL HAGIOGRAPHY

Art was among the first manifestations of saints' cults. Whether in the form of shrine architecture and ornamentation, or pictorial narratives, visual elements were used in saint's cults from the beginning. St. Peter's tomb was commemorated with a cult structure as early as the second century, and monumental architecture in honor of the saints was a major feature of the Constantinian building program.[49]

Pictorial hagiography, often in the form of scenes from the martyrs' Passions, is recorded and even survives in Rome from as early as the fourth century, contemporary with the earliest examples of formally written saints' Lives. The early pictorial narratives are usually quite short.[50] For example, a two-scene narrative in a *confessio* in Ss. Giovanni e Paolo in Rome celebrates three martyrs.[51] One particularly intriguing notation in the *Liber Pontificalis* (sixth or seventh century) mentions silver screens bearing images of the Passion of Lawrence.[52] The best evidence of a substantial early narrative cycle is the *ekphrasis* delivered by Asterios of Amaseia in 410 at the martyrium of Euphemia in Asia Minor.[53] Although some scholars doubt the existence of the four paintings that Asterios describes (in emotionally charged imagery), the episodes are closely paralleled in later illustrated narratives.[54] Thus, by the fifth century, the conventional forms of hagiographic narrative had already begun to take shape.

The first evidence for an important set of narrative pictures of a saint's Life in the West relates to those that celebrated the Life of Martin at Tours. Two sets of *tituli*, that is, explanatory captions, survive. The fifth-century set describes paintings in Martin's funerary church, while the sixth-century set seems to have been associated with frescoes in the main church—a significant (perhaps new) location for hagiographic imagery.[55] The first of these sets of *tituli* is organized as a pilgrim's guide and demonstrates a concern for how the narrative pictures of the saint—controlled through their accompanying text, their architectural setting, and the devotee's physical position in relation to the works—would be received by their audience. These images at Tours are contemporaneous with Gregory the Great's reorganization of the tomb of St. Peter in Rome.[56] Much material dating from the eighth century onward survives in Rome. Santa Maria Antiqua preserves eight scenes from the Life of Quiricus and Julitta in a private chapel,[57] and Santa Maria in via Lata houses six scenes from the Life of Erasmus.[58] Other fragments date from the ninth century.[59]

In the North, several illustrated Lives in varied contexts survive from the second half of the ninth century. The Life of Ambrose is depicted on the back of his tomb, the Golden Altar in Sant'Ambrogio in Milan, while the Life of Christ dominates the front. A condensed Life of Bishop Arnulf appears in a single initial in the Drogo Sacramentary (see fig. 55).[60] Other evidence points to the Carolingian promotion of pictorial hagiographic narratives, which are now lost.[61]

Finally, at the turn of the tenth century, apparently at Reichenau, the illustrated Passion of Romanus, book X of the *Peristephanon,* was included in a luxury copy of the *Opera* of Prudentius, now in Bern.[62] It is the oldest of the hagiographic manuscripts considered in this study. Illustrated cycles of the Lives of saints, of course, continued to decorate liturgical objects, and a few are worth mentioning here that will not be otherwise considered. An ivory book cover in Amiens with scenes from the Life of Remi seems to date from the tenth century.[63] An eleventh-century ivory casket from Spain illustrates the Life of Millán.[64] Sumptuous reliquaries from the eleventh through the thirteenth century feature scenes from the Lives of Hadelin, Remaclus, Anno, and Heribert.[65] St. Mark's Life appears on the Pala d'Oro within his eponymous cathedral in Venice,[66] and Adalbert's Life is depicted on the bronze doors of the cathedral at Gniezno in Poland.[67]

Many more Lives—on shrines, in wall-paintings, and in books—have disappeared, but what survives clearly attests to a widespread production of pictorial hagiography and to a conventional, or shared, basis for its iconography. Viewers were familiar with conventional compositions, such as the martyr brought before the judge or the martyr's decapitation, that individually had a relatively static significance. It was, however, through the interactions of scenes in narrative and their cumulative effect that hagiographers were able to convey complex meanings. Such narratives are best preserved in books, and books, for the most part those dedicated to one saint, will be the focus here

Libelli—literally, "little books" that recount the life and deeds of a single saint or, occasionally, two saints[68]—survive from the late tenth century (the *libellus* of Wandrille, and that of Kilian and Margaret), and appear more abundantly during the eleventh and twelfth centuries (Amand, Aubin, Benedict, Cuthbert, Edmund, Liudger, Lucy, Martin, Maurus, Omer, Quentin, and Radegund; see appendix). Pictorial cycles dating from the later period are significantly longer: for example, the Life of Amand (Valenciennes, Bibliothèque municipale, MS 502), contains thirty-four miniatures, more than twice the number contained in any surviving cycle predating the eleventh century.[69] The cluster of books in this period represents a high point in their use for the artistic elaboration of the cult of the saints. Although the tradition of *libelli* continued into the thirteenth century, the many changes create a somewhat confusing picture. The use of select manuscripts, instead of a survey, allows a sharper focus for this later period.

Although *libellus* has become the customary term among hagiographers for manuscripts that contain the Life of a single saint, the term is also used in various fields of medieval studies to refer to other types of small books. Art historians, following the lead of Francis Wormald, have taken up the term to differentiate these simple hagiographic books from the other major category of illustrated hagiographic manuscripts, those containing collections of saints' Lives (which will be considered briefly in chapter 4).[70] The majority of *libelli* treated here were created in monasteries, and many have as their subject the patron saints of those monasteries. While each contributes to an understanding of the hagiographic genre, each also uniquely represents the historical circumstances under which it was produced and exemplifies the importance of a particular saintly patron.

Unillustrated hagiographic *libelli*, in contrast, seem to have fulfilled comparatively modest functions. They could serve as the monastery's repository for the liturgical material concerning a particular saint—including the *vita*, office, hymns, prayers, and sermons. Alternatively, the *libellus*, whether limited to the *vita* or containing the entirety of the saint's dossier, might be a means of disseminating the text or texts: the saint's Life could be copied from a circulating copy. Some of these have turned up with creases down the center as if they had been carried in a pocket or saddle bag.[71] In either case, the manuscript itself is usually more functional than luxurious.

How do such modest manuscripts compare in function with illustrated hagiographic *libelli*? First, the illustrated *libelli* are generally sumptuous in design and materials. Such ornamentation was intended in part to dazzle the laity, who might not recognize the saint without a glorious "vestment," but also to honor the saint by cloaking the account of his or her life in splendor. Throughout the Middle Ages, authorities as diverse as Jerome and Abbot Suger argued that the making of a shrine, book, or church celebrating a saint demanded visual glorification—the lavish application of gems, gold, artisanal ornament, and images.[72] Consequently, *libelli* do not always strictly qualify as "little books" and often are extensively decorated in gold and silver. The very inclusion of illustrations gives them far greater status than their unornamented cousins.

A second, no less important but less obvious difference between the two varieties of *libelli* concerns the dissemination of texts. The saints celebrated in illustrated *libelli* were rarely wanting in documentation. Illustrations were usually added to centuries-old accounts of well-established saints of great renown. Illustrated *libelli* might have spread the fame of particular saints, but they were not responsible for their initial introduction.

A third difference between the two forms of *libelli* concerns their respective audiences. Illustrated *libelli*, although of monastic manufacture, were not always

Figure 4. A disobedient boy, lost at sea, is pardoned by St. Omer, *Life of Omer (Audomarus),* for the canons of St. Omer, third quarter of the eleventh century. Bibliothèque de l'Agglomération de Saint-Omer, MS 698, fol. 10v.

Figure 5. Scenes from the Life of St. Omer, Saint-Omer, Gothic tomb of the saint.

intended for monastic use. Rather, they were made with an eye to the world outside the monastery. This comes as no surprise, since in the medieval controversies over images it was repeatedly argued that the religious, especially monks, did not need images to assist them in their spiritual meditations. Others, however, needed images, and nuns were often included among such "others."[73]

Finally, the special consideration that ornamentation conferred gave illustrated *libelli* the status of extra-ordinary objects: the strength of their association with the saint and the honor due to his or her venerated person transformed these objects—often kept in the treasury and designated as "shrine-books"—into relics.[74] They contained documents and records of donations to the monastery, apparently so that the saint would take particular care to ensure the security of any gifts, promises, or privileges recorded within his or her *libellus*. Furthermore, episodes preserved in the narrative cycle of illustrations in the manuscript could be transferred to imagery on the shrine of the saint, as they were for St. Omer (compare fig. 4 and fig. 5), indicating that at times the imagery itself had acquired a certain authority.

THE USES OF *LIBELLI*

Just as the use of relics had a history, the uses and functions of the illustrated *libelli* also changed through time.[75] Differing circumstances of culture, society, and religion resulted in changing patterns of how sanctity was conceived, and the illustrated *libelli* both reflected and helped to forge these patterns.

Roughly three periods in their production may be distinguished. The first and earliest group of *libelli* seem to have been made to spread the fame of a saint, often a saint whose cult had political implications. The second group consists of books produced by monasteries during what is generally considered the heyday of monasticism—the eleventh and twelfth centuries; these were intended to glorify the monastery's patron saint while generating income from ever-increasing numbers of pilgrims.[76] The third group, the last significant hagiographic illustrations produced by monastic artists (although later illustrated Lives continued to be commissioned by monasteries from urban workshops), added yet another potential benefit to those exploited by earlier manuscripts. With the rise of the monarchy and the court, the Lives of saints were directed to a new audience of readers in order to curry favor and devotion in that arena.

The correspondences between the earliest illustrated *libelli*—those of the tenth century—and relics suggest that we look to contemporary practices surrounding relics to further our understanding of the books' functions. Indeed, the dissemination of the saintly body is linked to the spread of a saint's fame through the dissemination of the text of his or her *vita*. Although most of a saint's body was likely to remain in a single recognized and powerful *locus sanctus,* the sites in which other, minor relics had been placed came to share in that power, albeit with a dependent spiritual status.[77] The process of dismembering saintly bodies and distributing their relics created a network of holy power. Dependent on a well-developed doctrine of intercession,[78] these networks served political ends and were frequently exploited by both the Carolingians and Ottonians.

The oldest surviving illustrated Life, Hannover Niedersächsische Landesbibliothek MS I 189, contains the Lives of Kilian of Würzburg and Margaret of Antioch and was made at Fulda in approximately 970. Although no other complete tenth-century *libellus* survives, the Hannover manuscript seems to have had a "fraternal twin," documented in an antiquarian's notes, that was also made at Fulda for the monastery of Essen.[79] That manuscript had a very similar layout and contained two *vitae,* the Life shared by the twin doctors Cosmas and Damian, and the Life of Pinnosa, a companion of Ursula. Two other tenth-century Lives, those of Agatha and of Romanus of Antioch, are each included in larger collections that contain no other fully narrative illustrated saints' Lives.[80] A *libellus* of Wandrille, now at Saint-Omer, contains only a partial set of illustrations in an inserted quire, made in a different format.[81] In none of these examples, except perhaps that of Wandrille, does the manuscript appear to have been made by a monastery for its own celebration of the cult of its patron saint.

That these tenth-century *vitae* were intended to spread their subject's fame beyond the monastery is suggested by the fact that all of the saints concerned (again, excepting Wandrille), were martyrs and that most were universal saints and patrons of the Church. Only the *libellus* containing the Life of Pinnosa was intended to complement a *corpus,* the relic body that had been recently translated to Essen. Nevertheless, in a sermon on another saint translated to Essen, a Saxon cleric overtly discussed such movements of relics in terms of the political implications of the change of patronage and envisioned the union of Francia and Saxony, ancient enemies, in an effective network of patronage devoted to the saint.[82]

The Hannover manuscript likewise seems to have been produced to propagate the cult of Kilian, a saint promoted during the same period by imperial interests.[83] However, because in certain respects it resembles a prayerbook, it evidences other purposes as well. Four prayers, including one to Mary and another to the Apostles, following the Lives of Kilian and Margaret, contain feminine Latin endings—"ora pro me peccatrice"—clear evidence that the manuscript was made for women. This fact sheds light on the role that gender played in how images were used and what functions they served. The inclusion of images in spiritual exercises by nuns during the late medieval period, as Jeffrey Hamburger has shown, sometimes reflected a gendered approach to artistic patronage.[84] Clerics charged with the care of female religious argued that pictures helped these "weaker intellects" focus their attention. A similar, albeit early, medieval sensibility may well be at work in the Hannover manuscript, in which eucharistic images seem to be fashioned to address a female audience, probably nuns (see pp. 122–26), and the Life of a bishop precedes (i.e., in some sense controls) that of a virgin.

Thus, apparently the book was made not for liturgical use but for private reading or devotion. Such private reading of saints' Lives was not unknown during the early Middle Ages. In fact, Greek Lives were translated to Latin with no other justification than that of edification.[85] The Lives of Margaret, Romanus, and Agatha, among others, came to the Latin West from Greek originals, and it has recently been argued that Prudentius's version of the Life of Romanus was specifically intended for private reading.[86] The spiritual use of these cycles of illustrations, however, was not limited to the lessons of an individual saint's Life. In addition to their moral or devotional intent—edification or prayer—the Lives were used more generally to help teach the cult of the saints in areas recently converted to Christianity. Just as Gregory of Tours used his stories to eliminate *rusticitas* and, in effect, teach the peasants how to deal respectfully with the saints, so these books teach the proper veneration of the saints.[87]

If the Hannover manuscript was made for the monastery of Essen, or perhaps one of the other convents that housed the imperial and noble widows and daughters of the Ottonian empire, it was well designed to serve both political and spiritual functions. We can only surmise that other, no-longer-surviving *libelli* of the period had similarly multivalent uses.

The second group of *libelli* constitutes the bulk of the surviving manuscripts; their functions seem more precise. The books cluster in the eleventh and twelfth centuries and were made for monasteries by resident monks, with the exception of one example clearly made by a lay artist (or artists) invited to work at the monastery under the monks' close supervision.[88] These *libelli* celebrate the Lives of monasteries' patron saints, who were usually confessors—most often bishops, but sometimes monks.[89]

Often elaborately illustrated, the *libelli* of the eleventh and twelfth centuries find their analogue in contemporaneous relic shrines encrusted with gold and gems and occasionally decorated with scenes from the saint's Life. Indeed, it was during this period that the Limoges and Mosan enamel work reliquaries began to be produced in such remarkable profusion (see figs. 45 and 46–47).

The monks who executed these works sought to glorify their monastery's patron saint: a famous patron might generate significant income from visiting pilgrims, or, perhaps more important, increase the monastery's prestige and influence, together with attendant political or judicial advantages. Many of the shrines, and thus the *libelli,* seem to have been in open competition with those of other monasteries. No doubt for that reason a recurring miracle story, a *topos,* in which the supplicant seeks a cure in one shrine after another, became popular during this period. The use and form of the *topos* may be revealingly contrasted with a similar story from the early Middle Ages. Gregory the Great, writing in the sixth century, tells of an exorcism performed by Benedict after a demoniac's earlier unsuccessful visits to martyrs' shrines, commenting, "but the holy martyrs did not grant [the demoniac] this favor, preferring instead to reveal the wonderful gifts of the servant of God."[90] This gracious commentary, balancing the merits of martyrs and confessors, contrasts markedly with the twelfth-century *miracula* of Edmund: Edmund's hagiographer gloats that a series of such competitive miracles demonstrates that the saint is especially powerful in England.[91] Leopold Genicot argues that subtle changes in how *topoi* were recounted can be important for historical interpretation.[92] The competition *topos* gives evidence of a holy geography that came to fruition during these centuries, and a turning away from the appeal of the universal martyr toward the local and more self-serving powers of the confessor saint and those who control his or her bodily relics.

The illustrated Lives reflect the centrality of issues of power during the high Middle Ages through the thematic prominence of demonstrations of the saint's patronage toward his own people. Focusing on this group of Lives, composed in the eleventh and twelfth centuries, Barbara Abou-el-Haj has shown how saints are depicted helping and protecting their devotees and cites the example of Edmund protecting his monastery from theft and unfair taxation after his death (see fig. 100).[93] The last miniature of the Guthlac Roll shows a crowd of figures with the texts of donations inscribed on scrolls; the roll may have been made in order to safeguard the monastery's threatened rights and possessions,[94] just as the illustrations of the *libellus* containing the illustrated Life of Omer consistently defend the rights of the collegiate church dedicated to Omer against the claims of the Abbey of Saint-Bertin.[95] The illustrated manuscript thus constitutes one of the primary documents of the ongoing battle against misappropriation. The Life of Radegund, Magdalena Carrasco has argued, was illustrated for the nuns of the Abbey of Sainte-Croix in order to assert their institution's status as a *locus sanctus* over that of the Church of Sainte-Radegonde, which held the saint's body.[96] Finally, Barbara Abou-el-Haj has explored more generally how these books were used as one of many sorts of props in the calculated "staging" of a given saint's power.[97]

Historical geography may explain the political character of eleventh- and twelfth-century saints' Lives. The production of *libelli* during the tenth century was concentrated in Imperial and recently pagan German lands; most eleventh- and twelfth-century *libelli*, by contrast, were created in Gaul, present-day France. The work of "putting together" traditions that defended rights and privileges (which might include assembling a cartulary as well as writing and illustrating a saint's Life)[98] was particularly strong in areas that were literate and accustomed to a Gallo-Roman form of patronage but that lacked a strong central means of political control. In these areas, the saint slipped easily into a symbolic role of power similar to that of the secular lord.[99]

In content, the narrative imagery of these manuscripts also clearly reflects claims of possession and privileges—a sort of pride of patronage that confirms the saintly status of their subject. Burial scenes depict and prominently demonstrate the location of the holy body (see fig. 85). The Lives of saintly monks and bishops show the patron's personal participation in the foundation and building of monasteries and local bishoprics (see fig. 60). Most important, the sanctity of the confessor is demonstrated by his conformity to authoritative types of monk and bishop saints, for example, attested in images of bishops serving the Mass and officiating over the liturgy as the authentic and local representatives of the ecclesiastical hierarchy (see fig. 57).

A related purpose of these *libelli* seems to have been to increase the saint's sphere of influence, his or her holy territory. However, rather than merely increase the saint's renown (as did the tenth-century *libelli*), books from the second period consistently and specifically encourage pilgrimage to the shrine of the saint. The act of "promoting" the saint had decidedly economic implications.[100] One striking example, the Guthlac Roll, contains numerous illustrations of a psalter and a flail that are not mentioned in the Life of its subject, St. Guthlac (see fig. 86).[101] These sacred relics, as Kimberley Kelly has demonstrated, were housed within the monastery of Crowland, where the roll was created: the illustrations advertise their presence.[102] It is not yet entirely clear, however, how such "promotion" would work, since these illustrated books were single exemplars. In the case of a text that existed in multiple copies and could thus have been distributed beyond the monastery (such as the *Liber Sancti Jacobi,* celebrating the shrine of St. James in Compostella), a far-reaching effect is easily imagined. In the case of the *libelli,* less obvious means must have served to promote the saint's, and the monastery's, fame. Clearly the illustrators of the books had some expectation that their project would have a certain success. That success would surely have been reinforced by the book's taking its place in a cultural context encompassing a variety of forms of physical and social representation, including compilations of miracles, wall-paintings, confraternities and their rituals, and even pilgrim badges.[103]

The last group of manuscripts that I will consider date from the thirteenth century and consist primarily of the manuscripts of Matthew Paris. They exhibit many of the characteristics of the *libelli* of the eleventh and twelfth centuries but were directed to a different, specific audience: the nobility and the court. The patronage of saints remains central in these books but takes a slightly different object and rationale. Matthew Paris recommended the saints he represented as powerful personal patrons for the nobility. The expectation was that members of the court would support the saints' foundations with favors and gifts.

The manuscripts of this group contain Lives written in vernacular poetry and illustrated by Matthew himself. One is a *libellus* of the patron of Matthew's monastery, Saint Alban. Another two (which I believe were copied from sketches provided by Matthew) are the illustrated Lives of Thomas à Becket and Edward the Confessor. The flyleaf of the St. Alban manuscript preserves notes in Matthew's hand that reveal that he lent it and other saints' Lives to ladies of the nobility.[104] Of value as a contemporary comparison to Matthew's manuscripts is a *libellus* of St. Denis made for (but not at) the monastery at Saint-Denis. It similarly includes verse versions of the saint's Life in the vernacular, which suggests that it was also intended for reading to a noble lay audience.[105]

Lending monastic books to the nobility calls to mind monasteries lending their relics to noble persons, or even the personal ownership of relics, a practice that became quite common in the late Middle Ages. A relic of Margaret (a patron of childbirth), for example, was customarily lent by the monastery of Saint-Germain-des-Près to the queens of France when they were in childbed.[106] One might contrast such practices to those described in earlier miracle stories, in which nobility and royalty traveled to the saint or his shrine in order to effect a cure. By the fourteenth and fifteenth centuries, saints could apparently no longer make such harsh demands on the nobility. Even those nobles who chose to go on pilgrimage had an easier route.[107]

These manuscripts for the court display many of the elements seen in earlier books. The *libellus* of St. Alban was created to celebrate the martyr's shrine at the monastery, where a cross supposedly used by Amphibalus and given to Alban had recently turned up. Matthew adds an account of the peculiarly shaped cross to the textual narrative and illustrations in this new version of the saint's Life, in service, perhaps, to the monastery, where such a relic would presumably have attracted pilgrims (see fig. 130). This strategy ties Matthew's Life of Alban back to the *libelli,* but the new audience also shapes the content. Stephen Jaeger has demonstrated that courtly virtues originated not among the laity but among ecclesiastics at court.[108] Indeed, I would argue that Matthew conceived of courtly behavior as appropriate to the saints.[109] Matthew characterizes his subject, St. Alban himself, as graced by such virtues, as is Edward the Confessor in *his* Life. In both text and pictures, Matthew gently teaches courtly ideals and virtues, approaching his noble audience with an entertaining and subtle religious tract. In some ways he is doing as his tenth-century predecessors did, spreading the glory of the saints, but his means are radically different.

Matthew's thirteenth-century narratives are based on earlier types and retain qualities of genre common to the earlier *vitae,* but there are significant changes as well. By the end of the thirteenth century, hagiographic texts and pictures had fully converted to "romance." They shifted to the vernacular and appeared in poetic formats more typical of secular literature. Pictures work with text to encourage private reading or performative reading in small groups. After Matthew's exemplary efforts, monks were no longer the primary patrons of illustrated *libelli* and no longer made them. Production shifted to lay workshops.

The thirteenth-century manuscript of the Life of Denis is another example of a manuscript specifically addressed to the court. It may be the first in a series of manuscripts describing the Life of Denis, each more luxurious than the last,[110] and was apparently commissioned by the monks of Saint-Denis for a courtly audience in order to promote the patronage of the saint for his country and king, as Charlotte Lacaze has shown.[111] Remarkably, these thirteenth-century manuscripts, like the earliest group, are not closely associated with a shrine. They can be read by a distant audience, and their value lies more in narrative effect than in their *virtus*—that is, the power associated with holy relics.

Why were illustrated saints' Lives produced? The key points are clear. *Libelli* increased the glory and fame of the saint; they drew pilgrims (as well as prestige) by proclaiming the power and merits of their saints and relics. At the end of the tradition, *libelli* were used by monastic interests to catch the ear of the court. One could call this last project a great success, but because it soon moved outside monastic spheres of production it must be taken as an end point for this study.

2

WORD AND IMAGE

Narrative Problems in Pictorial Hagiography

☞

Events must be not only registered within a chronological framework of their original
occurrence but narrated as well, that is to say, revealed as possessing a structure, an
order of meaning, which they do not possess as mere sequence.
—Hayden White, "The Value of Narrativity"

[God's] beauty is seen in all created beings;
Scarce otherwise you shine greatly and wondrously in the saints.
—*The Book of Sainte Foy,* trans. Pamela Sheingorn

For God's sake, speak, Mother; go on and do not break the thread
of your life-giving narrative.
—*The Life of Mary of Egypt,* trans. Benedicta Ward

HISTORICITY AND CHANGE mark the development of hagiography during the
Middle Ages, but relatively unchanging conventions and methods of construction
also find expression throughout the genre's history. The two aspects of pictorial
hagiography—historical and conventional, diachronic and synchronic—are an essential background against which to examine the individual narratives that serve as
case studies in this book. Here we turn to the conventional as it is expressed in narrative forms. The reader should note that the following remarks apply generally to
both textual and pictorial narrative; considering them together helps to clarify key
points, and only at the end of this chapter will the particular strengths and qualities of pictorial hagiography be highlighted.

A saint's Life is not a biography in the modern sense, that is, a recording of historical facts or the events of an individual life.[1] Rather, it is a project that aims to match a collection of words to one central fact: the ineffable holiness of a saint. Stephen Nichols describes the purpose of narrative in similar medieval stories as "not to inform people more accurately about their world and neighbors, but to show how the world mirrored God's immanence, and therefore the subordination of the human to the divine."[2] A meticulously composed construction, the saint's Life not only "makes the saint," but ideally in some sense, *is* the saint.[3] This distinction has several important implications.

First, as a construction, the hagiographic narrative is not necessarily fiction, but neither does it necessarily respect "fact."[4] In the preface to a Life of Gregory the Great, one hagiographer writes of his own efforts: "Then after we have established our work on a firm basis [by describing the virtues of the saint] we can raise the structure little by little to its crowning point."[5] The metaphor of a solid foundation and a careful building of effects points to the hagiographer's intent to create a narrative that will rise above mere words and deeds to reflect the grace of the saint, the holy coronation that the saint receives at death, and his admission to the heavenly court. Authors of saints' Lives typically lament the inadequacy of their work even as they search for the means to indicate the way above and beyond words.[6]

But if saints' Lives are constructed, their goal is not and cannot be an ambition to create the perfect object—either text or image. A second consequence of the constructed nature of saints' Lives is that their authors seek above all to create an effect in their audience. In the process of doing so, authors "disappear" in service to the audience's needs. As the recipients of truth claims and rhetorical embellishments, as spiritual *doppelgängers* to the listeners and viewers displayed within the text, as the object of the work's intent to move (or even to effect conversion), the audience shapes the form and justifies the existence of saints' Lives. Readers and viewers are always implicitly present in the narrative structure of hagiography even if they are rarely explicitly mentioned in the texts themselves. In some sense, hagiography is simply a series of effects directed at an audience.

Nevertheless, these effects are not trivial or superficial. Nichols describes one sort of effect in narratives and liturgies celebrating the Passion: "Emotion, the movement of the psyche in response to perception of events, serves a primary purpose in religious ritual participation. Affective response 'proves' the 'reality' of the divinity by demonstrating its power to dwell within the participant and thus to exist at a basic level of human response."[7] Such effects of identification and response, whether emotional, metaphysical, or spiritual, are equally essential to the operation of hagiographic narrative.

Thus a third, perhaps surprising, consequence of the construction of hagiographic Lives is that they are highly rhetorical at the same time that they claim to be true. Augustine counsels preachers in *De Doctrina Christiana* to limit rhetorical artifice and to use simple narrative,[8] but saints' Lives, quintessentially "simple" narratives, teem with rhetorical manipulation. These devices are essential to creating the requisite simulacrum of reality (that is, sanctity) and to the act of persuasion.[9] Guibert of Nogent complains of inexpert hagiographers whose work failed, for "even when stories about the saints are true . . . they can be expressed in such a ragged, pedestrian style . . . that they are believed to be quite false."[10] Guibert focuses on truth as an essential element of hagiography, making it dependent on "proper" forms of writing. Although Guibert's own rhetoric is learned and ornate, other hagiographers are more subtle and effective, hiding their devices behind the curtains of the production.

It is in the context of a need for rhetorical effect that the important issue of facticity can be better understood. Hagiographers make claims for truth even in the most suspect of circumstances. One monk makes the broad claim that "if anything we have written did not concern this man—and remember, we did not learn about them from those who saw and heard them but only in common report— . . . in his case we have little doubt that they were true of him too."[11] How can assertions of truth be reconciled with such patent fabrication? Moreover, why is truth so important to hagiography? To answer these questions, we must first examine the hagiographer's larger narrative goals.

Hagiographic narrative aimed to move its audience in a specific way, avoiding mere pleasure for a deeper spiritual effect. Truth takes an important place in this effect. Hans Robert Jauss, in analyzing the aesthetic intentions of narrative as it developed from Aristotle's *Poetics* through the Middle Ages, underscores a general dismissal of the imaginary among medieval authors in preference for the exemplary. He also argues for their rejection of catharsis in favor of compunction, a powerful and effective emotion in the Middle Ages, far from today's sentimental guilt.[12] Exemplarity and compunction worked together. The exemplary, as Jauss explains, was founded in fact and came to be considered superior to the imaginary. For one, it effectively avoided "concupiscentia oculorum," the pleasure, or concupiscence, of the eyes—what Augustine (*Confessions,* VI:8) describes more generally as the concupiscence of all the senses. In "true" or exemplary tales, therefore, aesthetic distance is collapsed through the operation of pity and the identification of the reader/viewer with the human subject of the true narrative: the audience does not take pleasure in the tale or images themselves. Most important, pity or compunction, founded in fear and even terror (*pavor*), prompts action. Gregory the Great explains the working of compunction in terms of "wounds . . . striking the hardness of the heart. . . . But by striking, [God] cures, . . . [the soul] is wounded in its most intimate place by a feeling of affection, it burns with a desire of contemplation, and, in an astonishing manner, its wound gives it life."[13] Ideally, then, terrifying and true narratives inspire a *conversio morum,* a profound change of heart.[14] In this way, the exemplary narrative, founded in "truth," is didactically superior even to doctrine— that which is only "thought." The narrative is extraordinary yet authentic, and it breaks the norms of generic expectation rather than simply fulfilling them. It can, as a consequence, inspire change and action.[15]

This operation of truth lies at the very center of the hagiographic narrative effect. Thus, saints' Lives must be true in order to work, although that truth may consist more of spiritual and rhetorical verity than historical fact. As extraordinary but authentic constructions, Lives may indulge in sensational oddities and extremes—from wearisome repetition to outrageous violence—but in the end, if accepted as truth, they genuinely move their readers. Caesarius of Heisterbach, in recounting the circumstances of his decision to become a monk, reported, "He exhorted me most earnestly to conversion, yet with no effect, until he told me [a miracle]."[16]

Excepting these few requirements of effect, but surely because of them, there is no single authoritative template for creating hagiographic narrative. A Proppian structuralist analysis defining fixed elements—roles and functions—is a tempting approach, but it ultimately fails to reveal the complexity or interest of the Lives.[17] Although often disparagingly tagged as indistinguishable from one another, saints' Lives do not comprise a set of basic episodes or scenes. Indeed, the sense that the Life is true because it is so extraordinary precludes absolute sameness. The norm is established only to be disrupted. The hagiographer works with the basic elements of a tradition of sanctity—oral reports, liturgical offices, popular devotions, miracle accounts, icons and pictures, perhaps even unadorned relics. From these "texts" he forms new narrative that will generate among the faithful the honor due the saint and the proper response of compunction.[18] Generating these effects, fulfilling expectations, and otherwise satisfying the desires of the reader entails certain familiar narrative paths. Rather than mere constraints, however, these familiar narrative sequences, or *topoi,* establish the saint's Life as a genre and also help produce its effects.

Genre depends upon predictability, formula, and repetition, but it also grows from reality and depends upon the variation, even violation, of its own formulas and norms in order to survive and develop. As defined by Jauss, the operation of genre is neither one of restriction nor of abstraction. Genres are unifying rather than dividing, not "a sequence . . . closed within themselves, encapsulated from one another . . . [but rather the] reciprocal relations that make up the literary system of a given historical moment."[19] Jauss emphasizes that genre has a situation in history, a "locus in life"; it is subject by its very nature to historical analysis because it is only comprehensible in terms of its generation from "typical situations and behaviors of a community."[20] The modern historian, of course, stands outside this process yet seeks to understand it from within.[21] However, by working both with and against generic norms, saints' Lives stage their own reception; it is precisely by examining this staging and its effects that we may capture a fuller understanding of these narratives.

The "sheer amount of vellum scratched up" (to use Thomas Head's phrase) to produce saints' Lives demonstrates the force and power of hagiographic generic norms: saints' Lives were perhaps the foremost creative literary form of the Middle Ages. One notable expression of such creativity takes the form of humor. From as early as the ninth century, hagiography was a rich field for satire and witticisms. The "Mock Elegy of a Gelded Ram," written at the court of Charles the Bald, plays on expectations about saintly bishops.[22] In the tenth century, Hrothswitha of Gandersheim wrote the decidedly comical (and decidedly generic) virgin's Life *Dulcitius*.[23] Head has described a poem by Letaldus (eleventh century) as a mock epic,[24] and at the end of our period, parodies such as *Nemo* and *Invicem,* as well as references in secular literature, use holy Lives to comic effect.[25] Such humor consistently calls for a thorough grounding in hagiographic types and norms in order to produce its effects.

More profound evidence of the power of the genre lies in the way paradigmatic sequences and *topoi* controlled the lived as well as the written Lives of the saints. For example, early written and illustrated Lives of virgins took certain limited forms. Virgins protected their chastity and performed charitable deeds, often serving the sick and the poor or distributing food (see fig. 35). As late as the thirteenth century, among the record numbers of new women saints that Donald Weinstein and Rudolph Bell record, the same virtues and actions dominate the Lives of holy women.[26] Caroline Bynum has demonstrated a wondrously creative variation within narratives about food and charity,[27] but they are still in some sense the *same* stories. Given the ample documentation, even scrutiny, of saints during the thirteenth century, it may be assumed that the hagiography reflects something of lived reality. It seems that in their own lives women genuinely attempted to reproduce the virtues and stories that they had read and seen. They were *topoi* come to life.

Even a saint such as Francis, often described as having broken the medieval mold, and as having re-created the very idea of the saint, is a product of a shaping process derived from the hagiographic genre. Certainly he remakes conceptions of sanctity, but he achieves this renewal by returning to hagiography's origins in the Life of Christ and the Lives of the Apostles.[28] The events in the Life of Francis are a *real* expression of the saint's fulfillment of Christ's injunction, "If any man will come after me, let him deny himself, and take up his cross daily, and follow me" (Luke 9:23). Furthermore, Francis's stigmata, a manifestation of the Crucifixion in the saint's own flesh, reflect an increasing medieval preoccupation with the sign of the cross itself. Francis (or at least the Francis of the hagiographers)[29] does not escape the intertextual and generic net of the Lives of the saints. Rather, he draws it up, bringing many traditions together and in the process pulling in an abundant catch of converts and believers.

THE HAGIOGRAPHIC PROJECT
AND THE GOAL OF EDIFICATION

Hagiographers repeatedly state their intention to edify their listeners and to inspire the faithful to imitation.[30] What do these goals mean for their audience?

Gregory of Tours illuminates what he defines as the purpose of hagiography in his *Life of the Fathers.* Hagiography, he argues, is not the writing of a multiplicity of Lives but the singular *"Life* of the saints." Because the saints all share one Life, that of Christ,[31] their Lives must bring that identity before the reader. Gregory emphasizes that hagiography will not only serve the individual Christian soul but will also strengthen the Church as a whole. In building and fortifying the Church, the "Life of the saints" therefore becomes both a unified and unifying project.

Gregory assigns two meanings to the notion of edification: to teach and to build. Hagiographers adopt and rework Paul's metaphor of the building of a tabernacle or temple in the soul (1 Cor. 3),[32] but they also represent the faithful themselves as the "lively stones" of the Church, which constitutes a "spiritual edifice" (1 Peter 2:5; see fig. 10, top right). Although most strongly articulated by Gregory of Tours and perhaps first enunciated by Victricius of Rouen in the fourth century, the double meaning also appears in Byzantine hagiography,[33] and it became a major theme in the works of Gregory the Great, as recent commentators have noted.[34] Some hagiographers even characterize the saints themselves as the "ornament" of this built church.[35] The theme continued to shape the perception of the cult of saints well into the high Middle Ages. Thomas Head has associated the prodigious writing and rewriting of hagiography during the tenth and eleventh centuries with Rodolphus Glaber's "shining mantle of churches" to argue that the "edification" of the Church may have been linked to its literal reconstruction in stone.[36]

In the *Dialogues,* Gregory the Great focuses on another important goal of the ecclesiastical project of telling the stories of the saints. In seeking to renew the Lives of the saints for the present day, he emphasizes recent saints and their miracles. He does so because he is aware of the needs of his audience and the ability of the saints to act as effective preachers through their deeds.[37] His interlocutor, Peter the Deacon, begins the conversation of the *Dialogues* by decrying the absence of "signs and miracles" in the Italy of his day. Gregory evokes a metaphor of sailing too far and losing sight of land or harbor to mourn the loss of "what was once actually in our possession."[38] Peter wants to hear more stories because "the lives of the saints are often more effective than mere instruction for inspiring us to love heaven as our home." He is eventually reassured that saints are not a phenomenon of the past and exclaims, "What astounding miracles for our times!"[39] The project of hagiography was never-ending. As Gregory recognized, hagiography required constant renewal to have its desired effect, to keep it fresh in the memory, and to perpetuate its action on the Christian mind. Peter confirms this by concluding, "We have new miracles, then, in imitation of the old."[40]

The principle of endless renewal makes clear that the building of the Church also signifies its progress toward salvation. A miniature from a manuscript of the Song of Songs in Bamberg illustrates this progress (fig. 6).[41] Movement in the Ottonian miniature is not linear, historical time but an upward spiral—a combination of the repetitive circle of the liturgy and the ascent toward salvation, represented by the reception of the Eucharist at the hands of Ecclesia, the Church personified. The sainted women and clerics about to receive the cup are followed in the center of the spiral by lay persons, newly baptized by St. Peter, all representative of the earthly Church.

By recording the details of the exemplary lives of the citizens of the City of God, hagiography builds the same upward movement. As Peter the Deacon notes, "it is very edifying to see men working miracles, for we gain a glimpse of the heavenly Jerusalem in its citizens here on earth." Gregory's eschatology is dependent on Augustine's conception of the City of God, but he places greater emphasis on the place of the saints in the construction of the city: "Because the end of the world presses upon us, it is necessary to gather living stones for the heavenly building."[42]

Indeed, the notion of time itself in hagiography is based on the interconnectedness of saints' Lives. Because the Lives of the saints have as their origin the Life of Christ and his spirit, their connection to historical time is weak. The Christian experiences the saint more immediately within the liturgy, and therefore as part of the *circulum anni,* than as part of mundane chronology. Saints seem only as near or far as present or past testimony makes them. Universal saints, such as martyrs, were known to have lived long ago but their power to intercede remained vivid and contemporary. Local saints such as bishops and holy monks performed miracles in the here and now, or at least within palpable boundaries of memory and geography. Rather than participating in a historical time, saints remade time into a process of salvation. The eleventh-century writer Peter Damian, in discussing the translation of a saint, observes that "the things that happened a long time ago . . . somehow seem recent and new."[43]

For their medieval readers, saints' Lives effected a progress toward salvation because the acts and miracles that they recounted served to edify the faithful and convert the unbeliever or those "hard of heart." Peter the Deacon notes in response to a Life recounted by Gregory that "the graciousness of almighty God toward us becomes apparent in these delightful miracles," identifying the effect of miracles with the action of God's grace.[44] Earlier in the *Dialogues,* Gregory the Great explains that grace derives from the action of the saintly narratives: "as we compare ourselves with those [saints] . . . we are filled with a longing for the future life," and we "love heaven as our home."[45] This effect depends upon a unique characteristic of salvational time: the saints need not wait until the end of time to take up residence in the heavenly Jerusalem, for they reside there even during their life on earth.

The salutary effects of the saints' acts will end only when time itself ends. Gregory recognizes the importance of this point for the faithful by devoting almost the entirety of book 4 of the *Dialogues* to the judgment of souls and the doctrines of the Last Judgment. The importance of the place of saints in eschatology persists into the high Middle Ages in Guibert's continuation of Gregory's discussion in *On Saints and Their Relics.* It is clear, then, that although they themselves are outside of time, the saints work in and throughout time to lead souls to salvation. Progress is effected in the souls who are saved, the citizens who are added to the chorus of the saints in Paradise (see plate 3).

In sum, in order to achieve their goals, the Lives of saints are made to be both affective and effective—but little else. They are rarely concerned with intrinsic

Figure 6. Ecclesia, *Song of Songs, Proverbs, and Daniel*, Bamberg, eleventh century. Bamberg, Staatsbibliothek, MSC. Bibl. 22, fol. 4v.

literary or artistic beauty (although some achieve it); they take Augustine's plain style and speak to the common Christian or even the illiterate.[46] The *vitae* are the essence of the sort of teaching that Gregory the Great counseled for the Church in his letter to Serenus of Marseilles—filled with acts, not dogma, narrative, not preaching, and written always with the Christian, or potentially Christian, listener in mind. Thus, directed to a living audience rather than to any static ideal of historical or theological perfection, a saint's Life is effective only when its audience is moved.[47]

Notwithstanding the clear importance of these hagiographic goals of compunction and edification, the mechanism of achieving such general effects is not always easy to pinpoint. Fortunately, some hagiographers specify their intent. Gregory the Great reveals precise details about how the audience should listen and react to his narratives; indeed the form of the *Dialogues* builds the audience into the text. Gregory and his deacon Peter regularly discuss the saints' Lives that Gregory recounts.[48] Gregory explains the finer points of doctrine in response to questions, but it is Peter's reactions to the narratives that are of most interest: Gregory portrays him as reacting, and thereby *prescribes* such reactions among the audience of the *Dialogues* themselves.

Peter expresses varied feelings about the saints' stories—hope and fear, delight, eagerness, and pleasure, even awe, wonder, and astonishment.[49] He also describes complex changes that occur within himself while he listens. He says he is "nourished" by the narratives; events that previously seemed insignificant, he now realizes, are "incomparably sublime."[50] The narratives, he clearly tells us, have enlarged his understanding and profoundly changed his attitude.

Yet to be moved is not the same as to imitate, a troubling problem about saintly narrative that, again, Gregory the Great's interlocutor helps to resolve. Hagiographers often claim to be providing a story for the faithful to imitate, yet often the lives are inimitable in their perfection.[51] Peter models a personal yet accessible response when he exclaims, "Whenever I hear of deeds that I am unable to imitate, I am more inclined to weep than to comment."[52] Peter's tears, of course, are not tears of frustration but of pity and compunction for his sins and inadequacies. In the *Dialogues,* Gregory argues that weeping—the "grace of tears"—is useful to the soul, working to soften it and thus open it to salvation.[53] He also, of course, recounts stories that show how such tears can save a sinful soul.[54] Peter, as a learned cleric, is far from a naive listener, yet he is depicted as reacting unashamedly to the effects of stories that many call naive. Specific narrative devices achieved these effects, and they shed light on particular conventions of hagiography.

RHETORICAL STRUCTURES:
REPETITIONS, REVERSAL, AND FRAMES

Saints' narratives incorporate structures and devices that operate in any narrative. The familiarity of these structures to audiences means that they come to be expected. Such expectations may be fulfilled, or they may be frustrated or even changed by a surprise or a twist that in turn creates new expectations.[55] In this sense they are "active," and have "dynamic character, that is, [they are] further determined through each new concretization."[56] As we look, things change. Yet underlying any reader's response to a narrative is a series of typicalities, a "horizon of expectations" (Jauss's term), or "variance" (Cerquiglini).[57] These typicalities are easily recognized in saints' Lives because hagiographic narrative is particularly inclined to repetition.

The first and most important repetitive structure in the "Life" of the saints consists of their narrative repetition of the Life of Christ. Gregory's use of the singular "Life" emphasizes that Christ's Life is a root narrative, paradigm, or alternatively, a "generic dominant" that all saints share.[58] Martyrs most obviously model their sacrifice on that of Christ, but all saints in some fashion follow his life. The relation of text to life in saints' Lives imitates the relation of the Gospel to Christ's life. Stephen Nichols identifies these "structures of meaning" as "not just one element of narrative language, among many, but, along with historical or human structures, a fundamental paradigm for narrative meaning. The most solemn moments of the epic hero's existence were cast, rhetorically and semiologically, as a metaphor of a corresponding moment in the life of Christ."[59]

The *Dialogues* of Gregory the Great offer a cogent and authoritative reading of this use of metaphor. Peter, Gregory's interlocutor, notes that a particular saint's miracles resemble those in the Old and New Testament, concluding, "This man must have been filled with the spirit of all the just." Surprisingly, Gregory replies in the negative, insisting that only one spirit was present, that of the Savior.[60] When Peter compares another saint's act to a specific scriptural miracle, Gregory again demurs. He denies that similarities lie in superficial likenesses and points instead to the deeper spiritual nature of the story. Gregory is arguing an expanded notion of Christo-mimesis.[61] He shows that saintly likeness to Christ extends beyond the limited narrative of Christ's bodily incarnation. Rather, a saint may also resemble aspects of Christ *Logos,* that is, the second person of the Trinity and the universal plan of salvation.[62] Gregory explores the correspondences between the acts of the saints and those of Christ, not in superficial similarities but in moral or theological lessons.

Gregory's approach is an encouragement to look beyond a superficial typology to the lessons and metaphorical meanings of the stories.[63] The Life of a bishop, a prince of the Church, may have little to do with the specifics of the Life of Christ, but if he is a saint he carries the "spirit of the Savior," even if he lacked the opportunity to be a martyr.[64] Other texts and life models that carry that spirit impinge upon and redirect the Gospel narrative, as part of a synchronic system of types. Hagiographers took special care to identify the acts or miracles performed by their subjects with those of Christ. Joan Petersen identifies both Gregory the Great's and Gregory of Tour's "fundamental aims" as finding "an acceptable substitute for martyrdom as a goal for sixth-century Christians."[65] The intent is to find a new way—different in substance but not in spirit—to imitate Christ.

The centrality of repetition as a concept underlying narration may perhaps be more clearly understood through Paul's description of the saints as the members of a body of which Christ is the head (1 Cor. 12:12–14). Again, it is Gregory the Great who elaborates, in a commentary on the four beasts of Ezekiel's vision. Gregory argues that, in the body of Christ as the Church: "as the breast is joined to the head, so the apostles are joined to the redeemer. As the arms are joined to the breast, so the martyrs are joined to the apostles. As the hands are joined to the arms, so the pastors and doctors are joined through good works to the martyrs."[66] Gregory's Church is a hierarchy of sorts, but a hierarchy literally and organically connected in a unity of body: Christ and the saints are joined as one.

However, along with this paradigmatic and even anagogic use of repetition to create a unity of the saints and Christ, repetition is also used in saints' stories in less elevated ways that nonetheless benefit their audience. "Repetition gives the reader a cumulative understanding of the abstractions that control . . . meaning," according to Suzanne Lewis.[67] Hagiographic repetition most commonly takes the form of the number three: One occurrence is unique; two may be chance, but three repetitions confirm a pattern.[68] In the Lives of the saints, threes show, for example, that saints can persist in their faith, that they can withstand torture, or that they have the true gift of prophecy. Of course, the number three also points to Christological elements, including the three days that Christ lay in his tomb and the Trinity.

The importance of repetition for hagiography extends even beyond the boundaries of the text. For example, epitomes of individual saints' Lives are continually repeated in the context of the liturgy.[69] Such repetition is a source of narrative power, for it lends authority and builds a sense of certainty, a connectedness to the life of Christ and the Church. As Gregory of Tours noted somewhat defensively, "it was the habit of rustic men to give greater veneration to those saints of God whose martyrdom they could read over and over."[70]

More generally, new versions of a saint's Life can also work as a form of repetition. A Life filled with grace bears repeating, although perhaps with variations that bring it up to date and show its relevance for modern concerns. Just as new saints bring the life of Christ into modern times, so new versions of the saint's Life allow it to address contemporary spiritual and political issues. Moreover, Lives (and their versions) are not limited to texts but also include illustrated cycles, liturgical offices and hymns, and epitomes. These "re-tellings" have distinct qualities. For example, liturgical offices emphasize not only the sacramental nature of the saint's Life but also the saint's conformity to his or her particular type.

Saintly types, of course, are themselves established by repetition. Indeed, one sort of hagiographic repetition concerns the literal reiteration of saintly Lives by other saintly Lives. Such repetition may even reach the extreme of what a modern reader would call plagiarism. For example, the Life of Regina is identical in virtually all but the saint's name to that of Margaret of Antioch.[71] But if imitation is the highest form of flattery, hagiographic repetition is the most genuine form of authentication. A saintly Life repeated in one detail or many shows a certain divine perfection, especially within a type. Nonetheless, repetition is usually not so slavish, and it is precisely the variation within repetition that establishes different types of saints, as well as an interaction of those types, within the genre of the *vita*.

At a somewhat smaller scale, the *topos* is a more limited but important example of such repetition with variation. For the purposes of this study, I define the literary term *topos* relatively broadly, as a nonoriginal narrative unit, ranging from an adjectival phrase to a story sequence.[72] In pictorial hagiography, *topoi* often make reference to other, similar images, thereby enhancing recognizability and clarifying meaning. For example, in an illustration from the Life of Liudger (see fig. 65), the saint heals a supplicant while seated at dinner. The illumination's composition and the inclusion of a chalice and bread clearly allude to the Last Supper and thereby enhance the sacramental message of the miracle (see p. 159). Historians and even literary scholars have tended to disparage the literary achievement of hagiographic narrative, citing its profuse repetitiveness. Certainly, under this argument, if verifiable facts or novel expression are the measure of quality, then *topoi* are symptomatic of texts devoid of imagination and creativity. Leopold Genicot, however, points a way to see hagiographic *topoi* in a different light, demonstrating that precisely because of the similarities perpetuated by repetition, small differences—which contemporary readers would have easily recognized—assumed an increased and interpretable importance.[73] It is abundantly evident that *topoi* are reused purposefully by hagiographers. They are reliable carriers of meaning that either usefully represent certain tenets or principles of sanctity or predictably serve to arouse feelings of awe, sympathy, or respect. Simply put, they are effective.[74]

Topoi can vary significantly in length, although longer *topoi,* composed of multiple episodes, can more conveniently be called "sequences." Such sequences often create meaning through juxtaposition or through the expected completion of a story episode. For example, the narrative unit that depicts the torture of St. Lucy is coupled in her Life with the defeat of her pagan persecutor (see figs. 41 and 42). The two-part sequence clearly demonstrates the saint's spiritual and even mundane victory through suffering.

The complex role of sequences demonstrates that although medieval narrative is generally episodic in nature, such episodes are rarely simple;[75] one literary study compares medieval texts to elaborate scene-painting that details emotion within static units.[76] Sequences or units can also be more referential than action-oriented, more symbolic than descriptive, and inextricably but obscurely linked to other units of the narrative. Although narrative "continuity" or "logic" may be weak or even nonexistent, hagiographic sequences or units can be used by the hagiographer to build, if not suspense, at least expectations of holiness or horror. Repeated and ever-more-awful tortures, for example, create a strong cumulative affect in the audiences of the Lives of martyrs (see plate 1 and figs. 15 and 16). By demonstrating that the saint can withstand tortures or self-induced hardships, the hagiographer builds a foundation of holiness, block by block, in order to move his audience to compunction.

Textual figures or paradigms from the Gospels, the "generic dominant," often generate sequences in hagiographic texts. Christ enjoins his Apostles to preach and to baptize, and the two actions in sequence become a key narrative unit in the Lives of Apostles (see fig. 54). In the Lives of bishop saints, heirs to the Apostles, the most important unit of narrative becomes, by a small permutation, the liturgical performance in which the bishop preaches and baptizes (see fig. 57 and plate 4).[77]

Sequences can also contrast.[78] Within a single image or episode or between episodes, hagiographers often define their subject's virtue by juxtaposing it against a moral opposite: a lying pagan with a truthful deacon (see fig. 14); a possibly homosexual prostitute with a virgin (see fig. 40); a taunting, rude lord with a respectful, honorable convert (see fig. 140). Abstract polarities might also be opposed: pagan idolatry with Christian faith, or violence and destruction with Christian peace. Such contrasts heighten the audience's appreciation of the saint's virtue and therefore commonly appear in medieval saints' Lives. They are *topoi* on a large scale.

Unfortunately, it is not possible or useful to draw up a standard list of structures or forms to be found in hagiographic texts. Analysis of how sequences function over long and short parts of the narrative, and how these sequences are formed into a whole, provides greater insight into the structure of pictorial narrative.[79] Even if the narratives of saints' Lives are episodic and do not satisfy modern expectations for suspense, climax, and narrative closure, they have their own integrity and fulfill audience needs in forging an adequate picture of sanctity.

Although saints' Lives are not exactly "popular culture" in the modern sense, examples from popular culture work well to suggest how *topoi* and sequences function.[80] The television situation comedy *I Love Lucy,* for instance, shows how repetition creates expectation. In each episode a sequence of *topoi* or plot structures is repeated: Lucy bumbles into some fantastic and disastrous scheme but is rescued or forgiven by her loving husband, Ricky. Whatever the particular narrative permutations, the viewer feels superior yet also sympathetic and ultimately experiences a genuine satisfaction at the final return to balance and harmony. Such balance, however, is only part of what makes the ending satisfying. Much of the feeling of satisfaction comes in knowing the outcome in advance. Repetition of *topoi* and themes allowed the show to become an icon of American life, reasserting secure family values and familiar story lines, offering both a paradigm of all-American virtue and a serving of empathy in unexpected form.

Saints' Lives must have provided precisely this sort of narrative satisfaction by reaffirming values and fulfilling expectations. One need not identify with the saint, but predictability and repetition in these instances become compensatory virtues. Furthermore, such repetition does not necessarily grow tedious. Commenting on one of Gregory's stories, Peter says, "though I have heard this account from others, I admit that, every time I hear it, it sounds new."[81]

Notwithstanding its charms, at the bottom of this smug edifice of predictability lies a lever that turns it all on its head. Jauss would call it violation or norm-breaking; Nichols calls it paradox; most simply named, it is reversal.[82] Precisely because of the expectations created by repetition and genre, reversal becomes the most effective device of hagiographic narrative. Its use was familiar from the foundation narratives of the Christian Church: Christ the wretched, executed criminal is the victorious God. Christ the humble is king. In death is life. Nevertheless, however effective when first encountered, long familiarity might deaden the effects of these paradigmatic Christological narratives. The repetition, development, and reversal of similar themes in narratives of the Lives of the saints becomes the locus for a renewal of compunctive effect.

The discussion of reversals underlies much of the best modern scholarship on saints. Peter Brown begins his *Cult of the Saints* by exploring the shock felt by late Antique society at the Christian attitude toward the dead. The image of corrupt and horrible death is transformed into the possibility of pure and healing wonder. Caroline Bynum's work uncovers a "startling reversal at the heart of Christian imagery. . . . In the mass, priest and God are symbolically woman." God "lactating on the cross, bearing the soul in his womb, feeding the faithful from the hands of his special cooks and servants, the clergy," she argues, becomes feminine. Patrick Geary shows how theft could be sacred, and Evelyn Vitz finds that the subject of the saint's Life is God or even the reader as much as it is the saint.[83]

A reversal of expectations is always at the core of the medieval narratives of the saints: the day of death becomes the *dies natali*. Saints are humble yet victorious. They gladly welcome torture, which purifies and heals them rather than harming them. Again, Gregory, an influential exegete throughout the Middle Ages, describes such contradiction as indicative of meaning,[84] and in his *Dialogues* notes that "since [saints] are not ashamed to accept dishonor among men, they receive a spiritual rank among the most honorable citizens."[85] Such reversals extend to every level of narrative—even a single episode can work against expectations—and reveal the nature of sanctity. For example, among the miracles of the late Antique doctor saints Cyrus and John, cures effected through patently implausible means carry an indisputable significance: the saints' power is based on grace, not logic.[86]

Indeed, grace, in its power and unpredictability, is precisely the mechanism that lies behind the perversity of saintly narrative. Grace is not earned or deserved; it is *bestowed* by God, apparently at will, and those who receive grace must reveal it in their sanctity. Gregory the Great insists that "the deed depends on the gift and not the gift on the deed; otherwise grace would no longer be grace. Gifts precede every deed."[87] Nevertheless, the seeming perversity of how grace is bestowed is finally the most predictable of all the qualities of a saint's Life. The genre must continually expand and test its limits in order to achieve this, its most important effect.

One of the primary mechanisms by which reversals are effected in hagiographic narrative is the frame, a literary or artistic device that controls both the narrative and the audience's reception of it. Our desire as readers "frames" the hagiographic narrative and in effect induces its production, while also driving every aspect of the narrative.[88] However, in addition to the universal frame of the reader's desire, particular, even unique frames color individual narratives. A frame may consist of one narrative enfolding another, giving the nested stories interdependent meanings, as in the text *and* illustrations of the Lives of Romanus and Barulas (see plate 1).[89] Other frames define the authority of the Life's narrator, the saint, or the viewer. A pictorial frame associates St. Lucy with the Five Wise Virgins (see fig. 31); a pictorial detail shows Alban's true conversion through sight, a conversion that is offered up to the reader repeatedly in other narratives that interweave with the saint's own (see fig. 130).[90] In each of these cases, the act of reading or viewing (or both) is underlined and problematized.[91] Moreover, if the hagiographer makes an attempt to achieve a metadiscursive discourse, to go beyond mere words and pictures, the frame seems to provide the jumping-off point or, at least, a moment for reflection. It stimulates the reader or viewer to read with the heart or to look with the "eyes of faith." As Eugene Vance argues, such a frame forges a connection beyond discourse into the "edifice of discourses that are the living expression of the social order."[92] Even if the texts falls short of metadiscourse, it rejoins the notion of hagiography as a project of the edification of the Church and its locus in life.

PICTORIAL NARRATIVE

Narrative texts and pictures share many important qualities, but there are also essential differences that set pictorial narrative emphatically apart from texts. In particular, issues of reception, especially in a medieval context, call attention to differences. Furthermore, as it was perceived and used by medieval hagiographers, visual narrative had unique and powerful potential.

It is often assumed that pictures merely illustrate their texts—a notion apparently validated by the fact that pictorial narrative rarely, if ever, precedes verbal narrative (whether oral or written).[93] However, despite a secondary temporal creation, pictorial narrative is in no other way secondary. Rather than as illustration wholly dependent on an underlying text, pictorial narrative is best understood as a partially independent *version* of the story, one that locates reception and interpretation in a markedly different medium. Pictures strive against problems (and achieve effects) different from those of verbal stories because of various qualities particular to images: the difficulty of the representation of time, the related need for the activation of still images, the striking effect of imagery, and the relationship of imagery to visualization. Each of these qualities creates complex issues of reception, both in general and in particularly medieval terms. The relationship between any particular text and a corresponding pictorial narrative, however, is shaped first by a very simple principle—that of selection.

Depending upon which parts of a written story they choose to represent, artists can shape pictorial narrative in ways radically different from texts. The results are anything but simple. The text of the Life of King Edmund of East Anglia, written by a tenth-century French author, focuses on kingship. The pictures however, revise this theme in accordance with twelfth-century English and monastic ideals of kingship (see pp. 216–54). The text of his Life describes Edmund giving charity to widows and orphans and the poor, but the accompanying illustrations show him distributing coins to men whose staves, purses, and bare feet distinguish them as a particular type of indigents: pilgrims (see plate 6). These pilgrims reappear in the Life—now as Edmund's "people"—when the vanquished East Anglians confront their conqueror, a sinful pagan.[94] The artist has chosen what to represent and by so doing redirects the story of Edmund's deeds to center on spiritual pilgrimage and a "pilgrim king." Obviously, selection is a simple, but often overlooked, means by which an artist differentiates picture from text. Most other differences between words and pictures are more clearly grounded in dissimilarities between the media.

Perhaps the most striking and most often discussed point of difference between words and pictures is how time is represented. In texts, by means of minimal conventions, events can be aligned in sequence and read in real time to provide a convincing simulacrum of time's passage.[95] In contrast, a sequence of pictures does not pass through and away from consciousness in the same way, and its elements cannot smoothly be connected to one another. Conventions of pictorial narrative must make up the difference and alert the viewer to an intention of chronological continuity. Some common conventions are the repetition of characters or settings, a uniformity of picture size and format, sequential ordering, or, at a minimum, placement in proximity to a text.[96] Without a few of these elements, the process of narrative storytelling in pictures does not have the opportunity to begin.[97]

But even if some or all of these conventions are present, the connective action of story that seems natural in texts remains insistently artificial and representational in medieval miniatures. Otto Pächt addressed the issue in a still provocative book, *The Rise of Pictorial Narrative in Twelfth-Century England,* illustrating his arguments with examples from the Life of St. Cuthbert.[98] In a few examples in the *vita,* a central figure of Cuthbert is flanked by before-and-after scenarios (see fig. 75, in which Cuthbert reassures a boy that he will eat, and an eagle supplies the meal). Pächt contends that, because the figure of Cuthbert himself is not repeated, the artist has ingeniously included the element of time within the very substance of the single picture: time has passed and, in effect, Cuthbert stands as the agent of change. We see miraculous cause and effect arrayed on either side of the saint.

Although this argument suggests a means to read time in this miniature, it is flawed as a general model for interpretation in three ways. One is hagiographic: the saint is not really the agent of change in a miracle but instead serves as a medium for the power of God.[99] A second difficulty concerns Pächt's conception of this formal device as a major innovation; in fact, it rarely occurs. In a more common configuration, the saint is repeated within the image, included in both episodes. Finally, Pächt describes the artist as using a sort of artistic magic to include the intangible "time" into the tangible substance of the miniature, but ultimately the trickster artist must still rely on his viewer to perceive and register the presence of what after all is not magic but illusion, the product of reading and viewing conventions. It seems impossible to escape the conclusion that time is located in the viewer's imagination in precisely the same way that it is in the reader's imagination. Although Pächt's particular example is flawed, he rightfully draws attention to hagiographic narrative as innovative and important.

The converse of the problem of how to represent time is the impression of simultaneity that pictures produce. Gregory the Great, in the *Moralia in Job,* notes that words are understood in sequence but that the visual is encompassed in a single glance that illumines the mind.[100] Gregory is not entirely correct—looking also takes time and interpretation[101]—but he does underscore two key elements of the medieval understanding of sight: the notions of stasis and totality. The latter, the forceful impression that sight "reveals all," is at the origin of much of the power attributed to art during the Middle Ages.

The abundance of details necessary to compose a visual image lies at the heart of the effects of stasis and totality. A text need not describe the color and cut of a character's clothing, nor specify details of setting. Visual narrative, on the other hand, cannot avoid being concerned with these particulars. A great deal of persuasive strength, moreover, resides in such seemingly inconsequential detail. These elements can set narrative context and mood; they can create a predisposition in viewers, who do not notice how and why a particular image seems so somber, so

impressive, or so lively. Visual details might even implicate political or religious beliefs. All these effects are masked and difficult to observe, for as David Summers
puts it, "a [picture] naturalizes the manifest contrivance of the organization in which
it plays a part and thus conceals the whole level of ideological significance of that
organization."[102] The naturalizing action may lead a viewer to belittle a picture as
mere illustration, but that same action thereby operates without the viewer's
awareness. As Summers notes, it is the art historian's particular task to apprehend
and analyze these effects.

Roland Barthes argues that there is no "noise" in literary narrative, no extrane-
ous or meaningless detail.[103] Similarly, the details of pictures, though seemingly
unimportant, are not accidental. (Pictures are not snapshots.) The artist has made
choices, whether innovative or conventional, in representing each element, and
while visual details may enter the viewer's consciousness less forcefully than do descriptions in texts, they are never meaningless. They are an essential part of what
fulfills narrative's object, turning "knowing into telling."[104] Gregory's "single glance"
may not be phenomenologically correct, but it does describe the powerful encompassing action of the visual.

The qualities that time assumes in pictures, both stasis and simultaneity, are clearly
indications that pictures rely on active engagement by the viewer. This engagement,
however, is not merely a function of the perception of time; it implicates many other
aspects of how images are received.

The letters to Serenus from Gregory the Great (justly characterized as the Church
Father most sympathetic to the visual)[105] concerning the use of images by the institutional Church are central to all discussions of pictures in the Middle Ages.[106]
Gregory commends pictures, "books for the illiterate," as a means of teaching, but
is careful to differentiate the viewing of pictures from idolatry: "To adore images
is one thing; to teach with their help what should be adored is another." He
specifically endorses hagiography or religious stories, arguing that "tradition permits the deeds of the saints (or holy persons) to be depicted in holy places." Herbert Kessler has asserted the missionary value of such material,[107] but, as Lawrence
Duggan and Celia Chazelle have argued, pictures were never intended to serve as
independent visual "texts."[108]

Indeed Gregory's approach to images transcends the didactic. Gregory's concluding comment—"From the sight of the event portrayed [viewers] should catch
the ardor of compunction"—has been labeled an afterthought,[109] but this notion
of compunction (already familiar from the *Moralia* and the *Dialogues*), is central to
his conception of the Christian use of images. The potential affective element of

images is precisely what makes them so appropriate for teaching. In his well-known tract *Pastoral Care,* Gregory grants extraordinary power to the visual, focusing on the process of sight in which the viewer literally takes the visual to heart: "It is also well said that [the images] were painted, because, when the images of external things are drawn into consciousness, what is revolved in the mind by thinking in pictured imagery, is, as it were, portrayed on the heart."[110] Gregory here delineates two crucial effects of the emotional power of pictures. The first is the sense of illumination and direct access to knowledge that the "totality" effect can give. The second is the perception of the exterior world being brought to the interior consciousness through an act of seeing accompanied by emotion.

Gregory's descriptions of "draw[ing] into consciousness" and "revolv[ing] in the mind" (or in the Letters, "gathering" [*colligere*])[111] as modes of active engagement with images constitute a conceptualization that is valuable not only for medieval issues of reception but also more generally. It may be that the need for activation is both the strength and the weakness of pictorial narrative.[112] The weakness perhaps is obvious: pictures seem lacking in movement, in action, in "telling in time." The less apparent strength comes into play when the viewer is called upon to remedy the deficit by making an investment in the narrative.[113] When, in Gregory's understanding, the act of sight brings the exterior to the interior, it is a moment of commitment. By allowing a sight or vision to be portrayed (*depingitur*) or engraved on the heart through contemplation, the viewer takes a spiritual action. The figure of the engraved heart is thus a common medieval *topos* that denotes this commitment. At the same time, however, it suggests a model of an unmediated transfer of knowledge,[114] because for Gregory, although seeing is acknowledged as a conscious action, it never demands the effort of interpretation that we understand it to require. For Gregory, any necessary labor on the part of the viewer is conceived as the work of memory or "visualization." Ideas are "revolved in the mind" until they are impressed whole and essentially unchanged.[115] Although Gregory elides the act of interpretation, his notion that the viewer makes the pictorial story his or her own is one that has once again found favor among modern scholars, particularly in terms of visualization.

Gregory's remarks about vision do not, of course, arise *ex nihilo* but creatively conjoin Stoic thought and biblical text.[116] These origins are illuminated by Jaś Elsner, who has studied two distinctly different currents in ancient visuality. He has articulated how patterns of reception for symbolic art differ from those of the viewing of mimetic art, a difference based on differentiating the "truth" from the "lies of nature." Philostratus, in the *Life of Apollonius of Tyana,* argued that *phantasia* (a stoic concept) "is wiser than mimesis. For imitation will represent that which will be seen with the eyes while *phantasia* will represent that which cannot, for the latter proceeds with reality as its basis."[117] Elsner explains that the rhetorical exercise of *ekphrasis* originates in this Stoic concept of *phantasia*—visualization or presentation of an object. In practice *phantasia* also came to mean "the situation in which enthusiasm and emotion make the speaker see what he is saying and bring it visually before his audience."[118] *Phantasia* even had the capacity to imprint and alter the soul. It was thought that it could, in effect, induce in its audience the original vision of truth or reality through verbal or pictorial means. Thus visualization in the ancient world was seen, at least by some, as an instrument for conveying truth.[119]

Visualization—the conceptual formation of imagery in response to either text or image—helps the viewer or reader to take in and understand an idea. In modern controlled experiments, visualization's effect on memory has been explored from several different aspects. Visualization assists in memory retrieval, particularly in the case of concepts that lend themselves to image, and it can mediate between verbal stimulus and response.[120] Memory is further assisted by the conjunction of verbal and visual, and to a certain limited extent by emotion, as well as "bizarreness."[121] There is evidence, moreover, that visualized images built up over time can be remarkably accurate and can even take time to "scan."[122]

These characteristics play an important role in how medieval narrative was shaped for the viewer. Joaquin Pizarro has noted the scenic quality of hagiographic narrative, which builds individual scenes through distinctive details.[123] Gabrielle de Nie has argued that it is this scenic quality in dreams and mental images that allows them to "be regarded as actual vehicles of God's communication with man."[124] So, even if, as Ellen Esrock has shown, visualization is not entirely respected in the modern literary world,[125] it was an essential aspect of early medieval narrative, needed to render both text and picture effective. The following examples clarify this function.

In his Lives of the bishops of Ravenna, the ninth-century writer Agnellus claims to tell the story of early bishops of the city from their portraits alone: "And if any among you should wonder how I was able to create the likeness I have drawn, you should know that a picture taught me."[126] If such extravagant imagination is inaccessible to historical investigation, it nonetheless demonstrates that the early medieval viewer was encouraged to let images come alive in his mind—to let them tell their stories. The fourth-century poet Prudentius's description of the martyrdom of Cassian in the *Peristephanon* not only shows the possibilities of visualization but also evidences the ease of narrative movement from image to text and vice-versa.[127] Prudentius describes a vision that appeared to him after he prayed before

Figure 7. Prudentius prays before the shrine of Cassian,
Peristephanon IX, in *Prudentius Opera,* Reichenau (?), c. 900. Bern,
Burgerbibliothek, Cod. 264, p. 119.

a picture at Cassian's martyrium. The vision was "in colors" and so remarkably detailed that it told Prudentius the story of the saint's Passion. The text claims that the
pictura refert—that is, in both senses of the verb, it tells and actually "brings to
mind."[128] The painting was apparently complete in one scene, yet, in fulfillment of
the imaging/imagining process, the artist of a Reichenau manuscript from c. 900
chose to illustrate Prudentius's description of the Passion of St. Cassian with two
scenes filled with "bizarre" detail and a "frame": a depiction of Prudentius himself
praying (figs. 7–9).[129] Thus, we have a sequence: Prudentius's pious prayer evokes a
vision, which in turn inspires the poet to compose an *ekphrasis* and narrative, which
in turn leads to a set of narrative illustrations. At each step—image-poem-images—
a narrative impetus expands and retells the story by supplying further details. The
effect grows in drama and potential impact at each stage of visualization.

Visualized images do not simply inhabit the memory; they also, Gregory claims,
have the power to move the soul. Augustine summarized the process in comments
to his congregation after a reading of the Passion of Cyprian: "we heard with our
ears, we watched with our mind, we saw his struggle, we felt fear for him in danger, we hoped for the assistance of God."[130] Augustine is not speaking of pictures,
but he describes a sequence of sensations that progress from apprehending, to vi-
sualizing, to experiencing emotion, and finally to turning toward God. Prudentius's
affective identification with the martyr similarly shows the powerful effect of a picture and an ensuing "vision" on the writer's emotions and faith.[131]

Figure 8. Cassian teaching and Cassian tried, *Peristephanon* IX, in *Prudentius Opera*, Reichenau (?), c. 900. Bern, Burgerbibliothek, Cod. 264, p. 120.

Figure 9. Cassian is martyred, and his soul taken to heaven, *Peristephanon* IX, in *Prudentius Opera*, Reichenau (?), c. 900. Bern, Burgerbibliothek, Cod. 264, p. 121.

Indeed, visualization was perceived as so powerful that it was called upon to battle the enemies of the Church. In 1025, at the Synod of Arras, Gerald of Cambrai used Gregory's arguments about the power of imagery against heretics who contested the veneration of the cross. Gerald is perhaps more specific than Gregory, claiming that the Crucifixion "excited the interior soul of man . . . inscribing the passion and death of Christ on the membrane of the heart so that each one will recognize within himself what he owes to his Saviour."[132] Nevertheless, Gerald's debt to Gregory is evident, and his comments incorporate the Church father's remarks into a complex understanding of the interaction of images, visualization, and affective devotion.[133]

These effects of visualization and reception finally draw us back once more to the problem of edification and imitation. Precisely what is the viewer taking into his or her own heart? How are these saints' Lives edifying? How is one to imitate them? What change in the soul is effected by the engraved heart? In the *Dialogues,* Gregory answers that hagiographic texts strike the soul with compunction, and it is clear that the potential action of pictorial hagiography is all the more immediate because emotional response constitutes a central effect of the visual.[134] Furthermore, while the visualization of saints' Lives can make their audience turn toward God, Gregory still points to the possibility of *imitating* the saints. This imitation can include not only the mimesis of a saint's actions but also the imitation of qualities such as saintly vision and prayer.

Gregory's description of the movement from exterior to interior that takes place during vision implies a change—not in what is viewed, but in the viewer. For vision and visualization to have its full effect, we must use our sight correctly. Augustine commands us to "arouse the reason of the heart, wake up the interior inhabitant of thine interior eyes, let it take to its windows, examine the creature of God. . . . Stir up, I say, the eye of reason, use thine eyes as a man should."[135] In the *Dialogues,* Gregory argues that true wonders are apprehended "with spiritual vision, purified with acts of faith and abundant prayers"[136] and then describes a saint who gazed on a miracle: "all the powers of his mind unfolded, and he saw the whole world gathered up before his eyes in what appeared to be a single ray of light."[137] The simultaneity of the vision calls to mind Gregory's comments in the *Moralia.* However, in this miraculous vision, attendant on a divinely granted vision of the ascent of another saint to heaven, the unified and illuminating nature of sight is even more powerfully and concisely figured (see fig. 125). Even if such powerful revelations are limited to saints, the occurrence of such a miracle argues that purified sight—the eye used as it should be—is open to truth conveyed by vision.[138]

How does one purify sight? Early medieval writers offer two alternatives that remain in force throughout the Middle Ages: Paulinus of Nola proposes liturgical purification, while Gregory recommends "acts of faith and abundant prayer."

The comments of the fourth-century writer Paulinus concerning the rite of baptism survive in two letters to his follower Severus. In the first, Paulinus expresses his reluctance to supply Severus with a portrait: "what consolations of real affection are you trying to get from appearances without life?"[139] Skeptical of corporeal sight and distinguishing between inner and outer eyes (see pp. 103–4), he argues that Christ "came, to enlighten the blind and to make blind those who see, so that our eyes which had been opened to sin should be blinded, and on the other hand so that the eyes which had been blinded should be opened."[140] Finally Paulinus assures his student that he, Severus, already owns best portrait of his friend and teacher, "painted . . . in the fleshly tablets of your heart."[141]

In a second letter, Paulinus relents and sends a verse for a portrait that Severus has commissioned and placed in his baptistery at Primuliacum along with a portrait of St. Martin. Paulinus disparages his own portrait ("Martin is here so that you may see a model of perfect life, whereas Paulinus schools you in how to merit forgiveness"),[142] but he forgives Severus for his zeal. Paulinus traces a virtuous motive in Severus's actions, writing that the newly baptized, "refashioned by water and by God," see with new and innocent eyes—"the eyes which had been blinded [are now] . . . opened." Severus has sought "to give a healthy formation to the persons renewed by baptism, [by placing] before them two completely different portraits, in order that on leaving the sacred font they might simultaneously see the exemplar to avoid and the model to follow."[143] This schematic credits sight with the literal shaping of the newly reborn soul.

Paulinus's remarkable text not only illuminates issues of vision but also specifically endorses pictorial hagiography. Paulinus first argues that sight will reconfigure the soul and then recommends that the model for reshaping should be the representation of a saint. He praises the portrait of Martin, which "arms our faith by good example and courageous words," and "manifest[s] . . . the shape of right living and the aggregate of virtues." All this is imputed to be somehow present in a single portrait supplemented with verses. Viewers in late Antiquity had more confidence than their modern counterparts in the notion that physiognomy reveals the true nature of the soul,[144] but Paulinus's explication nonetheless ascribes altogether remarkable powers of revelation to a simple portrait. An active process of visualization, making use of both text and image, is obviously meant to be at work, and pictorial hagiography holds a very important place in this process.

In contrast to Paulinus's argument that sight has great power to impress the "fleshly tablets of the heart" if it is preceded by the liturgical and sacramental purification of baptism,[145] Gregory recommends "acts of faith and abundant prayer." Gregory thus counsels action that might be continuing, incremental, and devotional rather than unique and sacramental. Furthermore, Gregory's is a path that the saints could mark out for Christians in their actions and their stories. Rather than recommend the impress of character in a single moment and a single picture, Gregory recommends action. His approach is more conducive to the development of narrative, especially pictorial narrative, in the service of a "change of heart."

In place of admirable but unattainable heroic acts, however, Gregory counsels viewers to follow the saints in faith and prayer. Indeed, the illustrated Lives of the saints provided a readily imitated gestural vocabulary of prayer and humility and a means that could purify not only the eyes but the entire body. Again, Gregory's writings seem to support this approach, for he argues that it is the body, not the words, of the saint that contains a message for the faithful, and that the inward soul is manifested by outward signs.[146]

That people of the Middle Ages imitated the gestures they saw depicted in illustrations of moral exemplars is not an implausible suggestion. Jean-Claude Schmitt has amply demonstrated a continuing medieval belief in the notion that gesture reveals and even controls the soul, and Joaquin Pizarro notes that gesture is one of the richest elements of the scenic detail of early medieval narrative.[147] A number of medieval writers, moreover, proposed programs of gestures, the regular performance of which would eventually result in a reformation of the soul. A particularly telling story is related of one of the followers of St. Francis. Brother John fastidiously copied the saint's gestures and movements, even to the point of absurdity: "when St. Francis stood in a church or in any remote place for prayer, [John] wanted to see and look at him so that he might copy all his gestures. If St. Francis bent his knees or clasped his hands to heaven or spat or coughed he did the same."[148] Francis begins to admonish John for his "simplicity" but comes to marvel at it, for John ultimately dies in "holy perfection." John peers at Francis, even during the saint's most private moments, as if he were a tableau vivant or perhaps already an icon, if yet living. His story attests that the visible actions of a saint, no matter how mundane, are worthy of imitation. The story dates to the thirteenth century, but it evokes and crystallizes earlier sentiments, as *topoi* often do. It is not a major extrapolation to argue that, if imitating the gestures of the saints themselves is an ideal, viewing and imitating their gestures as revealed in pictures may be equally beneficial.

The illustrated Lives of the saints provide ample evidence of the importance of perfected gesture.[149] We have images of the saints praying, resisting temptation, suffering patiently and humbly through the worst torments—and praying again. Perhaps it is precisely the vision of saintly bodies, so human and often so pitiable, with which the viewer can identify most intimately. Particularly in the case of prayer, which is discussed at length in medieval sources, there is much to be learned. For example, Peter the Chanter in the twelfth century argues that prayer is best taught at schools of theology, yet he allows that all members of society—not only masters of theology—should pray.[150] Though the illiterate were not able to read the Chanter's learned treatise on prayer, they could imitate the pictures they saw within it, as well as similar ones in the illustrated Lives of saints. Theatrical performances even posed actors in the prayerful attitudes of saints for the edification of the faithful.[151] As Peter insisted, when the faithful "mastered these rules [of comportment in prayer] as they are practiced by the perfect, we will be able to enter heavenly society."[152] Ultimately, a profoundly meaningful imitation is sought. The strictly visual reading of pictorial hagiography shows how through imitating the bodies of the saints (even if not their literal suffering or martyrdom) the opportunity for the powerful action of empathy knows no bounds. By reading the *bodies* of the saints, medieval viewers, even illiterate ones, may have found a means of access to these narratives.

CONCLUSION

In the foregoing, I have emphasized that the genre of hagiographic writing was well-known to the medieval audience but remains generally unfamiliar to the modern reader and viewer. Only by becoming familiar with elements of this generic form and its "horizon of expectations" will the modern reader-viewer begin to understand the Lives and be capable of recognizing innovation.

Above all, the Lives of the saints are not records but constructions, designed by the hagiographer for effect, and they achieve their effects through rhetorical devices and narrative manipulation. Even while involved in such artful construction, however, the hagiographer never represents his efforts as anything but the truth—a truth that has particular qualities within the hagiographic context. It is achieved through the entirety of the constructed Life rather than in any individual detail, and it aspires to a reality above mere mimetic description. Furthermore, it has two important functions. First, as edification, truth teaches individual Christians and builds the strong and secure "edifice" of the church of the saints. Second, it inspires its Christian audience to compunction by revealing pain and horror undiluted by aesthetic distance. Compunction itself moves the soul and induces it to action and conversion.

As one version of narrative saints' Lives, pictorial hagiography is particularly useful in achieving these ends. Gregory the Great argues that pictures are not only instructive and didactic but also effective in a very literal sense because they strike the soul. They give an impression of simultaneity, stasis, and wholeness that allows the unmediated apprehension of their contents. Thus, unlike texts, they have the unique ability to directly penetrate the heart, where spiritual change can most easily be effected.

Pictorial hagiography takes unique advantage of these ideas. In making use of the process of visualization whereby the viewer takes visual information into the "heart"—that is, the memory—the artists created relatively static or "scenic" pictures that were filled with detail, richly resonant symbols, and references to other, similar hagiographic scenes. This referencing of *topoi* is one means by which genre becomes especially important to understanding how these narratives were received by their medieval audiences. A sort of intertextual reading or "interpictorial" viewing must have been the primary interpretive activity of the audiences.[153] The recognizability of the *topos*—whether a single scene, a sequence, or even a gesture—is founded on repetition and is crucial in conveying meaning. However, *topoi* also signify by means of small but telling changes and even through reversals. Indeed, reversals lie at the core of the most compelling hagiographic narratives, imbuing the stories with a sense of the seemingly capricious nature of grace.

Given the emphasis on change and innovation in all of the above, it may come as something of a surprise to the reader, that, in the following chapters, it will be of the first importance to underline the conventionalities and standard qualities of saints' Lives types in order to understand the genre. At the same time, however, we will not sink entirely into the torpor of sameness. I hope to give some sense of the twists and turns, the innovation in each hagiographic type that can come only after the typical has been mastered.

MARTYRS' PASSIONS

Bearing Witness

ॐ

For what is a martyr . . . except an imitator of Christ?
The vanquisher of rabid lust, the suppressor of ambition, and a candidate for death?
—Victricius of Rouen, *De Laude sanctorum, 6*, trans. Giles Constable

[Martyrs are] in image, by virtue of signs, what [Christ] Himself is by nature of divinity.
—Aponius, *In Canticum Canticorum explanatio*, 12, trans. Giles Constable

MARTYR STORIES WERE the first saints' Lives, and they remain the foundation of the genre. The reasons are clear and persuasive: the Lives of martyrs are unparalleled in demonstrating the compelling heroism of individuals who sacrifice their lives in the service of their faith. True to the Greek word *martureo,* they "bear witness . . . in favor of another,"[1] that is, Christ. Three elements are intrinsic to the testimony of martyrdom and occur in every Passion narrative. First, martyrdom recreates the sacrifice of Christ. Indeed, much of the drama of Passions lies in the suffering and death of the martyr's body as a parallel to Christ's sacrifice and bodily death. Second, martyrdom provides evidence of the most unshakable faith. Third, it secures a victory for Christianity against pagan persecutors.

Often the victory occurs in court. The original martyrs' accounts are presented as transcripts of judicial trials in which martyrs testify to their faith and provide evidence by withstanding questioning and torture.[2] After sentencing and a challenge to recant their testimony by sacrificing to pagan gods, the martyrs give up life itself. Whether purportedly literal transcripts or, later, more literary versions, Passion narratives are not, however, the trials of individuals. Ultimately it is not the martyr's faith but the Christian message of salvation that stands trial and, of course, finds triumph in the martyr's sacrifice.

Given that audience's sympathies are assumed, it is not surprising that trial and martyrdom serve to validate Christian faith. A basic structure—the ultimate reversal of an apparent defeat—dominates martyrs' Lives no matter how complex their themes and stories. It also serves as the foundation of the reversal of order that is an essential trope in the Lives of the saints—the martyr's death comes to be celebrated as the day of birth (*dies natalis*), because it celebrates a victory over the paganism that only *seems,* by lesser, worldly standards, to have prevailed. The implication of the reversal is that the martyr has found a source of strength greater than worldly power. Success is demonstrated by mass conversions inspired by the martyrdom and recounted in the Life. But victory is further reinforced and validated by the reactions of the *other* audience, the sympathetic reader, who may be inspired to compunction or, if a nonbeliever, to conversion. The modern notion of political martyrdom still carries much of this sense: a surprising reversal of power caused by the ultimate sacrifice as witness to a cause that wins converts.

Such stories of the deaths of martyrs have a powerfully direct effect; however, when Christianity was no longer actively on trial, authors of saints' Lives had to find substitutes for death as the witness of faith. Saints began to have to exert power in this world, not only in the next, and most did not die the violent deaths of martyrs. These saints constituted a new type: the confessor. At the same time that the confessor saint matured, the increasing complexity of the Church and its teachings demanded a narrative subtlety to match these expanded ambitions. The Passions discussed in this chapter originate after these developments, and for that reason, none is purely the story of a martyr; all are enriched by narrative effects borrowed from Lives of confessors. Nevertheless, the martyr type is still recognizable in them, even dominant—the martyr still makes a sacrifice and is marked with grace—and the core of the narrative continues to depend on the trial of the saint. Indeed, without these basic elements, the martyr's Life would lose its efficacy and its ability to reveal evidence of the sanctity of its object; of course, these same elements are also at the core of the pictorial expression of martyrs' Lives.

The narrative essence of a martyr's Passion is simple: the story ends with the death of the saint. But the reliable presence of this stark eventuality belies the apparent simplicity of Passion stories. True, the standardization of event—questioning, torture, and death—and the universal presence of the number three is at the least repetitive (and at the worst numbing), but illustrated martyrs' stories reveal a subtlety in demonstrating grace, virtue, and witness that is far from formulaic. The events that constitute the martyr's Passion are not a standardized list but rather a series of successive revelations—in effect, demonstrations of purity. The Passion narrative is something like a prayer that gradually builds up to a sacramental pronouncement as a climax to the manifestation of grace. In the earliest texts, the climactic event may be simply the death of the martyr, but only the most abbreviated pictorial hagiography—single wall-paintings or individual pictures in books such as *menologia* or Passionals—reduces the account to such a bald demonstration. In martyrs' Lives of the high Middle Ages, the sacramental moment precedes or even follows the death so that the death itself is quiet, almost anticlimactic.

The Passion of Romanus of Antioch, this chapter's primary example of the subgenre, is not an entirely typical martyr's Life (although, as I have intimated, it is doubtful whether any Life dating to the Middle Ages can be described as typical). A study of its narrative is nonetheless instructive precisely because its fundamental deviation from the norm helps to clarify the expectations that a Passion narrative forges in its readers. The deviation consists in the fact that the most compelling "evidence" at Romanus's trial is not the saint's own testimony but the martyrdom of a child that takes place as part of the trial. Romanus is a martyr but he is also a *rhetor,* and in his Passion the trial of religions is explicitly presented as the case at hand. As a martyr, Romanus follows Christ's example in torture and death;[3] as a *rhetor,* however, he defends his faith as if he were a lawyer in a sort of universal court. Although one aspect of Romanus's Life promises a lively story while the other seems to call for speech making, the two are unified in the concept of witness, which encompasses both word and action. Romanus's Life for that reason will serve us well as a guide to the narrative of the Passion and its figurative meaning.

The Passion of Romanus of Antioch forms the subject of book X of Prudentius's *Peristephanon* and is preserved in a single illustrated example, Bern Burgerbibliothek Cod. 264, produced c. 900, probably at Reichenau. In the Bern manuscript, the Passion is part of the *Opera* of Prudentius, which, with the additional exception of the *Psychomachia,* remains for the most part unillustrated.[4] The Romanus illustrations are scattered throughout the text of the poem, and most are less than full page. Impressed linear marks indicate that the figures and scenes were either traced or carefully composed using a stylus, and the resulting miniatures are very different in style from the *Psychomachia* illustrations. The presence of the Romanus cycle does not seem to indicate a particular cult at Reichenau. Rather, because the poem is the longest and one of the most interesting of the *Peristephanon* collection and the only one to represent an Eastern martyr, its illustrations may have been copied for a purely hagiographic interest.[5] The illustrations may reproduce an earlier, particularly admired cycle of illustrations (perhaps Carolingian) that were originally produced for a separate *libellus.*

Other martyrs' narratives in *libelli* from the tenth to the thirteenth century define a context for the Life of Romanus and will serve as comparanda. The illustrated Lives of Agatha, Kilian, and Margaret similarly do not seem to have been created to complement a saint's shrine but may have been copied and illustrated for hagiographic interest or for political reasons. In each, pictures are interspersed throughout the text (see appendix). By contrast, the illustrated Life of Quentin was composed to complement the saint's bodily relics, which were at the center of a long-standing cult in the city of Saint-Quentin. The awkward pictorial execution, strained poses, and clumsy compositions have suggested to some observers that the miniatures in the twelfth-century manuscript in the Basilica of Saint-Quentin are copies of an earlier exemplar, again, possibly a Carolingian original. The pictures are generally full- or half-page and appear throughout the text between the chapters. Each is accompanied by a verse *titulus*. Finally, the Lives of Lucy (twelfth century) and Alban (thirteenth century), treated more fully in chapters 4 and 9, respectively, will be briefly considered here.

Martyrs' Lives compose the bulk of the earliest illustrated manuscripts, but they also continue to appear in later manuscripts, and the genre spans a broad spectrum of cult situations. Despite the physical variations among manuscripts examined here, the narratives themselves are very similar. Particular categories of sequential events, common to the structures of Passions, are useful in the analysis of both the Life of Romanus and the genre. Although no one of these categories is required in a Passion, most are usually present; each works uniquely in any given instance.

QUESTIONS OF ORIGIN AND STATUS: THE STATEMENT OF FAITH

Before a saint can witness for Christianity, his faith and origins must be demonstrated. In Passions framed as judicial transcripts, and even in later forms of martyrs' Lives, the prosecution asks, "What is your origin?" The saint replies, "free and Christian," a response focused on social status and membership in a group.[6] The reply accords with the *Gloria Martyrum* of Gregory of Tours, who (in the words of Raymond Van Dam) "rather than seeing [martyrdom] as an opportunity for individual heroism, . . . consistently placed [it] in the context of the ecclesiastical community."[7] The identification of status and membership in the community is important to pictorial hagiography as well. For the martyr to serve the purpose of witness fully, he or she must be given the authority to speak. Images assert this authority precisely and concisely by establishing community.

In the Bern manuscript, Romanus is introduced as a spokesman for his congregation—perhaps even their protector.[8] The Passion describes the saint as the deacon of a "Christian flock . . . united in the league of one spirit."[9] In the first miniature of the Bern manuscript (fig. 10), Romanus stands in the doorway of the church, holding a book that apparently represents the doctrine or Gospels of the Church, next to a woman who must be Ecclesia. The two defend their church against the king's emissary, who comes to challenge the Christians and to destroy their place of worship.[10] Romanus's actions may be intended to evoke the memory of early Christian deacon martyrs such as Stephen and Lawrence, who in their very public roles defended the books of the Church (symbolically, its doctrine) and cared for its people;[11] alternatively, his role may be envisioned as similar to that of medieval episcopal leaders, who as early as the fourth century were identified as defenders of, and spokesmen for, the Church.[12] In either event, Romanus's identity and authority are grounded in his role within a community.

In a similar construct that seeks to define community more figuratively, the first miniature of the Passion of Margaret of Antioch groups the virgin, together with other maidens, as a shepherdess. Remarkably, the sheep in her flock acknowledge her by raising their forelegs, intimating a shared innocence as well as depicting her community with the faithful (fig. 11). The first miniature of the Life of Lucy also situates her within the Church and its doctrine, in this case more literally: a welcoming cleric holds an open book, and the architecture of the church surrounds the scene like a frame (see fig. 33). Finally, in the first miniature of her Life, Agatha is dragged with few preliminaries from a double-towered building, which may represent a church, or, at the very least, symbolize her noble origins. The visual content of each of these introductions is very different, but each illustration stresses the place of the saint in the Church and distinguishes it from that of the saint's antagonist.

A prefect or a judge usually serves as the martyr's inquisitor. The representative of secular power was typically reinterpreted by the medieval artist as a contemporary leader, such as a duke or king; the Roman emperor Galerius is portrayed thus in the first miniature of the Life of Romanus (archaeological accuracy is never a part of these Lives). For their parts, the saints are depicted as eager to enter the contest; indeed in the Lives of Romanus, Margaret, and Agatha (figs. 10–12), they lead the way into court in front of the lictors, the Roman magistrate's men-at-arms, who are often represented as contemporary soldiers or other men of lower class.

Figure 10. Romanus defends the Church and is taken to court, *Peristephanon* X, in *Prudentius Opera*, Reichenau (?), c. 900. Bern, Burgerbibliothek, Cod. 264, p. 131.

Figure 11. Olybrius sees Margaret as she is tending sheep; Margaret prays to God,
Passions of Kilian of Würzburg and Margaret of Antioch, Fulda, c. 970. Hannover,
Niedersächsische Landesbibliothek, MS I 189, fol. 14v. (Courtesy Graz,
Akademische Druck- und Verlagsantsalt)

The next scene, the verbal confrontation in which the protagonists state their positions, is usually represented as an almost private debate: the Lives of Agatha (fig. 13) and Lucy (see fig. 38), for example, each contain only two figures. The Christian makes a doctrinal statement, typically in response to a demand to worship pagan gods (see fig. 12, left), then usually ridicules deaf, blind, and mute gods and asserts the salvific qualities of the Cross and of faith in Christ, reiterating Church doctrine (compare Ps. 135:13–18). This statement is delayed in the Life of Margaret by an imprisonment and in the Life of Romanus by three tortures. The schematic of the opening scenes in a martyr's Life may seem simple, but the narrative can be realized with extraordinary subtlety, as is particularly evident in the Life of Romanus.

Figure 12. Agatha is taken to court and refuses to worship idols, *Collection of Saints' Lives*,
French, late tenth/early eleventh century. Paris, Bibliothèque nationale,
MS Lat. 5594, fol. 68r. (Cliché Bibliothèque nationale de France)

Given Romanus's profession, it is fitting that his argument in defense of his faith is protracted and complex (indeed, it is the most persuasive verbal defense of faith presented in this group of Lives). The artist of the Bern manuscript responds to this emphasis on the debate by making a dramatic visual statement. Instead of depicting the protagonists alone, the artist adds a lictor, who has to restrain Romanus's ardor, while three men in cloaks—that is, men of a higher social standing—stand behind the prefect Asclepiades and apparently further discuss Romanus's arguments (fig. 14).

The saint responds at length to Asclepiades' jibe that Christ was nailed on a cross: "Because your understanding is blind you cannot imbibe our mystic doctrine. . . . Yet in the darkness I shall hold out a bright torch and he that is sound will see, while the purblind will cover his eyes." Romanus further argues that salvation comes through the Cross because God took on human flesh. He continues: "You think this is foolishness, you wise men of the world . . . he who is foolish in respect of the world might be wise in the knowledge of God." Finally, Romanus argues that the Cross was prefigured and prophesied—that ancient truth was made *visible* in Christ and fulfilled in the Cross: "At last the words of the prophets were made plain and in our time antiquity was justified, shining before our eyes from a visible countenance."[13]

Although no cross is mentioned in the text as physically present at the scene, the

Figure 13. Agatha with a prefect; Agatha imprisoned, *Collection of Saints' Lives,* French, late tenth/early eleventh century. Paris, Bibliothèque nationale, MS Lat. 5594, fol. 68v. (Cliché Bibliothèque nationale de France)

artist introduces one. By placing a cross, painted in gold so that it will shine as a "bright torch," in Romanus's hand, the artist creates a remarkable visual parallel to the textual argument about the triumph of truth in the symbol of the cross. The worldly, "wise" men who cannot see this truth are proved undeniably blind, and the reader-viewer is supplied an unmistakable witness.

Nevertheless, even with this concrete visual demonstration, the evidence for the Christian faith remains doctrinal and abstract. To flesh out its nature and achieve a clear demonstration of the truth and power of the cross, the narrative needs the human action or exemplum. The doctrinal statement establishes a frame that explicates the basis and force of Romanus's rhetoric, but at the same time it opens a space for a more concrete demonstration of the truth.

Romanus and Asclepiades seem to be portrayed in the miniature as relative equals, but details of the illustration belie this equality. With his left hand, Romanus defiantly begins to make the sign of the cross, a blessing gesture that transforms his speech into an instrument of exorcism against the power of darkness.[14] Light is often a symbol of truth in the Lives of martyrs, and here the gold of the pictured cross evokes

Figure 14. Romanus's disputation with the prefect, *Peristephanon* X, in *Prudentius Opera,* Reichenau (?), c. 900. Bern, Burgerbibliothek, Cod. 264, p. 135.

this association.[15] Perhaps without the restraining hand of Asclepiades' lictor, Romanus would even use the cross as a weapon, as does Margaret in *her* battle against demons. Instead, he only brandishes it defiantly.[16] We seem to be left with no choice but to admit the power of Romanus's statement. However, in the text, as Romanus abruptly ends his speech, he proclaims that he has been throwing "pearls before swine" and he will now be silent.

TORTURE AS WITNESS

In the life of Romanus, the saint's recourse to silence is not an admission of defeat but a powerful strategic move. Silent witness is central to martyrdom, for it reflects the destruction of language that is caused by the pain of torture: "Physical pain does not simply resist language but actively destroys it, bringing about an immediate reversion to a state anterior to language, to the sounds and cries a human being makes before language is learned."[17] However, it is also a commonplace that saints do not cry out. Their silence reverses nature and demonstrates their power but also corresponds to Christian (primarily Augustinian) notions of speech, in which truth resides in a region beyond or above language. Silence expresses the power of the saint's body to witness to truth. Indeed, the acts and miracles of the saints were even said (by Gregory of Tours) to be only properly *received* in silence, not with "chattering interpretations" but with "stunned" silence.[18] Representing silence through the medium of words raises considerable challenges, but pictorial hagiography particularly suits silent reception, for it has the ability to effectively "engrave" the saint's deeds on the heart of the viewer, bypassing the mental or physical "noise" of language.[19]

Because silent acts thus speak more loudly than words, the statement of doctrine by the saint in Passion narratives is usually followed by torture. The Life of Romanus, however, again varies from the pattern. The saint has already suffered three tortures before the end of his debate with the prefect and will eventually suffer three more (all the while chiding his torturers for their weakness),[20] but because physical suffering does nothing to stop the flow of his words, he is a poor object for the audience's pity and horror. This is the reason why a second martyr, the child Barulas, torn from his mother's breast, becomes Romanus's substitute. The horrific suffering and sacrifice of an innocent child serves as the unqualified affective center of the Passion and elicits the desired hagiographic effect of compunction. By means of this substitution, as we will see, the narrative moves from apologetics, the verbal countering of pagan beliefs, through what Romanus calls the "deep reasoning" of doctrine, to the "natural understanding" of an infant's miraculous words,[21] and finally to the mute agony of a martyr, the unthinkable suffering of the baby Barulas.

But first, as noted above, Romanus, far from maintaining his threatened silence, continues to speak. Remarkably, his words, not his body, are tortured. Just before his vow, he infuriated the prefect with his endless speech, and in a rage, Asclepiades ordered the third torture of the martyr, demanding that his "words" be tortured. The lictors used iron claws to score his cheeks and jaw, but Romanus was roused to exultation and proclaimed that his flesh was purified and "every wound . . . [is become] a mouth uttering praise."[22] Romanus's claim to silence is thereby vindicated, for the Passion clearly makes the argument that Romanus's testimony no longer has its origin in his own speech but is now miraculous. In its uses of speech and silence, Romanus's Life is not solely an example of a Christian witness: rather, it *exemplifies* Christian testament. Indeed, the Life of Romanus vividly recapitulates Augustine's theories of language and represents a special kind of speech, sanctified and purified.[23] In manuscript copies, the Life is titled "Romanus, Contra Gentiles," and it was recognized as a particularly effective argument for Christian belief.

Although the ability of the martyr's body to speak is a central idea of martyr-dom, the specific incident of the torture of Romanus's words is probably unique in a saint's Life. Clearly, Prudentius has particular rhetorical reasons for introducing it, but I use this extraordinary example to make the point that ultimately all torture contains some figurative meaning. Tortures tend to fall into a few limited categories in the Lives of most martyrs; they are scraped with claws, burned, and whipped, and each of these torments, in alluding to the Life of Christ, furthers the saintly progress toward purification. In order to better understand the full meaning of these figurative tortures, we must turn from the extraordinary toward the more typical.

Whipping or flagellation is, of course, modeled directly on the life of Christ and is the clearest form of *imitatio Christi* in many martyrs' Lives. The text often specifies that the saint is whipped until the ribs can be counted, in evocation of Psalm 90, which was associated with Christ's own torment and crucifixion.[24] In pictorial ha-giography, the saint is often depicted from the rear to correlate with the typical de-piction of the flagellation of Christ.[25]

The flagellation of Barulas as described in Prudentius's text is supplemented in the Bern illustration by the scraping of the child martyr's flesh with claws (see plate 1). Again, the skeleton of the body is laid bare. Removing the flesh and revealing the bones is, of course, a bloody and gruesome thing, but martyrs goad their torturers and exult that "the impure mortal flesh" is "filthy, it swells up, its runs, it stinks, it hurts, it is puffed up with anger, or unbridled in desire, . . . [and] is the prompter of sin." Torture cures this miserable flesh and frees the spirit, "the substance of glory."[26] The glossator of the Carolingian manuscripts of the *Peristephanon* in fact has glossed the Latin word for iron claws, *ungulae* with *fidiculae* (root: *fides*), noting that iron claws test the faith.[27]

Burning, the third most common torture in martyrs' Passions, was literally a test of faith or truth during various periods in the Middle Ages,[28] but it has a more figu-rative import in Passions. When we are told that St. Margaret is "tried" with torches and found "golden,"[29] the analogy is to the smelting of gold in a furnace in order to purify it; the gold itself, like the martyr, does not burn. Trial by fire is thus the clearest figurative proof of the purity of the saint. Romanus as well cannot be burned, and when it is attempted a miraculous rainshower douses the flames (fig. 15). In a variation of the motif of purification, Lucy is tormented with flaming oil (see fig. 41); in effect, she is anointed at the same time that her purity is proved.

Lucy's torture illustrates a "liturgical" effect that frequently appears in Passions. Many of the Lives of the martyrs include tortures that create a paradoxical sense

Figure 15. A storm prevents Romanus from burning; Romanus's tongue is cut out, *Peristephanon* X, in *Prudentius Opera,* Reichenau (?), c. 900. Bern, Burgerbibliothek, Cod. 264, p. 144.

that the martyr is participating in the rituals of the Church while being tortured. Margaret, like Thecla before her, is thrown into a tub of water; Margaret seems to be threatened with drowning, Thecla with "ravenous seals."[30] In both cases, the virgins take advantage of the occasion to pronounce baptismal formulas. The illustration from the Life of Margaret shows that the artist clearly understood the implications of the text: the tub is represented as a small baptismal font (fig. 16).

Figure 16. Margaret is tortured by burning; Margaret leaps into a tub, *Passions of Kilian of Würzburg and Margaret of Antioch,* Fulda, c. 970. Hannover, Niedersächsische Landesbibliothek, MS I 189, fol. 28v. (Courtesy Graz, Akademische Druck- und Verlagsantsalt)

Turning torture into benefit in this way is intrinsic to the working of all martyr's Lives, recapitulating the principle of reversal. Burning, whipping, and even execution are understood merely as steps in a ladder of perfection leading to the celestial home.[31]

The illustrated Life of Quentin presents a particularly vivid narrative of such perfection through torture. Lisa Bessette observes that the cycle of illustrations in the *libellus* of Quentin represents the martyr's persecuted body as progressively increasing in power. Like Anthony, who after torment by demons "had more power in his body than formerly,"[32] Quentin's body is gradually empowered through his physical punishment. He is transformed from a weak and small figure, incapable of speech, into a strong and dominant (although still mute) figure.[33] Quentin's final torture is unique in medieval pictorial hagiography. His body, much larger than the figures who encircle him, is doubly tortured: nails are driven into his fingers, and spikes are hammered into his shoulders (see plate 2). The artist has taken advantage of the opportunity to draw a parallel to Christ's torture with nails at the Crucifixion, but the cross itself is absent, for the martyr's body quite literally *represents* the Cross. Quentin holds his arms out to the sides; one of the tormentors actually stands on the martyr's rigid arm while hammering.[34] The effect is much like a late medieval image of the Man of Sorrows displaying his wounds, but at this early

MARTYRS' PASSIONS

date the illustration finds its sole contemporary parallel—and a somewhat incomplete one—in the Anglo-Saxon Aethelstan Psalter image of the Last Judgment, which includes the *arma Christi*. Alternatively, perhaps the extended arms allude the priest's gesture at Mass, suggesting that Quentin offers again a quasi-liturgical sacrifice of his body.

Quentin's body and its torture bear witness to the power and meaning of the cross, much as did Romanus's words. Quentin's *vita,* however, in effect combines the *topoi* of disputation and torture-as-witness without the complications of the frame narrative in the Life of Romanus. At the top of the miniature, Quentin's frontal pose and his gaze confront the viewer with the message. Below, the artist has repeated his meaning, now contained within the trial narrative, in which Quentin confronts the prefect Rictiovarus. Instead of a speech gesture, however, the artist represents Quentin once more calmly displaying his hands, which are bristling with nails. Both pictures supply mute but effective witness: every wound cries out with a "mouth," to use Prudentius's metaphor, and words are not necessary.[35] Furthermore, the prefect's attempt to reverse the saint's faith is itself turned on its head: Rictiovarus's challenge is literally written upside down across the page.[36]

RELEASED FROM BONDS: PRISONS, VISIONS, SACRAMENTS, AND DEATH

Another reality that the martyr's Passion inverts is the horror of prison. Martyrs regularly find themselves imprisoned: Margaret and Agatha three times, Romanus and Barulas once. Each narrative emphasizes the dankness and darkness of the prison, yet in all these accounts the saints rise above the conditions—even quite literally. Often the saint ascends a small flight of stairs to enter the prison (see fig. 13); in other instances prison is depicted as a tower. In *Ad Martyres,* Tertullian describes the nature of the martyr's imprisonment: "Ye have been translated from a prison [that is, the world] to a place, it may be, of safe keeping. It hath darkness, but ye yourselves are Light. It has bonds, but ye have been made free by God. An evil breath is uttered there but ye are a sweet savour."[37] The transformation of the prison is clearly complete in the last illustration to the Life of Romanus, in which the saint is finally martyred. Earlier in the *vita,* Romanus's prison is pictured as a hall-like, barrel-vaulted structure; at the saint's death, it has taken the form of a domed mar-

Figure 17. The martyrdom of Romanus, *Peristephanon* X, in *Prudentius Opera*,
Reichenau (?), c. 900. Bern, Burgerbibliothek, Cod. 264, p. 149.

tyrium from which Romanus's soul ascends to heaven (fig. 17). The illustrator of
the Life of Quentin, following the model of St. Peter, identifies an angel as the agent
of the saint's literal and figurative release from his prison (fig. 18) and gives form
to Tertullian's assertion that the prison "has bonds, but [the saint] has been made
free by God."

Situated in a locus set apart from (or even above) the world, imprisonment often
becomes an occasion for meditation and vision. Both Agatha and Margaret receive
visions in prison: Agatha is healed of her horrible wounds by a man who appears
to her, and Margaret is promised martyrdom and sees a vision of the Cross. In both
instances, the visions illustrated in the miniatures represent more than the actions
or events described in the textual narratives. The events assume the character of
sacraments that bring the narrative to its climax and seal the promise of grace for
each saint. Agatha's vision takes the form of a *senex* or *medicus* who ultimately reveals himself as St. Peter (fig. 19). The healing of her breast is visually reminiscent
of the *Unctio Infirmis,* a sacred and liturgical anointing of the sick, and the text reports that her once physical breast is now replaced by a spiritual breast, the source
of metaphysical rather than bodily sustenance.[38]

After defeating a dragon and a black devil (that is, lust and sin in animate form),[39]

MARTYRS' PASSIONS

Figure 18. Quentin is freed from prison by an angel, *Authentique or Passion of Quentin (Quintinus),* Saint-Quentin, c. 1050–1100. Manuscrit de l'Église paroissiale déposé à la Bibliothèque municipale de Saint-Quentin, p. 19.

Margaret sees a cross extending up to heaven and topped by a dove (fig. 20). At the base of the cross is a gold disk—probably a liturgical paten. Margaret's imminent sacrifice is thus likened to the sacrifice of the Mass, which recapitulates the sacrifice of Christ.[40] The miniature of Margaret's vision shares elements with the illustration accompanying Psalm 115 (interpreted in the Middle Ages as the martyrs' prayer) in the Utrecht Psalter (fig. 21). The Psalms were often quoted in Lives, and Psalm 115 may be the most frequently cited in martyrs' Passions:

Figure 19. Agatha is healed by St. Peter, *Collection of Saints' Lives,* French, late tenth/early eleventh century. Paris, Bibliothèque nationale, MS Lat. 5594, fol. 70r. (Cliché Bibliothèque nationale de France)

> I will take the cup of salvation, and call upon the name of the Lord. I will pay my vows unto the Lord now in the presence of all his people. Precious in the sight of the Lord is the death of his saints. O Lord, truly I am thy servant and the son of thine handmaid: thou hast loosed my bonds. I will offer to thee the sacrifice of thanksgiving, and will call upon the name of the Lord. (Ps. 115 [116]:13–17)

We have already seen an instance of the loosing of bonds in the Life of Quentin. The same image appears in the Utrecht Psalter, where a martyr stands below the Cross, catching Christ's blood in a chalice and in turn proffering a paten. Chains or ropes drop from his arm; his execution, as well as that of others, is underway. If the martyrdom is here the vow and sacrifice that the martyr makes in the presence of the people, that sacrifice is being offered by the paten, which can be compared to the disk in Margaret's Life and the promise of her immanent sacrifice, just as Quentin's torture (see plate 2) was also likened to the sacrifice of the Mass.

These images of sacrament, whether in the narratives of martyrs' Passions or in

Figure 20. Margaret defeats the black demon and sees a vision of a cross topped with a dove, *Passions of Kilian of Würzburg and Margaret of Antioch,* Fulda, c. 970. Hannover, Niedersächsische Landesbibliothek, MS I 189, fol. 26v. (Courtesy Graz, Akademische Druck- und Verlagsantsalt)

the prayers of the Psalms, reach out to the reader-viewer to make a direct and impressive analogy to Christ's sacrifice. For Gregory of Tours, these are the sort of miracles, figuratively associated with the liturgy, that serve as the "sacraments of divine teaching," the witness of which impels belief and even conversion.[41]

In addition to the notion of the sacrifice of the Mass reiterated and thus explicated by the saint, these images make one other important point: that the sacraments are mediated and controlled by the Church. Pictures in the Utrecht Psalter and the Passion of Margaret include images of eucharistic vessels. In the Passion of Romanus, and particularly in the depiction of the torture of Barulas (see plate 1), the idea is taken even further and depicted more explicitly.

The miniature, which draws an analogy between the child martyr's body on a gibbet and that of Christ on the Cross, includes a building, placed directly below the figure of Barulas. A passage preceding the torture episode, elaborating a Pauline metaphor (1 Cor. 3:10–14), seems to explain the presence of this building:

> [God] has established [a temple] for himself in the soul of man, one that is living, clear, perceptive, spiritual, incapable of dissolution or destruction, beautiful, graceful, hightopped, coloured with different hues. There stands the priestess in the sacred doorway; the virgin Faith guards the first entrance, her hair bound with queenly ties,

CULAINFERNIINUENE RUNTME   DNS · HUMILIATUSSU ETLIBERAUITME ·   PLACEBODNO · INREGI ONEUIUORUM ·

Figure 21. Martyrs sacrifice themselves, Psalm 115 (116), *Utrecht Psalter,* Reims (Hautvilliers),
c. 820. Utrecht, Rijksuniversiteit, MS 32, fol. 67r. (Reproduced by permission
of the University Library, Utrecht)

and calls for sacrifices to be offered to Christ and the Father which are pure and sincere,
such as she knows are acceptable to them.

The building in the miniature may be located within the soul itself, as it is in the
biblical and the poetic description, but it is probably also intended as an evocation
of the universal Christian Church. Gregory of Tours speaks of saints who "deserved
to become the temple of the Lord themselves, but who have also in the souls of
many others prepared the tabernacles of the grace of the Holy Spirit."[42] In other
words, a saint can prepare others to receive God's grace. The image, once again, is
that of the "edification"—the building—of the Church through the Lives and examples of the saints.

    In the miniature of Barulas's torture, the Church is envisioned as literally nour-
ished by the blood of the martyr. The spectators, men and women alike, are moved
to tears and faith by the sight of the child's suffering. Yet one person, the child's
mother, resists tears and "calls for sacrifices." When her baby is said to cry from
thirst, she scolds him:

    You ask for water to drink, though you have nearby the living spring which ever flows
    and alone waters all that has life, within and without, spirit and body both, bestowing

on those who drink. You will soon reach that stream if only in your heart and inmost being your one eager, ardent longing is to see Christ, and one draught of it is ample to allay all the burning of the breast so that the blessed life can no longer thirst.[43]

Clearly this is no ordinary mother. In this narrative of her baby's Passion, Barulas's mother is cast as the Church personified—Ecclesia. Borrowing yet another metaphor from Paul (1 Cor. 3:1–2), Barulas, the "babe in Christ" testifies that he has learned Christian doctrine from the twin founts of wisdom of his mother's breasts. The strokes of the whip during his torture draw "more milk than blood."[44] So, if the mother is Faith, or Ecclesia, the child's sacrifice of blood and milk becomes nourishing truth. The blood of the infant martyr, in his likeness to Christ, waters the Church as a "flowing source."[45]

Many images of martyrs' tortures show the reactions of sympathetic audiences, but here the Church is defined as central in channeling that reaction. It is an edifice that transforms the raw pain and sacrifice into spiritual food and drink that is soothing to the soul, allaying thirst forever; it is a faith that calls always for further sacrifice of the pure victim. In Gregory's terms, it is a spiritual edifice, a temple, that through its perfection and the indwelling of the Holy Spirit, fosters the preparation of tabernacles in the hearts of others. Unlike Lucy's last sacrament, which takes place in an actual church and is assisted by real clergy, Barulas's sacrifice is figurative but all the more insistent on the role of the Church in mediating the effects of the martyr's Passion.

The sacramental elements contained in these images underscore an institutional involvement through the intervention of the Mass, doctrine, or the clergy (in person or embodied as "Faith"). But they do so simultaneously with a stress on the affective: the personal sacrifice of the martyr, the personal revelation, and the intimate reaction of the spectators. This unexpected combination is surely the origin of their power. Although Lives of saints may be intended to augment the prestige of the Church, they capture their audience's attention at the outset by explicating the benefits to the individual believer. It is the emotional content of these scenes that effectively conveys their message of the Church's power to the viewer.

Was the institutional presence of the Church in saints' Lives a new development in medieval hagiography? It may be that the earliest (and no longer extant) illustrated martyr's Passion did not lay stress on the mediating role of the Church, although this seems unlikely.[46] Saints' Lives, as narratives directed at a collective audience and as vehicles to "strengthen the Church," have always been based in community.[47] Already in the fourth century, rather than arising from the devotions of individuals, the cult of saints was very much the purview of the bishop and the clergy, as Peter Brown has shown.[48] The oldest surviving illustrated Lives regularly associate sacrament with martyrdom and in so doing demonstrate the consistent intervention of liturgy in the genre of hagiography.[49] Many different episodes may serve in this purpose—tortures, visions, healings, even elements of the Mass itself—but the message remains the same.

In this context, the death of the martyr plays a special role because it is the final sealing of the Holy Spirit (in some texts) or the "consummation of martyrdom" (in others). For the most part, the artist is at some pains to demonstrate that the martyr ascended directly to the "celestial home." Romanus and Margaret are carried aloft by angels (figs. 17 and 22). Kilian's grave is marked by a blooming tree. Quentin's and Edmund's souls are received as doves by the hand of God (fig. 23).

Death, moreover, is often shown to be marked by the quality of the martyr's life. The martyr's Passion is in its nature like a prayer, so the artists of the Passions of Margaret, Quentin, Lucy, and Kilian depict the saints praying fervently as the sword descends (see figs. 22, 23, 42, and 70). (The sword, the Roman means of execution reserved for nobility, is the instrument of death for the vast majority of martyrs.) Barulas, the baby who embodies natural understanding, dies in a manner that is visually reminiscent of the sacrifice of the Innocents: he is beheaded while suspended by his feet (fig. 24). Romanus prays as passionately as other saints, but he is strangled in one last attempt to stop the words of faith from issuing from his throat (see fig. 17). Lucy, described in her life as an "immovable mountain" of faith does not bend under the thrusts of a sword (see fig. 42). The body of Quentin, an apostolic missionary, a "fisher of men," is thrown into a river after he is beheaded. Each of these deaths reiterates the central issues of the given Life.

NARRATIVE EFFECTS: BEYOND *TOPOI*

Our discussion has brought us literally to the end of the Lives of martyrs but not, perhaps, to a complete understanding of their composition. The Passions betray undeniable elements of repetition, but their composition entails more than filling blanks in a generic *curriculum vitae*. Hagiographers sought to build a Life—to construct a narrative. To understand the subtle interplay of scenes of different weight and pur-

Figure 22. Margaret prays and is martyred, *Passions of Kilian of Würzburg and Margaret of Antioch,* Fulda, c. 970. Hannover, Niedersächsische Landesbibliothek, MS I 189, fol. 32r. (Courtesy Graz, Akademische Druck- und Verlagsantsalt)

pose, the effect should be followed through the complete Life of a saint. Thus, we return to the story of Romanus's Life in order to fit the episodes we have already examined into a proper narrative discourse. Finally, a similar consideration of the narrative of Quentin's Passion will provide an effective contrast and demonstrate the wide variety of such narratives.

Prudentius seeks above all to establish his subject's authority to speak—that is, to witness—for Christianity. Once he is able to establish the validity of Romanus's speech, the saint's invocation and explication of the trial and martyrdom of the child Barulas as an exemplum of his arguments can rise above its literary and artistic presentation and become, in effect, both true and real for the reader. Romanus's true speech thus works as an authenticating frame for the "acts" of the infant's Life.

Figure 23. Quentin is beheaded, *Authentique or Passion of Quentin (Quintinus),* Saint-Quentin, c. 1050–1100. Manuscrit de l'Église paroissiale déposé à la Bibliothèque municipale de Saint-Quentin, p. 45.

Figure 24. Barulas is beheaded, *Peristephanon* X, in *Prudentius Opera,* Reichenau (?), c. 900. Bern, Burgerbibliothek, Cod. 264, p. 142.

In order to demonstrate that the saint's testimony is true, Prudentius first identifies Romanus as a spokesman for the Church and then proceeds to validate the purity of his speech.[50] In doing so, the hagiographer takes pains to establish how speech is produced by the throat, tongue, and lips. The narrative then details the successive torture of the organs of speech in reverse order, descending into the corporeal source of the words.[51] The torture is ineffective, and Romanus's speech is thus proved not only true and pure, but indeed divine.

The particular corporeal itinerary of Romanus's tortures establishes ever-deeper levels of speech and truth. The saint's lips—or words—are tortured before his long speech on doctrine. Then the infant Barulas is chosen from the crowd and *he* speaks, albeit briefly, with natural wisdom as an innocent. When torture silences the miraculous speech of the baby,[52] Romanus resumes his role as speaker to explicate the meaning of the suffering body. The climactic and sacramental illustration of this scene shows Romanus not only speaking but actively disputing with his antagonist Asclepiades. The two stand to either side of Barulas on his gibbet, framing a picture that becomes the perfect proof of Romanus's arguments. Unable to defeat the Christian rhetorician, the pagan prefect tortures him again, finally ordering that his tongue be cut out. Removing the tongue is a *topos* in saints' Lives and serves as the ultimate demonstration that the saint's ability to speak is a miracle granted by God.[53] After Romanus's tongue is removed, he is fully purified *and* still speaking. In desperation, the prefect has him throttled, breaking his throat and finally silencing him (see fig. 17). But this is still not the end: Prudentius is careful to note the martyr's final testament in heaven, and the last illustration shows Romanus ascending to his celestial home.

Romanus's martyrdom and physical silencing entails a transfer of the duty to testify. Perhaps not surprisingly, the burden falls upon written documents of various types and value. Asclepiades' court records are drawn up but quickly "blackened" and "buried" by time.[54] By contrast, "the page that Christ has written upon is deathless and in heaven not a letter fades away." An angel has "recorded the words of [Romanus's] discourse" and drawn "exact pictures of [his] wounds." "This book is in the heavenly register," and will serve at Romanus's judgment before the Lord.[55] Furthermore, his recorded merit will enable Romanus to act as intercessor for those who pray to him. The illustrated manuscript that depicts Romanus's Passion thus takes on an important role as the simulacrum of the celestial register and a careful record of the martyr's wounds. It stands as an efficacious witness to the martyr's testimony and heavenly status as powerful intercessor.

More broadly, this analysis suggests that in recounting the Life of Romanus, Prudentius is not merely telling the story of one unusual martyr; rather, he is explicating the nature of all martyrs. The illustrator, in creating a pictorial retelling of the martyr's Passion, does so as well.

As Romanus himself testifies, however, his veritable torrent of words is neither typical nor desirable in the story of a martyr. Indeed, most martyrs witness silently—with their bodies—and paradoxically it is their *in*action, embodied in their muteness, that speaks to their faith. Nonetheless, the narratives of these less prolix martyrs are equally purposeful in their construction and use familiar *topoi,* combined to make a complex and resonant narrative. In depicting a series of gruesome tortures, the artist of the Quentin *libellus* traces a "corporeal" narrative that is perhaps in some ways more suggestive of the essential power of the martyr than was the verbal display offered by Prudentius.

The pictorial narrative of the Life of Quentin is notably static. The martyr's body is consistently depicted as still, calm, and enduring. In one illustration of whipping, Quentin's skin is horribly pierced, but rather than standing he lies prone and still (perhaps in imitation of the Apostles).[56] His elongated and gracefully curving body contrasts with the frenzied and twisted bodies of his torturers, violently thrown down (the text recounts) by an intervening angel (fig. 25). The torturers gesticulate

Figure 25. The flagellation of Quentin, *Authentique or Passion of Quentin (Quintinus)*,
Saint-Quentin, c. 1050–1100. Manuscrit de l'Église paroissiale déposé
à la Bibliothèque municipale de Saint-Quentin, p. 16.

wildly and twist in torment with the sort of physical abandon that was repeatedly condemned by the Church.[57] Their confused entanglement makes Quentin's calm center all the more striking. It is as if Quentin is elsewhere. A phrase in the Life of Polycarp, an early and influential Passion, aptly sums up Quentin's attitude: tortured martyrs were said not even to be "present in the flesh, or rather that the Lord was there present holding converse with them."[58]

Other illustrations of Quentin's sufferings show the saint's calm, still, and nude body turned toward the viewer and displayed as a powerful testament (see plate 2). One image displays the saint's back, as if no part could be left untouched by the torture or unrevealed as witness to faith. The Passion of Polycarp describes the martyr's flesh as "adorned" and notes that even before Polycarp's martyrdom Christians were "always eager to be the first to touch [it]."[59] Martyrdom transforms saints' bodies into "otherness," but an otherness that is by no means grotesque. Indeed, the bodies become infinitely desirable (although in principle this desirability is inversely related to the saint's sexuality).[60] Quentin's body, stripped and exposed in the spectacle of torture, is emphatically set apart visually from those of his tormentors. Yet, in a reversal of the display of mundane torture, in which the victim is unmade and all power resides in the tormentor,[61] this is the beginning of the remaking of the saint's body as a sanctified and powerful body that ends in the transformation of his corpse into a holy relic.

Quentin suffers torture and is still, but paradoxically he also acts, and these actions constitute his narrative. Like Polycarp, Quentin works his way toward sanctity through "converse" with the Lord, that is, through prayer. Thus, at the same time that the narrative emphasizes the immobility of the saint's body, it allows one body part limited independence of movement—the hands. Quentin's animated and enlarged hands describe a subtle but distinctive narrative of their own. In the first miniature of the Life (p. 9), the hands describe gestures associated with speech, but then at once are entrapped: in three scenes of torture, the hands are tied fast (pp. 11, 13, and 16 [fig. 25]). In a dramatic reversal, the ineffectual bound hands are set free. Quentin is released from his chains by the angel (p. 19 [fig. 18]) and begins to pray in a wide and inclusive gesture that makes a first reference to the priest's invitation to the Mass (p. 20.)[62] The hands seem to grow in size. The saint is immediately entrapped in a series of tortures in which the hands are conspicuously bound (pp. 29, 30, 32, 34, and 37), but once again the hands break free, this time simultaneous with the saint's own active intercession through prayer, the only energetic stance allowed him in this cycle (p. 42 [plate 2, bottom]). Quentin's spiritual freedom, however, is expressed as a expansive gesture of public prayer made while the saint is still bound and suffering torture but portrayed as miraculously powerful and autonomous (p. 42 [plate 2, top]).[63] The final two actions of the saint's Life consist again of prayer, first private prayer received by the hand of God, and then prayer during the final moments of martyrdom (pp. 44 and 45 [fig. 23]).

Once more it is instructive to compare Quentin's Passion to the archetypal martyr's Passion—that of Polycarp. In that brief text, the martyr's "converse" with God is similarly a focus of the narrative and is clearly and succinctly explicated. Three sorts of prayer are described. Polycarp prays for the benefit of the community (one of the martyr's contributions to the "building" of the Church); he prays in private, indeed so intensely that he is "unable to stop"; and he prays publicly and therefore liturgically, likening his own death to the sacrifice of the Mass.[64] As narratives of edification, the Passions of both Polycarp (in a text) and Quentin (in pictures) provide models of prayer and its power for imitation by Christians. Ultimately and insistently, these are Lives that advocate prayer, both public and private, through all of life's adversities.

Martyrs are skilled at praying on their own souls' behalf, but their merits also allow them to intercede through prayer on behalf of the souls of the Christians who pray to them. The structure of the earthly trial that underlies the Passions of the martyrs is completed and superseded in Prudentius's story of Romanus by the trial in a heavenly court. In that version, the martyr's victory is not simply assumed or stated: it is proven, and the saint is explicitly granted the power to intercede with the Supreme Judge. Prayer, whether private, public, liturgical, or intercessory, is the end and the goal of the Lives, and in these prayers the reader attempts to follow the saint. The pictures of Quentin's Life use *topoi* to create a narrative that emphasizes and explicates prayer and perhaps thus teaches the reader how to pray.

What I am suggesting is that the reader of saints' Lives responds to the text not only intellectually but also emotionally *and* physically in modeling his or her self *and* body after that of the saint. Such responses may be necessary for the proper reading of edifying texts. Just as viewers were encouraged to pray like the saints and as Brother John modeled himself on St. Francis (see p. 56), so these texts and pictures recommend that their audience respond physically and even viscerally to a saint's actions. Such encouragements to response may be one of the most effective devices of the hagiographer's narrative strategy.

A primary example lies in the painstaking depiction of bloody and horrible tortures and their implements. Although in the Lives, as above, the typical weapons of

Figure 26. The flagellation of Margaret, *Passions of Kilian of Würzburg and Margaret of Antioch*, Fulda, c. 970. Hannover, Niedersächsische Landesbibliothek, MS I 189, fol. 18v. (Courtesy Graz, Akademische Druck- und Verlagsantsalt)

torture are figurative, they have other meaning as well. Elaine Scarry has argued that the pain of others is incomprehensible except insofar as it is located in the "sign of the weapon." She quotes Michael Walzer's comments on war: "I cannot conceptualize infinite pain without thinking of whips and scorpions, hot irons and other people."[65] The language of pain is replete with metaphors for weapons and the agency of the "causes of hurt." We speak of burning, stabbing, or pounding pain. One of the principal characteristics of saints, however, is that they do not feel pain; viewers, on the contrary, confronted with the sight of whips, claws, and torches and the display of wounds and blood cannot help but conceptualize and experience the unfelt, unexperienceable pain of others. The presence of weapons and wounds cues a response of pity and empathy in the viewer.

Moreover, the audience *in the text* is said to weep and moan and be horrified by the tortures of the saints. They are swept away in the events, and they are converted. Pictorially, this is most evident in the Life of Margaret (figs. 26 and 27), where the cringing reactions of the onlookers may be one of the most vivid displays of emotion in early medieval art. This remarkable spectacle guides the response of the sympathetic audience that views the text and the pictures. Although already converted, readers and viewers experience compunction and are strengthened in faith and in their status as a community. Rather than enjoy the sight through *concupiscentia ocu-*

Figure 27. Margaret, scraped with claws and imprisoned, *Passions of Kilian of Würzburg and Margaret of Antioch,* Fulda, c. 970. Hannover, Niedersächsische Landesbibliothek, MS I 189, fol. 20r. (Courtesy Graz, Akademische Druck- und Verlagsantsalt)

lorum, they are moved, and their "change of heart" is formed and paced by the narrative. Thus, through the viewing of the images, the audience is allowed the opportunity to model his or her body on the courageous body of the saint as part of a complete conversion to the text. In imitation of the bodies of the saints, the viewer can learn prayer, patience, courage, and humility.

Finally, even if there is little suspense, little action, too much talk, and even too much story, the Passions of the martyrs are carefully constructed and often profoundly moving narratives. In the end, the act of martyrdom itself witnesses—that is, tells a story—and the textual and pictorial narratives hope only to shape and elucidate the circumstances of that compelling event for an audience of the faithful.

THE VIRGIN AS CORPUS
Bodily Offering

ॐ

The Apostle . . . says: "I exhort you, therefore, brethren, by the mercy of God to present
your bodies as a sacrifice, living, holy, pleasing to God—your spiritual service" [Rom.
21:1]. If then, the body, which is less than the soul and which the soul uses as a servant
or a tool, is a sacrifice when it is used well and rightly for the service of God, how much
more so is the soul when it offers itself to God so that, aflame in the fire of divine Love,
and with the dross of worldly desire melted away, it . . . becomes beautiful in His sight
by reason of the bounty of beauty which He has bestowed upon it.
—Augustine, *The City of God,* X:6

The one and same Lord who as head of the Church is the bridegroom,
as body is the bride.
—Bernard of Clairvaux, *Sermones super Cantica Canticorum,* 27:7

CERTAIN FEMINIST scholars speak of woman's gender as not single, but double.[1] Virgin martyrs represent what might be called "doubled bodies." That is, insofar as the virgin martyr does not easily resolve into a simple image for a single
audience, she represents an example of "both at once." As the essential medieval
body, she is both menacing and comforting; she both fully inhabits the body and is
"safely and miraculously beyond it."[2] The significance of her exemplary body includes both the physical courage and suffering that she shares with male martyrs
and her particular qualities of corporeal purity and humility. These latter qualities,
enacted in a Life, provide a model of the refinement of the body and its physical
senses that is essential to the perfection of the soul. Thus, the hagiographic role of
the virgin saint is to renew the flawless, but also human, body of Christ in this world.
By attaining a perfection that mirrors that of Christ, the virgin's body not only becomes an icon and model of the path to salvation but also serves as a matchless

offering to God. In her "doubled" roles, the virgin saint was uniquely suited for two different audiences, male and female.

For all Christians, virgins represented the saintly type that found its highest narrative achievement in stories of the preservation of the body, threatened and attacked but ultimately miraculously inviolate.[3] Perhaps precisely because of the reputed insatiability of female sexual desire, the women who controlled that desire became heroic models of sexual abstinence for both genders during the Middle Ages.[4] For women, the preservation of and attention to the actual body may have been the only viable route to spiritual fulfillment, as it clearly was for certain saints of the late Middle Ages.[5] For men, virgins' bodies were symbols of the desirable purification of the senses and the body through which union with God could be achieved.[6] To become a bride of Christ was an equally important goal for both sexes, and virgins' bodies were objects through which the power of the holy could be accessed.

Virgin saints are almost always martyrs. Since all martyrs' bodies are sources of holy power, in what specific sense does gender differentiate the Lives of virgin saints from those of male martyrs? Medieval hagiography evokes important differences between the sexes, but scholarly literature has not yet adequately characterized these differences.

One of the most enticing approaches that has been offered for distinguishing the hagiographic treatment of virgins from that of male saints finds a defining difference in the "corporeality" of virgins.[7] Unfortunately, this characterization does not ultimately prove useful, for corporeality is little more than a suggestive category and, as argued in chapter 3, applies equally to male and female martyrs. Other scholars have detected a pornographic subtext in the frequent representation of virgin saints as nude or undergoing torture.[8] Certainly rape and attempted or implied sexual violence are features of virgins' Passions,[9] and the nude, tormented body plays its part in these stories and their effects (although it does so as well in the stories of male martyrs). Whereas modern sensibilities tend to read the accounts of virgin martyrs as chronicles of sexual crimes,[10] a more dispassionate approach is in order. We must attempt to survey the surviving evidence fairly to assess the place of the virgin's Life in narratives of the Middle Ages. Read without regard to generic prescriptions, these illustrations and texts may have occasionally functioned as erotica, but this was clearly not their primary role.

One way to understand the culturally specific functions of such Lives is to look at how they fit into the larger context of sanctity. A useful source for considering this bigger picture is the class of manuscripts that collect abbreviated saints' Lives:

illustrated Passionals. These manuscripts, whose purpose was usually liturgical, comprise a large number of texts, and the distribution of images by gender is a good indication of saintly cult as it was actually celebrated. Let us here consider three manuscripts (chosen because they are readily available in complete, published form): the Stuttgart Passional, the Weissenau Passional, and the Pamplona Bible.[11] All three were made in the twelfth century and were lavishly illustrated. Notwithstanding the titles of two of the manuscripts, which imply that they concern themselves only with martyrs, none of the works is so restricted; indeed, all three depict a broad range of narrative moments and holy actions other than martyrdom. Thus we may expect a representative, although perhaps not a statistically valid, survey.[12]

The artist of the Stuttgart Passional seems to have been distinctly shy of depicting female nudity: the manuscript contains only one nude among some twenty-four female saints. Male nudes are more numerous—eight among more than a hundred male saints. Male and female saints are tortured and martyred in similar proportions. The Pamplona Bible, by contrast, depicts six male and five female nudes, a much larger proportional representation of female nudity than in the Stuttgart manuscript; just under 8 percent of the male saints but nearly 15 percent of the female saints are nude. The Pamplona Bible depicts men and women tortured in approximately equal numbers. In the less abundantly illustrated Weissenau Passional, one virgin and two male martyrs are depicted nude; one virgin and two male martyrs are tortured.

Given that male saints outnumber female saints in hagiographic literature, in one case (the Pamplona Bible), the artist depicted a higher percentage of nude women, even though the actual numbers were lower. Furthermore, female saints represented in illustrated twelfth-century hagiographies are more often early Christian martyrs; male saints, by contrast, often comprise historically recent confessors and monks, who were not tortured or martyred and therefore would not have been depicted nude. Nevertheless, these numbers do not suggest an intrinsic preference for representing female nudity and torture.

One difference in the representation of male and female saints in Passionals, however, does seem significant. Many more female saints are depicted simply in the act of prayer; illustrations of male saints more often show these figures making liturgical gestures, usually the "blessing."[13] Only one illustration, in the Weissenau Passional, depicts a female saint making this highly charged gesture.[14] However, two female saints are shown receiving the host, one in the Pamplona Bible and one in the Weissenau Passional.

This survey may correct some preconceptions, but it tells us little about how individual images were meant to affect their viewers. The dynamic of the virgin martyr's story and its function within its genre are revealed much more clearly in the cycles of narrative images of the Lives of Lucy, Agatha, Margaret, and Radegund.

Notwithstanding their limited number, manuscripts containing illustrated narratives of virgins provide a relatively generous sample. Of the twenty-some illustrated narratives treated in this study, four, or about 20 percent, constitute the Lives of female saints. This figure—although subject to a wide margin of error, as a statistic based on such small numbers and the vicissitudes of survival—does exceed the overall 17.5 percentage women saints in the statistical survey of medieval saints calculated by Donald Weinstein and Rudolph Bell. It far exceeds the 8.3–11.8 percent they arrived at for the years 1000–1200, the chronological core of our study.[15]

There are several reasons for this relative abundance of female imagery. First, three of the four female saints commemorated in pictorial cycles are by no means contemporary with the date of the manuscripts' composition; rather, they are martyrs of early Christianity. Saints venerated in lavish artistic production are usually saints of the distant past, and illustrated narrative *vitae* constitute updated versions of Lives encrusted with venerable age and authority. The sanctity of women, even more so than that of men, tends to be of the most ancient variety. The faithful were encouraged to use saints as models, and women above all were encouraged to return again and again to the models of virgin martyrs.[16] Perhaps because women's roles (at least those recommended by the Church) changed so slowly from late Antiquity through the Middle Ages, new models of female sanctity were perceived as unnecessary and perhaps even threatening.[17] Ironically, this conservatism encouraged the concentration of cult power among a limited number of virgin saints. "Lists" or "catalogues" of such saints include Barbara, Thecla, Susanna,[18] Catherine, Margaret, Agnes, Juliana, Lucy, Cecilia, and finally the mother-virgin represented by Ann.[19] The unmistakable star-quality of Catherine, Margaret, and Barbara, the *Nothelfer* (holy helpers) of the late Middle Ages, epitomizes the extraordinary renown of certain saintly women.[20]

As these lists readily suggest, the power of female saints was not limited to assisting women, and the imagery of a select group of virgins was more popular than might be expected given the relative dearth of female saints. The four extant illustrated manuscript Lives of women clearly demonstrate this quality of cross-gender appeal. Lucy's illustrated Life, for example, was made for the male monastery of St. Vincent in Metz, along with a luxurious but no longer extant reliquary of 1090, to honor the venerable relics of Lucy, donated in the tenth century and preserved in one of the monastery's oratories.[21] The relics were renowned throughout Christendom because, as chronicles note, the saint was celebrated in the Canon of the Mass.[22] Two of the narrative Lives of virgins illustrated in other manuscripts—those of Agatha and Margaret—may have been intended as objects of private meditation to encourage emulation and piety; the Life of Agatha may have been intended for an audience of monks, but that of Margaret was certainly written for women.[23]

Although the Passions of virgins thus functioned to induce meditative prayer and were open to symbolic interpretation by either sex, women seem also to have valued them as literal models of sanctity. As a result, the very earliest Lives, which map specific and relatively narrow paths to female sanctity, were taken up by generations of women through succeeding centuries. The resulting patterns of sanctity had particular characteristics: Weinstein and Bell note that most female saints were lay figures, and that their religiosity centered on acts of service, charity, and self-denial;[24] virginity, of course, was the first and most crucial act of self-denial. The extraordinary creativity of female religiosity during the late Middle Ages, as explicated by Caroline Bynum, is all the more remarkable in its adherence to this same relatively narrow range of possibilities. The *virtuose* that Bynum describes creatively exploit the possibilities that were present even in the most formulaic of early Lives.[25] Thus, although the genre of virgins' Lives is clearly established through the repetition of elements, the disparate audience of the Lives produced a wide variety of receptions and more surviving examples than might be expected.

The fourth and final surviving illustrated woman's Life is not true to type. Radegund is neither an early Christian saint nor a virgin: she is a queen and through her rank holds the twin options of action and self-determination. Nonetheless, on initial examination, her Life seems more like than unlike virgin Lives. Radegund serves God and fulfills her service primarily in private. She retreats from worldly life to found a monastery, although she does not become its abbess. Only within cloister walls and after her own death is her sanctity fully revealed. Nonetheless, her Life exhibits carefully controlled innovation. Indeed, although it begins by holding fast to the carefully circumscribed role of female sanctity, the Life of Radegund expands that role significantly when the narrative turns to its subject's retreat from the world (see pp. 265–70). Precisely because it veers away from the context of virgin saints, discussion of the Life of Radegund is best deferred to a later chapter. Only after understanding the pictorial types of monk and king, to which it also relates, will the limitations and innovations of Queen Radegund's Life be apparent.

Because it includes, in addition to a narrative of nine scenes, not just the typical iconic frontispiece but three iconic images that occur in the middle of the book, the pictorial Life of Lucy—our primary example in this chapter—demands a discussion of the relative functions of iconic and narrative imagery. As we will see, however, Lives of virgins exhibit an iconicity that makes the functions more alike than different. Perhaps all Lives of saints have something of this effect, but because of the relatively static nature of their witness, it seems stronger in the illustrated Lives of virgin saints and is an important feature of the type.

Although I have already asserted that they may be alike, it is useful to oppose the terms *icon* and *narrative* in tracing how representation works. Narrative finds a unique manifestation in medieval illustrated saints' Lives, but iconicity is also insistently present in most if not all of these Lives. For example, in the Life of St. Margaret, an icon appears in the form of a frontispiece that precedes the story (fig. 28). A second, mixed, form is familiar from its use in Byzantine icons: a portrait of a saint might be surrounded by a narrative frame, as in numerous icons of St. George.[26]

But ultimately, narrative, especially during the early Middle Ages, can itself become icon, creating an intrinsically mixed narrative/icon that explores its subject through an episodic structure. That is, a series of episodes that support narration may also be emblematic of various virtues or truths that are revealed as essential to the subject as a holy being. Together the episodes shape an aggregate picture, or icon, of the saint. The goal of this iconic function should not be misunderstood: the virtues are not necessarily intended for emulation nor are they, in fact, fully imitable. Rather, they have a different purpose. In this type of presentation, virtues and truths lift the mind toward their ultimate source: God. By defining a strong foundation, iconic virtues participate in the obligation to "raise the structure little by little to its crowning point." Byzantine icons were believed literally to carry the prayers of the devout from the representation to its archetype, and the devout viewer could lift his or her thoughts from the degraded likeness, expressed in language or art, to contemplation of the divine truth. The same ascent is described in the West.[27] In the case of narrative "icons," the reading of the pictorial narrative similarly lifts the mind of the viewer and carries a series of prayers from the representation to the archetype. The process becomes almost a sort of intercessory prayer by means of pictures. The Life of Lucy shows how this remarkable effect was achieved.

Figure 28. Frontispiece to the Life of Margaret, *Passions of Kilian of Würzburg and Margaret of Antioch,* Fulda, c. 970. Hannover, Niedersächsische Landesbibliothek, MS I 189, fol. 11v. (Courtesy Graz, Akademische Druck- und Verlagsantsalt)

The illustrations of the Life of Lucy are contained in an unpretentious *libellus* (now in Berlin), which also includes a prose Life of Lucy; a verse Life, sermon, and letter by Sigebert of Gembloux; and liturgical offices in honor of Lucy. The Latin *vita* is early Christian, as is the core of the liturgy.[28] Originally from the Belgian monastery of Gembloux, Sigebert, a schoolmaster at Metz and an important figure in hagiographic literature, wrote the texts associated with Lucy during the late eleventh century; the illustrations in the Berlin manuscript date to about 1130, that is, sixty years or more after Sigebert's texts were composed.[29]

It is evident from the inscriptions on scrolls in the miniatures that the illustrations are primarily based on the early Christian prose Life, and they represent a standard virgin martyr's Life. However, verse Lives were sometimes claimed to be useful for meditation, while sermons were preferred for moralizing.[30] Therefore, it is not surprising that it is Sigebert's more poetic evocation of the saint in his sermon and verse Life that explains the ordering and appearance of the illustrations and how they might have been used by the monastic audience. Sigebert's descriptions focus on the same qualities that the artist uses to visually epitomize the saint.

Although the manuscript was made for monks, the monastic community does not seem to have constituted its sole audience. The small size of the Berlin manuscript and the fact that no monastic documents are included (as they typically are in other monastic *libelli*) suggest that the book did not have as its primary focus the safekeeping of the evidence of saintly patronage. The Lucy manuscript in this respect resembles the tenth-century Life of Margaret or the thirteenth-century manuscripts of Denis and Alban,[31] which were not tied to the shrine of a saint, contain no miracles specific to the contemporary shrine, and apparently circulated (in the case of the Alban manuscript quite literally) among a wider readership

A few details of the Berlin manuscript suggest a female readership outside the monastery,[32] but the dedication page that prefaces the verse Life places emphasis on the originating male audience: a tonsured monk labeled Rodolfus who offers a book inscribed with the prayer "pro me et fratribus me[is]" (on behalf of myself and my brothers). It is tempting to identify this Rodolfus as the scribe or even the artist, but there is evidence that more than one scribe and more than one artist participated in producing the manuscript. Rather, this Rodolfus must be one of the monks of the monastery of St. Vincent who sponsored the production of the book.[33] One might expect Lucy's portrait icon to be paired with the image of Rodolfus, at or near the beginning of the manuscript, but it is not. This oddity demands an explanation.

The portrait of Lucy (fig. 29) appears in the center of the *libellus,* just before the

Figure 29. Saint Lucy, *Passion of Lucy,* Metz, St. Vincent,
c. 1130. Berlin, Staatliche Museen, Kupferstichkabinett, 78 A 4, fol. 61r.
(© Kupferstichkabinett—Sammlung der Zeichnungen und Druckgraphik—
Staatliche Museen zu Berlin—Preußischer Kulturbesitz)

office and after Sigebert's epistle. In the epistle, Sigebert reminds the reader that the Life should be read in terms of the "spirit" rather than the "letter," particularly because he had discovered uncertainties regarding the date of Lucy's martyrdom.[34] He is therefore cautioning the reader that minor misinformation should not detract from the belief in the power of the saint herself, who stands "spotless . . . before the throne of God."[35] Facing this very statement is the powerful portrait image of the saint. Although not a frontispiece for the Life, perhaps it should be considered a frontispiece for the office it precedes.

The form of the representation is iconic. Lucy stands under an elaborate arch, the only figure in the manuscript to be represented in an entirely frontal attitude; the effect is regal and severe. She is recognizably a martyr in heaven "before the throne of God," crowned, in jeweled court dress, and perhaps intended to hold a palm.[36] Sigebert describes the heavenly virgin's costume eloquently in his verse Life—gemmed collar, pearls that hang over her forehead, a dress of rare tapestry edged with gold—and likens the virgin's limbs to ivory.[37] Such dress and imagery are associated with saintly virgins and might even be said to express their identity as royal members of the heavenly court. Lucy's frontal symmetricality and style of dress recall several images of female saints depicted in another twelfth-century German manuscript, the Stuttgart Passional. Furthermore, similarly rich costumes clothe virgins in all the narrative cycles, even in the most incongruous situations, such as the miniature in the Hannover manuscript that introduces Margaret as a shepherdess (see fig. 11). Therefore, although Lucy is represented here individually, her court dress and the setting imply her presence in the court of heaven with the cohort of virgins.

As an icon, the portrait of Lucy resembles frontispieces to the Lives of virgins. On that of the Hannover Life, Margaret is represented in court dress with a companion identified as Regina, being crowned by Mary (see fig. 28). The frontispiece to a lectionary in Boulogne-sur-Mer (fig. 30) groups virgins in a court around Mary in much the same way that All Saints' images group the virgins together.[38]

Much like the chorus of anonymous virgins depicted in the famous mosaics on the north wall of San Apollinare Nuovo,[39] these images emphasize the likeness and the timelessness of virgins. What "marks" these young and beautiful women is their lack of specificity and individuality, and it is surely no accident that the icon of Lucy is the only illustration in the Berlin manuscript that is not profusely labeled. The iconic similarity among early and high medieval depictions of virgins does not, however, diminish the power of these figures; to the contrary, it increases their partic-

Figure 30. The Virgin in heaven, detail of frame from frontispiece
to the Life of Folquin in *Legendary,* eleventh century. Boulogne-sur-Mer,
Bibliothèque municipale, MS 107, fol. 87v.

ular power as intercessors. Such an image, a true icon, devoid of almost all detail
and individuality, functions as an empty receptacle for prayer, transmitting it onward to its object. The icon takes its shape *from* the prayers of the devout rather
than shaping those prayers. In this way, the Lucy image is eminently appropriate as
a frontispiece for the prayers that follow it, for it is a holy vessel.

That this miniature of Lucy prefaces the elements of the liturgy rather than the
Life itself is particularly fitting, for materials associated with the liturgy are the most
iconic of the textual versions of the Life of any saint. By reason of their performance, the liturgical texts have narrative qualities,[40] but their primary effect is a portrayal of the saint in terms of the static, descriptive attributes that are common to
the class of virgins. The offices of Agatha, Agnes, Cecilia, and Lucy, thought to have
been composed by a single early Christian cleric,[41] characterize each of these virgins with the same virtues, building an especially powerful and holy representation
of their type. As with the use of literary *topoi,* repetition does not drain meaning
but instead reinforces it.

The primary virtues with which Lucy is credited in the office center, of course,
on her virginity, emphasizing her immovability on issues of faith and chastity, and

her status as *sponsa*, or bride, of Christ. We read (or would have heard) such epithets as *mons immobilis* and *sponsa Christi*, but perhaps Lucy's foremost identifying quality derives from her name, *Lucia*, or light. It is not unusual for a saint, and especially a virgin saint, to have a symbolic name: Fides (Faith), Agatha (Good), Agnes (Lamb), Margaret (Pearl). In the Lives of each of these saints, name is synonymous with nature. So with Lucy; in the office at nocturn we hear:

> *Ad Luce [or Lucis] nomen Lucia sortita*
> *nos fide tua absolve culpae*
> *tenebris et lucis apta gaudiis.*

> Inasmuch as Lucia has been assigned the name of light,
> release us in respect of your faith
> from the shadows of guilt and fit [us] to the joys of light.[42]

The play on the metaphor of light as faith and darkness as sin is central to the liturgy of Lucy's feast as well as to the medieval conception of Lucy as a holy figure.[43] It is no surprise that later medieval legend attributed to her *vita* a torture in which her eyes were removed and later miraculously restored. In late medieval and Renaissance images the saint offers her eyes on a dish (perhaps a paten), demonstrating her sacrifice.

Lacking the convenient attribute of the eyes on a platter, the twelfth-century artist of the Berlin manuscript creates a different pair of non-narrative images intended to reflect Lucy's foremost quality. These are the other two iconic images mentioned at the outset of this section. At first glance these frontispieces, which represent the parable of the Wise and Foolish Virgins, seem to have little to do with Lucy herself, yet there are some fundamental correspondences at work. The Wise Virgin's lamp—the light of her faith—is the attribute that allows her to enter into heaven, and each is characterized as a *sponsa Christi*. Furthermore, the virtue of the virgins is reinforced by their collectivity, and their courtly dress implies their rightful place in the court of heaven among the chorus of virgins (fig. 31).[44]

Do these two miniatures of the Wise and Foolish Virgins serve only to manifest Lucy's nature as expressed in her name? I believe that they are intended to serve a more specific function, much like that of the icon: to lift the viewer's thoughts toward the divine through the anagogical movement of Christian allegory just as the icon works to convey one's prayers and thoughts heavenward. The same might be said of any allegory, but *this* allegory works in several particular ways to elevate the believer's thoughts above the mundane.

Figure 31. The Wise Virgins, *Passion of Lucy,* Metz, St. Vincent, c. 1130. Berlin, Staatliche Museen, Kupferstichkabinett, 78 A 4, fol. 18r. (© Kupferstichkabinett—Sammlung der Zeichnungen und Druckgraphik—Staatliche Museen zu Berlin— Preußischer Kulturbesitz)

Starting in the early twelfth century (that is, contemporary with the Berlin *libellus*), the image of the Wise and Foolish Virgins was associated with the decoration of church portals and with the theme of the Last Judgment, with which the parable is often paired.[45] Thus, both in iconography and through architectural placement, the parable of the Wise and Foolish Virgins alludes to the physical and spiritual transition from earth to heaven.

Furthermore, throughout the Middle Ages, the Wise and Foolish Virgins were associated with the use of the senses.[46] The five senses could be either the occasion for sin (the five Foolish Virgins), or virtue (the five Wise Virgins).[47] Origen associates the virgins of the parable with those of the Song of Songs (1:3), in which the virgins love the Heavenly Spouse because of his divine "odor," which they perceive with not an earthly but a heavenly sense of smell. Spiritual or heavenly smell was one of the five spiritual senses that, according to the Alexandrine theologian, were revealed in Scripture. Origen's exegesis of the parable is amplified by Augustine, who argues that the senses must be grounded in faith and that the oil of the Wise Virgin's lamps represents "good works."[48] Through these associations of the Five Wise Virgins with the five spiritual senses, the identification of women with the senses and body was not only deepened and strengthened but also cast in a positive light. Moreover, by means of the parable and its exegesis, women and their bodies came to assume a prominent place in the monastic discourse on reading.

In the *Golden Epistle,* William of Saint-Thierry, companion and biographer of St. Bernard (and contemporary of the Lucy manuscript), advises novices that reading is a carnal activity, involving the senses and feelings. He counsels them to re-direct physical means of apprehension toward the spiritual activities of thinking and meditation. In proper reading, the very strength of the reader's response allows the text to "take hold of the mind and save it from distraction."[49] Following this paradigm, the inclusion of the Wise Virgins in the Lucy *libellus* becomes a commentary on, as well as a guide to, the redirection of the aroused senses that the narrative of a virgin saint's Life seeks to shape and control.

But these sorts of ideas are not limited to the twelfth-century work of William of Saint-Thierry. Sigebert's introduction to his sermon on Lucy contains similar sentiments, and the discussion alludes directly to the senses of sight, hearing, smell, and taste in explicating the meaning and value of reading Lucy's Life. It is possible that the schoolmaster was thinking specifically of the exegetical meaning of the five Wise Virgins, but quite certainly, as a hagiographer, Sigebert is treating the means of access to the heavenly. Perception and learning, he argues, can only occur through the involvement of the senses. Here, the saint's Life offered to his monastic audience follows the regimen that Augustine recommended for the perfection of the senses. A virtuous life (and its narrative embodiment in a *vita*) begins in faith, is amplified by good works, and finally focuses on purification and sanctification in preparation for a union with God.[50]

There is additional and even clearer evidence that Augustine's interpretation of the Five Wise Virgins was brought to bear on the reading of saints' Lives. In the richly illustrated twelfth-century monastic Weissenau Passional, a selection from Augustine's commentary on the Wise and Foolish Virgins prefaces the texts and images of the Lives of the saints.[51] There Augustine's text is used explicitly as a preparation for reading and viewing the Lives of the saints.

Iconographic evidence suggests that the parable of the Five Wise Virgins was also important in the reading of pictorial hagiography. In the *Zwiefalten Legendary* (1162) in Stuttgart, lamps border the image of the Ascension of St. Benedict, perhaps the foremost figure in medieval accounts of the perfected senses (fig. 32).[52] The burning lamps allude to those carried by the Five Wise Virgins; their inclusion in a miniature that depicts Benedict's entrance into heaven symbolizes his readiness to be united to the Lord. Their number may represent the saint's myriad good deeds, as they do in Augustine's exegesis. While the monastic illustrator of the Life of Lucy in effect argues that monks should emulate the Wise Virgins, the Stuttgart artist proves that the paragon of monastic life has succeeded in doing so.

In all these ways, the exemplum of the Five Wise Virgins in the Berlin manuscript becomes an exhortation to use one's senses well—to look to the saints to prepare the way to heaven, or as in Sigebert's text, to taste, smell, even eat the saintly. In this complex layering of meaning, the Wise and Foolish Virgin miniatures enlarge on the possibilities offered by the more conventional types of non-narrative images, such as Byzantine portrait icons. They begin to explore what an image can *do*. In suggesting meditation and forming the viewer's experience, they follow a path that approaches the operation of narrative images.

The Wise and Foolish Virgin miniatures thus stand midway between icon and narrative episodes in the sense that their images propose a certain kind of approach to narrative. They counsel the believer to read or look with senses fixed upon the holy as a means of access into the spiritual significance of the Life. In this way, they provide an interpretive frame for the narrative images. In this context, however, unlike the frame created by the speeches of Romanus, it is a visual frame for a visual

THE VIRGIN AS CORPUS

Figure 32. The Death of Benedict (*left*), *Zwiefalten Legendary,* Zwiefalten, 1162. Stuttgart,
Württembergische Landesbibliothek, Cod. Hist. 2.415, fol. 30v.

narrative. Because in the Middle Ages women were uniquely associated with the body, it is not surprising that such a sensory frame should appear here. Again, William of Saint-Thierry advises that "it is not man who is for the sake of woman but woman who is for the sake of man, and it is not spiritual things that are for the sake of carnal but carnal that are for the sake of spiritual."[53] If the perfected senses are to be represented, the perfection of body represented by a holy virgin is particularly suitable. When we turn to the narrative of the Life of Lucy, we will see a further staging of the virgin's body as the arena for the viewer to consider his or her own virtues, especially that of chastity.

THE VIRGIN AS NARRATIVE: THE COMPANY OF VIRGINS AND THE POWER OF FAITH

The pictorial narrative of the prose Life of Lucy begins with Lucy's visit to the shrine of Agatha in Catania in the company of her mother, who is suffering from a flux of blood (fig. 33). The site is labeled *Cathinensis civitas,* yet the tonsured monk who tends the shrine reminds one of the manuscript's origin in Metz. This miniature, the first in the manuscript, situates the story in the liturgical and monastic setting to which the viewer will be returned at the completion of the narrative. Lucy and her mother stay at the shrine overnight praying, prostrate on the floor, barely touching the shrine—imitating, as the text notes explicitly, the faith of the woman with the flux of blood who touched Christ's robe (fig. 34). Thus the narrative begins with a call to faith before action, as does the Life of Romanus (see fig. 14). It also emphasizes Lucy's comradeship with another virgin saint, as did the frontispiece of Margaret's Life (see fig. 28).

The second miniature further solidifies the alliance. In the upper register of Lucy's vision, Agatha appears in royal dress and calls Lucy her virgin sister. A multicolored band separates the top from the bottom of the miniature, placing Agatha securely in heaven; below, Lucy and her mother pray. Through the text and this illustration of the Christo-mimetic miracle—the cure of the flux of blood—Agatha is linked with Christ. Therefore her avowal both emphasizes Lucy's place in the chorus of virgins and firmly establishes Lucy's grace and sanctity.

The miracle represented in this miniature additionally confirms Lucy's holy nature. The mother's emission of blood marks her nature as fixed in a sexual and

Figure 33. Lucy arrives in Catania at the shrine of Agatha, *Passion of Lucy*, Metz,
St. Vincent, c. 1130. Berlin, Staatliche Museen, Kupferstichkabinett, 78 A 4, fol. 1r.
(© Kupferstichkabinett—Sammlung der Zeichnungen und Druckgraphik—
Staatliche Museen zu Berlin—Preußischer Kulturbesitz)

Figure 34. Lucy prays at the shrine and has a vision of Agatha, *Passion of Lucy*, Metz, St. Vincent, c. 1130. Berlin, Staatliche Museen, Kupferstichkabinett, 78 A 4, fol. 1v. (© Kupferstichkabinett—Sammlung der Zeichnungen und Druckgraphik—Staatliche Museen zu Berlin—Preußischer Kulturbesitz)

maternal body. In contrast, Lucy is identified by both her faith and her virginity as separate from this sort of femininity, and her posture helps to establish this otherness. Although prostrate prayer is appropriate to shrines, in the twelfth century it was a humiliating posture for a noblewoman to assume. Furthermore, it was figured as "copulation" with the earth, in recognition of sin.[54] For Lucy's mother it is an effective posture to ask for a cure, but for the virgin and blameless Lucy, it marks a moment of transition from a sinning body to the pure body of a bridesmaid of Christ, welcomed by her saintly sister Agatha. It is as though the believing woman with the flux of blood represented in the Gospels had been split in two, corresponding to two possibilities of woman's sexuality.[55] Now that Lucy's bodily perfection and sisterhood with a heavenly virgin have been established, subsequent miniatures detail the sainted virgin's actions.

In the next miniature Lucy tells her mother that she intends to distribute her worldly goods to the poor, and she does so (fig. 35). These actions place new emphases on the text of the early Christian prose Life. Rather than simply distribute her inheritance in the form of goods or money, Lucy donates food. Furthermore, the recipients of her largesse are not only the poor but also the sick. Although the new emphases in this episode are not typical of early Christian virgin saints' Lives, they do herald important developments in narratives about women of the high Middle Ages.

In the upper register of the miniature, Lucy argues with her mother: "If you are thankful to God for healing your body, then you should give Christ what you possess" (Si tibi gratum esse dei salutem tui corporis habens da Christo quod possides).[56] Given that it was Lucy herself who, through faith and as Christ's deputy, cured her mother, she now stands in a position of authority. Below, Lucy hands bowls full of bread or grain to a crowd of beggars, an act of charity of the kind that becomes perhaps the most characteristic narrative image of female saints during the high Middle Ages.[57] For example, in the Stuttgart Passional, in which each saint is represented by a single image, one virgin's Life is epitomized with a similar image of donation.[58] Bynum has argued that the holy status of later medieval women was associated with food for two reasons. First, the association was consonant with reality: from a domestic standpoint, women controlled food in the medieval economy, and often it was the only gift that they had to give.[59] Second, the association was profoundly symbolic, since even women's bodies were given over to nurturing.[60] The pictorial hagiography of the Lives of virgins brings together both ideas. Lucy gives away her inheritance in the form of food, while in a more symbolic

Figure 35. Lucy tells her mother of her intentions and gives away her possessions, *Passion of Lucy*, Metz, St. Vincent, c. 1130. Berlin, Staatliche Museen, Kupferstichkabinett, 78 A 4, fol. 2r. (© Kupferstichkabinett—Sammlung der Zeichnungen und Druckgraphik— Staatliche Museen zu Berlin—Preußischer Kulturbesitz)

Figure 36. St. George healing the sick, fresco, Tours, Saint-Martin.

gesture, Agatha gives her breasts as a sacrifice; in her *vita,* they become symbolic of spiritual food—the host.

In the pictorial Life of Lucy, the charitable act of distributing food rather than money is one element of divergence from the early Christian *vita.* But an additional aspect of Lucy's donation, also not mentioned by the prose Life, is intimated by the miniature: its healing value. One of the beggars making an appeal to Lucy is a double clubfoot on crutches; another man may be represented as having a skin disease— much of his face is darkened with a wash of color. The presence of the cripple ties the scene to the pictorial *topos* of healing as, for example, in the eleventh-century fresco of St. George healing beggars at Saint-Martin in Tours (fig. 36). Male saints in similar representations of charity regularly heal in addition to distributing goods and money (as St. George and King Edmund [see plate 6] are represented doing). Sigebert refers to Lucy bathing the sores of the sick in this episode of the verse Life, and in his sermon on the saint, he praises the cures that her relics effected.[61] Sickness was usually associated with sin during the Middle Ages; here Lucy personifies her saintly quality in offering, in Sigebert's words, "medicine for vices."

Sigebert's characterization of Lucy as *medicamentum* rather than *medicus,* passive rather than active, recasts the male role of healing. Lucy makes no gesture of power in the miniature but merely offers food to be consumed. In effect, she offers what she possesses, and through that offering is able to induce miraculous healings. Sigebert's sermon and its powerful linkage of the themes of sacrifice, food, and medicine offer a useful insight into the function of this image in the narrative. Lucy is not presented here primarily for her acts of charity. Rather, she *is* charity itself. She makes of herself an offering—of food, of healing, and eventually, of her body itself through martyrdom. In the last two miniatures of the opening sequence and the first three of the next, other aspects of the virgin body reinforce the purity of purpose of the virgin's Passion.

THE VIRGIN ON TRIAL

The fourth miniature finds Lucy's fiancé accusing her of following the Christian faith before Paschasius, the pagan prefect (fig. 37). In the lower register, the fiancé grasps her wrist, a gesture that has been taken to signify male possession or even rape.[62] Lucy counters by clasping a fold of her gown before her belly, a gesture reiterated in many virgin's Lives that seems to copy an Antique gesture signifying modesty or even chastity.[63] If, as in other Lives, the trial constitutes a defense of Christianity, here the virgin's Life refocuses our attention to issues of chastity and bodily defense.

At the close of the opening sequence of miniatures, Lucy is brought before Paschasius in the tribunal, and her formal interrogation begins (fig. 38). Above the prefect, seated on his large and imposing throne, is an equally imposing pair of curtains, extravagantly looped over a pole and occupying the top third of the miniature. This theatrical drapery in effect sets the stage for the main body of text, which immediately follows in the manuscript layout. In the miniature and the text, Lucy vigorously declaims and defends her beliefs. After the interposition of the texts of the manuscript and the three "iconic" images, the pictorial narrative resumes at the end of the manuscript. The last miniatures give final proof of the virgin body's purity and power.

Lucy refuses to relinquish her Christian beliefs, and Paschasius consigns her to a house of prostitution. What the artist chooses to show in the ninth miniature is that Lucy could not be taken to the brothel, even by the brute strength of a yoke of oxen (fig. 39). She becomes a *mons immobilis,* as Sigebert characterized her, an

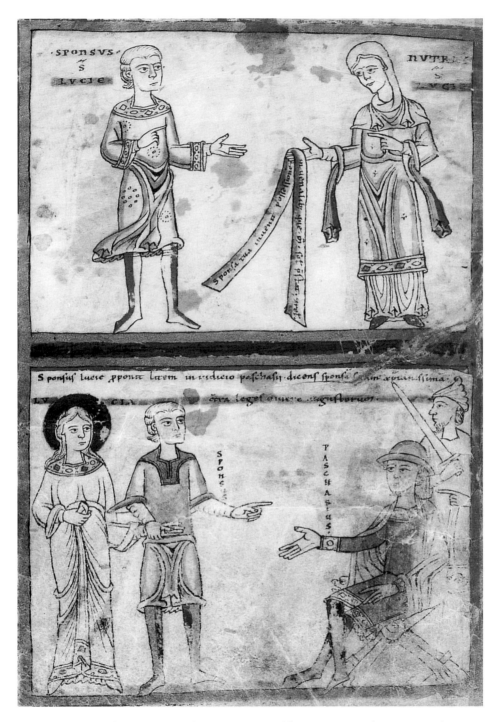

Figure 37. Lucy's fiancé argues with Lucy's nurse and betrays Lucy to the Roman authorities, *Passion of Lucy,* Metz, St. Vincent, c. 1130. Berlin, Staatliche Museen, Kupferstichkabinett, 78 A 4, fol. 2v. (© Kupferstichkabinett—Sammlung der Zeichnungen und Druckgraphik— Staatliche Museen zu Berlin—Preußischer Kulturbesitz)

Figure 38. Lucy before Paschasius, *Passion of Lucy*, Metz, St. Vincent, c. 1130. Berlin,
Staatliche Museen, Kupferstichkabinett, 78 A 4, fol. 3r. (© Kupferstichkabinett—
Sammlung der Zeichnungen und Druckgraphik—Staatliche Museen
zu Berlin—Preußischer Kulturbesitz)

Figure 39. Lucy is condemned to a brothel but cannot be moved, *Passion of Lucy*, Metz, St. Vincent, c. 1130. Berlin, Staatliche Museen, Kupferstichkabinett, 78 A 4, fol. 66r. (© Kupferstichkabinett—Sammlung der Zeichnungen und Druckgraphik—Staatliche Museen zu Berlin—Preußischer Kulturbesitz)

Figure 40. Agatha is forced into a brothel, *Collection of Saints' Lives,* French, late tenth/early eleventh century. Paris, Bibliothèque nationale, MS Lat. 5594, fol. 67v. (Cliché Bibliothèque nationale de France)

immovable mountain of Christian resolve. Such heroic resistance to rape is not unusual in the Lives of virgins. Similarly, but perhaps less dramatically, the virgin Agatha resists the coercions of the procuress Artemisia after being confined to a brothel for "training" (fig. 40). Both miniatures reveal virgin bodies that are "untrainable" in the normal sexual functioning of the body. The virgin saints' bodies are above any taint of sexuality, and both artists resist any salacious element in their miniatures. Indeed, Lucy is quite literally a mountain, towering over her diminutive persecutors.

Miraculous resistance is the most common outcome of incidents of attempted rape in the Lives of virgins. As Katherine Gravdal has stressed, an emphasis on virginity is inseparable from the narrative features of rape, prostitution, seduction, and forced marriage (or the resistance to these actions), that characterize the Lives of virgin saints and define them as preeminently female narratives.[64] In such a context, it is the virgin's renunciation of her sexuality that confirms her sanctity—that makes her, so to speak, the man, or *vir,* of *virginitas.*

One version of the saintly sexual struggle (exemplified in the Life of Margaret) brings the virgin to trial only after she has resisted seduction by a prefect or another figure of male authority. Lucy's trial begins with a suggestion of resistance to intimated corporeal coercion (the clasping of the wrist). If, however, the theme of rape is brought to the fore in the image of Lucy's consignment to a brothel, it is precisely to reverse it by defeating any possibility of lust or sexuality. Lucy's reaction makes this meaning clear. In the Berlin miniature, the virgin does not even pollute her eyes by looking in the direction of the brothel to which her enemies are attempt-

THE VIRGIN AS CORPUS

ing to drag her, for her virtue is inviolable. Instead, she looks out to the spectator—perhaps a monk, perhaps a woman—challenging that viewer to emulate her fortitude. It may well be a male audience that Lucy is challenging to move beyond the arousal that misguided sight can provoke.[65]

The virgin's ability through her body to reverse the worldly system of power and resist lust is further emphasized in the next two miniatures, which depict her torture. In the first (fig. 41), Lucy is stripped to the waist, her upper body exposed. As Tertullian argued in *On the Veiling of Virgins*, "every public exposure of a virgin is [to her] a suffering of rape."[66] Unable to consummate a true violation of Lucy's body, Paschasius rapes her with his eyes, leering at the virgin from the upper register while stroking his beard.[67] (Surely Paschasius's characterization as evil makes this a warning against improper looking.) Below, Lucy maintains an extravagant posture of prayer, kneeling with her arms raised high and her eyes averted. Two tormentors pour oil on her and subject her to flames. On the facing page, in a miniature that depicts her martyrdom by the sword (fig. 42), Lucy appears in precisely the same posture, albeit reversed. In effect, she has not moved, even though everything around her has changed. Now the virgin martyr occupies the upper register and Paschasius, defeated, is led off in chains. Sigebert characterizes the events in his verse Life: "Faith is crowned, perfidy abdicates."[68]

One element in Lucy's depiction does change in the second miniature: she shifts her eyes to look out at the viewer, once again calling attention to her strength as an exemplum and moral authority.[69] Within the image itself, five viewers respond to the challenge, looking with fixed attention at the virgin's heroic body. Unlike the leer of Paschasius, however, these viewers look with the "eyes of Faith."[70] These believers, converted by Lucy's testimony to Christ, as in the text, are now purified and see properly. A transformation has been effected in the presence of Lucy's nudity: sexuality has been defeated; lust is led away in chains and replaced with purity. Through its power, the virgin's body has accomplished a radical shift in its surroundings while it alone (even as it is tortured and mortified) remains unchanged.

Similar calls for transformation or change in the perception of the body are embedded in other virgins' Lives. These variations reveal the power of this imagery. During Agatha's torture, the sexual perception of the nude female body is recalled at the very moment that it is denied. Agatha's torture seems intrinsically sexual because it involves her breasts (fig. 43).[71] However, reminding us that a body can offer more than one powerful message to its viewer, during her torture the saint herself calls out to her tormentors: "Are you not confused to cut away that which you sucked on your own mother?"[72] The suckling breast to which Agatha makes reference is

Figure 41. Lucy is stripped and tortured, *Passion of Lucy,* Metz, St. Vincent, c. 1130.
Berlin, Staatliche Museen, Kupferstichkabinett, 78 A 4, fol. 66v. (© Kupferstichkabinett—
Sammlung der Zeichnungen und Druckgraphik—Staatliche Museen
zu Berlin—Preußischer Kulturbesitz)

Figure 42. Lucy is martyred with a sword; Paschasius is led off in chains, *Passion of Lucy*, Metz, St. Vincent, c. 1130. Berlin, Staatliche Museen, Kupferstichkabinett, 78 A 4, fol. 67r. (© Kupferstichkabinett—Sammlung der Zeichnungen und Druckgraphik—Staatliche Museen zu Berlin—Preußischer Kulturbesitz)

Figure 43. Agatha's breast is removed, and she is imprisoned, *Collection of Saints' Lives,*
French, late tenth/early eleventh century. Paris, Bibliothèque nationale, Ms. Lat. 5594, fol. 69v.
(Cliché Bibliothèque nationale de France)

also, of course, an image of the nourishing Church, and she herself refers to her
"interior breast" that nourishes her senses.[73]

Another image in the Life of Agatha may be intended to prompt the viewer to
reflection (see fig. 40). In the scene in which Agatha is condemned to a brothel, the
artist represents powerful enticements that the saint confronts and resists. Remarkably, the inducements have nothing to do with sexual encounters with men.
Rather, what Agatha emphatically rejects is friendship—absorption into an intimate,
close-knit, and animated community of women. Moreover, if there is any hint of
sexuality among these chastely garbed women, it can only be in the close embrace
of two of the women. Is this an intimation of homosexual love? If so, it is surely
condemned by its context. But given the male audience of the manuscript, it is clear
that it is not only sexuality but also profligate physical intimacy and even women
in general that this image condemns.[74] Women are depicted as consorting in packs,
chattering and pointing, and having no control of their bodies. Perhaps this image
is intended to permit thoughts of (and monkish guilt about) sexuality and physical
companionship to surface. But if so, they are immediately condemned, controlled,
and reassuringly defeated by the power and model of the saintly virgin.[75]

To read these images in this way is to begin to see how they attempt to manip-
ulate the response of their audience. They initially present the worldly beauty of

the saint and perhaps the enticements of sex or female companionship, but that presentation is clearly subordinate to other elements that reflexively shape a response negating any mundane desires. Perhaps the effect is clearest in the Life of Margaret, in two miniatures discussed in chapter 3 (see figs. 26 and 27 and pp. 88–89) for their modeling of viewer response. In those miniatures, the saint's torture is also displayed with frontal nudity, yet Margaret looks out, meeting our gaze. The spectators within the image model our prescribed response: they cringe in conspicuous horror (their response is documented in the text), shocked by the whipping that so cruelly cuts the virgin's beautiful body.[76] To strengthen the effect, in the next miniature even the hard-hearted Olybrius and the saint's tormentors turn away, hiding their eyes. Such a reaction, embedded in the image, parallels reactions embedded in texts— whether the actual empathetic responses of Peter in the *Dialogues,* or various calls for empathy in Passion texts, or William of Saint-Thierry's "feelings [that] give rise to prayer."[77] As Gregory notes in the *Dialogues,* it is compunction and tears that will soften hard hearts and lead to conversion. The tears shed by the audience within the image from the Life of Margaret in fact lead to their conversion in the subsequent narrative. Similarly, the empathy and "tears of compunction" of the external viewer of the image are intended to displace the mundane attractions of sexuality and substitute a movement of the soul toward faith. Furthermore, they negate the allure of physical beauty and replace it with the recognition of its heavenly cognate, divine perfection.

The second image of Margaret's torture brings to the fore this important aspect of the effect of the story. Margaret's beauty is raised as a factor that makes her torture—indeed her entire tale—all the more horrible. Her beauty, of course, is by no means unique: all virgins, it would seem, are beautiful. It is one of the first qualities noted by hagiographers.[78] Undoubtedly it is the beauty of a virgin's body that makes her sacrifice so affecting and complete. What is important to understand, however, is that although this beauty may at first appear as a mundane and superficial quality, ultimately beauty functions as a sign of purity and divinity. This cognate of divine perfection is not only an attribute that reflects the virgin's inner or spiritual beauty but also a sign of the divine itself.

The idea is implicit in Bernard of Clairvaux's description of the bride in his *Sermons on the Song of Songs:* "What can be a clearer sign of [the bride's] heavenly origin than that she retains a natural likeness to it in the land of unlikeness, than that as an exile on earth she enjoys the glory of the celibate Life, than that she lives like an angel in an animal body?" (27.6).[79] Medieval viewers were prodded to recognize certain truths: God created beauty in the world, and humankind has the opportunity to recognize God's agency in the beauty of his creation. However, beauty can equally function as a seduction and distraction, serving as an end in itself, a mere pleasure for the luxuriating senses and *concupiscentia oculorum*.[80] Only if looked at properly and with the desire of faith, will beauty lead the soul on a spiritual path.[81] The eyes and all the senses must discover God in the world.[82] In the Passions of virgins, the spiritual exploration of feminine bodies follows the same dynamic that one must follow in thinking of the body they imitate—the body of Christ. In the later Middle Ages, Angela of Foligno explicitly warned of the danger: "because it sees God 'humanated' . . . , the human soul sees the soul of Christ, his eyes, his flesh, and his body. But while it looks . . . , it should not forget also to turn to the higher . . . , the divine."[83] But already Augustine had written, "Let us love, [only] that beauty which seeks the eyes of the heart."[84] Ultimately, the beauty of the virgin's body plays a crucial role in this anagogical action of the narrative, both drawing the eye and at the same time reminding the viewer of beauty's origin.

The Lives of virgins attempt to effect a change. Not all of the images use beauty as enticement to effect a reversal of perception, but each supplies the potential for recognizing difference—not difference in the virgin, who remains emphatically unchanged and uninvolved (except perhaps through the challenge of her gaze), but difference within the viewer. In each case, the viewer is confronted with sexuality and earthly beauty and led to reject it. The narratives prompt the viewer to take a path of purification that the monks or female viewers might follow in their own souls. We found a similar process of purification recommended by the iconic image of the Five Wise Virgins, but that was more abstract, more meditative. In making use of emotion, the narrative finally perhaps taps the richer, more productive vein.

VIRGIN AS SACRIFICE AND CORPUS

Lucy's Life lacks a burial or ascension. In place of an angelic demonstration of her reception into heaven or a miraculous sign of her sanctity at the time of her burial, the last illustration of the Berlin Life uses what at first seems a relatively simple scene of the saint's reception of the host as *viaticum* (fig. 44). However, in this miraculous last burst of physical strength after receiving the mortal blow of the sword, Lucy effects an identification of her own body as sacrifice with that of the Eucharist.

Figure 44. Lucy receives the Eucharist, *Passion of Lucy,* Metz, St. Vincent, c. 1130.
Berlin, Staatliche Museen, Kupferstichkabinett, 78 A 4, fol. 67v. (© Kupferstichkabinett—
Sammlung der Zeichnungen und Druckgraphik—Staatliche Museen
zu Berlin—Preußischer Kulturbesitz)

The ceremony is performed by a tonsured monk and returns the viewer almost sensibly to the twelfth-century present and the reassuring care of the liturgy, while at the same time marking out the miraculous nature of Lucy's body not merely receiving the host but also palpably participating in the sacrifice of the Mass.

The comparison of the virgin's body to the host is by no means unique to the Life of Lucy. It recurs in images in the Lives of Margaret, Agatha, Valerie, and other virgin saints, and it becomes a typical metaphor for the Virgin Mary in the later Middle Ages.[85] The episode in the Life of Lucy is perhaps closest to a miracle in the Life of Agatha in which the saint is healed by St. Peter, who is described as a *medicus* and depicted liturgically garbed and tonsured (see fig. 19 and pp. 74–79). A young deacon, not mentioned in the narrative, accompanies St. Peter and carries a large candlestick with a burning candle, as does a cleric in the Lucy miniature.[86] Both miniatures may make reference to the ceremony of the Last Rites.

Although images of the Mass may be viewed as sacramental and visionary in the context of martyrs' Lives and are typical of the genre, these images in virgins' Lives attain a special prominence and a new significance. Bynum has shown how nuns of the later Middle Ages ecstatically identified themselves with the Mass.[87] I would argue that this identification has a long tradition in the Lives of virgin saints and their pictorial hagiography.

The martyrdom of the virgin Valerie on Limoges reliquaries of the twelfth and early thirteenth centuries presents a striking example of the continuation of this tradition (fig. 45).[88] Two reliquaries, one in St. Petersburg, the other in London, preserve the same multi-episode narrative (and twenty-one other reliquaries depict the narrative, or a variation of it, in condensed form). Valerie's Life is remarkably succinct in its appearance in both text and images.[89] The text of her Life (not attested before the tenth century) recounts how she was converted by the Apostle Martial, committed herself to a new bridegroom (Christ), and rejected her previous suitor, the duke of Aquitaine. She distributed her wealth to the poor and to the Church. In two of the four primary episodes depicted on the St. Petersburg reliquary, on the lower register she is first called before the duke and condemned to death; she is then martyred by the sword. Only in the upper register is a significant new variation on the typical Life of the virgin saint introduced.[90] There, in the center, Valerie, a cephalophore, miraculously carries her own severed head, offering it to St. Martial in an event that is likened by the artist to a Mass.[91] The paten on the elaborate altar, although decorated with a cross, is empty, and Valerie's offering is explicitly depicted as the sacrament.

Figure 45. Reliquary of St. Valerie, Limoges, c. 1175–85. St. Petersburg,
State Hermitage Museum.

In offering themselves at the end of their lives, virgins support the Church metaphorically and even physically. Both Lucy's reception of the host and Valerie's offering are depicted in detailed and geographically specific ecclesiastical settings.[92] Moreover, Valerie's offer of her body explicitly confirms the sanctity of the new church founded by the confessor-saint Martial in Limoges—the presence of her body, buried in Martial's own tomb, created a *locus sanctus* marked by martyr's blood.[93] Similarly, but less explicitly, the depiction of the final image in Lucy's illustrated Life claims a special sanctity for the church at Metz by virtue of the presence there of the virgin's holy body.

Thus in Valerie's short life, and in those of Margaret, Agatha, Lucy, and at least two women in the twelfth-century Passionals, virgin saints typically conclude their lives as "living hosts." Their perfect bodies become perfect sacrifices. In most of these images, the primary action is that of the virgin receiving the host. She offers herself in spirit, but she is depicted being offered the sacrament by a priest. In this formulation she herself does not celebrate the liturgy but takes a more passive role; what is significant is that in her passivity she is both subject and object of the sacramental event.

The virgin saint is unique because, as a woman, she can be both host and recipient of the host. The image of Lucy receiving the *viaticum* offers striking confirmation of this doubling. The profile view allows the artist to focus the scene on the host as it is delivered into the saint's mouth, effectively focusing attention on the sacramental action. Nevertheless, although it is the only profile representation of the saint in the manuscript, the saint is not in any way diminished; she is still a dominating presence. It is clear that Lucy herself is part of the sacrifice. In his verse Life, Sigebert characterizes both Lucy's sacrifice and the narrative of her Life as *puram hostiam,* a pure host or offering. The phrase and the image derive from the office that describes Lucy as a saintly living host.[94] Furthermore, Sigebert implicitly characterizes Lucy as the host in his sermon when, in a twist of the Augustinian metaphor of saints as teeth, he describes meditating on her Life as literally ruminating— grinding the elements of the Life with the teeth and swallowing the sweetness of the saintly *exemplum* as a medicine to relieve the harmful humors of the vices. He emphasizes, moreover (in an analogy to the theology of the Eucharistic host), that in this grinding, nothing is worn away except perhaps the teeth themselves.[95]

It is finally the virgin's body itself, as revealed in its perfection in the narrative of her Life, that becomes the embodiment of the perfect offering. Her *corpus* is both body and host offered to the readers of her Life. Thus, she perfectly reiterates her model, the body of Christ, sacrificed as an offering for Christians.

CONCLUSION

In its inclusion of episodes of accusation, torture, and violent death, a virgin's Passion is very like that of other martyrs. Only in certain emphases in select miniatures is the nature of the virgin clarified and explicated. If maleness was taken for granted as superior and natural (or perhaps in the case of monks, obliterated, "un-gendered"),[96] the femaleness of a virgin saint had to be closely defined in order to demonstrate her sanctity. Of course, the virgin's gender is not at all that of the average woman but something emphatically other. Indeed, she victoriously rises above and beyond her sex and provides a model of celibacy for both sexes. In pictorial narratives, the miniatures that convey these meanings work as icons of virtue. Whether literally iconic or narrative in form, together they create a vision of the virgin as an especially palpable form of sacrifice. Sigebert calls the Life of Lucy "sweet medicine" and its illustrations demonstrate how, with the gifts that any woman can offer—food and body—the virgin rises through her corporeality to achieve union with God. In modeling this role, she serves as an especially effective icon of intercession, a passive but efficacious vessel for prayers.

These functions of the virgin's Life shed light on the effect of saintly narratives on their audiences. Earlier, I suggested the presence of a female audience for the Lives of virgins, and it is a medieval and a modern commonplace to note that young women read such Lives as models. However, our analysis must nuance that under-standing.[97] As a type, virgins are static, and they liberally share their natures with other virgins: a virginal intertextuality and interpictoriality. In these ways, virgins' Lives seem appropriate for a female audience; certainly medieval women did model themselves upon these saints. Nevertheless, the Berlin *libellus* was created for a male foundation and apparently remained there. Attempting to define a single-gender audience for that book or any virgin's Life is certainly a mistake. In *Gender and Religion,* borrowing terminology from Victor Turner and insight from Paul Ricoeur, Caroline Bynum and Paula Richman argue that in their polysemic character, symbols may function in different ways for different audiences.[98] By the same token, the narrative of Lucy's Passion may have provided a model for young women, but it also served the male clerics who cared for Lucy's relic body, and who made and owned her book.

These men, as their onetime teacher Sigebert suggests, would ruminate on the Life, focusing on individual moments and qualities. What might have been seen as a menacing and erotic body, exposed in images of torture, is revealed to be a body that has miraculously overcome the appetites of the flesh. It becomes an example to those monks who seek similarly to overcome the ever-menacing sin of lust. If the senses are clarified, the beauty of the virgin becomes not an occasion for pruri-ent interest but an icon of the possibilities of purity. The beauty of her flesh, per-haps so tempting, is shown through narrative to reflect the beauty of her soul, as she stands immaculate before the Lord. Only a woman, the quintessential body of the Middle Ages,[99] could offer that body to the Lord as a sacrifice and thereby become the image of the purity of body that was a goal for all religious.[100]

John Coakley has traced an interesting and further development of the monastic use of the special qualities of female sanctity, arguing that among the mendicants holy women were perceived as "experiential" and uniquely capable of active contact with the divine. Men were expert witnesses but "felt divine contact was elusive." Therefore for the special friends of female visionaries and the interpreters of female revelation, "the cultural language of gender . . . served the men both to express and, although only vicariously, to transcend the divide between a life of evangelical action and a life of experiential contact with God."[101] Perhaps this is a development of earlier notions of the virgin's perfected senses.

Finally, as Augustine muses in his sermon on the Wise and Foolish Virgins, "I do not think . . . that this parable . . . relates to those women only who . . . are called Virgins . . . but if I mistake not this parable relates to the whole Church."[102] Augustine's musings apply equally well to the stories that have been our subject. Through virgin saints, any Christian may see a reflection of the body of the Lord. As icons in action, these narratives perfect the senses and carry the reader or viewer through the image in this world, up toward the archetype and the divine. Lucy, like her sisters, is the living host whose Life and nature serve as sweet medicine to those who read it.

5

THE LIVES OF CONFESSORS
Bishops

ॐ

THREE IMPORTANT TYPES of saints represented in Lives of the early and high Middle Ages can be grouped under the heading of the confessor—the bishop, the monk, and the royal saint. Confessors lacked the certainty of sanctity provided by martyrdom, a fact that obligated their hagiographers to *demonstrate* their subjects' saintliness. As a result, although sanctity operates as a given in these Lives, the accounts are marked with repeated, almost ponderous, assertions of holiness. Furthermore, unlike the clear structure and universality of the narratives of martyrs' Lives, confessors' Lives are distinguished by their variability and particularity. This "infinite malleability" characterizes confessor saints in their functions and actions in society, as well as in their depiction in "literary sources, liturgical texts, . . . and the visual arts."[1]

Among confessor saints, bishops and monks are particularly well represented in illustrated manuscript Lives of the high Middle Ages; indeed they constitute the majority of such Lives. The reason is not difficult to discern.[2] Monks were the primary caretakers for saintly bodies and their associated relics and were therefore the most ardent promoters of cults, as well as, ultimately, the primary audience for Lives. It is not surprising, therefore, that monastic manuscripts celebrated patrons and fellows. Moreover, the Lives of bishops also take a prominent place in monastic hagiographic output: bishops were often monks at the outset of their careers and founders of monasteries later.[3]

Although the Lives of monks resist easy classification, episcopal Lives, while ranging widely in terms of date and place of production, clearly adhere to a distinctive, stable, and identifiable type. Even more so than the texts, the pictures are easily identifiable as belonging to that type. An exploration of the episcopal subgenre will help us to understand how artists attempted to demonstrate the sanctity of bishops through such Lives, and, not incidentally, by these means sought to advance the power and prestige of the Church.

THE BISHOP'S LIFE

> He did not lust with greed after raiment of scarlet or purple
> but was content with his woolly tunic.
> He did not ride his horse in pride through the green pleasances
> but journeyed on his own four feet, as he should.
> Spotless was he, nor empty were his words—
> Baa or baee, mystic were his utterances.
> (Sedulius Scottus, *Mock Elegy on a Gelded Ram*)[4]

That a Carolingian poet should choose to create a parody on the Life of a bishop speaks to the ubiquity and importance of the type during the early Middle Ages. At the same time, albeit humorously, the poet introduces us to the problematic nature of episcopal office. The bishop was a man who was both in the world and withdrawn from it—above reproach but also open to the criticism to which the powerful are uniquely subject.

Above all, a sainted bishop's Life is marked not only by personal sanctity but also by the honor of the episcopal office. Gregory of Tours praised one holy man, saying that his personal character even "equaled the grace of the episcopacy."[5] Nonetheless, despite this doubling of possibilities, a bishop's sanctity is also distinctly confined—as the shepherd of his flock, he is the servant of his people. Apart from unusually famous figures such as Ambrose, Martin, or Denis, the bishop is by nature tied to a locality. Bishops eventually assumed the function of the Roman landowner in late Antique patronage systems and often came from the same noble ancestry.[6] In Ottonian conception, the bishop was a "prince of this earth," with all the attendant responsibilities.[7]

In death, as saintly patrons who staked spiritual claims, bishops literally divided the geography of Europe into separate spheres of patronage and influence. Gregory of Tours's narratives make clear that regions were particularly "nourished" by the local saint as leader and intercessor. Boundaries of influence could be drawn and evil kept outside.[8] Indeed a saint was "granted" to a locale as its special intercessor, and a town might not be "big enough" for two.[9] The universal nature of the illustrated books of martyrs seemed to make these Lives suitable to a wide and disparate audience; bishop saints, by contrast, had a fiercely partisan audience, and illustrated books containing their Lives were made with the express intention of lauding their sanctity and power, in preference to that of other saints.

These local and advocatory *libelli* were made for a specific monastery or church where the relics of the confessor were preserved. Often, in the last pages and on the flyleaves, deeds and charters that would have come under the specific protection of the saint were recorded, "for safekeeping." Gregory of Tours's *Glory of the Confessors* contains an abundance of miracle stories that show a saint defending "his" property, and the illustrated Lives are similarly replete with pictorial representations of saintly defense.[10]

Nevertheless, the impressive holy power of these patrons was never completely taken for granted. Because the Life, as a constructed image of sanctity, took on the burden of proof, the hagiographer had to demonstrate that the confessor was indeed blessed with grace. One strategy might be to pile up virtues and miracles; a more effective one was to show how the bishop shared the qualities of other saintly bishops—how he conformed to episcopal type.

Although bishop saints even within the hagiographic type would have had to adjust to many different historical particularities, their representation in Lives contains several elements that appear consistently in the subgenre. The bishop is consecrated as an officer of the Church and takes his place in its hierarchy. He preaches, baptizes, and prays. He cares for his people, often with acts of exceptional charity, often with medicine for their souls. The latter can be either figurative and equated with preaching and guidance or literal—expressed as miracles of healing or saintly patronage. At his death he bequeaths a heritage of sanctified land and purified community.

Nonetheless, as with martyrs, a list of actions or qualities falls short of adequately characterizing these narratives. It was in the preface to the Life of a confessor that a hagiographer argued that he had to *build* a narrative that suited the glory of the subject (see p. 30). Creating an ideal in the *vitae* of bishop saints does not center on recounting actions performed but rather on illustrating the nature of the episcopal office: its significance and its place within the Church. For example, although episcopal Lives are marked with a sacramental quality, the sacrament does not lie in the saint's own sacrifice, as it does in the Passions of the martyrs, but rather in the bishop's celebration of the liturgy. Thus, the Life of Christ was alone not sufficient as a model for the Lives of bishops; hagiographers had to seek other narrative models such as the Lives of the Apostles, New Testament texts, and, of course, liturgical ceremony. Indeed, it is finally in the celebration of the Mass that the bishop saint finds the fullest narrative expression of his sanctity.[11]

THE BISHOP'S PLACE IN THE CHURCH: EPISCOPAL OFFICE ON EARTH AND IN HEAVEN

Even before recounting the events of its subject's life, the episcopal Life situates itself in relation to those of other saints. Relatedness is a central theme for such Lives, for bishops are quintessentially involved, in Gregory of Tours's phrase (*Glory Conf.*, 80), in building "unity of the Church." Gregory lays particular stress on his intent in writing the "Life" of the saints: to "strengthen the Church" and to make the "aims" of the saints clear.[12] Furthermore, he does not simply seek to build the universal Church but also to construct a smaller *communitas*. As bishop of Tours, Gregory defines his congregation as the beneficiaries of the virtues and deeds of a particular patron saint, Martin of Tours, but he also demonstrates how Martin functioned in the larger community of saints, a network of sanctity, based, as Peter Brown would have it, on "observed human relations" and "human interactions."[13] Gregory illustrates the principle with stories in which confessors of great prestige intercede on behalf of new members of the heavenly community—Martin for the virgin Vitalina and again for Pelagia—and incidents in which choruses of saints, dressed in white robes and chanting psalms, celebrate the feast of a fellow saint at his or her tomb.[14] The illustrated Life of Amand depicts one such welcome of a fellow saint: the virgin Aldegundis has a vision of Amand ascending into heaven accompanied by ranks of fellow saints clad in white (see plate 3).

Through the events of his Life, the bishop displays the character and hierarchy of the social order. In the early and high Middle Ages, the bishop, as the epitome of ecclesiastical power, not only leads his earthly church but is responsible as well for the souls and spirituality of his congregation. He plays a dominant part in guiding and consecrating female sanctity. Martin, as a living but already holy bishop, interceded with his prayers for the new virgin saint Vitalina. As a saint already resident in heaven, he returned to earth to attend the funeral of Pelagia. Similarly, bishops are continually called upon to assist virgin saints by blessing their tombs or persons. On the reliquary of St. Martial in the Louvre, the bishop blesses the new convert Valerie (figs. 46 and 47) and in effect administers the Last Rites (she is to be martyred as a consequence of her conversion).[15] Although she ultimately consecrates Martial's church through the gift of her martyr's blood, she is always depicted as subservient to him in his capacity as official representative of the Church. On her own reliquary, Valerie even presents her severed head as an offering to him (see fig. 45).

Needless to say, these examples are pointedly gendered, but the significance of the bishop's place in the ecclesiastical hierarchy supersedes gender and even extends beyond death. In the illustration of Aldegundis's vision of Amand's ascent (plate 3), the bishop's prestige is revealed through clear pictorial differentiation. The saints that flank him—souls that the holy bishop has converted—wear simple white robes. Amand, however, wears glorious liturgical garments, holds a crozier, and is far larger than any of the other figures (his head is uncovered because episcopal miters did not become common until the twelfth century). While the other saints energetically march in groups and raise their hands in supplication, Amand stands calmly alone, both hands firmly grasping his crozier, locking eyes with the angel who welcomes him to heaven with the offer of an enormous gold crown. Even within the saintly chorus, the bishop saint thus holds an elevated position replete with power; at the same time, however, he is bound by obligation to the souls he shepherds.

In discussing the type of the bishop saint, it will again be expedient to focus on an individual saint. The illustrated Life of Kilian of Würzburg consists of eleven framed miniatures, which immediately follow the relevant texts, breaking into the single-column format. The manuscript seems to have been intended to further Ottonian efforts to spread the cult of this episcopal saint, but in this case there is no evidence that it complements the celebration of the cult of Kilian's body.[16]

To reveal the variety within the Lives of bishops, much of which derives from their origins in diverse geographical areas and political situations, the discussion of Kilian will be supplemented with comparative material from several other Lives.[17] Kilian and Amand were apostolic bishops, both of whom began with no fixed see. Another apostolic figure, Quentin, was never bishop, but his holiness and importance to the local see is demonstrated in his *libellus,* which makes use of many

Figure 46. Reliquary of St. Martial, front, Limoges, c. 1165–75. Paris,
Musée du Louvre. (Photo RMN/Arnaudet)

of the same narrative strategies that appear in episcopal Lives. Aubin is perhaps
the bishop saint whose power is most clearly represented as founded in the Eucharist.[18] Other bishops, such as Cuthbert, Liudger, Martin, and Omer, began as
monks, and their Lives will be discussed in this chapter as well as the next. Although
the surviving pictorial hagiography of Arnulf, Denis, and Ambrose is either frag-
mented or not contained in *libelli,* aspects of the imagery are of great interest here.
Finally, as we have seen, Martial's Life is epitomized on a small thirteenth-century
reliquary from Limoges that is particularly interesting for its apostolic and missionary message.

Figure 47. Reliquary of St. Martial, reverse, Limoges, c. 1165–75. Paris,
Musée du Louvre. (Photo RMN/Arnaudet)

BUILDING A BISHOP'S LIFE:
ACCLAMATION, CONSECRATION, INVESTITURE,
AND APOSTOLIC PRESTIGE

The first images of a bishop's Life establish his authority and his right to hold his
office. The most important of these images, regardless of its position in the narrative, is the depiction of the bishop's election and consecration to his office. The texts
of episcopal Lives often make much of their subject's being spontaneously chosen
by the will of the people, but this means of selection seems to have been rarely (if

ever) pictured.[19] Instead, illustrations almost invariably depict liturgical recognition by the Church, essential in establishing the authority of the bishop, and a fitting initiation for the bishop's liturgical Life. If such recognition can be linked to apostolic origins, it is all the more effective in establishing the bishop's prestige.

Two miniatures in Kilian's Life depict the pope himself examining and consecrating the bishop and describe Kilian's relationship to the hierarchy of power. In the first (fig. 48), the saint submits to ceremonial questioning by the pope; in the second (fig. 49), Kilian is consecrated by the pontiff, who stands within the church behind an altar marked with a cross. The illustration establishes that the pope derives his power from Christ, represented by the cross on the altar; the pope, in turn, passes the power "to loose and to bind," as the text notes, to Kilian. The historical authority of the pope, which derives from St. Peter himself, is further indicated by the compositional reference of this miniature to the familiar image of the *Traditio Legis,* in which Peter first received *his* authority from Christ (fig. 50). Finally, the presence of three of Kilian's episcopal brethren, who stand across from the saint and recommend him for consecration, further situates Kilian within the fellowship of bishops.

The liturgy of such a consecration in the tenth century, as recorded in the Romano-Germanic Pontifical, makes specific reference to many of the details illustrated in the Hannover miniature. Nevertheless, the Fulda artist strays from specifics of the liturgy as often as he adheres to it.[20] Ultimately, the artist's principal reason for using liturgical formulations is not to create an accurate liturgical record but to represent Kilian as ever more firmly embedded within the structure of the Church. Here, Kilian takes his place within a historical and communal patronage system of spiritual authority.

Similar scenes of consecration within a church appear in the Lives of Liudger and Ambrose. Barbara Abou-el-Haj has discussed somewhat different imagery in the Life of Amand, focusing more specifically on the process of investiture.[21] Whether or not her assessment of partisan special pleading in the context of the investiture conflict can be supported by the slim visual evidence, it is clear that Amand's assumption of the bishopric is a more political event, since it is marked by the presence of a king (fig. 51). In terms of medieval practice, which traces its roots back to the sixth century,[22] and the religious law of the eleventh century, this reflects historical reality more accurately than does a purely ecclesiastical appointment. Kings or emperors appear on the shrines of Heribert and Remaclus, on the bronze doors that recount the Life of Adalbert, and in the Omer *libellus.*[23] Bishops

Apostolicum uirum iohannem pontificantes. quoniam defunctus e. A sco papa cononę predictus di pontafex ke llena. Amabiliter cchonorabiliter. suscepatus e.

Cum autem beatus papa conon audiuit. unde uenerat &ad quod uenerat. &ad quę locum ęxinde prompta uoluntate fiar fuerat. Audito illius fide pariter cchoc-

Figure 48. Kilian examined, *Passions of Kilian of Würzburg and Margaret of Antioch,* Fulda, c. 970. Hannover, Niedersächsische Landesbibliothek, MS I 189, fol. 3v. (Courtesy Graz, Akademische Druck- und Verlagsantsalt)

trina dediglli ado & scopetro principe
apostolorum licentiam & potestate pdi
candi ecdocendi. Et quoscumq: scea con=
uertere potuisset doctrina liberalatq;
firmissima hoc faceret potestate

psi nanque exinde pergentes itinere
seques trati sunt. tamen corporaliter
non spiritualiter. Et adherebant suo epo
kyliano. colonatus prbr. & totnanus

Figure 49. Kilian is consecrated as bishop, *Passions of Kilian of Würzburg and Margaret of Antioch,* Fulda, c. 970. Hannover, Niedersächsische Landesbibliothek, MS I 189, fol. 4r. (Courtesy Graz, Akademische Druck- und Verlagsanstalt)

Figure 50. *Traditio legis*, mosaic, Rome, Santa Costanza, fifth century.
(Alinari/Art Resource, N.Y.)

might be represented serving as both spiritual and secular princes, especially in German Lives, and some examples show both ecclesiastical consecration and political investiture.[24] Nevertheless, illustrated saints' Lives made in monastic centers generally avoid representing power structures outside the Church. The textual Life of Ambrose, for example, records the acclamation of the people and the participation of the emperor in his consecration; the ninth-century Golden Altar of Sant'Ambrogio in Milan, by contrast, shows Ambrose being welcomed into the Church exclusively by his fellow bishops (fig. 52).[25]

It is a peculiar mark of both Amand and Kilian's historical episcopacy that each man was first appointed not to an established see but to the office of a missionary bishop. Kilian's pictorial Life, in fact, defines its subject as a missionary from the first illustration (fig. 53), which, of course, precedes his consecration. In the company of eleven others, Kilian "takes up his cross" and departs from his homeland, Ireland, to spread the word of God.[26] It is only when he finds a likely region for conversion (in effect for spiritual "acquisition" by the Church), the pagan city of

oratione dedituf: sermone cautuf

S iquof exiam capriuof uel puerof tranf

Figure 51. Amand is consecrated as bishop, *Life of Amand,* Saint-Amand at Elnone (Saint-Amand-les-Eaux), c. 1050–1100. Valenciennes, Bibliothèque municipale, MS 502, fol. 11r.

Würzburg, that he turns to Rome and seeks the pope's approval. The pope's consecration of Kilian (as well as his approval of the mission) gives Kilian's Life apostolic overtones. Such associations are an important element of many episcopal Lives.

On the Limoges reliquary chasse in Paris, Martial's apostolic mission is similarly affirmed, by St. Peter himself, in this case. Peter grants Martial his staff, and following Peter's model the saint uses it to resurrect the future bishop saints Aurelian and Andrew (see fig. 47 [at lower left] and fig. 46 [lid]). Some hagiographers explicitly designate the miracle of resurrection itself as an apostolic act.[27] Martial's wearing an unadorned toga, in marked contrast to the ornate miters and copes worn by other

Figure 52. Ambrose is consecrated as bishop, *Golden Altar,* back, Milan, Sant'Ambrogio, c. 870. (Foto Marburg/Art Resource, N.Y.)

bishops on the reliquary, further conveys his apostolicity. Such simple yet remarkably effective illustrative affirmations belie the complex textual and liturgical maneuvering that, as Richard Landes has shown, was used to establish Martial's apostolic prestige and garner power for Saint-Martial, his foundation in Limoges.[28]

Assertions of apostolicity and the prestige that it confers do not end with the granting of the saint's mission. As Lives of apostolic bishops, the stories of Kilian and Martial both make pointed reference to visual models that originate in the Lives and Acts of the Apostles. Three basic actions that give characteristic shape to apostolic Lives—preaching, baptizing, and the working of miracles—are repeated endlessly in these and other episcopal Lives. Persecutions, tortures, imprisonments, and

Figure 53. Kilian arrives at Würzburg with his companions, *Passions of Kilian of Würzburg and Margaret of Antioch,* Fulda, c. 970. Hannover, Niedersächsische Landesbibliothek, MS I 189, fol. 2r. (Courtesy Graz, Akademische Druck- und Verlagsantsalt)

martyrdom, the typical dramatic narrative reactions to the basic actions in the Lives of the Apostles, also often recur in Lives of bishops.

Specific compositions contained in cycles of apostolic Lives may have served as precedents for Western saints' *vitae.*[29] The representation of the actions of preaching and the working of miracles in these compositions closely follows even earlier precedents from the Life of Christ: Christ or the Apostle stands to the left making a gesture of blessing, often accompanied by one or two witnesses. To the right is the audience or the person or persons to be healed—kneeling, blind, on crutches, or lying in a bed. Often an audience consists of a standing group who argue among themselves, representing reaction and conflict.[30] Since Christ himself did not conduct baptisms, and therefore his Life does not provide a visual precedent, baptismal images adopt an even simpler composition for representing that ceremony. Again, the apostle is on the left and the catechumen is on the right, usually in a barrel-like tub; witnesses or waiting catechumens sometimes appear as well.

One particular combination of these apostolic scenes, however, seems to have had special significance. A Carolingian ivory in the Museo Nazionale in Florence presents

Figure 54. Peter preaching and baptizing, Carolingian
ivory plaque, Florence, Museo Nazionale.
(Alinari/Art Resource, N.Y.)

actions of preaching and baptizing described in the Book of Acts (fig. 54). This pictorial combination becomes paradigmatic of the missionary acts of the Apostles who follow the injunction of Christ: "Go ye therefore, and teach all nations, baptizing them in the name of the Father and the Son and the Holy Spirit" (Matt. 28:19).[31] As such, the two actions often serve as a visual core for the Life of a bishop, as in a historiated initial D depicting the Life of Arnulf in the Drogo Sacramentary (fig. 55).[32] In a remarkably brief summation of episcopal duties, the bishop is pictured preaching, baptizing, and exorcising. Similarly, on the Golden Altar in Milan, Ambrose himself is baptized by other bishops and in turn preaches to his congregation (fig. 56).

Figure 55. Arnulf of Metz, historiated initial, *Drogo Sacramentary*, Metz, c. 850. Paris, Bibliothèque nationale, MS lat. 9428, fol. 91 r. (Cliché Bibliothèque nationale de France)

The latter image, in particular, speaks to Ambrose's episcopal prestige through its apostolic associations. Not only is it close to models from the Lives of the Apostles—Ambrose preaches in apostolic simplicity to a small audience—but the presence of an angel attests to the special efficacy of the bishop's speech. The angel whispers in his ear, demonstrating that Ambrose's words emanate directly from a divine origin.

One other example, Amand preaching to the sacrilegious Basque (fig. 57), reveals how illustrated Lives of bishops explore and expand the *topos* of apostolic preaching. At the outset of the episode, depicted in the upper register, the unbelieving Basque jeers at the bishop. The text recounts that "one of the ministers, shallow, tricky and arrogant, rising and joining mocking words with loud laughter . . . began to disparage the servant of Christ and to treat the gospel which he proclaimed as worth nothing."[33] Amand and the minister face off in a debate that calls to mind that of Romanus and Asclepiades (see fig. 14). The Basque's slinking, animal-like movements mirror his unregulated speech; Amand's words, by contrast, are represented as deriving directly from the Gospels—the bishop's gesture of speech, a pointing finger, is superimposed over the book. The depicted audience awaits the outcome and the nearest onlooker crosses his arms as if taking a neutral position.

Figure 56. Ambrose preaching, *Golden Altar,* rear, Milan, Sant'Ambrogio, c. 870.
(Foto Marburg/Art Resource, N.Y.)

In this depiction of preaching as a spectator sport, the sainted Amand, of course, vanquishes his foe. In the lower register, preaching takes on a different, "liturgical" aspect, demonstrating the power of the bishop and perhaps serving as an inverted substitute for the rite of baptism. The bishop stands frontally, dressed in his cope, and holds a gospel book in one hand and a crozier in the other. The power of his "liturgical" stance (what Barbara Abou-el-Haj has called the "image of power")[34] possesses and destroys his adversary. The Basque is literally repelled (in a reverse somersault) by the bishop's speech and the truth of his words; in a doubled image, he is possessed by a demon and begins to rip his own clothing. Except for a single companion behind the bishop, the audience has disappeared. The Basque's only supporter is an arabesque-like tree (trees often figure as pagan cult objects) that

Figure 57. Amand preaches to a sacrilegious Basque, *Life of Amand,* Saint-Amand
at Elnone (Saint-Amand-les-Eaux), c. 1050–1100. Valenciennes, Bibliothèque municipale,
MS. 502, fol. 23 v.

seems to caress his dying head. Preaching is revealed in this miniature to have two
somewhat divergent aspects—it can be persuasive, or failing that, in a medieval ad-
justment to the apostolic model, it can be empowered with the potency of the
liturgy. In this miniature, the saint serves as agent, but it is the Church that wins
the victory.

The primary role of apostolic elements in these narratives, however, is not to provide hard evidence of the bishops' connections to the apostolic origins of the Church. Certainly, throughout the Middle Ages, "documents" of various sorts concerning the apostolic status of patron saints were adduced as evidence in advancing the prestige and authority of one episcopate over another.[35] Art was particularly valuable in service of these efforts because it could create a persuasive image or effect without entailing the necessity of proof or overt forgery—Martial's reliquary is a good example. Nevertheless, the images of consecration, preaching, and baptism in the *vitae* do not serve these particular ambitions except in the most general of ways. Rather, apostolic imagery in bishops' Lives reinforced an ecclesiastical spiritual hierarchy; in the illustration of Kilian's consecration, for example, St. Peter and the Apostles are the source of the Church's authority. Any likeness or connection to the Apostles that can be established by an episcopal narrative helps to justify the bishop's place in his office and secure his exalted position within the spiritual company of Christ's companions.

PREACHING AND THE POWER OF THE LITURGY; BAPTISM AND BUILDING THE CHURCH

Scenes of preaching and baptism are not used solely with the intent of establishing connections to apostolic precedents; these scenes also lay the foundation for establishing the sacramental nature of the bishop's Life. If images of consecration serve to assert authority and community, then the case for the holiness of the saint was most convincingly set forth for the medieval viewer in depictions of the bishop's performance of the liturgy.

The Life of Kilian expands the apostolic significance of the paradigmatic pair of preaching and baptism to make just such an argument.[36] Two scenes, which the artist has taken pains to position on facing pages and to make the largest in the series, epitomize the core of Kilian's Life as bishop. They also position the imagery of preaching and baptism with respect to other themes and events in the saintly bishop's Life: his acclamation by the people of Würzburg, the accomplishment of his mission in the baptism of the populace, and the fullest revelation of his sanctity. But above all, it is the details that invest the miniatures with liturgical power and meaning. In the "preaching" miniature (fig. 58), Kilian wears a pallium and cope and stands behind a lectern or altar. He is accompanied not by two witnesses as in

Figure 58. Kilian preaching, *Passions of Kilian of Würzburg and Margaret of Antioch,* Fulda, c. 970. Hannover, Niedersächsische Landesbibliothek, MS I 189, fol. 4v. (Courtesy Graz, Akademische Druck- und Verlagsantsalt)

apostolic scenes of preaching but by two lesser clergy, his deacon and presbyter, who assist by holding a book and crozier. Kilian is represented in a frontal position with arms spread wide, a gesture commonly associated with the liturgy. Below, the members of his audience gesture as if speaking; some raise their hands as if in approval or acclamation. Clearly, Kilian is engaged in a liturgical ceremony of some kind. In portraying the scene as a liturgical celebration, the artist may have been influenced by his own experience. During the early Middle Ages, preaching as an activity independent of worship was rare (perhaps even nonexistent), and liturgical performance took its place: "worship ritual—the pattern of prayer and gesture— was the school for most Christians."[37]

The Hannover miniature is clearly not a picture of simple preaching; neither is it a literal representation of liturgical ceremony. Just as certain frontal images in the Life of Amand (in particular the second episode of his encounter with the Basque) are liturgically transformed into images of power, this image positions Kilian in the center of the power and sanctity that the celebration of the liturgy bestows on the officers of the Church. Medieval celebrants were thought to be especially worthy: "When the priest has invoked the Holy Spirit and sacrificed this beloved host, . . . where, tell me, do we place him in our esteem? . . . Tell me what must be more pure, more holy than a soul in which resides such a spirit!"[38] In the Fulda miniature, preaching has been transformed by a generalized evocation of that same glory of the liturgy in order to reveal an image of the saint perfected and sanctified.[39] The halo, appearing for the first and only time in the Life of Kilian, marks the moment.

Such displays and *topoi* of glory and power in the Lives of bishops are ultimately intended to exhibit charisma, the inevitable persuasive power of the Christian truth, doctrine, or liturgy.[40] They are immediately followed by conversions (or, alternately, punishment, as in the case of Amand and the Basque). In Quentin's Life, scenes of preaching and conversion or baptism are linked by *tituli* that leave no doubt about such inevitability: "Here Quentin preaches the dogma of salvation to the populace," is immediately followed, in the next miniature by a *titulus* referring to the faith and salvation of that populace and a picture showing their baptism; preaching is immediately followed by belief.[41] With its implication of inevitable consequence, the confessor's Life follows a pattern familiar from the Passions of the martyrs: charismatic preaching or liturgy has the power to produce converts, just as the persuasiveness of martyrdom has the ability to convert pagans.

Baptism, of course, follows conversion as the seal placed on the new believer's soul. Hence images of baptism complete the construction of an image of the bishop's sanctity. Baptism also asserts the power of the Church and of the Church's servants to mark the elect—to seal the newly converted unto God. In this sense, the miniature of Kilian baptizing the people of Würzburg (plate 4) again makes a complex argument for the value and power of the liturgy.

In the upper register of the miniature, Kilian baptizes a single figure who stands in a barrel-like tub. Once more, the miniature amplifies the cursory account in the text, which states only that the saint "baptizes" the people. Kilian's deacon and presbyter serve as assistants in the liturgical celebration, and they hold what appear to be a sacramentary and a chrismatory (a container for the anointing oils) as Kilian administers the chrism that is the final seal of the baptism. Below, three other Christians who have already been baptized are notable for their dress—and undress. In the center, one man pulls on the white robe of the new initiate; at each side of him, two men gesture to call attention to the various elements and actions of the scene. They are stripped to the waist, clothed only in loincloths and peculiar headdresses. It is the liturgical association of these headdresses that particularly focuses the significance of the scene. The pointed headdress with gold circlet is identifiable as the veil and the diadem that certain Carolingian liturgical texts require initiates to wear at baptism. They specifically symbolize the baptismal initiate's assumption of a new Christian status and signify his ceremonial likeness to priest and king.[42]

These elements and actions in the Hannover miniature demonstrate how the liturgy of baptism effectively marks and purifies the Christian neophyte and raises him to a new and glorified status.[43] This illustration addresses the audience directly: it assures its viewers that the bishop is holy and can lead them through the liturgy; furthermore, it promises that participation in the liturgy sanctifies every Christian, just as it does the clergy.

Other representations of bishops performing baptism similarly convey the import of a ceremony that establishes the community and sanctity of the Church. Amand, for example, unites political and spiritual power in baptizing the son of King Dagobert: the infant miraculously intones the word *Amen* at the conclusion of the ceremony, sealing a political promise of conversion as well as miraculously affirming the efficacy of the liturgy.[44] Omer baptizes an important local landholder who then donates his land, which will become the monastery of Sithiu, that is, Saint-Bertin (fig. 59). The miniature is labeled with a *titulus* that reads, "In which St. Omer baptizes Adrovaldus, whom he had converted from pagan errors through preaching."[45] The connection is explicit: Omer converted the pagan from the error of his ways through preaching, and baptism seals the pact. The narrative implies that Omer had been traveling as a missionary: the artist of the miniature, however, depicts a chalicelike font over which three lamps are suspended: the setting is clearly a church, with all the pomp and grandeur entailed by such a location. Omer has acquired not only a soul for the Church but also a valuable tract of land, and the grant of the land is depicted in a second, abundantly decorated ceremonial in which the bishop "marks" the newly acquired properties with Christian buildings in order to literally secure the gains of baptism.[46] In combination, the two miniatures show that the bishop builds his community, builds the Church, and builds churches through baptism.[47]

The association of building with conversion is an important one, in part because building churches and founding monasteries were activities that established episcopal prestige and extended the Christian community. A ninth-century bishop,

Figure 59. Omer baptizes Adroald, *Life of Omer (Audomarus),* for the canons of St. Omer,
third quarter of the eleventh century. Bibliothèque de l'Agglomération de Saint-Omer,
MS 698, fol. 15r.

Figure 60. The Franks tear down their temple and build a church, *Life of Amand*,
Saint-Amand at Elnone (Saint-Amand-les-Eaux), c. 1050–1100. Valenciennes,
Bibliothèque municipale, MS 502, fol. 18r.

Desiderius of Cahors, even claimed that "the building of very many churches was
among the divine obligations."[48] However, before a site could be fully appropriated
for Christian use, the bishop first had to correct pagan error by destroying any cult
site. Several miniatures that illustrate episcopal building contrast destruction with
construction, as in the Life of Amand (fig. 60);[49] or display the authority of the saint
to command and direct builders, as in the Life of Liudger.[50] Thus building, figuratively or literally, can manifest authority, sanctity, and even correct doctrine.[51]

These miniatures demonstrate the power and unity of the Christian community
as forged in preaching (that is, liturgy) and baptism in three ways: the eagerness of

the populace to join as a group with the bishop and the Church; the subsequent sanctification of the people through the liturgy; and, in the images of Omer and Amand, the joining of political power with spiritual power. Each of these themes highlights, in addition to the strength of the community itself, the rightful and efficacious place held by the bishop as leader of his flock. The bishop's power (both in life and after death) to acquire and hold lands, as well as to convert, persuade, or chastise people and princes, is essential to the construction of his sanctity. Of course, it is equally important in enabling his community to assert and maintain its rights.[52]

BISHOPS AND THE MIRACULOUS

Although the paired actions of preaching and baptizing most succinctly epitomize the episcopal mission, apostolic models recommend a third action to be performed by the saintly bishop. As shepherd of his flock and heir to the Apostles, it is through miracles, especially those of healing, that the bishop demonstrates his sanctity and his service to his community. Unlike the apostolic model of the primitive Church, where miracles directly express the power of Christianity, the bishop's most important miracles are those that demonstrate his control of divine power through his place in the Church. Most of these miracles involve spiritual healing and, implicitly or explicitly, result in conversion or a strengthening of the ties of faith. In such miracles the bishop serves as a "holy doctor." Christ and St. Peter are his models in a healing role that, Raymond Van Dam has argued, is allied to the bishop's function of teacher or master in the classical mode.[53]

The most commonly represented episcopal miracles of healing are three that occur in the Life of Christ: curing paralytics, giving sight to the blind, and exorcising the possessed.[54] A more unusual but highly significant miracle is the raising of the dead. This miracle, of course, recalls Christ's resurrection of Lazarus and is signaled by some hagiographers as the true sign of apostolicity.[55]

In the illustrated cycles that survive, the curing of paralytics generally occurs as a posthumous miracle: the paralytic comes on crutches to the tomb of Omer or Albinus, for example, and leaves walking.[56] The miracle attests to the saint's healing and miraculous nature and his efficacy as a patron.

In contrast to the posthumous healing of paralytics, healing the blind is a miracle that seems particularly suited to the living bishop. By leading the supplicant to see

Figure 61. Liudger cures the blind Bernlef, *Life of Liudger of Münster,* Werden, c. 1100. Berlin, Staatsbibliothek, Cod. lat. theol. fol. 323, fol. 12r. (Staatsbibliothek zu Berlin, Preußischer Kulturbesitz)

"the true light," the bishop in some sense brings a sinner into the fold. In the Life of Liudger the saint cures a supplicant, Bernlef, by making the sign of the cross in front of his eyes (fig. 61). The bishop asks whether the man can see and, indeed, Bernlef can suddenly see the cross described by the saint's blessing.[57] Similarly, Albinus cures two blind persons, including a woman whom he cures with the sign of the cross (fig. 62); in doing so, he drives out a demon, thus suggestively linking two types of miracle.

Possession by demons is much emphasized in early medieval texts, in which demoniacs are cured in droves by bishop saints. Peter Brown evokes the disorder of the late Antique cult site, with demoniacs rushing around screaming declarations

Figure 62. Albinus cures a blind woman, *Life of Aubin (Albinus),* Angers, Saint-Aubin,
late eleventh century. Paris, Bibliothèque nationale, MS n.a.l. 1390, fol. 1r. (Cliché
Bibliothèque nationale de France)

about the presence of demons, or announcing the power of the saints in strangled voices.[58] Such exorcisms demonstrated the power of the Church—not only because exorcism was a liturgical ritual, but also because the disorder of possession contrasted with the power, grandeur, and solemnity of the Church and its representative—the bishop, whether living official or dead saint. However, as Brown notes, "the drama of exorcism was not merely a drama of authority: it was a drama of reintegration."[59] By the bishop's action, the individual was simultaneously restored to his humanity and rejoined to the Church.

Numerous pictorial exorcisms demonstrate the potential power of the miracle. Liudger drives out a demon from Helgoland (fig. 63), purifying an entire island with a single miracle. In part, the miracle is already constituted simply by recognizing the presence of such a demon,[60] yet such a geographically ambitious miracle once more reveals the bishop's power over space and community, not merely over the individual.

A bishop's power to exorcise demons could equally be inverted. Kilian, who accomplishes no miracles during his life, is represented after death effecting miracles of possession—the opposite of exorcism. Kilian's executioner and the woman who ordered his death are possessed by madness and commit suicide. Notably, the representation of the madwoman calls to mind the vices of discord or heresy controlled by the virtues, as described and illustrated in the *Psychomachia*.[61] Finally, Duke Gozbert, who acquiesced in the arguments of a pagan in setting the murderer free, is driven from his throne and his country (fig. 64). In a similar instance, Amand effects the possession of the sacrilegious Basque as punishment (see fig. 57). By such means, bishops regulate their communities—in these cases not by bringing in converts but by casting out sinful members.

However, even more than exorcism or healing miracles, it is Eucharistic miracles that reveal the purest nature and potential of the episcopal Life. One of the *tituli* that Fortunatus composed for the dedication of the sixth-century basilica of Saint-Martin at Tours describes a miracle illustrated in a fresco: while Martin was celebrating Mass, his hands were suddenly and miraculously encrusted in gold and gems.[62] The original fresco is lost, but the fact that such a miracle was chosen for illustration and poetic elaboration in the Life of a bishop emphatically demonstrates that the glories of the Mass merited adornment and deserved a magnificent setting. Hincmar of Reims in his episcopal statutes of 852 advises priests not to allow the sacraments to go before the populace "without the sacred vestments of priesthood, but among these holy things let it be sent to them, returning from communication

Figure 63. Liudger drives a demon from Helgoland, *Life of Liudger of Münster*, Werden, c. 1100. Berlin, Staatsbibliothek, Cod. lat. theol. fol. 323, fol. 9v. (Staatsbibliothek zu Berlin, Preußischer Kulturbesitz)

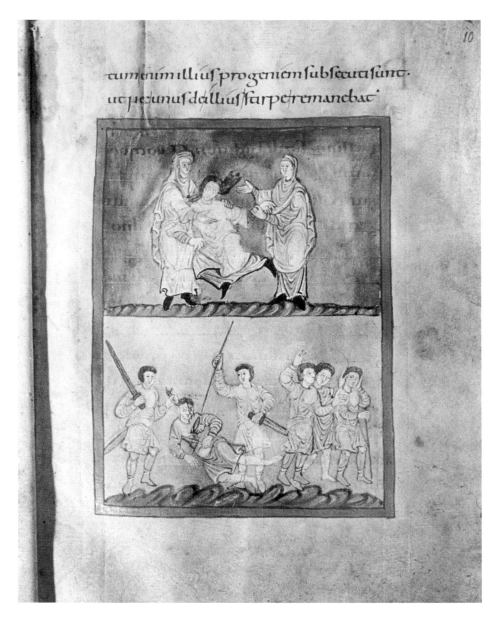

cumeium illiuf progemem subsecuta sunt.
ut petunuf dei illiuf sarpe remanebat·

Figure 64. Geilana goes mad; Gozbert is killed by his swordbearers, *Passions of Kilian of Würzburg and Margaret of Antioch*, Fulda, c. 970. Hannover, Niedersächsische Landesbibliothek, MS I 189, fol. 10r. (Courtesy Graz, Akademische Druck- und Verlagsantsalt)

with the divine."[63] The miraculous appearance of gems on the hands of Martin suited his role as a celebrant, but they also suited his position as bishop.

In fact, like the miracle of Martin's Mass, many episcopal miracles reiterate the identification of bishops with the power and meaning of the liturgy. In the *Glory of the Confessors,* Gregory of Tours recounts numerous miracle stories involving bishop saints that concern wine (or grapes) or oil.[64] The liturgical significance that might remain only allusive in texts is highlighted in illustrations with gesture and detail. In a Life thoroughly saturated with liturgical symbolism, Albinus excommunicates a sinner, who then dies when the consecrated host is presented.[65] In two different episodes, Omer cures infants of their blindness by means of baptism. In the first of these, the font is miraculously supplied with water after Omer strikes it with his crozier; the water flows out in four streams, reminiscent of visual depictions of the fountain of life, the nourishing source of the wisdom of the Church. In a series of miracles that occurs only after he is consecrated as a bishop, Cuthbert effects cures twice with holy water, once with oil, and once with consecrated bread, and performs a miracle in which he tastes water and thereby gives it the flavor of wine. In the Life of Amand, a blind man is healed with the water in which the bishop has washed his hands before the Mass.[66] Finally, Liudger heals a blind beggar while presiding at a feast that is visually reminiscent of the Last Supper (fig. 65).[67] The beggar disdains the food arrayed on the table and asks instead for the spiritual food that he knows Liudger is capable of giving. Through the use of symbolic substances and settings, these miracles repeatedly emphasize the complete identification of the bishop with his role, especially as celebrant of the Eucharist.

Symbolic gesture is another means of making the same identification. Many of the healings and exorcisms accomplished by bishops are executed with the sign of the cross, a ritual gesture made with the fingers and hand (see figs. 61 and 62). However, this gesture is not exclusively thaumaturgical; it is also distinctively liturgical and an important source of the bishop's power. With the sign of the cross and an impression of the hand, the bishop seals the soul to the Lord at the final moment of the ritual of baptism. Furthermore, the repetition of the gesture by the laity could renew the seal. The church fathers commended the sign of the cross, and the faithful were instructed in its use by the clergy:

> The cross repels every crime,
> and darkness flees from the cross.
> Consecrated with such a sign
> the mind does not know how to bend.[68]

Figure 65. Liudger cures a blind man, *Life of Liudger of Münster,* Werden, c. 1100. Berlin, Staatsbibliothek, Cod. lat. theol. fol. 323, fol. 13r. (Staatsbibliothek zu Berlin, Preußischer Kulturbesitz)

With this powerful sign, bequeathed to them by their bishop, the faithful could keep out demons and sins or destroy demonic power.[69] Because of its efficacy against evil, the sign of the cross was used by priests, laymen, and even women—Margaret destroyed the dragon, an incarnation of evil, with the sign.

However, the use of the sign of the cross as a means of healing is distinguished from the more common protective gesture. The "medicabilis divinae potentiae dextera"—"the divine healing power of the right hand of God"—was reserved for God's special representatives.[70] It might occasionally be used by a nun such as Radegund, but she more often performs healing miracles with other forms of touch or gesture (see chapter 8). Textual Lives, *tituli,* and miniatures specify that it is bishops who most often cure with the sign of the cross.[71] In the miniatures, martyrs use the sign of the cross almost passively—that is, protectively—against the encroachment of evil. Bishops, by contrast, use the sign actively, as a liturgical gesture that they wield by prerogative: as God's instruments—the limbs, the arms of the body of the Church—bishops transmit God's power.

Perhaps the most telling pictorial example of the sign's power is the representation of Martin's gesture, which in the Tours manuscript of his Life revives a hanged slave (fig. 66). There, a circle of hands explicates the origin and magnitude of the saint's power. The hand of God blesses and enables Martin, who in his earthly mission, in turn makes the sign of the cross over the limp body of the dead slave. The arrangement of the dead man's arm and Martin's hand suggest that the saint is raising the man by grasping his wrist, but in fact, he does not touch him at all: rather the limp arm of the man is lifted and overshadowed by the power of Martin's gesture.

In its full significance, the interaction of gestures in the miniature is even more complex. As Magdalena Carrasco has observed of other such scenes, the imploring gesture of the dead man, although here contrary to reason and the text, is essential in evoking the miracle.[72] It implies the faith that is essential in initiating the miraculous, and it is a pictorial convention in miracle scenes. In this miniature it has the wonderful quality of describing a rising line, as if the limp lower part of the body, having slipped from the broken rope, is now being raised upward through the arm and its conjunction or crossing with Martin's arm. Martin duplicates this "crossing" configuration with the sign of the cross.[73] Thus Martin's gesture is triply motivated—by the request of the dead slave, by the power of God, and by his own status as bishop. All of this is contained within the circle: the hand of the slave, the hand of God, and the crozier that Martin holds in his left hand.[74] This perfect circle might be seen to represent the ideal toward which the representation of miracles in bishops' Lives aspires: the joining of service, sanctity, and office.

uiri dextera in pedes constitit. atq;

ita cum eo usq; aduestibulum domus.

turba omnia inspectante processit.

SVBEODEM FERE

VII·

tempore: MARTINVS adepisco
patum turonicae aecclę petebat;

Figure 66. Martin revives a dead slave, *Life of Martin of Tours,* Tours, c. 1100.
Tours, Bibliothèque municipale, MS 1018, fol. 18r.

THE ACTIVE LIFE: THE BURDEN
OF OFFICE AND ARTISTIC PROBLEMS

As an active "limb" of the Church, the bishop, of course, remains part of the world. Among the Lives of saints, that of the bishop is most clearly marked by its public nature. Monks, hermits, and virgins might retreat to the contemplative life, but the bishop must continue to serve his community. The active life becomes both the burden and the privilege of bishops,[75] and although these responsibilities are stressed in the texts of bishops' Lives, artists seem to have found them difficult to represent.

One common literary *topos* is the bishop's reluctance to assume office. Many saintly men did not wish to assume the office to which they were called, and to represent this reluctance Lives attempt to conjoin episcopal glory and episcopal humility. Of Egbert of Trier,

> the humble heart of a devoted monk hid under the costume of a bishop, as if he frequently paraded with Martha in public in order to carry out the ministry of God, but nevertheless turned himself with Mary completely over to the study of the divine word[76]

and, of Martin of Tours,

> [after entering the episcopate, he] remained the same as before. There was the same humble heart and the same poverty-stricken clothing; [yet], amply endowed with authority and tact, he fully sustained the dignity of the episcopate without forsaking the life or the virtues of the monk.[77]

Indeed, Martin founded a hermitage-like retreat—a sort of episcopal finishing school for humility—and was joined there by other ascetics, many of whom later became bishops.[78]

Pictorial hagiography has no trouble representing one side of this equation: the dignity and authority of the bishop. It revels in scenes of the celebration of the liturgy, representations of miracles in the midst of crowds, and depictions of glorious vestments and ornament, all of which clearly represent the public nature of the office of the bishop and its association with the Church. The other side, humility, seems to have been more difficult to depict. Nevertheless, at least one artist was able successfully to combine the representation of humility and authority. In the miniature of Bernlef healed by Liudger, the artist conveys the bishop's humble demeanor by adding details not specified in the text (see fig. 61). Liudger, dressed in a brown cowled rough cloak, dismounts while his entourage remains on their horses; he stands on the ground before the kneeling petitioner holding the reins of his horse, an animal that commonly served as a medieval symbol of pride. The gold background of the miniature and the appearance of the hand of God proves that a miracle is taking place, contrasting the impression of the bishop as a simple man with the glory of his miraculous sanctity. This expressive image, however, is altogether exceptional, and illustrations of episcopal humility are rare. Indeed, medieval artists more often equate the splendor of the office with the splendor of gold- and silver-laden miniatures.

Depicting a bishop's humility or his reluctance to assume his office seems to have been a challenge that medieval artists were unwilling to meet, but they also seem have been reluctant to depict the bishop performing certain of the obligatory services of episcopal office. In particular, the bishop had to serve as a just judge in the secular world. Although this role may have begun as a continuation of the role of the late Antique landowner and was to some degree Christo-mimetic, eventually it evolved into the duty of serving as arbiter in ecclesiastical courts.[79] The judgment of saintly bishops, of course, was not limited to courts but prevailed even after death. Gregory of Tours tells of a grave-robber who was captured and held in an embrace by the corpse of a holy bishop. The bishop held the man until he could be judged by a secular authority—in fact, until that judge guaranteed clemency. Gregory also notes that at the tomb of St. Nicetius of Lyons "the chains of poor people are broken."[80] Similarly, in a miniature in his Life, Omer causes the heavy chains of a prisoner to fall off at his tomb (fig. 67).[81] The miraculous reversal of secular judgment in which a hanged man is released from the bonds of death by a living bishop is a common *topos* in texts of bishops' Lives and is represented pictorially in the Lives of Liudger and Amand (fig. 68).[82] However, these and other examples of leniency and forgiveness may be contrasted with an image in the Life of Edmund, in which a group of thieves, caught in the act, are literally frozen to the walls of a church by the saint's miraculous intervention. They are not pardoned: to the contrary, the thieves are condemned in an episcopal court and put to death in a particularly gruesome hanging.[83] The somewhat ambivalent message of episcopal miracles of judgment on the whole seems to emphasize compassion and charity rather than punishment (at least, unless the saint's property is directly threatened) and may represent an alternative power established on behalf of the bishop's people and the poor in opposition to secular authority. Nevertheless, even though it was an important part of his office, the bishop is never depicted actively engaged in the role of judge. Thus,

Figure 67. Omer frees a prisoner, *Life of Omer (Audomarus),* for the canons of St. Omer, third quarter of the eleventh century. Bibliothèque de l'Agglomération de Saint-Omer, MS 698, fol. 34v.

Figure 68. A man is hanged and brought back to life by Liudger, *Life of Liudger of Münster,* Werden, c. 1100. Berlin, Staatsbibliothek, Cod. lat. theol. fol. 323, fol. 15r. (Staatsbibliothek zu Berlin, Preußischer Kulturbesitz)

three prominent aspects of textual Lives—reluctance to assume office, humility, and service as a just judge—are almost entirely absent from direct representation in pictorial hagiography, although they sometimes are depicted obliquely.

THE BISHOP'S LEGACY AND THE SANCTIFICATION OF HIS LAND

An aspect of temporal power that does find an important place in the representation of saintly bishops, in part because of their obligation to "build" the Church, is the bishop's legacy of land acquired for the Church. Kilian's Life ends with his martyrdom; the saint is beheaded while praying with his presbyter and deacon. In the Hannover miniature (fig. 69), the three companion saints bend in an attitude of *proskynesis* and are dispatched simultaneously by the executioner's sword. In the miniature that follows the illustration of the execution, a blooming tree—a symbol of life, sanctity, and fruitfulness—marks the site of the martyrs' entombment.[84] On the eleventh-century ivory cover of the *Kiliansevangeliar*, the Eucharistic meaning of the sacrifice of the martyrdom is even clearer: the blood that falls on the ground at the moment of execution nourishes a luxuriant grapevine (fig. 70). Notwithstanding the Eucharistic overtones of this image, the most important purpose that Kilian's martyrdom serves is to sanctify the land and designate his territory. With the shedding of blood onto and into the ground, Würzburg is consecrated to Christianity and a *locus sanctus* is created. Kilian's domain in the geography of the saintly patronage of the Church is thus marked and confirmed.

Although most bishop saints are not martyred, their Lives devise narrative means to mark out this episcopal sacred geography. This may occur through miracles at the tomb and in the surrounding area or, more often, through alliance with martyrs who have already sanctified the land with their blood. Peter Brown masterfully discusses the "impresarios" of local martyrs such as Paulinus of Nola and Ambrose. In the latter case, the bishop of Milan brings the martyrs Gervasius and Protasius within the purview of his bishopric, both bodily and spiritually, by moving their relics into his church and even into his own tomb.[85] By means of association (even, figuratively, adoption), translation grants the already saintly bishop the aura of the martyr.

Gregory of Tours implicitly acknowledges the importance of such sanctified territory in his *Glory of the Confessors*. The *Gloria martyrum* orders its subject hierarchically—Christ, Apostles, greater and then lesser martyrs; the *Gloria confessorum*, by contrast, is organized geographically. (Only Martin, Gregory's personal patron, is distinguished among the other confessors by his placement at the beginning of the book and by his appearance in many of the stories.) As a consequence of this geographically specified power, and as if to demonstrate that the bishop will never "leave," the illustration of bishops' deaths often prominently feature "local" architecture and the fervent prayers of the community (see fig. 3).

Localized power, however, has both positive and negative aspects. Saints Kilian, Omer, Amand, and Liudger, for example, were not widely venerated during the Middle Ages and even into the present day are not well known outside their immediate

Figure 69. The martyrdom of Kilian, Totnan, and Colonat, *Passions of Kilian of Würzburg and Margaret of Antioch,* Fulda, c. 970. Hannover, Niedersächsische Landesbibliothek, MS I 189, fol. 7r. (Courtesy Graz, Akademische Druck- und Verlagsantsalt)

spheres of influence. Cuthbert may have been more widely known because his territory was literally expanded by the movement of his relics; Ambrose's fame is due not to his miracles but to his theology. For the most part, however, except for a saint such as Martin, who is a national patron, bishops are most often quintessentially local saints. Nevertheless, within each saint's special domain, he exercises almost unlimited power as the intercessor for his people. Control—both secular and spiritual—over his episcopal territory may be the most important legacy of the holy bishop.

THE LIVES OF CONFESSORS

Figure 70. The martyrdom of Kilian, Totnan, and Colonat, Ivory book cover of *Kiliansevangeliar,* Würzburg, eleventh century. Würzburg, Universitätsbibliothek, Th. q. 1a.

CONCLUSION

Although bishops' Lives do not benefit from the sanctity guaranteed by the sacrifice of martyrdom, hagiographers found reliable means to assert their holiness. The imitation of Christ through the repetition of his healing miracles plays a part in establishing episcopal sanctity. The association of bishops with St. Peter and the imitation of apostolic models further demonstrates the worthiness of bishops to be the successors to Christ's companions. Finally, bishops visibly pursue the apostolic mission: they serve their congregations as the active arm of God, reaching out to heal, preach, and baptize.[86] Of all hagiographic images, *topoi* from bishops' Lives are the most recognizable.

At the same time that the bishop's Life is marked with power, it also is restricted. Although these limitations are not often chosen for overt illustration, they are often conveyed by more subtle pictorial means. Unlike the Apostles and martyrs, the bishop is a local saint with a limited geographic sphere of influence and renown. He takes his place in the ceremony and hierarchy of the Church and is justly and appropriately glorified by its majesty, wealth, and beauty, but at the same time must pursue humility and contemplation. He must assume the responsibility of judging, usually with compassion, but sometimes harshly. He makes the sign of the cross, marking the Christian, celebrating the liturgy, and effecting healing miracles, but the power of the sign is not inherent in him; rather, it is transmitted through his office and through the *dextera dei,* the right hand of God.

Early medieval bishops were glorious and powerful saints—certainly that is how they are portrayed in Lives composed centuries later—but they were not saints whom the faithful could easily emulate. As a consequence of the inimitability of their subjects, episcopal Lives provide little space into which their audiences might insert their sympathies. While martyrs' Lives offered abundant opportunities for identification, the virtues of bishops' Lives lie above and beyond the aspirations of the average viewer. In the end, the viewer might approach at a tangent,[87] or be humbled by the image of power (see fig. 58),[88] or, as the narratives direct, accede to a space in a "lower register" with populace. Nonetheless, by accepting the ideological representation of the power of the hierarchy of the Church and its access to the divine—by joining with those who acclaim and affirm the power of the bishop as officer of the Church (see fig. 57)—the faithful are guaranteed the intercession of these powerful patrons and perhaps may share, even if momentarily, the glory of priest and king (see plate 4).

Was anyone able to imitate these Lives? Even bishops, placed in ever more public and political positions of power, must have found such iconic episcopal Lives hard to imitate. Perhaps it is not surprising that during the late Middle Ages, with the intense scrutiny of papal canonization and its legal system, few bishops achieved sanctity.[89] Other sorts of confessors, especially those who could be viable models for the lay faithful came to the fore.

THE LIVES OF CONFESSORS
Monks and Abbots

⳰

No exterior addition other than contempt of the world or complete love
of God makes a true monk.
—Ivo of Chartres to Abbot Geoffrey of Vendome (1094)

UNLIKE BISHOPS, saintly monks cannot be readily described as perfected examples of a type: in many ways, they might be said to act emphatically against type. Nonetheless, even in the absence of strong narrative patterns, it is worthwhile to explore what might be essentially monastic about the pictorial Lives of monks and nuns. The issue takes on an added interest because the manuscripts of these Lives, like most others considered in this study, were made by monastic artists, and monks or nuns constituted a large part of their audience. In the end, as we will see, the special problems of monastic Lives suggest the challenges and changes to which the formulas of the hagiographic genre were subject.

One element that Lives of monastic saints might be thought to have in common is their purpose. Michael Goodich proposes that thirteenth-century monks' Lives were intended "to personify the particular rule of each order," and identifies the hagiographer's function as "largely didactic, aimed at presenting a perfect paradigm of observance in order to stir his fellow monks to similar austerities."[1] This purpose is articulated explicitly in the early Middle Ages: the monk Felix, for example, in his eighth-century Life of Guthlac, proposes that the text "serv[e] as a guide to this . . . way of life."[2] Two questions arise: Are monastic Lives really as uniform in their intentions as this agreement might imply? Can this didactic intention be discerned in monastic pictorial hagiography before the thirteenth century?

It is readily apparent that illustrated Lives of monks and nuns, even that of Guthlac, present a more complex character, in function and in realization, than the one assumed by Felix and Goodich. In theory, as confessors, monks might prove their sanctity by close adherence to monastic strictures and the contemplative life. But in fact, early medieval sanctity, for monks and for others, was proved in more public and miraculous ways. Thus, most celebrated monastic saints gain their recognition through an active public or authoritative role as bishop, abbot or abbess, or reformer. Furthermore, those saints whose Lives are illustrated are generally patron saints of great prestige and power, not humble monastic exemplars. Finally, and perhaps most important, these Lives were not composed or illustrated for consumption (and imitation) by a limited audience of fellow monks. For example, the Life of Guthlac—perhaps the quintessential monastic *vita*—was composed in the eighth century at the request of an Anglo-Saxon king, and it seems to have been illustrated (in the thirteenth century) as a sort of evidential testament concerning various gifts to the saint's monastery. In both instances, versions of the Life were created with an eye to specific audiences outside of the monastery.[3] The function of Lives is ultimately quite complex, a complexity often mirrored in their narratives. Our goal must be revised: not to find a typical monk's Life, but rather to discover the lines of the monastic mortar in the built structure of holy Lives.

Barbara Abou-el-Haj attempts to define core scenes in certain Lives of saints (including several monastic *vitae*) in events such as education, initiation, preaching or teaching and conversion of others, miracles, death and burial.[4] Certainly these events are key moments in most Lives of saintly monks and nuns, but (excepting miracles) they also occurred in the unrecorded lives of many religious who were not saints. This is precisely our problem and would have been an even more important problem for the medieval viewer. Beyond miracle, what separates the life of the saint from that of the average monk? How is the difference conveyed in artistic representation (if it is indeed conveyed)? Furthermore, what is *particularly* monastic? The variety of the Lives of monks and nuns offer special insight into these issues.

A useful approach to considering monastic Lives is to ask how each so-called core scene finds its place in the narrative. An investigation of the initiation, one of the most common of such scenes,[5] in three manuscripts demonstrates that variation is as important as commonality in monastic Lives. The Guthlac Roll (c. 1210) is unusual in that it consists of a series of pieces of parchment glued together to make a roll. Although most of the episodes are selected from Felix's early medieval text, the text itself is not copied out on the roll.[6] The pictures appear as a set of roundels reading from left to right along the length of the roll. The darker color of their ink suggests that many of the identifying *tituli* were added after the drawings were composed. It has been suggested that this unique object was used for display on the feast of the saint and also that it served as evidence in a monastic dispute concerning property rights.[7]

The scene of Guthlac's tonsure in the roll's third roundel (fig. 71) represents his monastic initiation at the double monastery of Repton. He kneels between an abbess and bishop, both of whom hold croziers and share a long bench. The bishop follows a liturgical ceremony, as implied by the open book held by an attendant, and cuts the saint's hair using a large set of shears that he holds in his left hand. The ceremony is markedly anachronistic, both exceeding the requirements of the text and exaggerating Guthlac's prestige. In Felix's text, the abbess, not the bishop, performs the simple rite, and we are told that Guthlac's stay at Repton was short, soon superseded by his eremitic experience as a recluse at Crowland Abbey. The miniature thus seems to be a formulaic version of initiation created by the roll's early thirteenth-century artist, perhaps to reflect life at Crowland. Its real significance, however, lies elsewhere. As we will see, it represents an important preliminary in the narrative of Guthlac's "ladder of perfection," serving as a precondition to his eremitical life.

A twelfth-century manuscript from Werden offers a very different model of the entry into monastic life by Werden's patron Liudger (fig. 72).[8] The saint seems to have entered as an oblate, given as a gift to the monastery by his parents. The practice of oblation was discouraged during much of the Middle Ages, and the *vita,* perhaps for that reason, emphasizes Liudger's religious precocity and eagerness to enter the monastic life.[9] The miniature depicts the saint's voluntary removal from the secular world, signified by his eager step into a new realm, and resembles a scene on the same subject from the Life of Adalbert on the bronze doors of Gniezno.[10] By the very act of representing the episode the artist emphasizes that Liudger has expressly chosen Werden as his spiritual home. The illustration is thus a fitting addition to a manuscript that is a testament to the saint's Life and patronage of the monastery. The manuscript is a luxurious edition of Liudger's Life, supplemented with other texts from the saint's dossier and enclosed within a precious late Antique ivory diptych cover from which it takes its peculiar elongated shape. Presumably because it was believed that the saint would keep the records safe, some of the blank manuscript pages were used to record the monastery's privileges.

A third example, the eleventh-century miniature that depicts Queen Radegund's consecration as a deaconess, takes an altogether different approach to presenting initiation (see fig. 118). Radegund's manuscript *vita* (discussed in greater detail on pp. 259–76) records that the queen's removal from the public sphere drew political

Figure 71. Guthlac tonsured, *Guthlac Roll,* Crowland, c. 1210. London, British Library, Harley Roll, Y. 6. (Reproduced by permission of the British Library)

objections, as well as threats of recrimination from her husband the king. The office of deaconess, moreover, was not part of the monastic orders. The miniature contrasts the confrontation of two groups or political communities (depicted in the upper register) with Radegund's simple and private act of submission in kneeling before the bishop (depicted below). Certainly, the artist fits the scene into the generalized functional slot of the initiation, but he also manages to convey the political difficulties of the consecrating bishop and the great sacrifice of the queen in renouncing her worldly glory.

The three examples share some important characteristics. All three emphasize

Figure 72. Liudger is given as oblate, *Life of Liudger of Münster,* Werden, c. 1100. Berlin, Staatsbibliothek, Cod. lat. theol. fol. 323, fol. 5r. (Staatsbibliothek zu Berlin, Preußischer Kulturbesitz)

the momentous separation of the initiate from his or her former life in order to begin a new one. In the Life of Liudger (as well as that of Adalbert), the two arches of the architectural background designate two different worlds—the sacred and the secular—and the saint is shown to move from one into the other. Humility is another element of taking holy orders, represented in two of the examples by the saint's kneeling posture and by the depiction of the physical signals of commitment assumed by the initiate—Guthlac's tonsure and Radegund's exchange of her crown for a veil.

However, ultimately the scenes seem more different than alike, and each represents an initiation that varies from the monastic ideal: oblation (Liudger), consecration as a deaconess (Radegund), and entry into a monastery only to leave it soon after (Guthlac). In each case, the primary narrative interest for the viewer arises from the way in which initiation is adjusted to complex narrative situations rather than any conformity to a standard.

THE LIVES OF CONFESSORS

Figure 73. Benedict is given a monk's habit and is fed by a monk, *Monte Cassino Lectionary,* Monte Cassino, c. 1070. Vatican Library, Lat. 1202, fol. 17v. (© Biblioteca Apostolica Vaticana)

Just as core scenes may have more narrative differences than similarities, sometimes the "core" is missing altogether. In chapter 6 of Bede's Life of Cuthbert, the saint is tonsured and admitted to a monastery, but no appropriate image of initiation appears among the fifty-five miniatures of the c. 1100 Oxford illustrated Life. Furthermore, one of the most important monastic texts, the Life of Benedict in Gregory's *Dialogues,* does not recount the moment of initiation.

The notion of core scenes thus entails several problematic issues. It implies that certain scenes must be present, that these scenes are relatively invariable, and that other narrative elements are superfluous. A more useful concept may be that of *topoi:* narrative elements that make use of recognizable visual formulas but that adjust those formulas to their surroundings. Indeed, as we have seen already in the Lives of martyrs, virgins, and bishops, it is in these adjustments that narrative finds its most expressive value. In their very wide range of variations, monastic Lives represent some of the clearest instances of medieval artists manipulating the possibilities of visual *topoi.*

In a striking example, the artist of the Life of Benedict (c. 1071), made at Monte Cassino, has clearly noticed and sought to remedy the absence of an initiation episode in Gregory's hagiographic text.[11] He creates an image that substitutes for the initiation by enlarging the significance of a fortuitous meeting (recounted in the text) in which a monk presents Benedict with a "monastic habit" (fig. 73).[12] The habit here serves metonymically for the ceremony: for contemporary viewers, it was "the clothing signifying mortification of the flesh, humility of heart, and remorse and contempt for the world."[13] The artist represents Benedict kneeling, receiving both the habit and a blessing from the haloed monk in a simulacrum of the ceremony of initiation, clearly recognizable in its key elements. Thus, again, a particular moment of separation is marked and a means of physical identification has been bestowed.

THE MONASTIC QUALITY OF MONASTIC LIVES

Despite the broad range of variables in its representation, initiation is perhaps the clearest example of shared imagery in monastic Lives. With the exception of the death of the monk mourned by his brothers, it is the most common scene in monastic Lives. What, then, are shared "monastic" elements of monastic Lives? The answer goes even beyond *topoi,* extending to characteristic narrative sequences and the representation of monastic virtues drawn from appropriate models. Of course, as with all saints, the primary model is the Life of Christ.[14] But since Christ was not a monk, monastic *vitae* required other narrative paradigms through which Christo-mimetic norms could be transformed to better represent such a life. The prototypes that come to mind are the Lives of the foremost monastic saints, Anthony, Benedict, and Martin, and another less obviously narrative but no less important model: the Rule of Benedict.

Perhaps because its subjects share and *learn* a communal life, certain elements of monks' Lives are intentionally and emphatically like those of other monks. In Felix's Life of Guthlac, the saint is shaped at various points in the text by a number of models. He learns from the diverse virtues of his fellow monks, picking the best of each to emulate. He reads, probably the Life of St. Anthony, and learns asceticism. But he also aspires to the virtues of St. Peter, is compared to St. Paul, and has a special relationship to St. Bartholomew.[15] Guthlac's textual Life thus indicates that the saintliness of a monk is not restricted to a likeness to saints of the same genre, although it is primarily based upon it. Nevertheless, none of the modeling activity of the text is directly reflected in the illustrations of the Guthlac Roll.[16] Only Bartholomew is pictured (in roundels 6 and 8) as he intercedes to save Guthlac from demons.

Few of the monks' Lives that might serve as exemplars or paradigms are illustrated between the tenth and the thirteenth century. Of those mentioned above, only the Life of Benedict is fully illustrated (in the Vatican manuscript that also includes an illustrated Life of Maurus).[17] A few scenes of Martin's *vita* survive in Touronian manuscripts.[18] Despite the paucity of material, however, this body of pictorial evidence is important to defining the genre of monastic Lives. We will consider the manuscripts of the Lives of Guthlac, Liudger, and Radegund, as well as examples of saints who began as monks or nuns: the Life of Cuthbert, Bede's text illustrated at Durham c. 1100–1120 (University College Library, Oxford, MS 165), with an unframed miniature prefacing each chapter;[19] the Life of Omer in the eleventh-century *libellus* made for the Canons of St. Omer;[20] and the Life of Maurus in a second *libellus* of the late eleventh century from Saint-Maur-des-Fossés (Troyes, Bibliothèque municipale MS 2273).[21] Both of the latter have miniatures within the text of the Life.

As a model for monastic Lives, Benedict's Rule may have been more influential than Lives of exemplary monks, and its importance inheres more in its use as a comparative text than in its specific recommendations. The first suggestion the Rule makes is that the monk emulate Christ in self-imposed suffering.[22] Indeed, in its detailed guidelines for an "angelic" life of self-denial, the Rule seems to hold out the promise that any monk who follows it perfectly will attain sanctity.

Not so. Again, the issue of a difference between conventional monastic life and the extraordinary Life of a saint looms large. The Rule exists to regulate the lives of all monks, even making provisions for those who must be chastised or excommunicated from the community. Hence, simply living the life of the Rule does not in itself transform a monk into a saint; however, the saint, in living the monastic life to perfection, demonstrates the fullest, even miraculous potential of the Rule. Three themes emphasized in the Rule deserve particular attention in this context, for they find expression in illustrated Lives in ways that seem to explicate their importance for monastic life and hence for the lives of monastic readers: obedience, the treatment of food, and the acceptance or rejection of community.

Obedience

Obedience, the foremost virtue of the monk or nun, is expressed emblematically in a famous episode depicted in the Vatican Life of Benedict (fig. 74). From his cell, Benedict miraculously sees Placidus drowning in a lake and orders the novice Maurus to save him. Maurus rushes to aid the boy, and only after returning does he

Figure 74. Maurus saves Placidus (*lower scenes*), *Monte Cassino Lectionary,* Monte Cassino, c. 1070. Vatican Library, Lat. 1202, fol. 31r. (© Biblioteca Apostolica Vaticana)

Figure 75. An eagle brings a fish to Cuthbert, *Life of Cuthbert*, Durham Cathedral Priory, c. 1100–1120. Oxford, University College Library, MS 165, p. 41. (Reproduced by permission of the Master and Fellows of University College, Oxford)

realize that he has run across the surface of the water. Placidus recounts that while he was being pulled from the water he saw a vision of a cloak above him that he recognized as Benedict's, and the miracle is therefore attributed not to Maurus but to Benedict.[23] Nevertheless, the instrumental cause of the miracle was clearly Maurus's great faith and obedience.

The episode was of great interest to the Benedictine order and was represented as early as the tenth century at San Crisogono in Rome in conjunction with a monastic revival in that city.[24] The miniature in the Vatican codex has been discussed by numerous scholars,[25] and particularly elegantly by Otto Pächt.[26] Pächt notes that the figure of the saint is not repeated in the two narrative parts of the miniature. He finds other examples of this in the Life of Cuthbert (fig. 75), and traces a direct influence from the Life of Benedict to that of Cuthbert with respect to the representation of time.[27] The composition of the Cuthbert miniature, however, has less to do with the passage of time than with the power of the saint to impel or induce miracles while remaining himself a still center of action: artistic composition is here subordinate to the import of the image (see pp. 46–47). A reading of the Rule of Benedict, moreover, grounds this interpretation in monastic practice. In discussing obedience, Benedict places particular importance on the immediacy of action:

> [monks] *immediately* put aside their own concerns, abandon their own will, and lay down whatever they have in hand, leaving it unfinished. With the *ready step* of obedience, they follow the voice of authority in their actions. *Almost at the same moment*, then, as the master gives the instruction the disciple *quickly* puts it into practice in the fear of God; and *both actions together are swiftly completed as one*. (Rule, 5:7–9, emphasis supplied)[28]

Instead of conflating a model with two scenes and implying the passage of time, what this compositional device conveys is the immediacy of true obedience impelled by saintly authority. The episode and its illustration thus realize the holy nature and miraculous possibility of obedience.

One of the striking aspects of the Vatican image is the action represented: the novice *runs* to do the saint's bidding. The miniature emphasizes running both in the pose of Maurus and in the *titulus* supplied in the Vatican manuscript: "Curre jubet. currit.—Puerum rapit. atque recurrit" (Run! he commands. He runs. He snatches up the boy. And runs back).[29] The Rule consistently associates images of running and fighting with the duty of obedience and the soul's improvement. The reference seems to be to 2 Tim. 4:7, which speaks of readiness for death: "I have fought the good fight, I have finished my course, I have kept the faith." The image of running appears four times in the Rule: "we must run and do now what will profit us forever" (prol. 44); "We run [to the kingdom] by doing good deeds" (prol. 22); "If we wish to dwell in the tent of this kingdom, we will never arrive unless we run there by doing good deeds" (14:22); and "Are you hastening toward your heavenly home?" (73:8). Battle is also an important metaphor in defining the character of obedience: "We must then prepare our hearts and bodies for the battle of holy obedience to his instructions" (prol. 40). Finally, the "labor of obedience" is contrasted with the "sloth of disobedience" (prol. 2). There can be no doubt that virtue, especially the virtue of monastic obedience, is embodied in the Rule by action, and expressed as vigorous movement toward a goal. The dying saint in Felix's Life of Guthlac similarly invokes the metaphor: "my spirit has run the course in the race of this life and is impatient to be bourne to those joys whose course has no ending."[30] In the illus-

Figure 76. The death of Guthlac, London, *Guthlac Roll,* Crowland, c. 1210. British Library, Harley Roll, Y. 6. (Reproduced by permission of the British Library)

tration of Guthlac's death, the little nude figure of the saint's soul virtually leaps from Guthlac's body and seems almost ready to escape the grasp of the angel who receives it. A "course" is delineated in rays of light leading to heaven (fig. 76).

The visual image of swift and miraculous obedience that is captured in the emblematic depiction of Maurus's rescue of Placidus did not remain unappreciated. It is repeated almost exactly in the illustrated Life of Maurus in the Vatican manuscript and also appears in the illustrated Life of Maurus in Troyes.[31] Variations of the composition appear in other saints' Lives as well. Pächt discerned a similar two-part composition in the Oxford Life of Cuthbert in a scene in which the saint commands a young boy to fetch their dinner, which has been supplied by an eagle—a miracle that alludes both to faith and to obedience (see fig. 75).[32] These repetitions of the composition reiterate the central importance of the virtue of obedience in monastic Lives.

Further reinforcing the importance of obedience, however, are hagiographic episodes that narrate its opposite. One such episode in the Life of Cuthbert is particularly illuminating. Two monks visiting Cuthbert at his hermitage on the island of Farne disobey the saint's seemingly casual command to cook and eat a goose before their departure, thinking that they have no need to obey because they have an abundant supply of food (fig. 77).[33] In the miniature, they sit slumped with dejected expressions; one wearily rests his cheek on his hand. The goose hangs as a reproach above their heads, and outside the hermitage their boat lies still, its sail deflated next to the rising waters. As a result of their disobedience of the saint's "casual" command, the monks are trapped for seven days by a terrible storm. The storm does not abate until the saint (who stands at the left of the miniature) chastises the monks and they finally plunge the bird into the stew pot. In contrast to miniatures that display a dynamic composition arranged from left to right in representation of obedient action that leads to betterment of the soul, this centralized and immobile scene demonstrates the stasis or stagnation of the soul that does not obey. These monks are punished for mistakenly relying on self-sufficiency instead of obeying the saint's authority.

Examples from other saints' Lives demonstrate the same stasis of disobedience. In the Life of Amand, through the intermediary of the Mass, Amand heals a monk literally paralyzed because of his disobedience.[34] In the eleventh-century Life of Omer, the saint forbids a young man to travel. Disobeying the command, the young fellow is caught in a storm at sea and is able to complete his journey only through the miraculous intervention of the saint (see fig. 4).[35]

Time is intimately involved in each of these explications of obedience. The miracles involve time-related events and the miniatures represent the succession of events through time, but in neither text nor image does time assume its normal narrative progress. Instead, it serves as a tool to mark the immediacy of the benefits of obedience and the stasis associated with sinful disobedience. Progress occurs not because of the passage of time but because progress is situated within the soul. It follows a narrative of the betterment of the monk's soul, the authentic narrative of these Lives.

Figure 77. Disobedient monks are delayed by a storm, *Life of Cuthbert,* Durham Cathedral Priory, c. 1100–1120. Oxford, University College Library, MS 165, p. 98. (Reproduced by permission of the Master and Fellows of University College, Oxford)

One other aspect of these pictures merits attention. Although obedience as a monastic virtue is clearly revealed in these miniatures, the saint is not the agent of the action. In no case, except perhaps that of the young Maurus (who only later is recognized as a saint), is the saint shown in a simple act of obedience. Rather, the saint assumes another role: he provides the voice of Christlike authority, one normally reserved by the Rule for an abbot.[36] If these miniatures model behavior for monks, the model is found in the responses of the saint's companions, not in the actions of the saint himself.[37]

Food

In addition to issues of obedience, the Cuthbert miracles introduce a second central issue of monastic concern: the proper approach to food. Miracles that involve food or drink appear in the Lives of monks with remarkable frequency. Although the Life of Cuthbert, with at least ten of fifty-five episodes relating to monastic sustenance, is exceptional in this respect,[38] other Lives also regularly treat food and drink. The concern with food is not surprising. Monastic life seeks to separate its

Figure 78. Benedict reprimands the disobedient brothers, *Monte Cassino Lectionary,* Monte Cassino, c. 1070. Vatican Library, Lat. 1202, fol. 43 v. (© Biblioteca Apostolica Vaticana)

practitioners from the sins of worldly life, and the sin of gluttony is a constant specter for the religious. The careful circumscription of diet in the Rule (see 4:36) reflects a real concern for the spiritual welfare of the monk, if not for his full belly.

Two episodes, one from the Life of Benedict and one from the Life of Maurus, seem to reinforce the actual strictures of the Rule regarding food, although this is not the primary intent of the artist in illustrating them. In the first illustration (fig. 78), again representing Benedict's prescience, the saintly abbot discovers that two brothers have dined while away from the abbey, a fact that they at first deny. (The miniature in the Vatican Lectionary emphasizes the sumptuousness of the forbidden meal.) Benedict promptly forgives the monks their trespass of the Rule (Rule, 51).[39]

The second miniature focuses on Maurus's departure from the abbey of Monte Cassino as he embarks on his mission to spread monasticism in France (fig. 79).[40] The primary action of the illustration represents the moment when Benedict gives the Rule to Maurus. Maurus, however, has already received the weight and measure and passed them to his companions on the journey. It is the latter two humble objects, so carefully depicted in the miniature, that are crucial to the maintenance of the food restrictions of the Rule by a monastic community. They are used to measure out the bread and wine that is each monk's daily allotment.[41]

Although these two scenes emphasize and clarify the Rule's practice concerning

Figure 79. Maurus departs with the Rule, *Monte Cassino Lectionary,* Monte Cassino, c. 1070. Vatican Library, Lat. 1202, fol. 127v. (© Biblioteca Apostolica Vaticana)

the consumption of food, they are among the very few to do so, especially as compared with the large number of scenes that deal with food in a more general or miraculous sense. In these latter scenes, the Rule and the artists go beyond the practical and, it would seem, begin to sacramentalize food.

Several aspects of the Rule suggest that eating is more than mere nutrition. The Rule requires that each monk in turn work in the kitchen as server, and this service begins with a benediction and prayer and ends with prayer (35:16–18). The cellarer is instructed to "look after the utensils of the monastery as carefully as if they were the sacred vessels of the altar" (31:10). A monk is not allowed to eat outside the abbey unless instructed to do so by the abbot (51:1), presumably out of concern that he will overindulge but also because the act of communal eating is considered spiritually satisfying. Eating in the company of one's fellows is so important that the first level of punishment or excommunication is the exclusion from the common table (24:3). If this is not effective, the monk "shall be deprived of participation both in the common meal and in the divine services" (25:1). The offender will not only eat alone but "the food which is given him shall be unblessed" (25:6). Short of corporal punishment or banishment for the incorrigible, these are the strictest measures that an abbot is directed to take. As the commentators on a recent edition of the Rule have noted, this attitude toward food is consonant with a notion of "sacramental sharing" characteristic of the early Church.[42] It is clear, therefore, that food takes on a sacramental quality within the monastic environment; this quality is explicitly confirmed in analogies between the food of physical nourishment and that of spiritual nourishment in miracles illustrated in the Lives of monastic saints.

The details in the composition of two illustrations from the Life of Liudger, bishop and founder of the monastery of Werden, links the food of the monastery with the Last Supper and the Supper at Emmaus (see fig. 65). The second illustration (fig. 80) may also allude to the imagery of the miraculous transport of Habukkak and his meal to Daniel in the den of lions,[43] although here it is the man who is brought to the meal and blessed by Liudger. Ultimately, these scenes have more to do with Liudger's control of the salvational substance of the Mass as a bishop than as a monk, but their treatment of food remains important for the monastic audience of the illustrated manuscript. Moreover, the scenes underline the analogy between spiritual and physical food.

For those who lived under the Rule, food also provided an opportunity for the refinement of virtue. Serving food offered a chance to demonstrate humility, and the motif thus finds its way into the illustrated Lives of the saints. Radegund, despite her former status as queen, gladly serves the poor, just as she joyfully washes their feet—two activities mandated in the Rule because "peculiar honor shall be shown to the poor and to strangers"(Rule 53:2 and ff; see p. 265). Cuthbert likewise serves a stranger and finds that he has waited on an angel. This miracle, at the same time that it demonstrates Cuthbert's humility and worthiness, also recalls Abraham's visitation by angels at the Oak of Mamre, a familiar typological reference to the Mass.

Finally, one last group of miracles related to food centers on the monk's faith that his sustenance will be supplied by God. This idea lies at the core of monastic

Figure 80. A hanged man comes to Liudger, *Life of Liudger of Münster*, Werden, c. 1100. Berlin, Staatsbibliothek, Cod. lat. theol. fol. 323, fol. 15v. (Staatsbibliothek zu Berlin, Preußischer Kulturbesitz)

and Benedictine spirituality; not surprisingly, such miracles are most numerous in the Life of Benedict himself. In the *Dialogues,* Benedict's earliest commitment to a life of denial is demonstrated by his withdrawal to a cave, where he is fed through the charity of a monk from a nearby monastery (see fig. 73). The text recounts that on Easter Day, God appeared in a vision to a wealthy priest and commanded him to share his feast with Benedict (fig. 81).[44] This scene, as pictured in the Vatican Lectionary, recalls any number of similar stories of holy men sharing food that they have miraculously received, including one on the Ruthwell Cross that depicts Anthony and Paul the Hermit fed by a raven, which in turn recalls the Old Testament ascetic archetype of Elijah in the wilderness fed by ravens.[45] Finally, the miracle of the eagle delivering a fish to Cuthbert is a similar example that found pictorial expression in the group of Lives that we discuss here (see fig. 75). The miniature in the Life of Cuthbert of the monks who tried to hoard the goose and

Figure 81. A priest shares a meal with Benedict; Benedict rolls in nettles and thorns to deaden his desires, *Monte Cassino Lectionary,* Monte Cassino, c. 1070. Vatican Library, Lat. 1202, fol. 18r. (© Biblioteca Apostolica Vaticana)

Figure 82. Benedict throws an oil flask down the mountain and prays before the overflowing jar of oil, *Monte Cassino Lectionary*, Monte Cassino, c. 1070. Vatican Library, Lat. 1202, fol. 63r.
(© Biblioteca Apostolica Vaticana)

were condemned for their disobedience (see fig. 77), on the other hand, is a remonstrance against lack of faith in God's care.

Gregory recounts a second story about Benedict's faith in God's provision and defines a variation of this sort of miracle. The episode occurs after Benedict has become the abbot of Monte Cassino, and thus represents food in an institutional setting. Here, the miraculous must work on a larger scale, and the *topos* is transferred authoritatively from the desert to the monastery. Through his gift of prescience, Benedict learns that one of his monks has disobeyed his orders by not distributing the last of the monastery's oil to the poor. The saint is so disappointed that he throws the last vial of oil over the wall of the monastery and down the precipice of Monte Cassino, but the flask does not shatter. When the saint prays over an empty oil jar, it fills to overflowing (fig. 82).[46] This miracle is paradigmatic in a number of respects: in its evidence of a steady supply of food for monastic needs, its demonstration of the virtue of monastic charity to the poor, and finally, in its indication of the sacramental significance of the miraculous oil.

On a similarly figural level, the feeding of monks or other religious by a miraculous catch of fish is pictured in a number of saints' Lives. Recalling Felix's comment that "salvation was not preached to the world by orators but by fisherman," the image suggests that faith in sustenance might in turn supply spiritual faith.[47] In the Lives of both Amand and Liudger, each saint receives an enormous fish that leaps to its capture (fig. 83).[48] In the Life of Edward the Confessor, St. Peter himself appears miraculously and supervises the netting of a good-sized salmon, which is given to a bishop (see fig. 143). Each of these cases illustrates faith that "the Lord will provide" all needs, both mundane and spiritual.

Whether as apostle, bishop, or abbot, the saint's function in these scenes of miraculous provision is to reassure the faithful (especially the monastic faithful) of God's care. More generally, whether serving, eating communally, or simply subsisting (Cuthbert lived by gnawing half an onion during the last few weeks of his life),[49] monks clearly live a life in which food plays a central role in defining spirituality.

However, once more, excepting the miracles that demonstrate a specific element of the Rule and the representation of the weight and measure, these miracles illustrate the saint rising miraculously above normal life to enter a supernatural realm where the average monk cannot follow. Although the representation of the elements of typical monastic life make these scenes more meaningful and more readily understood by their monastic audience, ultimately these elements are secondary to the spiritual meaning of the scenes.

Community and the Solitary

The last of the three themes from the Rule that stand out as essential to the monastic life is community. The communal experience was central for monastic spirituality. Monks ate, slept, worked, and prayed together. As emphasized in the paradigmatic monastic Life, that of Anthony, community gave monks "joy" and "eagerness to advance, each drew courage from the faith of the rest."[50] One portrayal of community can be found in an illustration from the Life of Cuthbert in which the saint, in conference with his monks, communicates with them as equals, illustrating Cuthbert's gentle yet persuasive establishment of the Rule in discussions among the chapter (fig. 84).[51] The death of a brother—for example, that of St. Maur in the Troyes manuscript (fig. 85)—also represents a moving portrait of a monastic community.[52] However, these images stand in striking contrast to the more usual depictions of religious hierarchies or solitary saints.[53]

The extraordinary and the saintly are most commonly represented by the solitary; scenes associating the joy of community with sanctity are atypical. Although the Rule is intended to govern the highest type of monastic life—the communal life of cenobites—even Benedict professes great admiration for the solitary monk:

Figure 83. Liudger receives a miraculous gift of fish from heaven, *Life of Liudger of Münster*, Werden, c. 1100. Berlin, Staatsbibliothek, Cod. lat. theol. fol. 323, fol. 14v. (Staatsbibliothek zu Berlin, Preußischer Kulturbesitz)

Figure 84. Cuthbert teaching, *Life of Cuthbert,* Durham Cathedral Priory, c. 1100–1120. Oxford, University College Library, MS 165, p. 50. (Reproduced by permission of the Master and Fellows of University College, Oxford)

the anchorites or hermits, who have learned how to conduct the war against the devil by their long service in the monastery and their association with many brothers, and so, being well trained, have separated themselves from the troop, in order to wage single combat, being able with the aid of God to carry on the fight alone against the sins of the flesh. (Rule, 1:3)

Benedict may have admired the eremitic life, but he did not follow the course that he recommended to his monastic brethren; indeed, he was a hermit only at the start of his career: he abandoned solitude in favor of leading a community of brethren.

Benedict's Life describes the saint's early career, waging "single combat . . . alone against the sins of the flesh." The combat is, of course, against lust, perhaps the most difficult trial of monastic life, especially for the young monk or nun. The Vatican Lectionary shows the extraordinary sight of a naked Benedict plunging into nettles and thorns in order to chasten and tame his flesh (see fig. 81).[54] A demon in the form of a black bird is represented in the preceding episode, but here Benedict is battling his own body. The saint's body is revealed, but only to obliterate it and its sinful desires. In the *Dialogues,* Gregory concludes, "with the passing of this temptation, Benedict's soul, like a field cleared of briars, soon yielded a rich harvest of virtues."[55]

Figure 85. The Last Rites and burial of Maurus, *Life of Maurus of Glanfeuil*, Saint-Maur-des-Fossés, c. 1050–1100. Troyes, Bibliothèque municipale, MS 2273, fol. 73 v. (Photo Pascal Jacquinot)

Of course, although Benedict's actions surely constituted a glowing model for his devotees, they were probably not intended to be followed literally. Benedict's Life offers an emphatically more active model for the pursuit of chastity than is apparent in the Lives of other monks or of virgins. The Lives of virgins primarily describe their subjects as withstanding assault; the women do not enter into battle like soldiers but are animate fortresses—Lucy is likened to a mountain. Felix's Life of Guthlac eschews both Benedict's chastisement of the body *and* the passive resistance of the virgins. Guthlac fights lust as an exterior threat.

Nevertheless, the text and pictures of the Life of Guthlac provide an excellent illustration of metaphors associated with the hermit's spiritual progress that originate in the Rule.[56] Consonant with the Rule's military imagery, Guthlac begins life as a soldier (although he will enter the more arduous fight as an anchorite). After initiation into the cenobitic life at Repton and training as a monk, he retires

Figure 86. Guthlac beats a demon with a flail, *Guthlac Roll,* Crowland, c. 1210. London, British Library, Harley Roll, Y. 6. (Reproduced by permission of the British Library)

to Crowland, where he conducts "war" against the devil in dramatic single combat. Guthlac's battle includes defeating temptations of the body,[57] but his struggle is dramatically externalized. It concludes with a scene in which the saint decisively defeats a host of demons, vigorously applying a flail while holding one demon's neck (fig. 86).

Two important elements are to be noted in this latter image. First, despite the saint's eremitic aspirations, this miniature is the sole representation of Guthlac separated from human company. Certainly the devil and his temptations are always present in one embodiment or another (as here), but in contrast to the text's proclamation of its subject's solitary life, Guthlac's extraordinary feats of virtue are consistently represented in human company as well—that of his disciple Beccelm (as witness) or of Bartholomew the Apostle (as supporter), or both. Beccelm also surely serves as a proxy for the viewer (who might well have been a monk of Guthlac's spiritual community). The surprisingly populous images of the Guthlac Roll describe a kind of community, albeit a narrow one, and in this they are typical of eremitic images.

A second element of note in the miniature is the flail, not mentioned by Felix. The text simply recounts that the saint vanquished the demons "in less time than it takes to tell."[58] The flail, first represented on the roll as a gift of the Apostle Bartholomew (in roundel 8), not only externalizes the saint's spiritual struggle but again establishes an important link to the saint's community. The flail's appearance in the manuscript may be a specific reference to the object's preservation at the monastery of Crowland as a relic of the saint. Another relic, the Psalter illustrated in this and other miniatures, was also preserved and was renowned as the origin of Guthlac's verbal "weapons." Both may have been the object of pilgrimage to the monastery.[59]

In sum, although Guthlac is represented as an exemplary model of the hermit resisting temptation, the sin that he is resisting is metaphorically outside himself: he fights demons rather than chastise his own body. Ironically, a specific community establishes how the battles of the eremitical Guthlac, armed with flail and Psalter, are represented. Indeed, the battles are shared—literally in the relics of spiritual war, visually in the images themselves—by a circumscribed community, supernatural and otherwise.

Other Lives similarly depict feats of virtue performed in "solitude," although the saints are not represented as completely alone. Cuthbert, like Guthlac, adheres to the Benedictine ideal of eremitic seclusion only after his term in a monastic community. The most compelling image of the saint's private prayer, however, occurs during his communal life. Cuthbert spends a night in the frigid North Sea in order to achieve solitude of both body and mind (fig. 87).[60] The saintly deed wins God's approval, expressed by two otters who lick the saint's feet when he emerges from the sea. However, as in Guthlac's Life, the saint's heroic privations are again witnessed; the miniature depicts a monk in the door of a building raptly watching Cuthbert from behind. Given Cuthbert's humility, without this witness the miracle might never have been reported.

Figure 87. Cuthbert prays all night in the North Sea; otters lick his feet, *Life of Cuthbert*, Durham Cathedral Priory, c. 1100–1120. Oxford, University College Library, MS 165, p. 35. (Reproduced by permission of the Master and Fellows of University College, Oxford)

The Life of Radegund avoids such extremes, which would have been inappropriate for a woman, not to mention a former queen. Instead, Radegund attains solitude through prayer and mental discipline, not hearing the noise of layfolk singing and dancing and unaware of the presence of her nuns (see fig. 120 and p. 268).

Even more common than the presence of community in solitude, however, is the use of architectural elements that define the hermit as a permanent member of the monastic fellowship. The depiction of monastic buildings, even when the depiction is emphatically anachronistic and contradicts the text (as it does in Guthlac's Life; see fig. 86),[61] defines the solitary saint as perpetually resident within the community. Images of saints working miracles outside the monastery often show them at a small window set in the high encircling wall of the monastery (see plate 7).[62] This formulation emphasizes both the saint's withdrawal from the world of sin and his or her proper and eternal place of residence.

These images make effective use of the monastic ideal of community in two ways. First, community contrasts with the holy solitude achieved by the saints. Each of these men and women, as saints, can go beyond community, often through prayer, sometimes as a warrior of God. However, as Benedict emphasized (but as he himself did not practice), most do so only by having first undergone the discipline of monastic life. The theme of separation of "the world out there" from the holy life of the monastery does not vary: the saints have simply progressed farther along the path of separation than the typical monk can (or should). Second, the monastic community insistently lays claim to these saints—as patrons but also as sainted members. Whether through the presence of witnesses or by being represented within a context of monastic architecture, even in the most solitary of experiences the saint is emphatically located within his or her community.

THE MONASTIC LIFE AS A TYPE?

For early medieval saints, Michael Goodich's notion that monastic Lives are meant to support monastic ideals does not hold true in a simple, straightforward way. Obedience, the control of food, and communal living were of great importance to all monks in cenobitic life; illustrations contained in saints' Lives use complex structures of narrative, reversals, and negations to represent the saint's relationship to these themes. Certainly monastic pictorial narratives support monastic ideals, but they do so primarily in indirect or superlative terms not intended for direct imitation. There is no scene-by-scene explication of the Rule, nor any literal correlation of monastic virtue to saintly exemplum.

Two moments shared by all monastics, however, do receive clear pictorial expression in the Lives of monks. Initiation and death almost always frame the monastic Life on earth and, as images, emphasize the saint's commitment to monasticism. As above, initiations are expressed in a variety of images but uniformly mark the departure from the secular world and the entrance into monastic discipline. Death scenes, in contrast, are remarkably alike in their depiction of the liturgical mourning of the community over its loss (see fig. 85). They also share the implication that community will continue to be important after death, represented by the care for the body and ongoing prayers on behalf of the dead.[63] For most monks, such prayers constitute the community's effort to support the soul's entrance into paradise. In the case of the saint, and particularly the abbot, such prayers soon turn from prayers *for* the soul to prayers begging intercession *from* the saint.[64] Thus, both initiation and death may serve less as models or records of monastic Life than as reassurance to communities that the saint, their patron, was once truly their companion and will be so forevermore.

THE ABBOT

The role of monastic leader is a common one for the saint to play, if only through a kind of circular logic: achieving the office of abbot was a recognition of saintly virtue. The Rule of Benedict specifies that the abbot is chosen for his "goodness of life and wisdom in teaching" (64:2).[65] Clearly all saints by definition adhere to the first of these qualities; the second, however, is an attribute distinctive to the holy abbot, for it reflects the prerequisites of his office. Three particular *topoi* are associated with the abbot's Life: teaching, building, and the legacy of the saint's death. There are, of course, striking similarities to the Life of a bishop in these *topoi*, not surprising given that many abbots were also bishops.

The abbot is usually marked by his teaching, and the saintly abbot by his teaching through prophetic—that is, miraculous—vision. We have already seen an instance of this in Benedict's reproof of the monks who ate outside the monastery without permission. Images of teaching also appear in the Life of Omer: in the first miniature of his Life, for example, Omer is instructed in the monastic life by Columbanus when he and his father are accepted at Luxeuil (fig. 88); in another, it is Omer who gives instruction in turn (see fig. 3).[66] As noted above, Cuthbert teaches in community (see fig. 84). Many more such examples could be adduced but I would like to concentrate instead on an episode in the Vatican Life of Benedict that once more seems paradigmatic. This episode, in fact, is repeated in the illustrated Life of Maurus in the same manuscript.[67]

The incident occurs almost immediately after Benedict has been elected abbot

Figure 88. Columban accepts Omer and his father at Luxeuil, *Life of Omer (Audomarus),*
for the canons of Saint-Omer, third quarter of the eleventh century. Bibliothèque
de l'Agglomération de Saint-Omer, MS 698, fol. 6r.

and has left his eremitic life.[68] Two boys, the now familiar Placidus and Maurus, are
brought to the saint by their fathers, Roman noblemen, "to be schooled in the service of God" (fig. 89). In the illustration of his Life in the Vatican Lectionary, Benedict holds a book and makes a sign of blessing over the two would-be students. The
titulus of the scene elaborates on Gregory's simple description of the event; it is the
request by the boys' fathers to Benedict: "Father, teach these for the Father of Fathers, through the legacy of the Fathers."[69] This formulation, of course, goes to the
heart of the notion of the abbot's relationship to his monks. The word "abbot" *(abbas)* is taken from the Greek word for "father." The illustration, together with its
accompanying *titulus,* overtly demonstrates the transfer of the boys from their natural fathers to their religious father, the abbot. The abbot himself, representing the

Figure 89. Placidus and Maurus are brought before Benedict; Benedict exorcises a wandering monk, *Monte Cassino Lectionary*, Monte Cassino, c. 1070. Vatican Library, Lat. 1202, fol. 30v. (© Biblioteca Apostolica Vaticana)

"Father of Fathers" (that is, God), in turn, passes on a religious heritage of authority from the "Fathers."[70]

The repetition of this scene in the Life of Maurus in the same manuscript, as John Wickstrom has argued, subtly changes the representation of abbot as father and expands the notion of monastic teaching. Through the pictorial device of the saint's hand placed on Maurus's head, Benedict "adopts" Maurus as his spiritual son. Furthermore, the artist adds a second scene that shows Benedict specifically teaching the Rule; its *titulus* reads: "My son, hear the words of thy father, the instructions of your teacher." These are the opening words of the Rule (prol. 1).[71] The essence of the monk's life is depicted here as the student's submission to teaching and the monk's reception and continuation of this monastic heritage.

The importance of monastic teaching continues as a central theme through the next several miniatures in the Life of Benedict. The miracle of Maurus's obedience, which appears on the page facing the image of Benedict as teacher (see fig. 74), emphasizes the interrelatedness of learning and obedience. Maurus's obedience in hastening to do Benedict's bidding contrasts with the episode directly below the scene of Benedict as teacher (see fig. 89). There, a young monk "wanders" when he should be praying. Benedict strikes the restless monk with his rod and the devil gives up his domination of the monk's soul.[72] Under the tutelage of Benedict, Maurus witnesses the presence and vanquishing of this devil. This brief succession of scenes thus effectively establishes Benedict as holy teacher, depicts Maurus as gifted and virtuous student (as opposed to the disobedient and aimless monk), and culminates in the fruit of this relationship—Maurus's swift and direct completion of the miracle of saving Placidus. Maurus, here represented as the perfect student, later becomes a saintly abbot himself. As Wickstrom noted, he is one of the few saints to exhibit growth and change, perhaps because of his unique status as *exemplum* of the student.[73]

In contrast to the image of the holy abbot as teaching father, abbesses are not depicted as teachers in the high Middle Ages. Although Radegund, founder of the abbey of Sainte-Croix, is described in texts as a teacher to her nuns, no images of teaching appear in surviving miniatures.[74] Instead, her role as leader of a community is conveyed through her touch. As abbot, Benedict's gesture of laying his hand on Maurus's head, reminiscent of the Old Testament blessing of Jacob by his father Isaac, is the only moment in which the sainted abbot touches one of his followers. By contrast, in at least four instances in the Life of Radegund the nun cures through touch. Radegund is also shown washing the feet of the poor, an act reminiscent to the Rule's requirement that the abbot wash the feet of his monks on Maundy Thursday.[75] What is striking in these illustrations, especially the foot-washing scene, in which Radegund seems almost to caress the leg and foot she washes, is the artist's emphasis on physical contact. While the sainted abbot effects cures through the sign of the cross, a gendered use of that sign (see pp. 159–61) that allows him to remain isolated and pure, Radegund uses a quite different gesture—she cradles a supplicant's chin in her hand (see fig. 123). This gesture resembles that of the abbess St. Gertrude healing in the Weissenau Passional (see fig. 124), and probably should be identified as a distinctly female gesture, especially available to the abbess. Thus, although not all the qualities of the abbot can be extended to the abbess, she has her own virtues.

In addition to teaching and healing, the Lives of abbots usually include prominent building activity. Because many abbot saints are also bishops, building might properly belong to the episcopal side of saintly character, but most of the buildings mentioned in the texts are identified as monasteries founded by the saint himself, as in the Lives of Liudger and Amand. In addition, Guthlac and Cuthbert are pictured lovingly building hermitages to which they then retreat (see fig. 86).[76]

The image of building is an important one in Gregory's *Dialogues*, as it is in the corresponding illustrations in Benedict's Life. As in the Lives of bishops, construction begins with the destruction of an idol, an altar, or a sacred grove, but then proceeds into an ongoing battle, because "such losses the ancient Enemy could not bear in silence."[77] In one episode, the devil appears under an immovable rock and causes a newly built wall to fall on a young monk. Here and in a similar miracle in the Life of Maurus,[78] the saint resurrects the dead monk. Not only do building scenes seem to function as part and parcel of the abbot's authority as founder and leader of monasteries, but to the extent they are represented as victory over the forces of the devil, they also assure the viewer that God approves of this form of the "building" or edification of the Church.

The third and most common theme in the abbot's Life is the celebration of his death. The death of the monastery's leader seems to represent an opportunity for expressions of community, not only in mourning but also in the community's care for its leader instead of vice versa. However, touch and ministrations to the body of the saint are not entirely welcome and are accepted only reluctantly. Through the many sicknesses and infirmities described in the text of his *vita*, Cuthbert (though not an abbot nonetheless a revered monastic leader) refuses to let any of his fellow monks care for him. Only at the last moment does he allow one monk into his cell; as he bathes the saint's festering wounds, the monk is granted the blessing of a cure of his persistent diarrhea. Similarly, in Benedict's last moments, the abbot continues to pray but allows a rare instance of bodily contact by permitting the monks to hold his arms aloft. Again in a saintly reversal, the illustration depicts the infirm and dying Benedict in the guise of the heroic Moses victorious in battle so long as he continues to pray (fig. 90).[79]

Perhaps abbots are reluctant to be touched because such care may be gendered as feminine. Throughout most of the Middle Ages, preparation of the body for burial was a woman's prerogative, even in the case of monks. For example, Guthlac's sister prepares him for burial in roundel 15 of the Guthlac Roll.[80] As heroic monastic figures, these leaders avoid the solicitous touch as a sign of bodily weakness; they accept it only after death or when they can provide a blessing in return.

At the death of their leaders, monks receive both spiritual and corporeal blessings. They may be granted heavenly visions comparable to those that a saint enjoys (as in the case of Liudger); certainly they receive an enduring patron. Benedict prophesies to Maurus, "I will be more present to you after my body is buried."[81] In turn, at Maurus's death, depicted in the Troyes miniature (see fig. 85), twelve monks administer him the Last Rite of communion and celebrate his burial with much grief and uncharacteristically intimate touching. As an elaborate lid is lowered into place, the body is clearly shown to be entombed in front of the monastery's altar where Maurus will remain readily available as patron. The minutely detailed depiction indicates that such joyous yet grief-filled deaths occasioned liturgical celebrations that must have been among the most profound monastic experiences.

CONCLUSION

Although virtually all of the illustrated manuscripts of saints' Lives from 900 to 1300 were produced by monastic communities, no one saint can be designated as purely and simply a representative of a model monastic life. Guthlac's illustrated vita might be taken as an excellent representation of the eremitic life, as might parts of Cuthbert's Life, but both go far beyond the Rule. Moreover, given that the manuscript was produced for Crowland, the site of Guthlac's hermitage, the artist of the Guthlac Roll had a vested interest in representing the eremitic aspects of the saint's Life. Maurus is the perfect student, but in both versions of his Life, he is presented as an adjunct to Benedict and eventually becomes himself a great miracle-worker and leader.

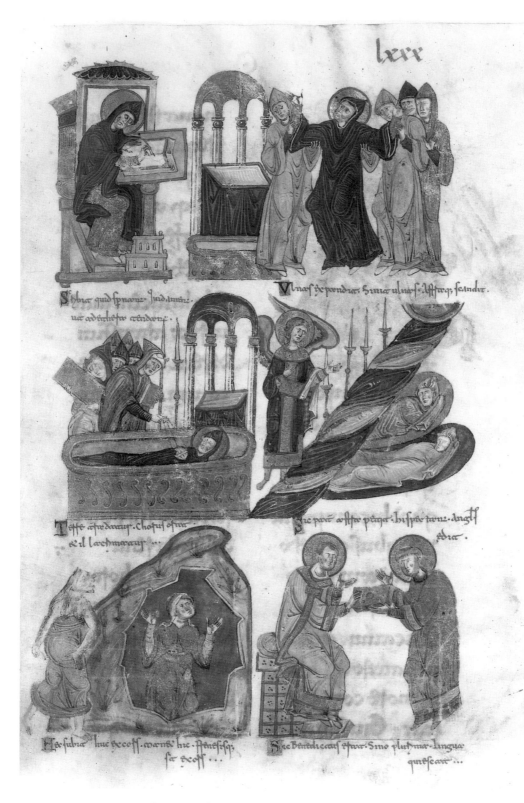

Figure 90. Benedict prays, dies, and ascends to heaven, *Monte Cassino Lectionary,* Monte Cassino, c. 1070. Vatican Library, Lat. 1202, fol. 80r. (© Biblioteca Apostolica Vaticana)

Of the manuscripts discussed here, only the Life of Benedict might offer the ideal mirror for monks. Of course, this is fitting given the saint's position as the Father of Western monasticism. Indeed, by including illustrations of both Benedict's Life and that of Maurus,[82] the Vatican Lectionary, makes an implicit argument for Benedict, and Monte Cassino, as the source of monastic observance because, even within the manuscript, Benedict's Life is shown to produce holy offspring. It is no surprise that the Rule is so amply attested in Benedict's Life, for he is, after all, the exemplary teacher and father—*abbas*. He even asserts his mastery of the monastic life before his community is founded. Nevertheless, in his perfection, Benedict must have been a hard act to follow. For example, the illustration of his explicit chastisement of his flesh is virtually unique in hagiographic illustrations before the late Middle Ages. It seems a monk could not hope to emulate him, only to learn from him.

For this question of imitability, it would be valuable to determine whether the later medieval and Renaissance pictorial hagiographies of Francis and Dominic are any more attentive than these earlier Lives to the real life of the brothers. Rona Goffen argues that the fatal flaw in the Franciscan order was its "cult of personality," implying an increased likelihood that followers imitated Francis in every detail of action (and we have seen one example of this in Brother John).[83] However, even Bonaventure, the saint's hagiographer, remarked on the foremost virtue of Il Poverello, "It is not granted to everybody to observe such poverty or to choose it, but it is given to all to admire it."[84] Bonaventure thus stressed the limited usefulness of extremes of virtue as a model for typical monastic life.

Perhaps we may turn again to the Rule to understand why monastic life is not in itself an imitation of sanctity but merely a possible first step to other more perfect models. It states:

> The purpose of this rule is to furnish a guide to the monastic life. Those who observe it will have at least entered on the way of salvation and will attain at least some degree of holiness. But he who aims at the perfect life must study and observe the . . . holy fathers . . . the New and Old Testament . . . the Lives of the Saints. . . . Thou who art striving to reach the heavenly land, first perfect thyself with the aid of Christ in this little rule, which is the beginning of holiness, and then thou mayst under the favor of God advance to higher grades of virtue and knowledge through the teaching of these greater works. (Rule, 73)

By these words, the Rule itself at its conclusion thus clarifies some of the distinctions that have been important to this chapter. It declares itself in favor of an interreferentiality of the holy life modeled on Christ, scripture, and other saints—a purposefully intertextual life. We have already witnessed such intertextuality in the Lives of martyrs, virgins, and bishops, but monastic life seemed to hold out the possibility of perfectibility based on a deliberate emulation of other saintly Lives—almost as if the overt formulas of the genre of hagiography were being offered up as viable actions for imitation. However, as the Lives of saintly monks and nuns make abundantly clear, such formulas are not ultimately effective in producing saints. Here, the Rule itself concludes by confirming that the life of the monk is a good life but that the life of the saint is extraordinary. Following the Rule takes one only so far up the ladder of perfection. The rest of the climb, as Maurus's vision of the death of Benedict demonstrates, is dependent on true sanctity and marked by the recognition and protection of angels (see fig. 90).[85] Saintliness is found in grace and miracles, not in human conduct circumscribed by rules.

QVAE CRVTIS ILLVD ETETI SPECTACVLVM ·
Quis ferre possit acris aut ferri rigor · —
Impacta quotiens corpus attigerat salix ·
Ionui rubebant sanguine uda uimina ·
Quon plaga ferat rosadis liuoribus ·

Ferunt minaces uerberantium genas
Illacrimasse sponte demanantibus
Guttis por barbarum frementia ·
Scribas & ipsas & coronam plebium ·
Iroceresq. sicas n stetisse insibus ·

Plate 1. The torture of Barulas, *Peristephanon* X, in *Prudentius Opera,* Reichenau (?),
c. 900. Bern, Burgerbibliothek, Cod. 264, p. 137.

Plate 2. The torture of Quentin, *Authentique or Passion of Quentin (Quintinus)*, Saint-Quentin, c. 1050–1100. Manuscrit de l'Église paroissiale déposé à la Bibliothèque municipale de Saint-Quentin, p. 42.

Plate 3. Aldegund's vision: Amand ascends into heaven with the souls he has converted,
Life of Amand, Saint-Amand at Elnone (Saint-Amand-les-Eaux), c. 1050–1100.
Valenciennes, Bibliothèque municipale, MS 502, fol. 119r.

Plate 4. Kilian baptizes the people of Würzburg, *Passions of Kilian of Würzburg and Margaret of Antioch,* Fulda, c. 970. Hannover, Niedersächsische Landesbibliothek, MS I 189, fol. 5r. (Courtesy Graz, Akademische Druck- und Verlagsantsalt)

Plate 5. Emma flees under Sweyn's oppression, *La Estoire de Seint Aedward le Rei*, London or Westminster, 1250. Cambridge. University Library, MS. Ee 3.59, fol. 4r. (Reproduced by permission of the Syndics of Cambridge University Library)

Plate 6. The charity of Edmund, *Passion of Edmund, king and martyr,* Bury St. Edmunds, c. 1130. New York, Pierpont Morgan Library, MS M. 736, fol. 9r.

Plate 7. Radegund exorcises a demon and cures a woman, *Life of Radegund of Poitiers*, Sainte-Croix, Poitiers, c. 1050–1100. Poitiers, Médiathèque François-Mitterrand, MS 250, fols. 34v–35r.

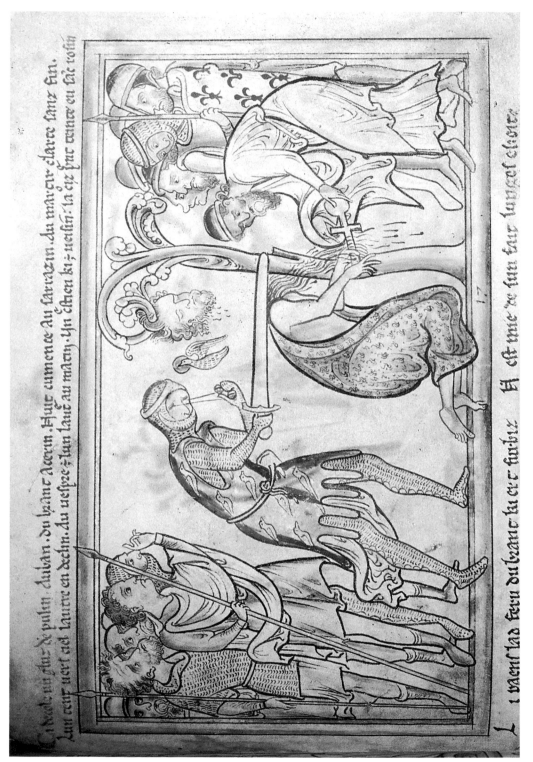

Plate 8. Alban is beheaded, *Passions of Alban (Albinus) and Amphibalus*, Matthew Paris at St. Albans, 1240 or later. Dublin, Trinity College Library, MS 177, fol. 38r. (Reproduced by permission of the Board of Trinity College Dublin)

LAY AND ROYAL SAINTS
Kings and Nobles

ॐ

It would be more holy and honest that he should recognize the right of armed force,
that he should unsheathe the sword against his enemies, that he should restrain the
boldness of the violent; it would be better that the bold should be suppressed by force
of arms than that the undefended districts should be unjustly oppressed by them.
—Life of Gerald of Aurillac, I:7, trans. Gerard Sitwell

UNTIL THIS POINT we have considered the Lives of holy persons whose actions and deportment reflect the Life of Christ in evident ways: martyrs emulate the sacrifice of his death, virgin saints emulate the innocence and purity of his body; confessors emulate his mission and miracles. In this chapter we turn to the Lives of men who wield power, do violence, and act in ways that Christ would have abhorred. Instead of focusing on the intercessory power of the heavenly court, the Lives of holy kings turn attention to the just use of power in time and in the world, in earthly court and kingdom. The duty of defending the realm was intrinsic to royal office: at least one medieval king was deposed because he was unable to bear arms or lead armies.[1] How, then, could a king be both good prince and holy saint? Certainly Christ's epithet is King of Kings, but his life is not a self-evident model for the actions of an effective earthly ruler. The Lives of bishops and monks to some degree address the problems of worldly power and introduce the issue of human frailty, but it is in the holy Lives of sainted kings that these tensions are treated with particular focus and clarity.

The saintly virtues of kings were celebrated as early as the sixth century, and the twelfth century has been justly called the "century of saintly kings," but it was not until the thirteenth century that kings came to be venerated on the basis of authentically virtuous lives.[2] During the early Middle Ages, cults founded to advance dynastic ambitions had developed around rulers of somewhat doubtful character.[3]

One theory holds that weak states created saint-kings in order to bolster their power.[4] The celebration of royal martyrs has also been associated with early pagan practices of leader sacrifice, or in the case of the subgenre of child kings, the sacrifice of innocents.[5] Indeed, František Graus argues that before the thirteenth century saintly kings were exclusively of two types: martyrs (killed as a result of their refusal to fight or because of the treachery of others) or pseudo-monks.[6] Although, as we have seen, monastic saints do not comprise a rigid type, many royal Lives are informed by the ideals of monastic sanctity—an unsurprising fact given that the authors of these works were usually monks.

One distinction important to historians of kingship, that between sacrality and sanctity, is also important to our hagiographic assessment. Sacral kingship is a principle of political theory that places the sovereign far above his subjects and endows him with certain powers by virtue of his office. Notwithstanding ceremonies of anointment and the sacral benefits of the office, however, kings had to achieve salvation and/or sanctity on the basis of individual merit.[7]

Whatever the political motivations underlying canonization or cult, in constructing the Lives of royal saints hagiographers had to address the issue of the proper action of the king. Very often they had little documentation or literary material out of which to shape their accounts. New narrative *topoi* had to be devised to demonstrate the sanctity of a king and the holiness of his actions. The exercise of worldly power was a particularly troublesome issue, because the use of physical force did not readily conform with the saintly ideal, creating an uneasy relationship that this chapter will examine at length.

By the high Middle Ages, the notion that personal conduct should be governed by order, duty, and limit began to assume an important place in the understanding of the social construct. Georges Duby's *The Three Orders* suggests the long-standing force of one such image of the proper functioning of the individual in society during the Middle Ages. That model conceives of society as made up of three all-inclusive orders: those who pray, those who fight, and those who labor. The medieval concept makes some egregious omissions—merchants come immediately to mind—and carelessly lumps others together. Nonetheless, this sort of categorization had tremendous power in defining how (and where) the ideals of the pious Christian life and the ideals of the societally productive life might intersect. From this fruitful field of thought sprang a crop of ideas about "orders" in the life of the earthly world—from the order of the pilgrim to that of the knight.[8]

Saints' Lives represent ideals of behavior cast in narrative form, of course, and they convey medieval notions of order. Clerics presumably turned to hagiography with the intent of expressing ideas about societal order, and they shaped stories to reflect particular ideologies. One example of such shaping, according to Thomas Head, appears in the Life of King Edmund of Anglia. Abbo of Fleury, when asked by the monks of Bury St. Edmunds to record the stories that he had heard from an aged St. Dunstan, gladly accepted the task of writing the king's Life because he took it as a welcome opportunity to present his own ideas on kingship.[9]

The basic problem of representing "those who fight" as saints is not hard to understand. The knight, or *miles,* was the instrument that kings used in asserting power. A hagiographic Life of a *miles* is problematic because the mounted, fully armed knight (or the king in knightly guise) constitutes a medieval icon of unbridled violence—the armored tank of the Middle Ages (see plate 5).[10] If such fierce "weapons" could be given a human, even holy, face by clerical hagiographers, then theoretically power and violence did not preclude a virtuous and even saintly life.

A remarkable (regrettably unillustrated) hagiographic narrative shows how the *vita* of a knight could be constructed to deliver this message. In the tenth-century *vita* of Gerald of Aurillac by his contemporary Odo, abbot of Cluny, the Life of a noble lord becomes a lay analogy for ecclesiastical orders.[11] Although the text's authorship colors its content (Odo was a widely known proponent of monastic reform), it also increases its interest. Monastic ideas and ideology were often powerful influences on lay society; C. Stephen Jaeger has gone so far as to argue that the notions of courtliness and the virtues of knighthood were first articulated in the Lives of the saints by clerical authors such as Odo.[12]

In his Life of Gerald, Odo makes startlingly original use of hagiographic *topoi* to define the proper exercise of worldly power. His metaphor of the "rhinoceros . . . bound with a thong" delivers a vivid image of an immensely powerful man, voluntarily yoked to serve God—in this case to "break the clods of the valley, that is, the oppressors of the lowly" (I:18; cf. Job 39:10). But perhaps Odo's most explicit characterization of the sacred use of power appears in his description of Gerald's own understanding of his office. Gerald knows that his duty is to "recognize the right of armed force" and to protect the weak against the violent (I:7). The saint realizes that he cannot or should not follow his own inclination and retire from an active life. Odo quotes scripture (Rom. 13:4) to argue that the judge "does not bear the sword in vain, for he is the servant of God to execute His wrath," but also mitigates this image of avenging violence by observing that such servants of God "might restrain by arms or by the law those whom ecclesiastical censure was not able to subdue" (I:8). Thus, in following his calling, Gerald takes his place in the order of knights: he is one of those "who fight" and by doing so works to preserve peace—in particular, the "peace of the church."[13] At this point, however, Odo introduces what will become an important *topos*. As a saintly lord and protector, Gerald "was so protected by God that . . . he never stained his sword with human blood" (I:8).

Odo's emphasis on the obligations of office and the compulsion to engage in an active life is, of course, reminiscent of the themes of obligations and demands of daily existence within one's order that dominate the *vitae* of monks and bishops. However, the similarities do not end there: saints who are kings, knights, monks, and bishops are all confessors and share certain hagiographic concerns of the saintly type. Furthermore, most Lives of kings, like the Lives of other confessors, were written by monastic authors.

For all these similarities, it nonetheless seems remarkable that Lives of knights and of monks first establish sanctity not through issues of power but through themes such as the proper consumption of food. Odo's Life of Gerald includes an abundance of references to eating. First, Odo tells us that the saint "ate only for refreshment, not pleasure" (I:13). Like a monk, Gerald had lections read aloud during meals (either he or a cleric provided commentary), and he disapproved of raucous feasting, that is, of "those who make a great noise, [for] they do not hear the cry of the poor" (I:15). Finally, we learn that after his death, Gerald's table itself assumed miracle-working powers and was moved to the church of St. Martin, "because the table had been consecrated by the many meals of the holy man" (IV:10). In Odo's conception, a holy life lived within the strictures of an order becomes something like that of a monk. One of the frailties of the human body—its need for food—is turned into a spiritual benefit through the use of monastic *topoi*.

However, monastic *topoi* in this secular Life are subtly adjusted to their new context. Monks' *vitae* described in the previous chapter tell of miraculous catches of fish; on four occasions Gerald is similarly miraculously supplied with fish, which he distributes to his entourage. However, as examples in late medieval art testify, when situated within the realm of feudal relations, the gift of a fish from vassal to lord typifies feudal obligation.[14] Thus, to the representation of faith in God's bounty, as in the monastic context, Gerald's Life adds the notion of the just distribution of the fruits of the feudal system. Pushing the *topos* to the limit, Odo tells of a miracle that occurred while Gerald was on pilgrimage to Rome: one fish, six inches long, provided sufficient nourishment for Gerald's entire company. The story echoes Christ's miracle of the fishes, but it also illustrates the bounties associated with faith.[15]

Gerald's decidedly monastic attitudes—his disapproval of raucous behavior and of feasting for pleasure—also take on specific meaning in the context of a lord's *vita*. Gerald's qualities make him a saintly exemplum and a warning to his gluttonous, ill-behaved fellow-nobles. Indeed, in his preface, Odo explains that he has written Gerald's Life in part to correct how his subject's saintly status has been understood. Other lords apparently rationalized "their luxurious lives by his example." After all, they said, he was "powerful and rich, and lived well, and is certainly a saint" (Preface). Odo shows that Gerald "lived well" only in the saintly, not the secular, sense.

Odo must have been fully aware of the tensions inherent between the "powerful and rich" and the holy, and he attempts to address many of them in his narrative. His solutions are proposed perhaps not with the belief that they will be carried out but as an ideal for conduct within the order of nobility. Thus they mediate between divine and worldly precepts. For example, recounting the freeing of serfs, Odo notes that Gerald freed many but not *too* many. "Let this be told that hence it may be clear how closely he adhered to the divine precepts, when he submitted in this way to legal and human ones" (III:4).

In addressing a somewhat more pressing issue—Gerald's obligation to protect his people—Odo observes that because of Gerald's peaceful nature, his vassals sometimes accused him of being "soft and timid" (I:24). Gerald found that "gentle words" soothed even the ill tempered and "forbore threatening" (I:25 and I:29; cf. Eph. 6:9). Though he seems more foolhardy than cowardly in avoiding violence by asking his men to join in battle using only the backs of swords and reversed spears, miraculous victories reward Gerald's piety and save his people from harm (I:8).[16] Consequently, despite his reluctance to use violence, Gerald fulfills his duties as knight and lord without "darken[ing] his glory" (I:8). Although some of his solutions may strain the credulity of the modern reader, it is clear that Odo labors consistently in his Life of Gerald to offer his medieval reader a possible resolution of the tension between saintliness and worldly obligations.

Illustrations of the Life of Wandrille, a Merovingian noble who retired to a monastery, can profitably be read in light of Odo's portrait of Gerald. Although the majority of the text is given over to describing Wandrille's career as a monk, the tenth-century illustrated *libellus* of Wandrille at Saint-Omer preserves a few introductory images of the saint's life before his taking religious orders. In the two surviving miniatures, Wandrille, a member of the Merovingian court, acts as an exemplary yet saintly noble.

In the first episode, Wandrille refuses to wield a sword or to produce heirs, two of the primary duties of a lord. The illustration shows the saint and his wife, who have agreed to a chaste marriage, prominently enthroned side by side. By means of a gesture, Wandrille refuses a sword offered to him by his vassals. Subsequently, in the text of the *vita,* the saint, traveling about his estates, comes upon a group of "the worst sort of rustics" who, unafraid of God, are in murderous contention over grazing rights. The saint prays and resolves all conflict in friendship and peace.[17] In the second of the miniatures, spread across facing pages, we see this encounter illustrated (fig. 91). On the right, the murderous band is fully armed, with helmets, standards, lances, and shields at the ready. The group prickles with hostility. On the left, Wandrille greets this warrior band with a languid lifting of his right arm, palm open in a gesture of peace. He has no weapons. His followers hold their lances down and clasp their shields under their arms. Wandrille's prayer and peacemaking are not shown; in fact, the confrontation seems to be between Wandrille and his men and the hostile band, rather than between two factions of rustics. Rather than following the text of Wandrille's Life, the episode has been remade in the image of Gerald's battles—victorious although fought with swords averted.

Below, a second episode on the same opening depicts an incident at court. Called out of his hermit's retreat by King Dagobert, on arriving at the palace Wandrille sees a poor man whose cart has overturned in front of the door. Courtiers ignore his plight, trampling the man underfoot. Wandrille "descended from his horse and took the pauper's hand," an action that provokes laughter among the courtiers. However, an angel appears and dusts off the saint's clothing: his character is revealed "as if a lamb among wolves,"[18] and Dagobert, in recognition of Wandrille's holy calling, allows him to retire from court to become a monk. The miniature in this case follows the text closely, but here it is the selection of the incident that speaks to an ideal of caring for the poor and a concern for civility among lay members of the court.

These two miniatures from the Life of Wandrille are inserted as an extra gathering into the *libellus* that contains his textual dossier. The fragmentary visual narrative may be a copy of the beginning of a longer, earlier illustrated Life (perhaps in another medium, such as wall-paintings in a Carolingian palace) that the peripatetic monks of St. Wandrille were attempting to record and preserve. It is somewhat surprising to see lay virtues extolled in the Life of a monk, but clearly clerics had an interest in such virtues, and saints' Lives became "some of the most polished weapons in an ideological struggle" concerning the proper use of power.[19]

Figure 91. Wandrille makes peace; Wandrille rescues a man from trampling, *Passion of St. Wandrille (Wandregisilus) of Fontenelle,* Saint-Bertin (?), late tenth century. Bibliothèque de l'Agglomération de Saint Omer, MS 764, fols. 8v–9r.

Wandrille, in his married celibacy, may have accomplished "the perfect form of marriage," according to the clerical conception of Jonas of Orleans.[20] And surely Wandrille's refusal to bear arms (when his civil responsibilities endorsed fighting) is a variation on the familiar *topos* of the soldier who turns his back on his profession in favor of the monastic life.

Gerald's Life suggests that the action of grace holds sway even in the realm of power and war. In delineating the ideal possibilities of a secular yet holy life of power, however, Gerald's Life and the lay episodes in the Life of Wandrille are clearly problematic. They provide models for saintly behavior in secular life, but they are not models for secular life itself. The *vitae* of kings have often been likened to "mirrors for princes," but those moralizing texts focus primarily upon political good. The ideal prince is not necessarily a saint, nor is a saint necessarily an ideal prince. The hagiographers of the Lives of kings have as their task resolving the conflict that opposes saintly virtue against political good.

THE ILLUSTRATED LIVES
OF KINGS OF THE HIGH MIDDLE AGES

Illustrated Lives of saintly kings are few in number but stand out among surviving *libelli* for their luxury. One prominent example, the twelfth-century manuscript Life of Edmund of East Anglia, recounts the deeds of a king who was a powerful monastic patron.[21] Given Edmund's status as martyr as well as king, it is probable that his martyred body made his cult and patronage more powerful than that of a mere saintly king. The text of Edmund's tenth-century Life by the French abbot Abbo of Fleury was illustrated between c. 1120 and 1130 by a visiting artist at Bury St. Edmunds, the home of the saint's relics.[22] The illustrations comprise a sequence of thirty-two lavishly colored, full-page framed display miniatures (sixteen paired folios or openings) that preface the hagiographic material. The manuscript also includes historiated initials that occasionally illustrate the same incidents as the full-page miniatures, but they are by a different workshop.[23] Excepting perhaps the more modest Lucy *libellus,* no other eleventh- or twelfth-century *libellus* is so clearly conceived as a display copy of pictures separable from their text.

To understand how Edmund's *vita* sets the stage for the important developments in royal Lives in the thirteenth century, we will compare it to the illustrations of Matthew Paris's Life of Edward the Confessor. (Matthew's work is treated more fully in chapter 9.) The text and probably a plan for the miniatures were created by Matthew in the mid-thirteenth century. The manuscript itself was written shortly thereafter in London or Westminster, probably commissioned by the canons of Westminster Abbey with a court audience in mind. Also of interest as comparanda to these manuscript Lives are the eight narrative metalwork reliefs on the Aachen shrine-reliquary of Charlemagne (declared a saint in 1165). The reliquary clearly expresses imperial German interests: it is ringed with German emperors rather than the conventional entourage of seated Apostles and thus offers a slightly different perspective on the virtues of a sainted king and the thematic concerns of thirteenth-century royal hagiography.[24] Finally, although the many richly illustrated Lives of St. Louis date well beyond the chronological upper limit of this study, several of the images shed light on royal hagiography of the high Middle Ages and will be briefly considered here.

Other comparative materials are equally scarce. Although Paul Binski uses the title of the Matthew Paris manuscript, the *Estoire de Seint Aedward le Rei,* to argue persuasively that "history" impinges on the hagiography of kings,[25] few illustrated chronicles exist, and these have a limited impact on pictorial hagiography.[26] Historical portraits and images of coronations of non-saintly kings are useful resources for visual comparison but provide little or no narrative context. The many versions and illustrations of the romance of Alexander the Great were instrumental in shaping an image of chivalric kingship, especially in the thirteenth century and later,[27] and they serve as an important precedent for some narrative pictorial strategies. Nevertheless, illustrations contained in history and romance manuscripts are most interesting—not as comparanda, but rather as contrasts to the Lives of saintly kings. As is the case with most saints' Lives, the authority of biblical texts (rather than the influence of contemporary materials) created the paradigms that in turn generated narrative.

Edmund of East Anglia is in many ways a problematic example of kingship. He did not produce offspring and failed to protect his kingdom, and his sanctity was based not on the strength of his virtue but rather on the fact of his martyrdom. However, we must be careful to separate appropriate royal political behavior from appropriate royal saintly behavior. In providing a Life to substantiate Edmund's sanctity, both its author and its illustrator had to supply actions that could be understood as exemplary and holy. Political issues that were paramount to the monastic point of view concerning the king's duties, such as righteous authority, royal mercy and charity, as well as the restraint of violence and protection of the weak, are, in fact, amply addressed in the events of Edmund's short Life in both text and pictures. The later medieval Lives of Edward and Louis produced in a court context, by contrast, are lengthy narratives that much more explicitly illustrate saintly royal conduct, and they reflect the ideal of "lived sanctity" in royal Lives of the thirteenth century and later. Nevertheless, they address many of the same issues that dominate the Life of Edmund.

THE CONSTRUCTION OF A ROYAL SAINT
AND ROYAL AUTHORITY: CORONATION,
CHARITY, MERCY, HUMILITY

The first problem that the artist of an illustrated Life of a royal saint had to address was how (and by whom) the king's legitimate authority had been established. In addition to having been selected to receive God's grace, a king's assumption of the throne must also be shown to have been affirmed by his people. The proof of legitimacy tends to take two distinct forms: demonstrations of legitimate royal ancestry and the testimony of a proper coronation by authorities of the Church.[28]

Edmund's authority in his illustrated Life is established by means of an abbreviated "prehistory" of the origin of his power, culminating in his coronation. Miniatures detail the story recounted in Abbo's text: the arrival of the Angles, Saxons, and Jutes in Britain, their battle against their enemies, the Britons, and their division of the country into three kingdoms.[29] A representation of Edmund's coronation in the presence of clergy and the nobility is the climax of this group of miniatures (fig. 92).

Similarly, the Life of Edward the Confessor in the thirteenth-century illustrated *Estoire* grounds Edward's reign in a political prehistory of his rule, detailing the kings who preceded him, showing enthroned portraits of the good, and deploring the wicked acts of the evil.[30] For example, the second miniature (plate 5) depicts the evil Sweyn (the Danish interloper) advancing on defenseless citizens—robbing, taking prisoners, and according to the text, "burning houses and monasteries" (ll. 182–86). At the far right of the miniature, the infant Edward is taken by his mother Emma to safety in Normandy; the image of the crowned mother is an unmistakable allusion to Mary's flight into Egypt.[31] After Sweyn is killed by a miraculous intervention (fig. 93) and the other contenders for the throne are eliminated by various means, Edward is crowned in the presence of the nobility and clergy (fig. 94). Already, in this example of the initial miniatures, the schematic quality of the Life of Edmund can be contrasted with the wealth of historical detail in the Life of Edward, although both accounts are equally careful to establish their subjects' royal origins.

Even the short cycles of the Life of Louis of France included in the Hours of Jeanne d'Evreux and that of Jeanne de Navarre lay emphasis on the king's royal genealogy.[32] Both depict the saint's princely childhood (in which his mother, Queen

Figure 92. Edmund is crowned king, *Passion of Edmund, king and martyr*, Bury St. Edmunds, c. 1130. New York, Pierpont Morgan Library, MS M. 736, fol. 8v.

Figure 93. Emma presents her sons to the duke of Normandy; Sweyn is killed by
St. Edmund, *La Estoire de Seint Aedward le Rei,* London or Westminster, 1250. Cambridge,
University Library, MS Ee 3.59, fol. 4v. (Reproduced by permission of the Syndics
of Cambridge University Library)

Blanche of Castile, figures prominently); mother and child appear as well in the illustrated Life of Louis by Guillaume de Saint-Pathus.[33] However, Louis' coronation is represented only in the Jeanne de Navarre manuscript, and the scene is markedly dominated by the activities of the clergy.[34] The large numbers of clergy may reflect Jeanne de Navarre's personal sympathies, but it also points to an increasingly elaborate set of rituals associated with coronation in the thirteenth and fourteenth centuries.

The second proof of legitimate rule—lawful coronation—is divergently illustrated in these Lives, but a close look at the ceremonial and its portrayal in the manuscripts elucidates several points in common among the various representations. It should be noted that the artists of these illustrations, as a rule, do not strive for historical accuracy in their depictions, but instead portray royal ceremony of their own era. The coronation image in the Life of Edmund is particularly imposing, especially given that Abbo relates no details about the event itself. Abbo's text lays stress on Edmund's Christian and Saxon origins and focuses on his three qualifications to be king: birth, election, and reception of the chrism.[35] In effect, however, only two

Figure 94. Edward lands in England and is crowned king, *La Estoire de Seint Aedward le Rei*, London or Westminster, 1250. Cambridge, University Library, MS Ee 3.59, fol. 9r. (Reproduced by permission of the Syndics of Cambridge University Library)

of these qualifications, birth and election, are represented in the pictorial narrative: birth (through the depiction of Edmund's ancestry) and election (through the presence of a cast of supporting characters in the coronation miniature). In the latter image, two bishops simultaneously invest Edmund with crown and scepter; grouped symmetrically around him are the laity and soldiers, representing the source of his secular power and the means by which that power is exercised. Two of the soldiers serve as Edmund's sword-bearers.[36] The presence of two bishops is characteristic of post-Conquest English coronations,[37] and it may have particular significance in the procedures governing election. At the coronation of William the Conqueror, two bishops addressed the crowd, asking whether William should be crowned, and the people acclaimed his coronation.[38] The presence of the "people" in the miniature of Edmund's coronation confirms his acceptance as a secular ruler. Abbo's observation that Edmund was "forced" to assume the office of king,[39] may be alluded to in the miniature by the modest gesture of acceptance that Edmund makes with his hand during the coronation.

The coronation image sheds ample light on royal ceremonial, but more intriguing is what it does not show. Certainly, the scepter, sword, and coronation robes associated with investiture are illustrated, but the regalia are incomplete: the ring and the rod are missing.[40] Furthermore, English kings were anointed from the tenth century onward,[41] and Abbo—a French author—places emphasis on the anointment of Edmund throughout the *vita*. The manuscript's English illuminator, however, has not pictured this sacral element of the coronation. The French believed that anointment conferred the status of *Christus Domini* on their kings (following the model of Clovis, anointed with the miraculous oil received by St. Remigius from heaven) and likened the office of king to that of bishop, who was also anointed with the chrism. The English came to accept this model only gradually, eventually discovering a miraculous oil of their own.[42]

Whatever his reasons for not illustrating the anointment, the artist of the Morgan manuscript nonetheless finds a means to assert the likeness of bishop and king. Edmund appears remarkably clerical in demeanor: his coronation robes are for all intents identical to an episcopal cope. The simulation of episcopal liturgical garments was used in English coronations to signify the equivalence of status of king and bishop in their paired anointings and to emphasize the entrance of the king into a quasi-clerical role.[43] English royal lawyers argued that the anointing of the king paralleled the sacring of the bishop—some of the liturgical formulas were remarkably similar—and that therefore the ceremony made the king part of the Church. The argument justified the king's involvement in the finances and governance of abbeys, but it also draws an analogy between the types of confessors. King and bishop both were officers of the Church, and kings were at one time titled "Mediator cleri e plebis," that is, mediator for Church and people.[44]

Finally, Edmund is depicted enthroned. The simple fact asserts Edmund's right to the throne, a right that will become a point of duty. He is depicted seated while others stand (a typical strategy of royal representation),[45] but his head reaches the same level as those of his courtiers: he is much larger than any other figure and given unmistakable prominence.

The simultaneous representation of Edmund's enthronement, coronation, and investiture conflates and simplifies what was in fact a complex ceremony. Such conflation is equally typical of contemporary liturgical images.[46] As a representational strategy, it entails a synthetic and richly symbolic but not overly detailed view of coronation and enthronement. Although it demonstrates its subject's power and authority, the coronation miniature—the first representation of Edmund in the narrative—begins a story of imperfect kingship on earth that is completed only in the perfection of Edmund's coronation in heaven at the end of his Life (fig. 95).

Figure 95. Edmund is crowned in heaven, *Passion of Edmund, king and martyr,*
Bury St. Edmunds, c. 1130. New York, Pierpont Morgan Library, MS M. 736, fol. 22v.

Perhaps it is for this reason that the representation of the sacrament of anointing, with its implications of royal perfection, might have seemed inappropriate to the twelfth-century artist. In other words, this is only the first, mundane, and finally incomplete ceremony of the saint's coronation: that coronation will be perfected in heaven.

The Cambridge manuscript of the Life of Edward the Confessor, dating more than one hundred years later than the Life of Edmund, supplies a much more detailed and liturgically correct account of coronation (see fig. 94). In this much longer Life, the king's sanctity is recounted through the detailed narration of his holy actions. Coronation is likewise pictured in a less symbolic but more detailed narrative fashion.

The image of Edward's coronation is paired in the same frame with an image of *adventus*. On landing in England, Edward is welcomed with joy by the nobility (l. 848); they greet him with open arms and "take Edward by the hands" (*titulus* 12). The image is reminiscent of ceremonies of acclamation and procession that precede the ecclesiastical ceremonials of coronation. The author of the *Estoire* compares Edward's arrival to Palm Sunday, and "as said to the son of Mary . . . [he was] elected king before he was born" (ll. 854–57).[47] In the second representation of the actual moment of Edward's coronation in Westminster Abbey, the clergy swarms around him. The archbishop of Canterbury grants the scepter and tips a vessel symbolic of the anointing over the king's head.[48] The archbishop of York blesses the crown, which is already in place. The abbot of Westminster, a constant presence in the ceremony, stands behind the archbishop of Canterbury, holding his crozier.[49] A few peers are present at the king's left, but the populace is nowhere to be seen. (In contrast to this liturgically specific image, later in the *Estoire* the traitor and evil king Harold crowns himself without benefit of clergy or proper ceremony and is handed the scepter by a lord.)[50]

Despite its abundant specificity, the image of Edward's coronation, like that of Edmund's, does not contain the full regalia that we would expect to see in a strictly historical account. Edward does not wear his ceremonial robes, the ring and rod are again absent, and—perhaps most significant—there is no sword. An almost identical coronation image appears in the *Flores Historiarum,* a Westminster history text, and there swords figure prominently.[51] Many of the rituals and activities associated with accession are embedded in the *Estoire* illustrations: preparatory prayer, *adventus,* the coronation of the queen, and feasting.[52] Hunting, considered essential to developing the skills of war, was also associated with coronation, but it is not represented in the *Estoire;* its absence, along with the absence of Edward's sword, is suggestive.[53] One may reasonably conclude that the absence of elements associated with blood and blood-sport frames an argument for the inherently peaceful nature of Edward's reign.

In works dating from the thirteenth century onward, the illustration of coronations becomes increasingly specific, especially so in France.[54] Although shunted to the side of the miniature, the representation of Louis' coronation in the Hours of Jeanne de Navarre, for example, contains an abundance of narrative details that illustrate the participation of the clergy in the ceremony. The liturgies and officers of the Church (whatever their form or identity) assume increasing importance as the source of legitimate royal authority. Although represented with a range of liturgical detail and narrative specificity, coronation is clearly an essential element of a king's Life, for it effectively demonstrates, in visual terms, the king's legitimacy as well as his dependence upon the Church. Further events and acts vary more widely among examples.

The next scene in the Life of Edmund stands alone in representing his works and virtues as king (plate 6). Its position in the narrative—facing the coronation and preceding Edward's martyrdom at the hands of the Danes—invests it with a heavy burden of significance, notably in the information that it conveys concerning the king's virtue.[55] The miniature illustrates Abbo's description of Edward's qualities: "He was liberal in his bounty to those in want, and like a benign father to the orphan and widow. He ever kept in view the dictum of the wise man: 'Have they made you a prince? Be not exalted but be among them as one of them.'"[56] This formula echoes the contemporary understanding of some of the most important of the king's duties—"that he defend and protect widows and orphans and strangers . . . [and] feed the needy with alms."[57] It also recalls Old Testament virtues associated with kingship (see Eccl. 32:1). The Morgan miniature, however, does not show widows and orphans as the beneficiaries of Edmund's charity in the way the *vita* suggests. Rather, it is four male "strangers"—pilgrims—who are here represented. In twelfth-century understanding, pilgrims were virtually identical to the poor,[58] and thus Edmund's performance of the duties of a king is sufficiently demonstrated. The miniature, however, goes beyond a minimal evocation of charitable virtue by means of an emphatic visual association of Edmund with the pilgrims. The miniatures of the *vita,* through the use of brilliantly colored panels and dividing lines, consistently create pictorial divisions and hierarchies among the figures they illustrate; this miniature, however, is exceptional in the sequence, for it has no interior

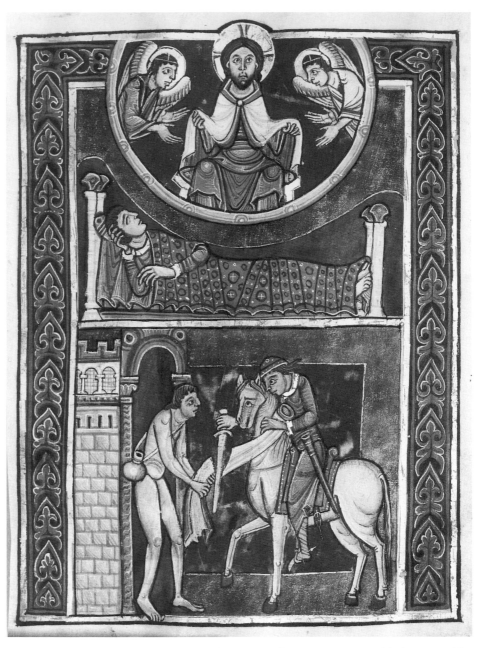

Figure 96. Martin divides his cloak with a beggar, St. Albans, c. 1120–30. Hildesheim, Basilika St. Godehard, St. Albans Psalter, p. 53. (© University of London, The Warburg Institute)

boundaries. Indeed, rather than order the treasurer who stands behind him to distribute coins, Edmund does it himself and actually *touches* the hands of the poor supplicants. He puts himself on their level in a literal illustration of the dictum that Abbo quotes: "be not exalted but be among them as one of them." In the Life of Gerald, Odo similarly emphasizes his subject's "love of the poor," his humility, and (particularly) his generous manner of giving alms: "Believing that he received Christ in the poor . . . How much those who send out their alms but do not bring the poor in to themselves diminish the merit they receive!" (*Gerald*, I:8; I:12; I:14). Gerald even "ate his morsel with the poor to the greater glory of God" (*Gerald*, II:27). Thus, a king's offer of large sums of money to the poor is not the sole measure of charity; more important is the spirit of fraternity in which the deed is done. This is the true sense of the action of one of the great exemplary saints, Martin (still in his knightly role—on horseback), who does not merely give his cloak to a beggar but divides it with the man, who is later revealed to be Christ (fig. 96). That Martin was a primary patron saint of the French kings suggests that he was considered a model appropriate to nobility. In sum, the artist has added the virtue of humility to this scene of Edmund's charity in order to portray the king's sanctity more fully.

The Life of Edward shows its subject engaging in similar acts of charity toward his people (including widows [fig. 97]), but the *vita* takes up the issue of humility separately; the longer narrative permits a more expansive visual treatment of the king's virtue. In scenes recounting an episode involving the Irishman Guil Michel, the text lingers on a description of his withered, deformed, and crumpled body (ll. 1925–43), yet we are told, as a demonstration of the king's humility, that Edward felt no hesitation in picking him up and carrying him on his back to the altar (fig. 98). As he did so, Guil Michel's crippled ligaments lengthened and were "fleshed out" (l. 1987), and the man was cured. The result was instantly recognized as a miracle and celebrated by singing the Te Deum. Although many of Edward's later miracles occur at court, this striking first healing takes place in the church at the command of St. Peter (ll. 1957–70) and is immediately claimed by the Church with the hymn of praise.[59]

Illustrated Lives of Louis of France even more explicitly identify the king's charity as the central constituent of his virtue. Joan Holladay has compared the illustrations in the Hours of Jeanne d'Evreux to images of the Seven Acts of Mercy.[60] In the next chapter, on queens, we will see that the same set of charitable acts had already structured the earlier Life of Elisabeth of Hungary. In his adoption of "feminine" qualities of sanctity, Louis breaks new ground for the construction of kingship that will be further explored in the late Middle Ages.[61]

Figure 97. Edward's ring is returned by pilgrims; Edward gives charity to the poor, *La Estoire de Seint Aedward le Rei,* London or Westminster, 1250. Cambridge, University Library, MS Ee 3.59, fol. 27r. (Reproduced by permission of the Syndics of Cambridge University Library)

A third episode in the Life of Edward extends the notion of charity into other duties of the king, such as judgment. While Edward feigns sleep, a thief twice steals into his chambers to plunder the royal treasury (fig. 99). When the rogue returns for a third helping, the king speaks up and warns him that the chamberlain is coming. Matthew Paris's text compares Edward's actions to Christ's forgiveness of the thief, but the account of Edward's charity and mercy mirrors the same *topos* in the Life of Gerald. Also pretending to sleep, Gerald allows a thief to escape, even finally warning him to "depart carefully lest anyone hear" (*Gerald,* I:25–26). Following apostolic example (1 Cor. 6:7), and showing a general contempt for wealth, both Edward and Gerald allow themselves to be defrauded, not a practical action certainly, nor one that many would be tempted to emulate, but a striking example of mercy and charity suited to a saintly king.

Figure 98. Edward carries Guil Michel and cures him; Guil Michel prays, *La Estoire de Seint Aedward le Rei,* London or Westminster, 1250. Cambridge, University Library, MS Ee 3.59, fol. 171. (Reproduced by permission of the Syndics of Cambridge University Library)

THE DUTIES OF THE KING: JUDGMENT AND DEFENSE

Edward's mercy in his act of charity implicates the duty of the king to judge. Unfortunately, in pursuing justice, mercy cannot always be the appropriate royal response. In contrast to Edward's mercy, scenes in the Life of Edmund point to a

Figure 99. Edward watches a thief in his chambers, *La Estoire de Seint Aedward le Rei*,
London or Westminster, 1250. Cambridge, University Library, MS Ee 3.59, fol. 10r.
(Reproduced by permission of the Syndics of Cambridge University Library)

harsher notion of judgment, but one that may conform more closely to Odo's rec-
ommendation in the Life of Gerald. Odo maintains that the judge serves as "the
servant of God to execute his wrath." The Church thus has primary authority to
judge and condemn, while lay judges have enforcement authority—to "restrain by
arms or by the law those whom ecclesiastical censure was not able to subdue" (*Gerald*, I:8). In two different posthumous episodes, Edmund strikes out to defend his

abbey. In one miracle story, sacrilegious thieves attempt to break into his church. Edmund's saintly power "restrains" them: they are literally frozen onto the church, where they are found the next day by the sacristan. The thieves are subsequently tried and hanged in one of the more grisly medieval scenes of execution. In a second episode, Edmund appears and strikes King Sweyn dead when he demands a tax from the monastery (fig. 100), a scene that has been compared to depictions of virtue defeating vice in the *Psychomachia*.[62] Saints can be remarkably vituperative after death, but these scenes represent a sainted king's intercession on behalf of the Church. After death, Edmund defends against thieves and unfair taxes, two commonly prescribed royal duties.[63]

The miracle of Sweyn's death at the hand of Edmund was considered such an important example of royal justice that it was cited in the pictorial prehistory of the Life of Edward (see fig. 93). In seeking to establish Edmund as Edward's forebear, the artist must have sought out the Life of Edmund and quoted the earlier image in his illustration: the compositions are too much alike to be explained as mere coincidence.[64]

A similar intertextuality also pervades royal Lives, hardly surprising given the small circle of clerics who were involved in their production. Osbert of Clare, a monk of Westminster and Bury, is known to have written at least three.[65] Considering the near certainty that the shared elements in the textual Lives of Edmund and Edward are not the result of chance, the knowledge and use of the pictorial hagiography of Edmund by the artist of the Edward cycle suggests a deliberate attempt to create an English royal hagiographic tradition, both textual and pictorial.

Edmund's posthumous choice of just execution over mercy and his violent defense of his kingdom against a foreign invader, Sweyn, brings us back to the issue defined at the outset as a central point of tension in the genre of royal saints' Lives: the place in a saintly Life of the violence required of "those who fight." A comparison of the Lives of Edmund and Edward to that of an ideal but nonsaintly ruler, Alexander the Great, provides an effective contrast. There are marked similarities among the Lives,[66] but much of the Alexander imagery concerns the emperor's prowess in battle and warfare; such imagery does not appear at all in the Lives of Edmund or Edward.[67] Although saintly chivalry is an important theme in the Life of Edward, the notion of the chivalric and saintly warrior remained relatively undeveloped in hagiographic literature, finding full expression only in fantasies such as the Life of St. George or the legends of Charlemagne.[68] Indeed, the narratives that recount the deeds and virtues of Edmund and Edward take pains to avoid attributing violence to their subjects' characters.

Figure 100. Edmund kills Sweyn for demanding unfair taxes, *Passion of Edmund, king and martyr,* Bury St. Edmunds, c. 1130. New York, Pierpont Morgan Library, MS M. 736, fol. 21v.

The aversion to violence is particularly evident in the Life of Edmund. Immediately after Edmund's act of charity to the pilgrims, Danish invaders arrive on the shores of England. The saintly king is embroiled in a war against his will. The attacking Danes are led by the fierce Ingvar, who, after winning a brutal but decisive battle, demands that Edmund capitulate and pay him homage.[69] Edmund refuses to submit his Christian people to such an indignity. These events lead directly to his martyrdom.

Edmund refuses to capitulate, but he in effect also refuses to fight, and as in the case of Gerald, the exercise of force becomes a central problem, one that cannot be satisfactorily resolved. Gerald miraculously wins his battles despite his refusal to harm his enemies. Similarly, Bede characterizes the pacifist saint and king Oswald as "victoriosissimus," rewarded by God with great conquests, and "miranda sanctitatis," triumphant in miracles, but for all his virtue Oswald is nonetheless ultimately defeated and slain.[70] Similarly, Bede even describes an alternate possibility: the saintly withdrawal from royal office. Coenred of Mercia quits the throne to become a monk, but in the high Middle Ages that route was censured: a king was obligated to accept his office (as the miniatures show Edmund doing).

In Matthew's *Estoire,* the problem of violence is rather more neatly resolved by means of a miracle. Edward has a vision of the Danish king, who is setting out on a naval assault against England (fig. 101). He prays fervently, the Danish king falls into the water and is drowned, and his armies are thrown into confusion. Through the power of his sanctity and his prayer, Edward protects his kingdom without the direct exercise of force.[71] Does the hagiographer thus imply that the king's prayer has itself the power to avert violence? Various elements of the text and images suggest otherwise. In his prayer, which takes place on the feast of the Pentecost, Edward, despite "his royal array . . . is humble . . . [and] abandons his heart to God" (ll. 1284–89). In response to the miracle, the king commits a striking lapse of decorum.[72] He smiles, perhaps even laughs.[73] Because kings were supposed always to retain a serene expression,[74] Edward's lapse—in church no less—marks the extraordinary nature of the event as a *miracle* at the same time that it disclaims any possibility of his agency—he is reacting with delight to the grace of God who sent the Holy Spirit "as to the apostles on this day (Pentecost)" (ll. 1314–17).

It might be thought that in avoiding war, saintly kings ought to be depicted as peacemakers, a role well suited to a monastic ideology. The Lives of Edmund and Edward, however, seem to offer no opportunities for peacemaking, for unlike Wandrille, these kings are the frequent target of sudden, unprovoked aggression by dis-

Figure 101. Edward has a vision of the drowning of the Danish king, *La Estoire de Seint Aedward le Rei,* London or Westminster, 1250. Cambridge, University Library, MS Ee 3.59, fol. 12r. (Reproduced by permission of the Syndics of Cambridge University Library)

tant enemies. The course of events is presented as inevitable, but in each case, the king's sanctity ultimately wins a victory for him and his people.

It is only later, in the fourteenth century, that hagiographers picture kings pursuing their own policies in waging war and making peace. Louis IX went on crusade and fought willingly; his Lives depict him as a warrior but do not lay emphasis on that role. Scenes of the Crusades are included in the Books of Hours of Jeanne de Navarre and Jeanne d'Evreux, but they depict the preaching of Crusade or acts of charity (such as caring for lepers or burying the dead) rather than actual fighting.[75] In the much longer Life by Guillaume de Saint-Pathus (comprising ninety-two images), Louis is shown in battle in at least one scene, but it represents the occasion of his capture at Damietta.[76] Ultimately the quintessential visual solution to the depiction of the sainted warrior king may be one that Martin Kauffmann has noted: Louis is shown *praying* on horseback.[77] In contrast to the icon of the armed and threatening warrior on horseback, the illustration represents the king seeking

Figure 102. Louis prays on horseback, *Life of Saint Louis by Guillaume de Saint-Pathus,*
Paris, 1330–40. Paris, Bibliothèque nationale, MS fr. 5716, p. 48.
(Cliché Bibliothèque nationale de France)

God's direction in his action (fig. 102; cf. plate 5). He is a reluctant and even gentle
warrior. Although theological dogma, prompted in part by the Crusades, sanctioned
just war, it was nonetheless not fitting to show a saint willingly engaged in the violence of warfare.[78] Here Louis' prayers mitigate and soften his image as knight.

Only in the depiction of the legendary Charlemagne was a sainted ruler allowed
a more enthusiastic pursuit of victory. The Life of Charlemagne, depicted in eight
reliefs on the thirteenth-century reliquary shrine in Aachen, sheds light on the role
of the sainted king at war. Remarkably, the reliefs on the reliquary do not offer evidence of Charlemagne's royalty—certainly, one would expect to see his coronation depicted. It may be that given his fame, his regal qualities were simply assumed.
The narrative begins instead with St. James appearing to the emperor and com-
manding Charlemagne to drive the infidels from the holy site of the Apostle's burial. Ensuing scenes show one already familiar approach to battle: the city of Pamplona falls without bloodshed as a result of Charlemagne's prayers. In another scene,
Charlemagne, fully armed with a shield marked with an eagle, vigorously leads his

Figure 103. Charlemagne leads his troops into battle, Chasse of Charlemagne, thirteenth century. Aachen Cathedral Treasury. (Courtesy Aachen Cathedral Chapter)

troops into a bloody and victorious battle, raising his sword high (fig. 103). Nevertheless, in the same relief, the emperor is also represented piously praying for the knights who have been chosen by God to fall in the battle. Charlemagne is not depicted with a halo in the sequence of reliefs until he expressly receives forgiveness for his sins in the miraculous Mass of St. Aegidius; in the subsequent relief he receives further proof of the righteousness of his deeds by receiving the holy relic of the crown of thorns. Although this narrative surely is an early example of hagiographic support for the glory of chivalry and the sanctity of warfare in service to the mission of the Crusades, it also clearly places limitations on violence: the mission is not chosen but granted, battle is pursued only when necessary, and the fallen are carefully blessed and remembered. Even the scenes themselves are literally ringed with identifying inscriptions that clarify Charlemagne's actions. Nevertheless, the emperor seems to win sainthood through the proper pursuit of the goal of Christian conquest. The legendary Charlemagne may ultimately have served as a better medium through which to introduce new ideas about holy war than the contemporary Louis.

Bearing in mind these general possibilities of the saint's relationship to battle—submission and martyrdom, miraculous avoidance, or the new concept of holy victory through just war—I would like to return to our primary example, the Life of Edmund, to further explore his choice and its narrative implications and representation. Edmund is neither victorious nor, apparently, holy enough to defeat the enemy bloodlessly through miracles: his defeat and slaughter by the Danes were undeniable facts. Edmund's pacifist nature and unsuccessful rule, in fact, disturbed some of his later hagiographers. As Robert Folz has pointed out, both earlier and later versions of the Life have the king fight but rue the bloodshed and therefore end the battle.[79] Because the issue of defeat clearly marks Edmund's Life as that of a failed worldly ruler, Abbo resolutely turns the emphasis of his hagiography away from temporal victory to show that the true significance of Edmund's kingship will be found only in the heavenly kingdom. The illustrations of the Morgan Life pursue this idea as well.

Edmund's ultimate victory is suggested in the depiction of his confrontation with the Danes. Abbo notes Edmund's pacifism and compares his martyrdom to the Passion of Christ, but the miniatures that illustrate Edmund's relations with the Danes do not simply depict a meek martyr. When he receives the demands of Ingvar, for example, Edmund considers them in the manner of a good king: he consults with his advisers, specifically his bishop (figs. 104 and 105). That this duty of the king was particularly important to the monastic producers of hagiographic manuscripts is evident in what the illustrations do and do not depict. The text makes clear that Edmund did not ultimately take the advice of his bishop to capitulate to the Dane's demands, but the miniature does not allude to disagreement. Instead, the depiction emphasizes the prestige and importance of the bishop as the king's adviser and contrasts this consultation with the arrogance of the Danish king on the facing page. The illustrations of the Estoire similarly depict Edward in consultation with his advisers regarding his proposed pilgrimage and his marriage (fig. 106). However, unlike Edmund, Edward always takes the advice of his counselors, even if it goes against his own wishes.[80]

The consequence of Edmund's refusal to capitulate is depicted in the next miniature as he is dragged off to martyrdom. Edmund's reluctant entry into the martyr's arena is far different from that of a typical martyr such as Romanus, Agatha, or Margaret. Romanus leads his captors, ready as a soldier of Christ to enter the fray and to debate the pagan prefect (see fig. 10). Edmund, by contrast, must be forcibly pulled from his throne (fig. 107). Edmund's hesitation, however, should be not interpreted as an expression of cowardice; rather it represents his refusal to abandon

Figure 104. Ingvar threatens East Anglia, *Passion of Edmund, king and martyr,* Bury St. Edmunds, c. 1130. New York, Pierpont Morgan Library, MS M. 736, fol. 10v.

Figure 105. Edmund consults with his bishop, *Passion of Edmund, king and martyr*, Bury St. Edmunds, c. 1130. New York, Pierpont Morgan Library, MS M. 736, fol. 11r.

Figure 106. Edward consults with his nobles about his vow of pilgrimage; two bishops are sent to Rome, *La Estoire de Seint Aedward le Rei,* London or Westminster, 1250. Cambridge, University Library, MS Ee 3.59, fol. 13 v. (Reproduced by permission of the Syndics of Cambridge University Library)

the foundation of his virtue—his place as enthroned king. In order to fulfill his duties to his office, he in fact resists the temptation to surrender to martyrdom. He attempts to retain his throne, although he will not use violence to do so.

After his captors have succeeded in dragging Edmund from his throne, a series of scenes ensue that, through a Christo-mimetic narrative corresponding to Abbo's text, establish the saint's victory in defeat and death. As in the dethronement, these episodes in some respects resemble the events of a martyr's Passion. However, most have some element that particularly suits Edmund's nature as king. When Edmund is led away by his captors (fig. 108), the miniature calls to mind the Psalms' imagery of animalistic tormentors, such as the "dogs that surround me" of Psalm 90, long associated with Christ's Passion.[81] But it is especially Edmund's status as a king (he still wears the crown),[82] and the contrast with his torturers, especially the cretin that spits on him, that makes this scene effective because it is repulsive for the audience. Other scenes of Edmund's torture also recall Christ's Passion. The forced disrobing is cast both as an imitation of Christ and as a symbolic removal of the signs of royal office. Afterwards, Edmund no longer wears his crown (fig. 109).[83] Another torture recalls the flagellation of Christ.[84]

Figure 107. Edmund is pulled from the throne, *Passion of Edmund, king and martyr,*
Bury St. Edmunds, c. 1130. New York, Pierpont Morgan Library, MS M. 736, fol. 12r.

Figure 108. Edmund is mocked and led away by captors, *Passion of Edmund, king and martyr,*
Bury St. Edmunds, c. 1130. New York, Pierpont Morgan Library, MS M. 736, fol. 12v.

Figure 109. Edmund is disrobed, *Passion of Edmund, king and martyr,* Bury St. Edmunds, c. 1130. New York, Pierpont Morgan Library, MS M. 736, fol. 13r.

One last episode in the martyrdom sequence may foreground Edmund's status as a soldier by likening his torture to that of another soldier saint, Sebastian (fig. 110). This miniature, if it is indeed intended to depict Edmund's bravery as a fighting man, is the only specific representation of his courage. However, again, the conventional power and strength of the warrior is denied to Edmund; bound and helpless, he is pierced with arrows. The image reiterates the message that the saint's strength is found in endurance and that only in heaven will he find his victory.

The royal office inherently militates against the imitation of Christ, yet imitate is precisely what Edmund has done. By depicting a king in a position of suffering, however, the Life of Edmund fails to supply a satisfactory model of an effective mundane king. His imitation of Christ has denied him his proper earthly power. The events that follow his martyrdom are those that finally clarify Edmund's power as saint and king, although perhaps in a manner unique among illustrated Lives of kings.

THE POWER OF ROYAL CULT: MIRACLE AND INTERCESSION

Kings are celebrated as saints because of the particular benefits they can offer to their followers. After death, their "kingdoms" might correspond to their original domain but they also rule a much larger and now spiritual realm in tandem with those who care for their bodies and celebrate their memories. The alliance of king and Church is even stronger after death than during the holiest king's life. It is depicted in each of the Lives we have examined.

From the high point of his coronation as a Christian king, Edmund is brought low in defeat by his pagan enemies—his tortured body is discarded, headless, in the wilds of the forest. However, a sequence of scenes in which his head is reunited with his body and placed in a shrine from which he once more rules serves to reestablish his power, now as heavenly king. The sequence derives its effectiveness from a combination of hagiographic and political principles. The retrieval of the saintly body is depicted in four scenes: Edmund's headless body is found; the head is discovered under a bush, protected by a wolf (fig. 111); the head is carried to the body in procession, with the wolf ceremoniously taking part; and finally, the head is perfectly rejoined to the body, with only a red line "like a thread" to indicate that the

Figure 110. Edmund is shot with arrows, *Passion of Edmund, king and martyr,* Bury St. Edmunds, c. 1130. New York, Pierpont Morgan Library, MS M. 736, fol. 14r.

two were ever separated (fig. 112). Each scene is dominated by an enormous and beautifully abstract image of a tree. These trees may represent the forest of Haglesdun, but they also serve as a sign of the uncivilized wilderness (as opposed to the domain of Christian rule and *cultus*), ruled by its "king" the wolf.[85] (A tree also dominates the image of Ingvar [see fig. 104].) With the removal of the body from the wilderness to civilization, the sequence of scenes that follow, which depict the translation procession and the placement of the body in an elaborate shrine within a building representing the abbey,[86] mark the beginning of Edmund's legitimate rule over his people from his rightful place on earth and as a saint in "heavenly glory."[87] The elaborate pictorial emphasis on the reattachment of the saint's head that precedes this restoration scene clearly has multiple meanings. In addition to its immediate significance in depicting the founding of the saint's cult, it is reminiscent of the political and legal metaphor of the ruling head joined to national body. According to this metaphor, only through the careful preservation of the whole and reunified body, that is, through the cult of the saint, will Edmund's subjects be joined as a national community and be served by their martyred "king."[88]

This interpretation, emphasizing Edmund's power amplified through cult, is supported by the curious omission of the most astonishing miracle in Edmund's *vita:* the moment when the king's severed head is graced with the power of speech. In the Morgan miniature, the head is markedly somnolent, the eyes and mouth are resolutely closed (see fig. 111). This passive image contrasts with the depiction of Romanus in his Life, who miraculously continues to praise God after virtually all his organs of speech have been silenced by torture. However, Romanus speaks on behalf of the Church and he speaks in the voice of Christ. In Abbo's text, Edmund instead speaks in the voice of the people. In the Anglo-Saxon vernacular, he shouts out his location: "Her, her, her" (quoted and translated by Abbo into the Latin, "Hic, hic, hic").[89] Abbo attributes the miracle to the "Word," that is, to Christ, but this remarkable event is left entirely unrepresented in the Morgan manuscript. The voice may have attested to the Word, but apparently it did not speak for the Church. That was done by the miracle of *cultus,* the wolf's protection and reverence of the body. It seems likely that Edmund's miraculous speech is silenced in the Morgan manuscript because cult and care for the body, the monastic prerogative, have become more important than the speech of the martyr. Once more, the monks have valued the office and significance of the king, especially in relationship to the Church, as opposed here to any individual example of a miraculous king.

Unlike Edmund, who accomplishes no miracles at all before his death, Edward

Figure 111. Edmund's severed head is discovered protected by a wolf, *Passion of Edmund, king and martyr*, Bury St. Edmunds, c. 1130. New York, Pierpont Morgan Library, MS M. 736, fol. 16r.

Figure 112. Edmund's head is joined perfectly to his body, *Passion of Edmund, king and martyr*,
Bury St. Edmunds, c. 1130. New York, Pierpont Morgan Library, MS M. 736, fol. 17r.

establishes much of the power of his sanctity through the healing and other miracles that he performs before and after death. Indeed, most royal Lives are marked with the miraculous, since even kings who never achieved sanctity often accomplished miracles through the effect of royal sacrality: miracles of the "king's touch," a cure for the skin disease scrofula, appear often in the Lives of French kings; the power to cure was granted to them by their anointment with the miraculous chrism of St. Remi.[90] Kings of other nationalities also had this power, including Edward the Confessor; one such miracle is illustrated in the *Estoire*.[91]

The miracles of the sacral king, however, are distinct from those of the sainted king. Edward's sanctity is signaled in his Life by his ability to cure through the intermediary of water, a miracle that seems to be particularly associated with saints who wield political power in life. In each miraculous instance, Edward washes his hands in a basin and his courtiers surreptitiously allow some person seeking a healing to wash with the water.[92] Gerald of Aurillac often healed his vassals with the same cure. He "refused through humility to lay hands on the sick . . . the sick used to steal the water with which he had washed his hands; and many were cured" (*Gerald*, II:10–13). The miracle is certainly not unique to knights and kings (it also appears in the Life of Amand), but it is particularly associated with Edward and the venue of the court. The miracle speaks to a particular sense of humility in the king or knight who refuses to believe that his sanctity can perform miracles yet at the same time allows that sanctity to benefit his followers.

Another royal act, not itself a miracle but associated with many miracles in Lives of kings, is that of pilgrimage. Pilgrimage had imperial associations that can be traced back to the Roman empress Helena, but it gained power as a *topos* indicating piety through the pilgrimage "habit" of early English kings and the renown of the legendary voyage of Charlemagne to Jerusalem (an important prototype for the Crusaders).[93] Both saintly and nonsaintly kings followed such models in taking up the crusade. Others went on "pilgrimage" to Rome or elsewhere.[94]

Although pilgrimage does not take place in the Lives of Edward or Edmund, Edward does vow to make a pilgrimage, and it is that vow that drives much of the narrative. His barons ask him to forego his promise (arguing that he is needed in his kingdom); as an act of pious substitution Edward proposes to rebuild Westminster, asking papal sanction for the remission of his vow. Eventually St. Peter himself blesses the endeavor by miraculously consecrating the church in person. Furthermore, the famous episode of the ring seems to serve as a "crypto" pilgrimage in the narrative. Edward gives a ring as charity to a beggar, and two Jerusalem pilgrims

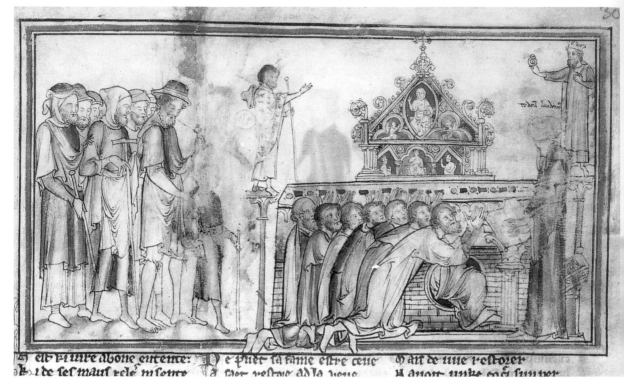

return it—they had been given it, miraculously, in the Holy Land by St. John, one of Edward's patron saints. This episode is the most famous single event from the Life of Edward. It was even represented by a pair of sculptures at the Westminster shrine (fig. 113).[95] Furthermore, the ring itself became, in legend, the coronation ring of Edward and a relic and focus of devotion at Westminster.[96] Thus, even if Edward was unable to go on pilgrimage, his efforts to do so were miraculously blessed by his special patrons, John and Peter.

Kings such as Edward had patrons that were important in their Lives; to what extent were kings effective patrons themselves? Although there are many similarities in the narrative construction of their Lives, the kings we are examining differ widely in terms of the potential power and character of their intercession, depending on

Figure 114. The death of Edward; Edward's soul is presented to Christ by St. Peter and
St. John, *La Estoire de Seint Aedward le Rei,* London or Westminster, 1250. Cambridge,
University Library, MS Ee 3.59, fol. 29r. (Reproduced by permission of the Syndics
of Cambridge University Library)

the origin of their sanctity as either martyr or confessor. Confessor kings seem to
be constrained by certain limitations. While other saints travel to Paradise in the
arms of angels, at their deaths confessor kings and knights require the further assistance of a saintly intercessor. Gerald holds St. Peter's hand as he climbs the stair-
way to Paradise (*Gerald,* IV:5). In the miniature of his death in the *Estoire,* Peter and
John intercede before Christ on Edward's behalf (fig. 114). Furthermore, until Louis,
the cults of royal confessors were not widely observed. That of Edward, for example, was largely dependent on royal ceremonial at Westminster.

In contrast, the martyr Edmund enjoyed a vigorous cult as a powerful intercessor. The last scene of his life is remarkable (see fig. 95). Although it has sometimes

been described as an ascension to heaven, it has eluded description as an illustration of a particular text. It seems, instead, to be a representation of the permanent heavenly status of the *saint* Edmund. He is received in heaven and crowned by the hands of angels but his feet remain on earth, venerated and kissed by two monks of Bury St. Edmunds. The picture could not reveal more effectively the full presence of the saint in his relics (and the effective *cultus* of the monks).

Of particular interest, however, is the coronation regalia that the angels bestow on Edmund. He receives the martyr's palm but also a scepter. He again appears in his coronation robes, and furthermore, rather than the simple fillet of the martyr, his crown looks distinctly imperial.[97] English kings were in the habit of giving their crowns to the abbey of Bury St. Edmunds (although they often ransomed them back for a high price).[98] Similarly, other kings donated their crowns to other churches, as if royal crowns, first put in place by bishops, were properly the property of the Church. Indeed, coronation churches such as Reims and Westminster had the privilege of holding the national regalia.[99]

The Morgan image, however, surely is more than a simple reflection of a specific crown, cult customs, or an attempt to explain the origin of the regalia. St. Wenceslas (fig. 115), also a martyred king and the Bohemian national patron saint, similarly wears an elaborate and distinctive crown in one of three illustrations in a tenth-century *libellus* in Wolfenbüttel.[100] In both cases, these crowns may be intended to represent the particular crown of a nation. The focus on politics and nation in the introductory illustrations of the Life of Edmund and in certain of his unillustrated miracles suggests that Edmund's crown is meant to signify his status as spiritual king of the English. Just as the hagiography of bishops developed a geography of Europe that focused on the episcopal city or territory, so the hagiography of kings focuses on the emerging concept and geography of nation. Edmund is a king of a "people," no matter how murky that notion may be.[101] Thus, at the same time that the image of Edmund seems unlimited in power and glory, Edmund's crown may imply that the sphere of his saintly influence is circumscribed by virtue of its association with nation—a limitation that never applies to a martyr's simple fillet.

CONCLUSION

Like the Lives of other saints, a king's Life was constructed to create a sufficient picture of sanctity. The Lives of Edward and Edmund despite their obvious differ-

Figure 115. Wenceslaus is crowned by Christ; Emma kisses his feet, *Life of Wenceslaus*, Bohemia (Prague?), before 1006. Wolfenbüttel, Herzog August Bibliothek, Cod. Guelf. II.2 Augusteus 4., fol. 18v.

ences, show striking similarities in their narrative strategies for such construction. Both Lives emphasize royal authority established through legitimate coronation at the hands of clerics. One of the two kings is anointed. Both kings scrupulously fulfill their office, which includes such duties to the people as charity, mercy, and protection of the poor. Both consult with clergy and attempt to maintain peace. Edward the Confessor's court is the picture of harmony, and he is a model of royal deportment. Edmund tenaciously clings to his duties and his throne even when threatened with death. Although the martyr Edmund refuses to fight, loses his kingdom, and is ultimately murdered, in the end it is demonstrated that his spiritual power as a saint is far greater than that of any worldly prince.

Nevertheless, at the same time that the Life of Edmund asserts confidence in the saint's power and prestige, it also reveals a peculiar and consistent limitation of that power. In the image of coronation, the anointing that would have made the king a sacred person regardless of personal saintly qualities and acts is not included. The king does not perform miracles while alive. The miraculous speech of the head of the king is silenced in preference for a glorification of cult. Finally, the ornate crown that seems to promise such far-reaching, even imperial power, may ultimately be limiting, in contrast with the universality of the martyr's crown. That royal power in the Lives of royal saints is so circumscribed may say something about the audience for royal hagiography. The readers and viewers of these Lives, although they included pilgrims, women, and monks, were clearly intended also to include kings.[102] In their efforts to shape and control the behavior of kings using hagiography, clerical writers and illustrators may have felt a need to supply restraints even for their own saintly creations—mundane power needed a constant check, even in the heavenly court.

Ultimately, kings would have found the clerical recommendations for royal action an uncomfortable fit, especially the proscription of violence. To find a suitable saintly role to emulate, kings of the thirteenth century and after, such as Louis, had to turn elsewhere. In part they turned to the well-established and more practical model of the saintly queen. In part they made use of the doctrines of just war created to facilitate the Crusades. Finally, they turned to the model of the chivalrous knight, a concept forged in a complex cultural mix of hagiography, legend, and romance. It is precisely this model that begins to find a place in the thirteenth-century hagiography of Matthew Paris.

THE LIVES OF CONFESSORS
Nuns and Queens

လာ

With [Radegund's] holy right hand she would protect her monastery with the sign
of the cross. Once while the blessed woman was making this sign, one of the sisters saw
a thousand thousand demons standing on top of the wall in the form of goats. When
the saint raised her blessed right hand in the sign of the cross, this whole multitude
of demons fled, never to be seen again.

—*The Life of Radegund,* trans. Jo Ann McNamara and John E. Halborg

THE HOLIEST WOMEN of the Church were virgins, for they produced "fruit a
hundredfold."[1] However, their prodigious and powerful sanctity, which derived from
the sacrifice of their bodies, remained almost entirely exemplary. If they were able
to drive off the many demons that threatened their purity, it was only by the de-
fensive performance of the sign of the cross. In contrast, holy female confessors,
although not as highly ranked in the saintly hierarchy, were able to enlarge their
sphere of influence and multiply the types and extent of their saintly powers.

In the miracle recounted in the epigraph, the Merovingian queen Radegund's
power is clearly amplified beyond control of the body, even if the cloister wall has
defined a new boundary.[2] During her earthly life, Radegund is able both to exploit
her status as a queen and to exercise a saintly power that derives from her vows.
Only in posthumous miracles, however, is her royal power fully joined with her
saintly power. Radegund's illustrated *vita* will serve as our primary example of a
woman confessor's Life, not only because of its own particular interest, but also because it became a model for the Lives of other women.[3]

Women other than virgin martyrs do not appear frequently in pictorial hagiography of the high Middle Ages. One reason is that the manuscripts of most saints'
vitae represent the efforts of monasteries to celebrate their local patron and to encourage pilgrimage. Few women's monasteries had the uninterrupted prosperity

that men's foundations often enjoyed, and founder's relics of longstanding veneration were rare. Furthermore, claustration seems largely to have prevented women
from participating in the economic life of the outside world, such as the economic
exchanges of saints' cults and pilgrimage, of which the creation of manuscripts
formed a part.[4] The absence of images of nuns or other nonmartyred female saints
in such manuscripts is for those reasons not surprising.

The outstanding exception, the eleventh-century illustrated Life of Radegund,
was apparently produced at an uncommon institution, the monastery of Sainte-
Croix in Poitiers. The book celebrates the life and certain relics of the monastery's
sainted founder and Merovingian queen (although in fact her corporeal relics were
not housed in the monastery).[5] Like the types of king and monk, the female confessor represented by Radegund, whether we class her as nun or queen, does not
conform in either text or illustrations to a well-established set of characteristics. Instead, the Life takes shape in a play of expectations between other types. Fortunatus, writing the Life of Radegund in the late sixth century, and Baudonivia, writing
another version shortly thereafter, relied on the Lives of bishops, kings, monks, and
others for inspiration. Nevertheless, Radegund's Life eventually became a type in
itself and a model for later women's Lives, especially those of queens.

The artist of the Poitiers manuscript, working five centuries after the text was
written, benefited from these developments. The artist's selection of scenes focuses
and condenses the textual tradition and by supplementing it with a more developed
conception of female sanctity, produces an eloquent series of images of female leadership and piety.

CHARACTERISTICS OF WOMEN CONFESSORS: TEXTS

Distinguishing the gender-specific qualities of women confessors is rendered difficult
by the cultural differences that separate the present-day audience from the works
in which these figures are portrayed. However, exemplary textual and historical
scholarship has examined the typology of women confessors in some detail, and
the results of these studies can be brought to bear on the question of their pictorial representation.

In her assessment of the gender-specific characteristics of Carolingian Lives of
women saints, Julia Smith begins by establishing the works' reliance on masculine

models and in doing so identifies several characteristics that came to distinguish the female confessor. Chastity, of course, was the foremost virtue of these saints, as it also was for male saints. However, Smith shows that, unlike her male counterparts, in achieving her virtues the female confessor did not reject her family but instead relied upon it for much of her success. Furthermore, her spirituality was characteristically intimate and personal and often centered on visionary experiences, in contrast with the male saint's public and institutional efforts.[6]

Seeking similarly distinctive traits characterizing the Lives of queens, Jo Ann McNamara has traced a tradition of royal Christian service extending from Helena, the mother of Constantine, into the high Middle Ages. Indeed, the texts take pains to establish a spiritual lineage of saintly queens.[7] McNamara has argued that queens are associated with virtues of mercy; specifically, they mediate the severity of their warrior husbands. The office of king obligated a ruler to protect his kingdom through acts of warfare, in which loot was acquired and prisoners were captured. In hagiography, the saintly queen's function was to redistribute this treasure to the poor and sick and to win the release of the prisoners.[8] Last, but by no means least, in those areas not yet Christian, the queen served through her pious example to convert the king to Christianity or to turn him from heretical doctrines such as Arianism to orthodoxy.[9] If he was Christian, the queen recalled her consort to his Christian duty.

In a treatment of queens from a somewhat later period, Patrick Corbet argues that an alternate type of the saintly queen as mother of a dynasty was well established by the year 1000 through the example of the saintly Ottonian empresses, including Adelaide and Mathilda.[10] He notes that Mathilda, although initially resistant to her marriage, comes to accept it and serves as an exemplary mother.[11] With the Life of Margaret of Scotland, the education of children began to find an important place in queens' Lives.[12] In the Life of Adelaide, however, Corbet finds a notion of sanctity that is not entirely based on its subject's role as wife and mother. Like many saints, Adelaide imitates Christ in her suffering, and her hagiographer characterizes such suffering as particularly royal: because she has suffered with Christ, Adelaide will reign with him (see 2 Tim. 2:12).[13] The comparison of the imperial court to the court of heaven is not unprecedented.[14] Baudonivia claims that Radegund collected relics into her own earthly but simultaneously heavenly "court," and Notker compares Charlemagne's court to the heavenly host.[15] Nevertheless, underlying the elaborations of such courtly imagery, Corbet maintains that ultimately royal sanctity is founded on humility.[16]

Claustration is necessarily a common (and essential) element in the Lives of nuns, but its character and meaning are linked to historical particularities. McNamara, for example, argues that nun's Lives show that women might use claustration as a means of protection.[17] Most of the royal saints considered by Susan Ridyard find their sanctity within monasteries.[18] In fact, despite much legislation intended to strengthen claustration, practice clearly allowed a semipermeable wall. Early medieval women's monasteries even served as bases for missionaries to "refuel," providing necessities such as food and books, and serving as hospitals for the sick.[19] On the other hand, living the life of "angels" within their monasteries, cloistered nuns could not serve as active proselytizers for the Church through worldly contact; rather, in their isolation, they were "living sermons" for the faith.[20]

A few further notes about gender-specific imagery in hagiography can be added to these observations. Medieval descriptions of secular women (and of royal women in particular) often stress their subjects' tastes for lavish jewelry and dress.[21] Women saints, by contrast, traditionally eschew personal ornament. The humble clothing that female saints choose to wear is often noted in their *vitae*, whether by other characters or by the hagiographers themselves. Although at times they concede to the demands of custom,[22] saintly women abjure the lavish clothing that would have served to enhance their beauty and status. Furthermore, their Lives are often filled with records of gifts of luxurious cloth and gems that they conspicuously remove from their bodies and donate to serve as ornament for churches, especially altars.[23] Sometimes this sort of gift is a product of the saints' own hands; saintly women are often characterized as weavers or embroiderers.[24] Finally, like virgin saints, women confessors are particularly associated with the sign of the cross, a gesture that renders their unadorned bodies, and particularly their hands, holy and powerful.

In some ways, these patterns of female sanctity—rejection of the world, humility, imitation of Christ and other saints, protection through the sign of the cross—are plainly reminiscent of the type of the virgin martyr. Nevertheless, the Lives of women confessors contain far more activity than the Lives of passive, suffering virgin saints. Indeed, hagiographers such as Fortunatus are fond of likening their heroines to Martha, who, of course, stands as the epitome of the active life.[25]

These gender-specific traits are characteristic of the long history of the Lives of royal and monastic women. Certainly, conventions of behavior changed between the sixth and the thirteenth century, but idealized, holy Lives did not change as quickly as did historical lives. Although typological differences are evident in the course of medieval hagiography, the elements that marked the individual as a saint remained to a large extent constant. Although, as an illustrated *vita*, the Life of Radegund is to some extent an isolated case, it exemplifies many of the qualities that we have just noted. Furthermore, an examination of the Life of Elisabeth of Hungary from her reliquary shrine in Marburg will help to further expand and solidify our understanding of the type of the female royal saint.

CONSTRUCTING THE NARRATIVE
OF A QUEEN'S LIFE: THE RADEGUND *LIBELLUS*

The twenty surviving miniatures of the eleventh-century Poitiers manuscript that illustrate Fortunatus's Life of Radegund include both half- and full-page illustrations; most of them appear at the chapter heads. Magdalena Carrasco has convincingly established that the manuscript was made at and intended to celebrate the *locus sanctus* of Radegund's monastery of Sainte-Croix.[26] To fulfill this purpose, the manuscript gives a particular shape to the Life of a holy woman, characterizing her as a powerful patron on behalf of her foundation.

Many of the gender-specific characteristics found in the text of the Life of Radegund are emphasized in the episodes selected for illustration. The pictures that illustrate her career as consort focus on a queen's Christian virtues: Radegund frees prisoners and brings her influence to bear on her husband Clothar's Christian conscience. In the next phase of her Life, having been ordained as a deaconess by Medard of Soissons, Radegund follows the example of Martha, serving humbly among the poor and the sick. Paradoxically, it is only after her claustration within the monastery that she founded as queen that Radegund's living power assumes its full expression. Her "holy right hand" is graced with miraculous powers of healing and can even resuscitate the dead. Finally, upon her death Radegund miraculously assumes the duties and authority of a powerful regent in her own right; she commands the building of shrines, the obedience of lords, and, again, the release of prisoners.

Radegund's relatively short Life offers us the opportunity to follow a narrative from beginning to end. An examination of the miniatures in sequence shows how the illustrations express the inherent conflicts that separate powerful queen from humble saint. The visual narrative of the Life of Radegund poses problems and, in succession, both refines and resolves them.

Tracing its subject's unwilling initiation into the role of queen, the first miniature of the *vita* (fig. 116) conveniently makes no reference to the massacre of Radegund's royal family in Thuringia and moves directly to the presentation of the young
girl as "part of the plunder." "Falling to the lot of . . . King Clothar," Radegund is
taken to a royal villa, where she is raised. There she speaks of her wish to be a martyr, cares for the other children, carries a cross, and frequently prays, displaying "the
merits of a mature person."[27] As shown in the lower portion of the first miniature,
"Radegund herself would polish the pavement with her dress and, collecting the
drifting dust around the altar in a napkin, reverently placed it outside the door rather
than sweep it away."[28]

The artist has focused on the young virgin's acceptance of her fate. As she is taken
off to the villa in the upper register of the miniature, she makes a gesture of acceptance. Another hand gesture, however—that of the king's man—makes an important point about the holy maiden's status: she is acquiescing against her will.
The gesture of a man grasping a woman's wrist has been shown to represent rape
or, at least, ownership.[29] In the Lives of virgins, the same gesture visually defines
them as unwilling victims when they are brought before their accusers.

In the second miniature of the Life (fig. 117), Radegund agrees to marry Clothar
but continues her life as a Christian, raising the crucial issue of her dual status as
religious yet royal. We are told that although a queen, Radegund refused to dress
or eat richly, prayed often, and frequently left the marriage bed. The artist has added
a somewhat implausible scene (given Radegund's status as war plunder) that expresses an undercurrent in many of the Lives of holy queens: the conflict between
saintliness and marriage. In the first compartment of the miniature, Radegund and
Clothar are engaged in vivid conversation, gesturing and looking directly at one another: Radegund seems to be negotiating the terms of her office as queen. These
negotiations may concern the queen's willingness to share the marriage bed.

Below, in one of the most humorous of medieval images (at least for the modern viewer), Clothar seems to be having second thoughts. While his wife "would
prostrate herself in prayer . . . so long that the cold pierced her through and through
and only her spirit was warm. Her whole flesh prematurely dead, indifferent to her
body's torment," Clothar is provoked to "harsher irritation."[30] The artist has caught
a very real pained weariness on Clothar's face, which contrasts with Radegund's
"frozen" yet pious expression.

In the next miniature, the first of several selected to illustrate saintly qualities
of charity and humility. Queen Radegund calls for the release of prisoners and

Figure 116. Radegund before Chlothar; Radegund in her oratory, *Life of Radegund of Poitiers*, Poitiers, Sainte-Croix, c. 1050–1100. Poitiers, Médiathèque François-Mitterrand, MS 250, fol. 22v.

Figure 117. Radegund at a feast; Radegund leaves her bed to pray, *Life of Radegund of Poitiers,*
Poitiers, Sainte-Croix, c. 1050–1100. Poitiers, Médiathèque François-Mitterrand,
MS 250, fol. 24r.

eventually obtains the benefice through a miracle—the chains fall from the prisoners' hands. Here Radegund is acting like a queen, but the source of power she displays is heavenly rather than mundane.

After the scenes depicting her marriage and her first act of charity, Radegund enters the monastery, but to understand the representation of her ordination, differences between the text and illustrations must be underlined. In the next, unillustrated but decisive event in the text, Radegund's husband Clothar kills her brother.[31] The saint flees the court and escapes to Noyon, where she demands that Bishop Medard allow her to accept vows of chastity. Medard hesitates, threatened by certain nobles. Finally, Radegund decisively "entered the sacristy, put on a monastic garb and proceeded straight to the altar."[32] Medard concedes and ordains her as a deaconess.

The text casts Radegund's ordination as a narrative of decisive, even headstrong, action; the accompanying miniature, by contrast, presents a static equation, emphasizing Radegund's exchange of crown and power for veil and servitude (fig. 118). In the upper register, composed without the architectural surround that designates an ecclesiastical setting, the queen seems to be Medard's equal. The noblemen who, in the text, "drag and harass" the bishop here merely whisper in his ear. The only physical contact occurs between Radegund and the man behind her, who tries to restrain the queen, and her stance is the only active element of this illustration. Perhaps she is meant to be running to the bishop, demanding his help, an allusion to the monastic *topos* of running toward Christ (see pp. 182–83). Below, however, the secular stage has been replaced by the holy space of the altar. Medard and Radegund are alone, and all action is stilled. Radegund humbly kneels before the bishop to receive his blessing. The image emphasizes a dramatic change in the queen's status—from secular to sacred, from active to contemplative, and from powerful to humble.

One strategy for representing this change lies in the artist's depiction of costume. In an image that evokes the many instances of exchange and donation of ornament documented in her written Life, the Queen is shown giving up her golden garments and crown and kneeling before a draped altar. Here a blue veil symbolizes her new status, as a woman consecrated to God. In each of the scenes in which she is depicted as queen, Radegund was represented wearing a long gold dress; however, as Fortunatus tells us, "soon she divested herself of the noble costume which she was wont to wear as Queen."[33] The miniature that depicts Radegund's ordination is exceptional in showing its subject dressed in muted purple with gold edging and

Figure 118. Radegund takes the veil, *Life of Radegund of Poitiers,* Poitiers, Sainte-Croix, c. 1050–1100. Poitiers, Médiathèque François-Mitterrand, MS 250, fol. 27v.

wearing a blue veil. In the scenes that follow, a new locus for gold ornament appears; after her initiation, the veil of consecration is consistently depicted as gold.[34]

The next scene returns to acts of mercy, as Radegund humbly feeds and serves the poor as well as washes their feet. These scenes, of course, allude both to Christ's washing the feet of the Apostles and to Mary and Martha's care for Christ. Magdalena Carrasco emphasizes the quasi-liturgical quality of Radegund's actions. In particular, Radegund's washing of the feet of the poor using a gold-colored chalicelike vessel is reminiscent of the monastic *mandatum*. Although the scene has evident links to monastic duties, it must be emphasized that Radegund, although ordained, has not yet retired to a monastery. Despite chronological confusion (perhaps provoked by the fact that Radegund is referred to as washing the feet of the poor on five different occasions in the two Lives, both before and after she founds her monastery), this illustration is clearly placed before her claustration and therefore may refer to Radegund's actions on behalf of paupers or lepers.[35] It would seem that the artist has chosen to depict this activity at this point in the narrative because of its public nature and also because it is not miraculous—no healings are implied.[36]

In the next miniature (fig. 119), Radegund goes into seclusion. Fortunatus asks rhetorically: "Weren't there such great gatherings of people on the day that the saint determined to seclude herself that those who could not be contained in the streets climbed up to fill the roofs?"[37] The artist depicts a crowd, but these people are not passive onlookers: they seem to follow in a procession that Radegund boldly leads. With a great stride, she climbs up into her cell. The short flight of stairs leading upward recalls similar symbolic ascents by martyrs (see fig. 13) and reinforces the textual analogy of the cell to a prison, tower, or even tomb.[38] The saint bids farewell to her followers, looking back over her shoulder.

A reference to the royal imagery of *adventus* seems to be intended. The *adventus* ritual, which marked the movements of late Antique emperors, survived in various ceremonies well into the Middle Ages and is depicted in the Lives of kings. The emperor's *adventus* to a country or city signaled its rebirth into well-being.[39] Similarly, Radegund's entrance into her cloister seems to imply rebirth for the saint and her community. She begins a new life by entering a symbolic tomb.[40] Dead to the old world, she is powerfully alive in a new life. Once more, she moves "swiftly" (as the active figure in the miniature implies), running to enter the monastic life.

Hereafter, Radegund's actions are restricted; they occur behind monastic walls. Apparently, however, in exchange for her freedom, the saint is granted tremendous power. She even disdains the abbacy to follow a monastic *topos,* "reserving no

Figure 119. Radegund enters the cloister, *Life of Radegund of Poitiers*, Poitiers, Sainte-Croix, c. 1050–1100. Poitiers, Médiathèque François-Mitterrand, MS 250, fol. 31v.

authority of her own in order to follow the footsteps of Christ more swiftly and heap up more for herself in Heaven the more she freed herself from the world."[41] In the lower portion of the miniature, Radegund's new piety and power are epitomized. Her commitments to fasting, prayers, faith, and seclusion allow her to experience her full saintly power. The saint gazes steadfastly toward an altar while encased in a set of three iron circlets that bind her body so tightly that, as the text specifies, the flesh swells to meet around them.[42] At the same time that she inflicts hardship on her body, her mind fills with faith. She achieves true wisdom, represented by the book she is shown holding—the first such representation, although the Life mentions her literacy in its first pages. The hand that holds the book is wrapped in gold cloth (as Bishop Medard's was wrapped on fol. 27v). It is the "holy right hand" that will work the series of uninterrupted miracles that follow.[43] These miracles "told the story that she herself would have kept hidden," that is, the story of her sanctity and power within her community.[44]

In a series of miracles that follow, Radegund cures the blind, the possessed, and the sick. Within the confines of the convent wall, her gestures mimic episcopal gestures of anointing, blessing, and even baptism.[45] Occasionally she holds a book. The opening on folios 34v–35r (plate 7) is typical. In each of two scenes, Radegund leans out of her cell to make a gesture of blessing, curing women of possession and madness in the presence of witnesses. Although these images of healing miracles vary in detail, Radegund's role remains the same; it is the circumscription of her actions that requires comment.

Radegund's hands are depicted as sharing the healing power of those of a bishop, but in her case that power is carefully limited. The miracle illustrations seem to argue that Radegund's power is bounded by the walls of the monastery itself. It is as if Radegund acquires her power not as bishops do, from a direct link descending from the right hand of God and through participation in the liturgy, but from her association—even *identification*—with the Cross and its relic that was, not coincidentally, housed in the monastery of Sainte-Croix.

We learn from Baudonivia's (unillustrated) Life that Radegund had been successful in petitioning the Byzantine emperor and acquiring a relic of the Cross. The acquisition of that relic serves to link Radegund with an important earlier queen: "Like Saint Helena, imbued with wisdom, full of the fear of God, glorious with good works, she eagerly sought to salute the wood where the ransom of the world was hung for our salvation that we might be snatched from the power of the devil. . . . What Helena did in oriental lands, Radegund the blessed did in Gaul!"[46]

Originating in the story of a relic housed in the monastery, Radegund's association with the sign of the cross is here firmly linked to her glory of "good works" and desire to defeat the "power of the devil." Once more, as in the Lives of Margaret and other virgins, the power of the cross originates in the virtuous body that imitates Christ, but now that power is also reinforced by the presence of a mighty relic. The saint's many acts of miraculous healing take place in the cloister where the virtue of the holy woman's body is strongest and most clearly apparent.

The series of miracles in Radegund's Life, for the most part depicted in half-page miniatures, culminates in the three final full-page images of the Life. In the first of these, Radegund's fellow nuns interrupt her in prayer. The second represents Radegund's last (and most important) miraculous healing. The third depicts a miracle on the occasion of her death. These three scenes are crucial to understanding the full meaning of the Life.

The curious scene of Radegund's interrupted meditations (fig. 120) itself interrupts the series of illustrated miracles. Describing the episode, Fortunatus writes: "One evening as the twilight cast its shadows, the layfolk were singing noisy songs near the monastery as they danced around, accompanied by musicians with cithars." A nun mentions the singing and Radegund replies, "God witness that I have heard nothing of any worldly song." Fortunatus concludes: "Thus it was obvious that though her flesh remained in the world, her spirit was already in Heaven."[47] Although the dancing and singing disturbed the other nuns, Radegund has heard none of it. All her senses are directed heavenward.

For the medieval audience, this episode would have been far from anecdotal, for it clearly demonstrates not only Radegund's monastic practice of solitary prayer but also the perfection of her soul. The image gives evidence of this significant saintly achievement. Radegund's senses have been "remade" to the extent that they admit only the heavenly. The perfection of the senses is reminiscent of the sanctity associated with the genre of the virgin saint, but in this context it is more than a passive corporeal model: it is the foundation for saintly power and action. In this way, the function of these perfected senses resembles that of the visions of Benedict.[48] Radegund's hard-won perfection signifies that she is ready to ascend to heaven, but first her sanctity and power will be revealed even more completely in the last miracle of her life. That miracle is the rarest and most esteemed of saintly wonders, a resurrection, which Fortunatus compares to the renowned miracle of the "blessed Martin."[49]

We learn from the text that the young sister of one of the nuns has died. Hearing

Figure 120. Radegund engrossed in her prayers, *Life of Radegund of Poitiers,* Poitiers, Sainte-Croix, c. 1050–1100. Poitiers, Médiathèque François-Mitterrand, MS 250, fol. 40r.

the nun weeping, Radegund takes pity on her and asks that the corpse be brought into her cell. There, the saint "handled the corpse of the dead little girl for seven hours. But seeing a faith He could not deny, Christ utterly restored her health. When the saint rose from prayer, the infant rose from the dead."[50] In the miniature, the decidedly mature and somewhat stiff girl is lowered feet-first into the confines of the saint's cell (fig. 121). In a departure from the events described in the text, at the moment of the girl's revival Radegund turns from her prayers, the two figures lock gazes, and Radegund grasps the girl's hand with her right hand. It is as if Radegund were pulling the girl from her death back to life using the same gesture that Christ used when he saved the souls of the dead in the harrowing of hell. The identical gesture is also used at times by sainted bishops in resuscitating the dead. In an illustration from the Weissenau Passional (fig. 122), Bishop Hilary uses his left hand to grasp a resurrected infant and holds a crozier with his right hand. Through the liturgical implement, Hilary's right hand serves as a conduit for heavenly power; Radegund's right hand, by contrast, works through touch—a more direct indication of the perfection of her saintly body.[51]

With the final and greatest miracle of her life complete and her earthly journey at its conclusion, Radegund "migrated from earth."[52] On that same day a tribune named Domnolenus dreams of the saint's journey. He "seemed to see the saint approach his town in state," again like a queen making an *adventus*. The saint asks two favors of the tribune—that he restore a shrine to Martin in his town and that he release certain prisoners. In exchange, Radegund cures the tribune's "wasting disease" by stroking Domnolenus's jaws and throat with her right hand. In the upper register of the last miniature of the cycle (fig. 123), the artist depicts Radegund pointing to the foundation of the oratory as revealed in the dream. In the lower register, Radegund and Domnolenus lock gazes and she cups his chin with her right hand as she points to the prisoners to be released in exchange for her gift of healing.

The gesture that Radegund makes with her right hand, "chin-chucking," is one that has aroused a certain amount of comment in art historical literature. Leo Steinberg, in his *Sexuality of Christ in Renaissance Art and in Modern Oblivion,* sees an erotic motif in depictions of the infant Christ making such a gesture toward his mother. Certainly these caresses to some degree encompass the sexual nature of human interaction, but as they appear in the Life of Christ and saints' *vitae,* they are not primarily erotic.[53] Gertrude of Nivelles, one of the foremost abbess saints of the early Middle Ages, makes the same gesture in the Weissenau Passional as she cures a girl of blindness (fig. 124).[54] In that miniature—a single epitomizing image at the head

Figure 121. Radegund revives a dead girl, *Life of Radegund of Poitiers,* Poitiers, Sainte-Croix, c. 1050–1100. Poitiers, Médiathèque François-Mitterrand, MS 250, fol. 41r.

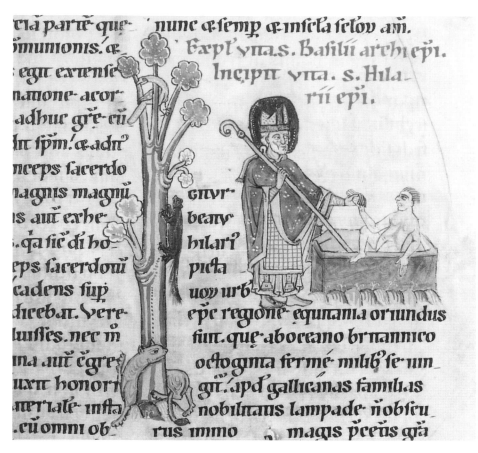

Figure 122. Bishop Hilary revives a dead infant, *Weissenau Passional,* twelfth century.
Geneva, Bibliotheca Bodmeriana, Cod. Bodmer 127, fol. 144r.

of the saint's Life—Gertrude cups the girl's chin with her left hand and signs the blessing with her right. The text of the Life of Gertrude recounts the saint's posthumous healing of a blind girl at her shrine (the girl is healed by lying on the saint's bed, preserved as a relic).[55] Because Gertrude worked no healing miracles during her life, presumably the artist of the Passional chose to represent the saint herself instead of her shrine in order to show her personal power.

In both of these healing miracles, the dead saint makes a very human, even tender, gesture. If anything, the gesture should be characterized as motherly. It is as if the saint claims the soul of the healed person as her own offspring in exchange for her role in leading it toward God. Similarly, the gesture of the infant Christ caressing

THE LIVES OF CONFESSORS

Figure 123. Radegund appears to Domnolenus and cures him, *Life of Radegund of Poitiers,*
Poitiers, Sainte-Croix, c. 1050–1100. Poitiers, Médiathèque François-Mitterrand,
MS 250, fol. 42r.

Figure 124. Gertrude of Nivelles cures a blind girl, *Weissenau Passional,*
twelfth century. Geneva, Bibliotheca Bodmeriana, Cod. Bodmer 127, fol. 176r.

his mother's chin reveals his love while paradoxically reversing the valence of the parental bond. Certainly there is something of Steinberg's "communion of souls" in this spiritual union of the saint or Christ with a petitioner. Rather than eroticism, however, this is a uniquely tender vision of saintly intercession.[56]

With regard to the structure of the Life's narrative, even more significant than the healing miracle in this last scene is Radegund's visitation to Domnolenus on the day of her death. The vision of a saint at the time of his or her death is a miraculous confirmation of the soul's ascent to heaven as well as a mark of the witnessing soul's sanctity. Benedict sees Germanus's soul ascend to heaven (fig. 125), and two monks in different places witness the ascent of Benedict's soul. Anthony watches Amun ascend.[57] On the day of her death, Gertrude of Nivelles is seen by a nun at a distant monastery.[58] Aldegundis is a witness to the ascension of Amand

Figure 125. Benedict has a vision of the death of Germanus, *Monte Cassino Lectionary*, Monte Cassino, c. 1070. Vatican Library Lat. 1202, fol. 79v. (© Biblioteca Apostolica Vaticana)

(see plate 3). Such sightings represent a common *topos* of sanctity. The vision of Radegund on her journey heavenward attests to the queen's sanctity and to her place in heaven.

Furthermore, in depicting Radegund's posthumous miracle, the miniature suddenly resituates the saint's actions beyond the walls of her monastery and places her back into the public and political sphere that she abandoned by entering into seclusion. Activities associated with a queen's public exercise of her office—sponsoring shrines, freeing prisoners, and keeping company with powerful men—are all activities that Radegund gave up during her cloistered life, according to her pictorial hagiography. It is only with her death that, in this final scene, Radegund resumes her full powers as a saintly queen.[59] The transformation offers a more expansive promise to the manuscript's audience. A powerful patron with full command of saintly and royal powers, firmly ensconced among the blessed in heaven, offers unlimited benefits to her monastic community and pilgrim petitioners.

The manuscript illuminations of Radegund's cloistered life demonstrate several of the qualities that scholars have identified as characteristic of women's Lives. In particular, her Life was largely private. Radegund turns her back on wealth and power in favor of humility, service, and the veil of a nun. She accomplishes her miracles primarily in the monastery and limits her charity to the local poor and sick. Her piety produces visions, as detailed in the textual Life but not in the miniatures, perhaps because of losses in the manuscript,[60] although she does achieve a certain mystic perfection during her earthly life as pictured in the interruption of her prayers in the second-to-last miniature. Radegund, however, clearly exceeds a typical woman's Life in her final miracle of the resurrection of a child.

What of the saint as queen? The cycle of another royal saint, illustrated in the thirteenth-century shrine of Elisabeth of Hungary in her church in Marburg, points to several continuities with the Life of Radegund in its images of the spiritual power of royal women saints.[61]

ELISABETH OF HUNGARY

It is clear from the form and ornament of the reliquary shrine of Elisabeth that the saint is meant to be shown taking her place within the larger edifice of the Church. The shrine is shaped like a church, and its primary faces are covered with portraits of the apostles and Christ. Mary and the Christ child adorn one end, and Elisabeth sits at the other. On the roof of the shrine-church, eight arches enclose narrative scenes dedicated to Elisabeth's Life—four to a side, each side reading from right to left, beginning on the back of the shrine and continuing to the front.

Perhaps the most remarkable quality of these narrative scenes of Elisabeth's Life is the absence of miracles.[62] Instead of the miraculous, the reliefs focus on Elisabeth's family and charities. The first relief shows Elisabeth's husband, Landgraf Ludwig, confirmed in his commitment to the crusade by Konrad II of Hildesheim. The Landgraf literally "takes up" the cross in this liturgical ritual, and the bishop is fully and gorgeously vested.

Figure 126. Elisabeth's husband leaves for the Crusades, *Elisabeth shrine,* Marburg, St. Elisabeth, thirteenth century. (Foto Marburg/Art Resource, N.Y.)

The second relief shows the spouses taking leave of one another (fig. 126). In this depiction, Elisabeth is shown, by her size and physical presence, to be the equal of her noble and crusading husband. Wearing his pilgrim's bag, Ludwig bids his wife goodbye with a lingering and direct gaze.[63] A clearer image of marital harmony, equality, and affection would be hard to achieve. In Elisabeth's Life, the scene clearly establishes the saint's marital status and, ultimately, her right to her husband's estate, dramatically preparing for the moment when that right is challenged and for the suffering caused by that challenge.

When, in the third relief, Elisabeth receives her husband's bones and a ring from pilgrims returning from Jerusalem, confirming his death, she immediately begins to disburse her estate. We see her clothing a half-naked beggar in the fourth panel, and the fifth scene, in which she herself is clothed in a nun's garment by a priest before an altar, repeats the imagery and composition of the preceding relief—Elisabeth assumes the place and pose of the beggar.[64] Through similarities in the poses of the three figures, the last relief of the back side is therefore repeated in this first relief of the front. While the back of the shrine recounts Elisabeth's secular Life, the front of the shrine tells the story of Elisabeth's consecrated life.

In the sixth relief, which depicts an episode in which the queen gave away her dowry, Elisabeth distributes coins to men and women, including the sick and the aged (fig. 127). She lines up the poor, threatening punishment if anyone changes places to receive a second handout and begins systematically to distribute the money. In the relief she takes a very active pose, her robes girded up by a plain knotted rope reminiscent of the Franciscan girdle. The saint has reached the second of the outstretched hands and has four more left to fill. The hand with which the saint makes contact is that of a woman holding a swaddled infant.

This is the first image we have seen of a woman distributing coins. As noted in the discussion of the virgin Lucy's Life, women are usually depicted distributing goods or food rather than money. The depiction of coins, particularly given the prominence of the woman with a child, is a reference to Elisabeth's royalty. Here she cares for the "widows and orphans" that good kings were sworn to sustain, as seen in the Life of Edward. The relief from Elisabeth's shrine suggests that she cares for all the people of her country, and the last reliefs of the cycle further develop this theme.

In reliefs 7 and 8, Elisabeth feeds the poor and sick with a spoon and gives them drink. In the eighth relief she bends to wash their feet.[65] These acts of charity are not novel—they are very close to those that Radegund performed (and Elisabeth even acquired a follower named Radegund). However, fully half of the reliefs of the eight-panel cycle focus on Elisabeth's work with the poor and sick, and this number is augmented in the stained glass windows of the Elisabeth-Kirche that also recount the Life.[66] The emphasis on charitable acts, a new element in this royal Life, is a product of devotional developments of the thirteenth century and reflects the prestige of the new mendicant movements.[67] Indeed, Elisabeth was often associated with the Franciscans (as evidenced by the the rope girdle), although in fact she was never a tertiary.[68]

Illustrations of the Life of St. Louis exhibit many of the same virtues that have been highlighted in the narrative on Elisabeth's shrine. The short illustrated Life of the king in the Hours of Jeanne d'Evreux includes several scenes that parallel those of the shrine, in particular, illustrations of the saint feeding the poor with a spoon

Figure 127. Elisabeth distributes coins as charity, *Elisabeth shrine,* Marburg, St. Elisabeth, thirteenth century. (Foto Marburg/Art Resource, N.Y.)

and giving alms. Jane Chung explains the similarity by arguing that Louis is, in effect, gendered female in these actions.[69] Joan Holladay argues that both Lives allude to imagery of the Seven Acts of Mercy.[70]

Beyond their acts of charity and their humility, another similarity clearly links Elisabeth and Radegund. In each Life there is at the outset a concern to define the saint's marital status. This may be a manifestation of Julia Smith's observation that female saints, rather than leaving family behind in their quest for sanctity, remain tied to their kinship groups or marital relations. Although Radegund escapes a cruel and brutal husband and never bears children, while Elisabeth loves her husband, has children, and is fully supported by him in her charitable activities, in each case marriage serves as a foundation for sanctity. Through her marriage but also her own familial connections, Elisabeth is part of a saintly dynasty that might be compared to that of earlier Ottonian saints, especially saints who are mothers.[71] Elisabeth, however, goes far beyond the early medieval Ottonian queens in her pious exercises, taking up a nunlike life after her husband's death. Nonetheless, given that the Radegund miniatures decline to comment on Clothar's cruelties, it may be argued that both cycles use images of marriage to similar ends: to establish the right of the women to their high secular status through their husbands. This medieval perception that a woman's importance is based on her husband's status intrudes even into the depiction of the Lives of the saints.

Ultimately, there may be little that can be deemed essential or unique to the holy queen in the pictorial hagiography that survives. In many respects, she is a feminized version of the male confessor in his various manifestations, albeit constrained and bounded. Yet images such as Radegund's freeing prisoners and founding a shrine and Elisabeth's disbursement of monies attest to the power of royal women, even if they are the exception rather than the rule. In comparison we might consider Balthild, a saint of uncertain virtue, who seems to have been celebrated on the sole basis of her (arguably) forced retirement at the famous convent of Chelles. Her cult was not significant enough to support visual expression. She may have been the only sainted queen to have actually exercised the powers of a queen during her life. Unfortunately, the saint's Life that praises her virtues has never succeeding in silencing the historical texts that vehemently abuse her character.[72] Rather than this sort of controversial and secular power, the power that Radegund and Elisabeth share derives from virtuous acts that demonstrate their saintly humility and charity.

CONCLUSION: AUDIENCE

Like all the illustrated Lives of confessors considered here, the Life of Radegund is addressed to a specific audience. However, whereas the Lives of kings seem to have been intended as admonitory messages to their living counterparts, it is unlikely that the Poitiers manuscript had a royal audience. Rather, the viewers of the manuscript were the nuns and their visitors at the monastery of Sainte-Croix, just as was the case with many of the other manuscripts celebrating monastic patrons. However, Radegund's Life did offer more actions for actual emulation by readers and viewers than other Lives of confessors. Women and nuns, subject to the same restrictions as the holy queen, could find a model for their own actions in the events and qualities of the first half of her Life—her acceptance of her fate, her eagerness to serve, her charity, and her prayers.

Furthermore, in the Life of Radegund, for the first time in a confessor's illustrated Life, a series of miracles that constitutes the second part of the narrative attempts to construct a heightened emotional response. Rather than the pity and compunction stimulated by the narratives of Passions, a confessor's narrative usually focuses on the edifying value of virtue. Indeed, Fortunatus concludes Radegund's Life and sums up her miraculous powers with a list of virtues, including piety and humility, faith and fervor. Unexpected, however, is the naming of two virtues—love (*dilectio*) and sweetness (*dulcedo*)—that cast Radegund's power as fundamentally different from that of other confessors.[73] In these particular virtues Radegund evokes the power of a mother, and the miniatures of her Life attempt to make the viewer feel her love.

To put it another way, in the absence of tortures, which elicit an automatic emotional response, miracles must suffice. Although their repetitious quality denies them the effect of astonishment, their number does create a sense of irresistible holy power—not a public power like that of the bishops, but a private and local power available to the saint's intimates. The sainted queen frequently uses the sign of the cross to cure, but almost as often she uses touch. She cares for the bodies of her "patients," washing them, holding them, stroking and even caressing them. Her approach to the body is unmistakably motherly, manifested in her contact, whether through the hands or through the eyes, with the people she cures. In addition to the physical cure, she give assurance of their spiritual welfare through the attention of her love. When the viewer finally arrives at the last of the miracles (see fig. 123), the look of love that Domnolenus returns to the saint might represent the look of devotion of the viewer herself. No doubt this is the saint's maternal power that Gregory of Tours aptly characterized:

> you cause the hearts of those listening to you to be so suffused by a heavenly glow, that the souls of the virgins called forth from everywhere, . . . come in great haste, longing to be refreshed in Christ's love at the spring of your heart; having left their families, they prefer to be with you whom grace, not nature, make their mother.[74]

9

THE END OF THE MONASTIC
TRADITION AND A NEW BEGINNING

Matthew Paris

ॐ

THE ILLUSTRATED Lives discussed thus far were created in the tenth through the thirteenth century. For the most part products of Benedictine monasticism, they represent the particular sanctity of the early and high Middle Ages. Despite their origin in a specific time and culture, these Lives, because they represent typical and powerful saints of their era, establish genres or types, creating the "horizon of expectations" for representations of sanctity in the later Middle Ages.[1] Nonetheless, it is also true that there are many and important new directions in the construction of sanctity that originate in the thirteenth century.

The "new" saints, as André Vauchez described the cults of the late Middle Ages, to some degree replaced the old advocates and diffused the importance of the established sanctoral.[2] By the end of the century, bishop saints, the dominant type in this study, are much diminished in importance. Mendicant spirituality, with its emphasis on pastoral concerns and urban society, eclipsed the rural and monastic centers of power represented by the Benedictines. Although, as Matthew Paris claimed, black monks were superior in their care of saintly bodies,[3] Franciscans and Dominicans were able to create saintly paradigms of great power. More important for our concerns, they were able to use art to their advantage in establishing the character and holiness of their saints, often even before canonization.[4] Such depictions had the advantage of attesting to sanctity without the necessity of a shrine. Because they were a specialty of Italy, they were even characterized in medieval sources as "Lombard style."[5] Narratives find an important place in this new and more actively public artistic expression, but they do not take the form of manuscripts. Rather, the primary form of Franciscan art is portraiture, "in the manner of a saint,"[6] supplemented with narrative on panel paintings or in frescoes. The form is reminiscent

282

of Byzantine narrative icons, but the effect is very different, created under a different conception of sanctity and for different use.

Although Franciscan sanctity responds to the sort of analysis that I have pursued in this book,[7] it also introduces new issues that have been the subject of much debate.[8] Instead of a consideration of Franciscan hagiography, the examination of a more conservative Benedictine hagiographer and his work will show the continued importance, in manuscripts, of the genres and types that I have discussed. Furthermore, compared to the paucity of data associated with earlier manuscripts, the work of Matthew Paris, a thirteenth-century monk of St. Albans,[9] provides an embarrassment of riches, both of manuscripts and of contextual information.

Matthew's work, both as historian and hagiographer, is in some ways profoundly conservative. Yet, at the same time, it is important for its innovations. As a hagiographer, Matthew defends the old ideas of sanctity while at the same time supporting new saints. He admires the spirituality of the Franciscans, even reflecting, through his own drawings, an appreciation for the innovations of their new hagiographic art.[10] Nevertheless, he is profoundly suspicious of mendicant influence and social mobility.[11] In sum, his work as a hagiographer is a thorough mix of the old and the new.

Matthew is well known to historians as a chronicler. His historical texts are extensive but not entirely accurate—he is too prone to letting his point of view color his accounts. The result has been called "epic moral drama,"[12] but it is also filled with specifics. Matthew was witness to many of the important events of his day, in some cases at the specific request of King Henry III. He was even directly involved on some occasions, as when he was called upon to make a diplomatic mission to Norway.[13] The magnum opus of Matthew's history writing is the *Chronica majora,* a continuation of the universal history of Roger Wendover, a fellow monk at St. Albans. Matthew eventually filled three large volumes of the *Chronica majora,* and even assembled an appendix of relevant documents, the *Liber additamentorum.*[14]

Despite this impressive work on chronicles, Matthew's reputation as an artist at one time exceeded his renown as a historian. He was thought to have originated an extensive school of manuscript production that dominated manuscript illumination in thirteenth-century England. Not surprisingly, more recent scholarship has shown that much of what was originally attributed to Matthew or his "school" was produced in the London or Westminster shops of professional manuscript makers.[15] The pendulum of art historical opinion has swung to an opposite pole, picturing Matthew Paris not as an innovator but as an eccentric working alone in a *retardataire* style.[16]

Although it is true that Matthew's autograph manuscripts in some respects betray a lack of the professionalism one might expect of an artisan—the Dublin manuscript of the Life of Alban is a patchwork of various bits and pieces of rough parchment—it is also clear that Matthew was not primarily an artisan. He was a precocious renaissance man, with a unique and creative mind, working in both literature and art. He continually sought new avenues for expression, from history to hagiography to romance,[17] and clearly enjoyed working out technical difficulties.[18] For example, although he seems to have had a shortage of good parchment, he did use fine parchment for the illustrations of his Life of Alban; the miniatures were glued in when necessary over the rougher, pieced pages. This particular care in producing his illustrations allowed him to maintain a consistent quality in his fine line drawings. (Unfortunately, it also allowed later admirers to remove some of them.) Moreover, the unfinished *Vitae Offarum* indicates that he took on ambitious projects he was not always able to complete.[19]

But before exploring Matthew's hagiographic narratives further, we must evaluate his responsibility for the illustrations, an attribution that has been contested.[20] The illustrated Life of Alban in Dublin (MS 177 is our primary example), the Life of Edward the Confessor in Cambridge (University Library MS Ee 3.59, discussed in chapter 5), and the fragment of the Life of Thomas à Becket in London (British Library Loan MS 88), along with the unillustrated Life of Edmund of Abingdon (British Library Loan MS 29/61), are all with good reason associated with Matthew Paris.[21] Shortly after Matthew's death, Thomas of Walsingham held his hagiography in equal esteem to his history, noting that he "elegantly illustrated the Lives of Saints Alban and Amphibalus, and of the archbishops of Canterbury Thomas and Edmund."[22] However, only the Dublin manuscript is in Matthew's hand. It is probable that the extant Lives of Edward and Thomas were produced by secular workshop artists in London or Westminster (rather than in St. Albans) following sketches or lost originals by Matthew. The text of the unillustrated Life of Edmund is a later copy.

The recognizably new style of hagiographic illustration that appears in all three illustrated manuscripts, that is, tinted line drawings in what are usually paired illustrations that stretch across the top of the page, corresponds closely to the format of the autograph Dublin manuscript with its double columns, rather than to the triple columns of the Lives of Edward and Thomas.[23] Furthermore, the shared use of distinctive images (boats, horses, etc.),[24] and the apparent copying of the Life of Edward from a detailed model,[25] makes a theory of common authorship of the

Lives plausible. To this may be added the uncontested evidence that Matthew wrote the Lives of Saints Thomas and Edward, and planned manuscripts for nonmonastic patrons.[26] Finally, the observation that he probably used sketches in creating the Life of Alban allows us a means of understanding the transmission of his designs.[27] Without compelling argument to the contrary, we must attribute to Matthew the design of all three of the illustrated Lives at issue.[28]

In this chapter, we will not focus on Matthew's Lives of new saints such as Edmund of Abingdon or Thomas à Becket.[29] We have already considered Matthew's development of the sanctity and political importance of the up-to-date chivalric king, Edward the Confessor, and will return to it here only briefly. Instead, in this chapter we will focus on Matthew's first and most important hagiographic project—depicting a monastic patron of the most ancient type: Alban.

In his verse rewriting of the Life of the first English martyr, Matthew ambitiously set out to revive and modernize a legendary saint. Furthermore, with the production in the 1240s and 1250s of this elaborate illustrated *libellus* dedicated to Alban, he performed a homage to the venerable patron of his own monastery.[30] Through his manuscript of the Life of Alban, Matthew made the old forms work in new ways, emphasizing witnesses to the saint's authenticity and attending to new sensibilities that valued spiritual devotion, pastoral care, and chivalric virtue. At the same time, however, Matthew defended the old institutions, especially that of Benedictine monasticism.

Clearly, Matthew set himself the task of competing with the new orders by creating an effective and compelling hagiography. The noble audience with whom the mendicants had found remarkable success in Italy and France was Matthew's audience as well. In his endeavor, Matthew was remarkably successful. His illustrated saints' Lives were in demand, copied, and read at court.[31] Notes on the flyleaf of the Dublin manuscript indicate that he lent it to noblewomen.[32] The extensive strip narratives, with added *tituli* and captions illustrating both vernacular and Latin texts, created a new sort of almost cinematic narrative. The quick succession of action scenes in this "painted movie" must have been exciting for its intended audience.[33] Although Suzanne Lewis has not come to the same conclusion, it would seem to me that Matthew's use of the window and the dense narrative structures of repetition and embellishment were the inspiration for the Anglo-Norman Apocalypse manuscripts about which she has written so brilliantly.[34] Even though I present him here as the last great proponent of monastic hagiography, Matthew's primary heritage is thus to be found in later manuscripts of city and court.

As in his hagiography, so also in his history texts Matthew had a distinctive approach. In her study of his illustrated chronicles, Lewis defines the dramatic and moral qualities of the historical text and images:

> Human action and change are perceived as a disturbance or disruptive force upsetting the natural fixed state of affairs. Hence action always leads to reaction, and events are explained as the inevitable consequences of moral antecedents. (98)
>
> [*Pictures* structure moral commentary, which] would otherwise be lost in the relentless stream of disjunctive chronological entries. (133–34)

This view of history, and the place of pictures in telling it, may be extended from the chronicles to the saints' Lives. Matthew thought of the Lives as a part, but a very special part, of his universal history. Thus, in the illustrations to both the Life of Edward and the Life of Alban (the Life of Thomas is a fragment), Matthew embeds the saint's story in a larger historical context, whether the story of a monastery or of a kingdom. As with history, so with hagiography; Matthew begins with fixed and immutable truths that, thrown out of balance by human action, can only be restored by divine intervention. The pictures take us through the story, leading us from action to reaction, to inevitable consequences, but with a remarkable array of visual embellishments, commentary, and gloss.

Indeed, the narrative of Alban's Life is so rich that it renders full analysis of its complexities impossible in this context. Here, I will try to indicate only a few of the particularly effective narrative devices and some of the major themes. I will attempt to emphasize the aspects of Matthew's narrative that conform to or contrast with those of the saints we have already discussed.

Matthew's innovations begin with compilation and layout. The Alban manuscript consists of a wide-ranging assortment of hagiographic texts concerning Alban and his teacher and fellow martyr Amphibalus, including Lives in two languages, miracles, and inventions, as well as charters for the abbey of St. Albans. However, there is some evidence to argue that the primary Life, the Anglo-Norman *Vie de seint Auban,* was originally a separate cluster of four gatherings.[35] If so, it may have been remade as a fuller *libellus* in 1257, a date that appears in the manuscript. As Florence McCulloch has argued, it may originally have been intended to show to King Henry III, when he spent a week at the monastery or, alternatively, to commemorate an invention at the tomb of Alban at which nobility were present.[36] Presumably, such an original showing would have added to its popularity in later years in Matthew's "lending library." Finally Matthew bequeathed it to the monastery.

Most illustrated pages in the *Vie* follow a well-defined yet complex format. The line drawings of the miniatures are contained in a rectangular frame that usually occupies the entire width of the top of the page. Underneath is an Anglo-Norman couplet that serves as a *titulus* for the illustration. Generally the illustration appears in close proximity to the portion of the Anglo Norman text that describes the action: on the same page, facing page, or following page. Below the two columns of the *Vie* on the page, Latin couplets usually appear, describing the events depicted in the scene. Finally, within the scenes themselves appear various comments made by the participants in Latin, with a single exception (in Anglo-Saxon).

There are, however, variations on this uniform presentation toward the end of the pictorial narrative. The pictures continue on folios 50v to 63r[37] with material that is relevant to the cult at St. Albans but not part of the *Vie* proper. Material concerning Germanus of Auxerre (who visited the shrine of Alban), and Offa, the royal founder of the monastery completes the illustrative cycle. The Anglo-Norman *titulus* couplets continue to explain this material for the viewer, although the versified Lives in Anglo-Norman and Latin are cut short. Therefore, for the last twenty-six pages of illustrations (out of a total of fifty-five), the miniatures only occasionally correspond to the texts contained on the lower part of the page.[38] Nonetheless, these pictures are essential for Matthew's explanation of Alban's place in history and constitute perhaps his most original contribution to the Life.

THE SPIRITUAL NARRATIVE:
FAITH, VISION, AND DEVOTION

The first four illustrations work in remarkably rich and inventive ways to create a devotional "frame" with which to understand the spiritual import of the narrative.[39] They begin with a double-portrait of the martyr-protagonists (fig. 128). The solid, simple presentation of the two seated figures, rather than "early" style, more persuasively evokes the special visual qualities of author portraits, conveying authority as well as a sense of introduction. Amphibalus the priest, barefoot, tonsured, and dressed in a brown cloak, makes a teaching gesture. Alban, dressed in an elaborate decorated cloak, hat, and blue shoes befitting his noble status, sits on a cushion with an air of comfort and authority.

The stately tone of the image is maintained in the next two openings, although

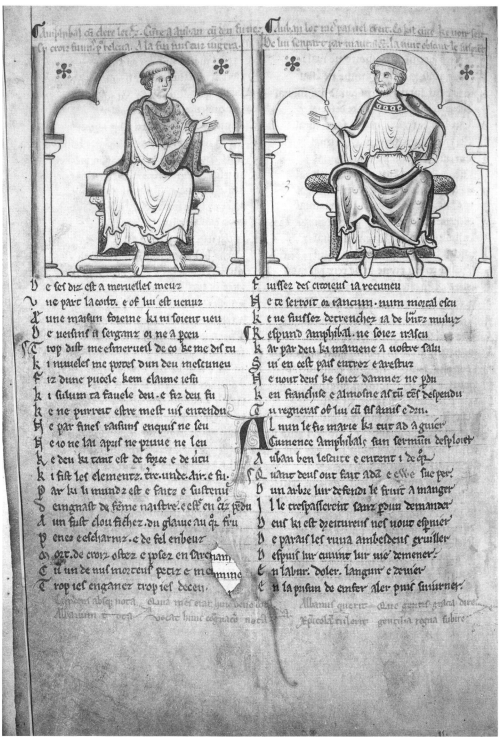

Figure 128. Alban and Amphibalus, *Passions of Alban (Albinus) and Amphibalus,* Matthew Paris
at St. Albans, 1240 or later. Dublin, Trinity College Library, MS 177, fol. 29v.
(Reproduced by permission of the Board of Trinity College Dublin)

Matthew also carefully and thoroughly explores the notions of witness and conversion with which we are already familiar from the discussion of martyrs in chapter 3. Through subtle manipulations of text and image, Matthew is able to make the concepts more intimate and imitable than did the earlier artist of the Life of Romanus, establishing a quality carried on in later medieval hagiographic texts.[40] Let us look at how he accomplishes this, first by summarizing the text.

The story begins with Alban taking the Christian priest Amphibalus into his home. In turn, Amphibalus preaches to the pagan lord about Christianity. The first *titulus* states that "Amphibalus, a learned cleric, told Alban how God was born, was put on the Cross and then arose to judge us all at the end." This *titulus,* used as a caption for the portrait of the saint, is separated and aligned with the figure of Amphibalus. The second *titulus,* similarly aligned with Alban, reads: "Alban heard it but did not believe what was told him was the truth. He departed from [Amphibalus] with displeasure." In the text, however, the reader discovers that Amphibalus has fully anticipated this reaction, for he allows that words alone may not be sufficient for conversion and promises further help: "Si deutant tan quor eslumine e esprent" (If you doubt, your heart will be illuminated) (ll. 184–85).

The next two illustrations detail Alban's conversion, set in motion by Amphibalus's preaching. On folio 30v the *titulus* explains, "Here Alban sees while sleeping what Amphibalus foretold. The body sleeps but the soul is awake [so] that in heaven he sees the great marvel." The text continues with a relatively full discussion of the story and Passion of Christ, including the Annunciation and other details such as the taunting by the Jews. The picture by necessity illustrates only two scenes from Alban's vision (fig. 129): Alban sees the Crucifixion and the Resurrection represented in smaller figures above a wavy band over his head. Such dreams, of course, were often considered a source of knowledge of the divine during the Middle Ages.[41]

Disturbed by his dream, Alban looks for Amphibalus to ask about what he has seen. Nothing in the text of the *Vie* or earlier Lives explains the details of the next and crucial miniature, in which Alban finds Amphibalus praying before the cross and secretly watches him through a conveniently placed window (fig. 130). On the previous page (30r), the narrator notes that while Alban was dreaming, Amphibalus spent the night in prayer before his cross (ll. 199–200), but makes no mention of a window or surreptitious spying. The *titulus,* however, is much more specific, indicating, "Here Alban sees Amphibalus through the window . . ." And indeed the illustration shows Alban peering at Amphibalus who, as the *titulus* puts it, "adored

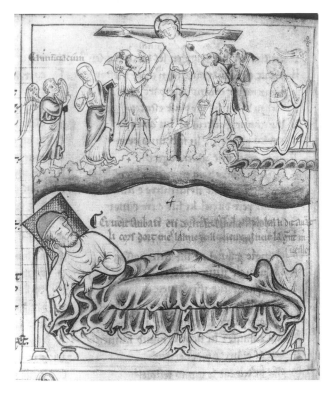

Figure 129. Alban has a vision in a dream, *Passions of Alban
(Albinus) and Amphibalus,* Matthew Paris at St. Albans, 1240 or later.
Dublin, Trinity College Library, MS 177, fol. 30v. (Reproduced by
permission of the Board of Trinity College Dublin)

the cross on his knees, sighing and crying . . . not sleeping." Once more, a martyr's
Life supplies a bodily model of prayer, but now with a new specificity.

Matthew's invention of the window is a master stroke, condensing a number of
meanings that are essential to the narrative. It focuses and directs the gaze of the
viewer and designates an "inside" and "outside" in the miniature. We follow Alban's
gaze and note that it aligns, not with the man, but with the object on which Amphibalus, in turn, fixes his gaze: the cross. Aligning ourselves with this perspective,
we join Alban in gazing upon the cross. By means of the window, the viewer is drawn
into the narrative in a uniquely intimate way: it forces us to admit our own curios-
ity that leads us to peer through the window with Alban. We are with Alban on the
outside and, with him, seek to join Amphibalus, who is within.

The inside remains a space apart, ruled by the sign of the cross. However, in this

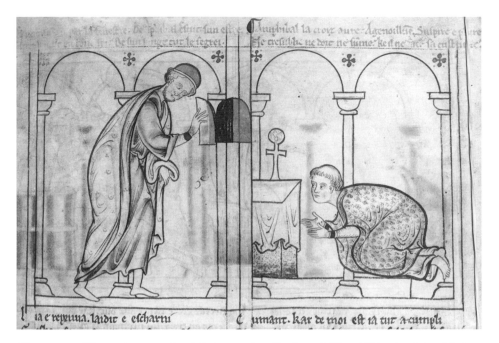

Figure 130. Alban spies upon Amphibalus praying, *Passions of Alban (Albinus) and Amphibalus,*
Matthew Paris at St. Albans, 1240 or later. Dublin, Trinity College Library, MS 177, fol. 31r.
(Reproduced by permission of the Board of Trinity College Dublin)

instance, unlike the cross in the Life of Romanus, the sign overcomes its semiotic
status and, in effect, becomes real. The peculiarly shaped relic-cross, said to be that
of Amphibalus, had been acquired for the monastery by abbot William of Trumpington (1213–45), and Matthew was the first to write it into the narrative of the Life
of Alban. Matthew's drawing of the relic in the *Gesta Abbatum* is a simple outline,
lacking the figure of Christ,[42] as are most of his representations of it in the miniatures of the Life of Alban. In this miniature, however, the crucified Christ appears
prominently displayed on the Cross.[43] This is, therefore neither a simple object nor
a mere sign; it is as if Amphibalus's prayers have allowed him a vision of Christ,
and, in turn, Alban is converted by this spectacle of the divine and its proper veneration. Thus, in contrast with the dream vision, which we were warned by the text
might be a nightmare, this vision is "real" and divine in origin.

The *titulus* declares that Amphibalus did not "change his habit" in praying
through the night. When Alban surreptitiously (albeit "in good faith") witnesses
this pure and unadulterated Christian piety before the cross, he completes a process
of conversion that began with preached words he did not believe, was elaborated

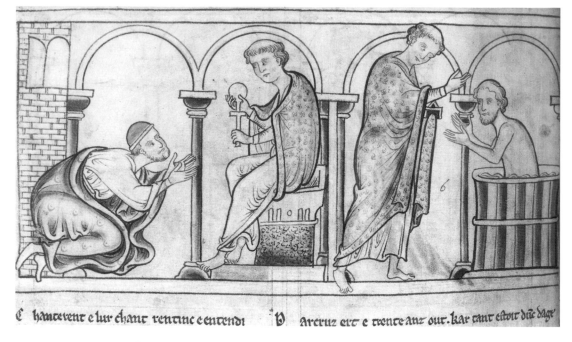

C hamcevent c lur chanr renrinc c enrendi   D arcruz err c rrenre anz our. kar rant estoir due dage

Figure 131. Alban is baptized, *Passions of Alban (Albinus) and Amphibalus,* Matthew Paris at
St. Albans, 1240 or later. Dublin, Trinity College Library, MS 177, fol. 31v. (Reproduced
by permission of the Board of Trinity College Dublin)

by his dream, and is finally accomplished through the sight of the cross. The fact
that vision completes the conversion is no accident. It reflects Matthew's sophisticated concern with the possibilities and function of vision, aspects that are both religious and artistic. Through Amphibalus's worship, the cross is shown to focus the
power and meaning of Christianity by its ability to evoke an affective or emotional
component of sight. Because Alban, who is "crying and sighing," is so visibly devoted in his worship, it is plain to the onlooker—both Alban and the reader—that
the cross is more than a sign to him; it is again, in some sense, real. Through this
vision Alban receives a model for Christian understanding of the Cross and experiences in his turn its affective meaning.[44]

   After this conversion through sight, the next opening shows the sealing of Alban's faith through doctrine and baptism. At the same time it reveals that some
witnesses pervert the evidence of their eyes; that is, they see improperly. This argument about vision is once more reinforced by the use of a window structure in the
next image (fig. 131). Here speech has become meaningful; it is no longer incapable

Figure 132. A Saracen spies on Alban, *Passions of Alban (Albinus) and Amphibalus,* Matthew Paris at St. Albans, 1240 or later. Dublin, Trinity College Library, MS 177, fol. 32r. (Reproduced by permission of the Board of Trinity College Dublin)

of conveying truth to Alban as it was before his vision. Alban is taught by Amphibalus, who now sits on a throne. As the text notes, Amphibalus held "school" in an underground house (l. 392), and the *titulus* clarifies that Amphibalus has told Alban "what the vision signified." The scene itself seems to be modeled on the teaching of a master in a university school rather than on mendicant preaching. In the next moment, in the same miniature, Alban is baptized. Again the *titulus* clarifies the action and adds that he was taught "everything that applied to salvation."

On the facing page, a pagan (identified in the text as a Saracen) peers into the house, again through a window (fig. 132).[45] As the *titulus* notes, he acts "covertly" rather than "in good faith" as did Alban, and plainly he inverts the movement of Alban's gaze and Amphibalus's actions. Furthermore, rather than being a secure source of doctrine and truth like Amphibalus, the master that the Saracen serves, depicted at the right of the miniature, is cockeyed and literally unbalanced. Clearly perfidious counselors have his ear as he tries to rule, but he lacks authority, even though he represents "pagan law" according to the *titulus*. The comparison across

Figure 133. Amphibalus gives Alban his cross, *Passions of Alban (Albinus) and Amphibalus,* Matthew Paris at St. Albans, 1240 or later. Dublin, Trinity College Library, MS 177, fol. 33r. (Reproduced by permission of the Board of Trinity College Dublin)

the opening between Amphibalus and the pagan governor resembles that of Edmund and the Danish king in the Morgan manuscript; here, however, the good now properly takes the right-hand side and the action has not yet really begun. We are choosing sides at this point, and clearly the actions and space of the Saracens are devalued. In the *tituli* describing the looking, the phrase "Ci veit," "here see," which is repeated twice for Alban—when he had his dream and when he saw Amphibalus—is conspicuously not attributed to the vision of a pagan.[46]

The next scene, in which Amphibalus passes his cross to Alban, shows how the cross becomes, in Matthew's retelling, the focus, even the impetus, of the narrative (fig. 133). The moment of stasis and perfect vision that represented Alban's conversion is disrupted by the actions of the Saracen. The rest of the narrative will show Alban's attempts to retrieve that perfection. Throughout, the cross literally "leads" the narrative, and, with rare but significant exceptions, Alban keeps his eyes fixed upon it.

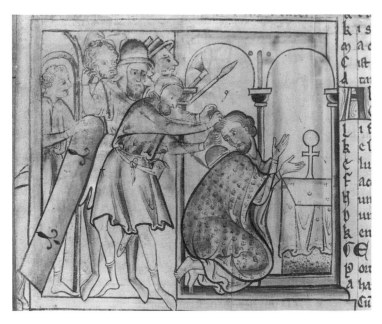

Figure 134. Alban is pulled from his prayers and arrested, *Passions of Alban (Albinus) and Amphibalus,* Matthew Paris at St. Albans, 1240 or later. Dublin, Trinity College Library, MS 177, fol. 33 v. (Reproduced by permission of the Board of Trinity College Dublin)

This fixing of the eyes on the relic-cross is reminiscent of the pious treatment of a holy relic that Matthew himself witnessed and described. Henry III took the relic of Christ's blood, which was encased in a crystal vial, and, "with the utmost honor, reverence and awe, he carried it publicly in front of his face, going on foot . . . without stopping to Westminster Abbey. . . . Even when he came to a rough or uneven section of road, he kept his eyes fixed always either on heaven or on the container itself."[47] Matthew notes that the relic of the blood was the most sacred of Christ's relics because its "effusion" saved the world. In addition to this description and an illustration in his chronicle, Matthew records the reception of this relic in his Life of Edmund.[48]

Immediately following his conversion and reception of the cross, Alban is literally wrenched away from his worship of the cross (fig. 134). He will subsequently be tried, tortured, and finally imprisoned for refusing to sacrifice to pagan gods. Although similar events dominated the narratives of early medieval martyrs, here they remain a minor part of the narrative, occupying only four miniatures in the Alban story.

Of more concern to Matthew are the events that follow Alban's imprisonment. In this portion of the narrative, Matthew turns a series of miracles in the Life into a sermon on the allegory of water, culminating in a representation of its salvific meaning for Christianity. Such allegorical meanings are typically associated with martyr's Lives. However, Matthew extends and elaborates the signification beyond its use in earlier medieval examples. Furthermore, his images do not usually refer to simple *topoi*, and his use of Biblical parallels is less directly typological than that of earlier examples. Lewis has argued that allegorical interpretation is essentially ideological: "[the ideological and the spiritual] must be seen as interpenetrating components of a single *mentalité* in which the dualities between active propagandizing and devotional meditation, external social realities and the internal world of the reader, tend to dissolve."[49] In depicting the pagans as unaffected by the deeper meanings of the events in which they play a part, Matthew's explication of allegories does seem to assume this sort of ideological stance.

First, the text specifies that while Alban languished in prison for six months the country suffered from a drought. In the early and high Middle Ages, both crop failure and agricultural abundance were attributed to the posthumous patronage of a saint. Here, as Vauchez has noted of other later medieval examples, *virtus,* saintly power, is transferred to a living saint.[50] So long as Alban stays in prison the drought holds. Matthew seems to find illustrating a lack of water challenging (fig. 135). The *titulus* notes the loss of life that resulted, so Matthew depicts a pile of dead and dying victims. But he also conveys the depredations of drought: one man is reduced to drinking from a beaker with a very narrow spout, out of which, presumably, water slowly trickles. The taste for the telling image is also evident in Matthew's illustration of the text in which, after noting the withering of leaves and grass, he observes that "oises e bestes . . . pantoiser." This line appears beneath the miniature in the manuscript, and so Matthew pictures, at the far right of the miniature, three men with their mouths open and two birds visibly "panting."

When Alban emerges from prison on the facing folio (fig. 136), it is only so that he can be taken to his martyrdom. He is led over a narrow bridge, and in the crush 772 people fall off the bridge and are drowned. The drought has ended and now it is the overabundance of water that has become a threat. Alban, of course, witnesses the catastrophe, takes pity and prays, briefly turning his eyes from the cross. The waters recede and the dead are resurrected. Despite this great miracle, only one pa-

Figure 135. Alban is imprisoned, and the country suffers drought, *Passions of Alban (Albinus) and Amphibalus,* Matthew Paris at St. Albans, 1240 or later. Dublin, Trinity College Library, MS 177, fol. 35 v. (Reproduced by permission of the Board of Trinity College Dublin)

gan is converted: Aracle. In this instance, it is the new convert who is clearly singled out in the illustration, for his eyes rather than Alban's are fixed on the cross.

The circumstances of this miracle seem quite naturally to lend themselves to a comparison with Moses' parting of the waters. Certainly, elsewhere Matthew seeks to draw parallels between Alban and the Old Testament figure; several marginal notes make reference to Moses and Matthew refers to a flame that appeared at Alban's grave as a "column of fire." His purposes here, however, are different; he draws an implicit analogy between Alban and Christ and in so doing completes his allegorical explication of water. The figure of Alban on the bridge bears a distinct likeness to conventional representations of Christ, with long hair and beard. Alban follows the Way of the Cross quite literally, as made evident by the cross that he carries. The path is narrow, and most others find it impossible to follow. The miniature moves with great animation across the page, culminating in the conversion of Aracle (fol. 37).

After showing the dreadful effects on the human body of the lack of water or its excess, Matthew Paris completes his *summa* on the nature of water with an image

Figure 136. Alban crosses a narrow bridge, *Passions of Alban (Albinus) and Amphibalus*, Matthew Paris at St. Albans, 1240 or later. Dublin, Trinity College Library, MS 177, fol. 36r. (Reproduced by permission of the Board of Trinity College Dublin)

of its miraculous appearance at God's command (fig. 137).[51] The pagans force Alban to climb a mountain, and when they suffer from heat and thirst they curse him for his "enchantment." Alban prays and remembers Moses: a fountain springs up. Again, rather than focusing on the miracles of Moses that he has cited in his text, Matthew refers to Christ in the image and the *titulus*: "God, said Alban, from whose side issued the water mixed [with blood] commanded a fountain to spring from this mountain. A fountain of living water sprang up. Each strove to drink of the water but the perverse sons of the devil were not grateful to God." In the miniature, Matthew alludes to the image of the fountain of life with its divided streams. That the pagans misconstrue the miracle and are not converted, he declares, makes their failure to believe all the more sinful. Matthew has used the water sequence both to make a spiritual argument about the saving grace of God, as well as to condemn those who are unaffected by the evidence of grace—the pagans who he characterizes as "Saracens." He concludes the sequence in an image of Alban's martyrdom.

Alban is martyred on the facing page. First, as the Christian martyr is beheaded

Figure 137. A miraculous fountain springs up, *Passions of Alban (Albinus) and Amphibalus*, Matthew Paris at St. Albans, 1240 or later. Dublin, Trinity College Library, MS 177, fol. 37v. (Reproduced by permission of the Board of Trinity College Dublin)

(plate 8), the executioner loses his eyes. The *titulus* supplies the meaning: "Night begins for the Saracen; for the martyr, light without end." Second, the slice of the sword releases a gush of blood that, according to the *titulus*, "tints" the cross "with a holy rosiness." Here the water symbolism is joined to the narrative of the cross. Alban's blood takes on the character of the pure fountain, the blood that was mixed with water at Christ's crucifixion. Later in the text Matthew underlines this by describing a martyr as a "fountain of blood."[52] Its particular power is here evident because this last event seems to affect the pagans, who in the miniature react with wonder and amazement.

The burial of the body of the martyr, as might be expected, closes the primary narrative of the cross, which has been transformed by the execution into a true relic of martyrdom (fol. 47r, misbound when foliated [fig. 138]). Yet rather than stress closure alone, Matthew's depiction puts the emphasis on the continuation of Alban's Life by portraying the martyr's effect on others. The grief of those witnessing the burial spans a range of intensity—from melancholy, through weeping, to

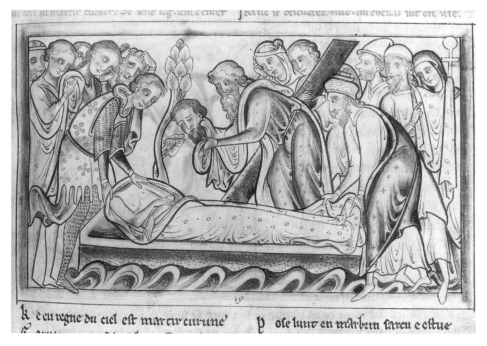

Figure 138. The burial of Alban, *Passions of Alban (Albinus) and Amphibalus,* Matthew Paris at St. Albans, 1240 or later. Dublin, Trinity College Library, MS 177, fol. 47r [misbound when foliated]. (Reproduced by permission of the Board of Trinity College Dublin)

one figure who in his rage and uncontrolled emotion looks remarkably like a lion. In his text and miniatures, Matthew frequently compares passionate and evil rage to the growls of a lion, but here even a Christian experiences this extreme of emotion. At the same time, Matthew draws an analogy between Alban's burial and that of Christ by likening the figure at the foot of the body to Joseph of Arimathea. He also includes women, rare in this cycle, surely for the same Christo-mimetic purpose.

However, two figures in the upper right corner do not share in the grief of the rest of the onlookers and deserve special attention because both refer to future developments in the extended narrative. The profile head with the exaggerated and ugly features and odd-shaped hat must be Saracen; certainly he resembles other such characterizations throughout the manuscript. Very subtly, Matthew breaks the elegiac mood by reminding the viewer that a witness will report these events to the Saracens and there will be retribution. In contrast to this figure of menace, to the left of the Saracen stands a man who represents hope. He holds the cross aloft. The cross occupies the uppermost right corner of the miniature to signal the true direction and meaning of the narrative. These details of rich characterization and complex storytelling are striking examples of why Matthew's work can be said to have a "cinematic" quality.

Ultimately, through his use of the cross in his narrative, Matthew has both thoroughly updated the martyr's Life and framed the viewer's reception of the narrative. His illustrations become a commentary on vision, recommending that the viewer look in a certain sort of way—with emotion and faith, in true emulation of Christ. Indeed, Matthew argues, if one looks properly, that vision has the power to convert the soul, and the devotion to the cross (as well as other visual devotions) can guide and direct a pious life.[53] Just as the icon of the Five Wise Virgins in the Life of Lucy framed the narrative and directed the viewer to look with purified senses, so also Matthew teaches the viewer how to look properly. If his advice is taken, surely the study of the narrative itself becomes a devotion.

A number of other modernizing elements of the narrative have been noted in passing. The vilification of nonbelievers as Jews, heretics, and "Saracens" is particularly characteristic of the period. Although pagans were important opponents in the narratives of earlier martyrs, throughout Matthew's text, pagans, embodied as these "others," are more harshly and specifically characterized. One reason may be that heretics and nonbelievers were perceived as a very real threat in Matthew's time.[54] Another is evident in Matthew's likening of events of the saint's Life to prophecies of the Apocalypse. The fountain of blood described in reference to martyrdom is one example, but Matthew further invokes apocalyptic imagery in his depiction of the final punishment of the nonbelievers. In the last moments of his story of the martyrs, the wicked and pagan are driven from the land (fig. 139). They are "deformed and distorted . . . maimed and blinded," as the *titulus* notes. The text elaborates further, noting insanity, possession, mouths twisted awry, eyes crossed, reversed fingers, and inflamed tongues (ll. 1768–78). Matthew has represented all of these but has emphasized the swollen tongues of the Apocalyptic punishment: "and they gnawed their tongues for pain. And blasphemed the God of heaven because of their pains and their sores and repented not of their deeds" (Rev. 16:10). Clearly, he sees such nonbelievers as a continuing threat to Christianity.

These "spiritual" narratives—the narrative of the cross interworked with an exploration of the mundane and salvational purpose of water—are important themes in Matthew's discourse because they clarify his understanding and purposeful construction of a martyr's Life. In many ways, they represent the continuation and development of older medieval symbols and ideas. Other themes that Matthew pre-

Figure 139. The wicked are driven from the land, *Passions of Alban (Albinus) and Amphibalus*,
Matthew Paris at St. Albans, 1240 or later. Dublin, Trinity College Library, MS 177,
fol. 49r. (Reproduced by permission of the Board of Trinity College Dublin)

sents, such as chivalrous virtue and the authentication of sanctity, more obviously
originate in contemporary concerns. They represent thoroughgoing changes in the
representation of sanctity in Matthew's time.

THE CHIVALRIC NARRATIVE

Although his illustrations emphasize certain themes by means of selection, and his
tituli direct the viewer's focus, most of the textual adjustments that Matthew makes
to the received hagiographic tradition of Alban's Life involve only modest expan-
sions and elaborations.[55] However, one section of text represents a major addition
on Matthew's part. The story of Aracle, the soldier who was ordered to execute Al-

THE END OF THE MONASTIC TRADITION

ban but instead was converted, is elaborated from a line or two in the Latin versions to a virtually freestanding narrative nested within the Life.[56] As such, the "hero" comes to serve as a model of saintly and martyred chivalry. In this narrative, Matthew significantly advances the idea of lay sanctity beyond the possibilities presented in the Lives of Wandrille or Edmund.

Aracle is unnamed in the earliest Latin Lives, which present merely the *topos* of the soldier who is converted by miracles and refuses to kill the saint.[57] In Matthew's version, however, he suffers a "passion" that makes him a martyr,[58] and thus he becomes a *saintly* knight. His acquisition of the name of a renowned Antique hero and his appearance as a noble knight in six illustrations surely must have appealed to Matthew's audience for reasons that a discussion of those scenes will make clear.

Aracle first appears in the scene of the miracle on the bridge, but his formal conversion and instruction by Alban are depicted on the left of folio 37r. The artist has patterned his composition after an image of a knight's initiation: Aracle kneels humbly before his patron, a sword depicted prominently in the space between them (fig. 140, left). But rather than enter the order of knighthood and the service of a king, Aracle symbolically enters the chorus of martyrs and the service of the saint, dropping his sword, as the text specifies.[59]

The illustration undertakes to show how Aracle is both noble and humble—a "gentil chevaler," according to the text.[60] His actions are nonviolent. He is beaten but holds to his faith (fig. 140, right); he is mocked but he does not rise to anger—in chivalric terms, he is "gentle of spirit," that is, slow to anger. In a second miniature and the text it illustrates (in which he has been healed miraculously by Alban's relics, fig. 141), Aracle is contrasted with the pagan soldiers and nobility, who are full of ire, rancor, and envy.[61] He even faults their bad manners as they mock him, saying, in the Anglo-Norman title, "This is not a subject for mockery which to others has value."[62] Aracle does not seek the approval of other knights (that is, vainglory) but rather the glory of truly pious actions.[63]

In each of the five miniatures (with six scenes) in which Aracle appears, Matthew characterizes the knight's virtue by visual means, often by contrasting him with the pagan nobles. He is represented as a beautiful, humble, and gentle beardless youth.[64] In contrast, the pagan nobles on their horses (see fig. 141) seem arrogant and, in one case (the knight with stars on his surcoat), even foppish or effeminate and elaborately dressed, perhaps a reference to knightly excesses.[65] A heraldic motif that appears on Aracle's cloak also appears in the *Chronica majora* on the robes

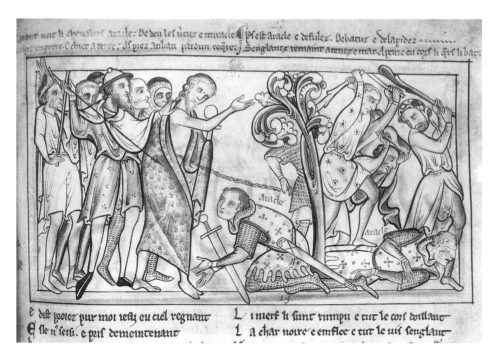

Figure 140. Aracle is converted by Alban; Alban is beaten by the pagans,
Passions of Alban (Albinus) and Amphibalus, Matthew Paris at St. Albans, 1240 or later.
Dublin, Trinity College Library, MS 177, fol. 37r. (Reproduced by permission
of the Board of Trinity College Dublin)

of a knight of whom Matthew approves,[66] just as, in fact, Alban's eventual executioner bears the arms of Fawkes de Breauté, who Matthew vilifies in his chronicles.[67] The comparison of Aracle's good with the executioner's evil is further emphasized in the Anglo-Norman *titulus,* which notes that the executioner is "a base man of bad lineage."[68] And yet, he bears the heraldic arms of a knight. Clearly Matthew is making the point that the status of knighthood alone does not confer virtue or even nobility.

Although most of these general ideas could appear in any hagiographic story—noting the saint's nobility or beauty or patience is a common element—it is the combination of virtues, Aracle's depiction in the miniatures as a good knight, and the fact that this somewhat obscure figure is prominently cast in the visual narrative, that re-creates Aracle as a hero tailored for Matthew's courtly audience. In addition to the story of Aracle, other elements strongly associated with chivalry appear in the Life of Alban. Legends about illustrious ancient ancestors of particular

Figure 141. Aracle is mocked by pagan nobles, *Passions of Alban (Albinus) and Amphibalus,*
Matthew Paris at St. Albans, 1240 or later. Dublin, Trinity College Library, MS 177, fol. 38v.
(Reproduced by permission of the Board of Trinity College Dublin)

regional importance are often a prominent feature in chivalric tales.[69] The story of
Charlemagne is elaborated in France as is that of Arthur in England.[70] In similar
fashion, Matthew defines the locale of his story as the Roman city of Verolanum,
populates it with ancient "Romans," and develops a hero with the evocative name
of Aracle (cf. Heracles).[71] Moreover, Matthew links these ancient Romans directly
to the monastery of St. Albans. They triumph over the "Saracens" in the end, and
the spiritual battlefield is left to the citizens of Verolanum, who, through "faith and
preaching, baptism and confession, prayers and discipline" expunge any guilt.[72] Remarkably like the description of a monastery in the Life of Edward, in which the
prayers and discipline of the monks are treated at great length,[73] these lines of course
ultimately refer to the monastery of St. Albans itself. Matthew even depicts a monk
in order to illustrate the passage (fig. 142). Thus, the monastery is seen as the cor-
rective for "modern" or chivalric excess.

The text thus addresses the evils as well as the virtues of chivalric practice. One

Figure 142. Faith, preaching, and baptism, *Passions of Alban (Albinus) and Amphibalus,*
Matthew Paris at St. Albans, 1240 or later. Dublin, Trinity College Library, MS 177, fol. 50r.
(Reproduced by permission of the Board of Trinity College Dublin)

last textual passage from the Life of Alban further demonstrates Matthew's intention not only to refer to the customs of chivalry but also to direct readers to the
correct forms of chivalric practice. A long passage recounting Alban's imprisonment
lovingly describes the luxuries that (presumably as a "haut mareschal") he has lost:
"bons vins," delicious meats, rich vessels, and servants.[74] He has manacles instead
of golden bracelets and lacks a fine coverlet of cotton or imported silk; indeed, he
has no bed. Although Alban ascended to his prison (in the manner of a typical martyr), he seems actually to suffer there. However, he undergoes his penance to purge
his guilt and keeps his true and good heart as a "leal chevaler" of the Lord.[75] Clearly
Matthew is aware of the secular temptations and excesses of the chivalric life, but
he devalues these pleasures by calling upon one of the premier knightly virtues,
loyalty to one's master—here God himself.

NARRATOR AS LAWYER:
EVIDENCE AND AUTHENTICATION

One last means of modernizing the Life of Alban is introduced by Matthew in order to address rising contemporary concerns about saintly authenticity. Aware of canonization procedures that used legal techniques to prove sanctity, Matthew used or created a number of narrative devices to enhance the *effect* of authenticity in his narrative. As Vauchez has shown, although canonization procedures during the later Middle Ages seem to correspond to today's levels of skepticism in gathering and testing evidence, in the last analysis, "the attitude of the popes and the cardinals [to miracles] was very much the same as that of the ordinary faithful. . . . They were ready to accept them as long as they were corroborated by witnesses who were in agreement, bore a resemblance to those described in the scriptural texts, and contributed to the edification of the Christian people."[76] In other words, the miracles were no different than they always had been, but the manner in which they were presented changed in important ways. Nevertheless, as Michael Clanchy has shown, we should not expect legal proceedings of the twelfth and thirteenth centuries to correspond to our ideas of evidentiary procedure,[77] and, in the end, strongly held belief and ancient authority carried more weight in canonization than mere evidence. Thus we find that Matthew calls upon witnesses and a plethora of supporting facts to substantiate hagiographic texts that, to a modern viewer, still remain a tissue of fiction. Nevertheless, an exploration of Matthew's narrative strategies will increase our appreciation for how he appealed to his thirteenth-century audience. If earlier medieval narratives are limited to author portraits, frontispieces, and pictured witnesses as evidence of authenticity, Matthew is able to expand into the presentation of charters and the use of particular narrative episodes to make his demonstration.[78]

Perhaps because of his work as a historian, Matthew was enamored of evidence. However, rather than sift it as would a present-day historian, Matthew amassed it, almost like a treasure hoard. The *Liber additamentorum* contains charters, writs, letters, records of the gems and jewels housed in the monastery of St. Albans, accounts and sketches of wonders, and even a drawing by another artist.[79] Matthew collects his evidence, as he tells us he has been commissioned to do by the king, in order to write a "plain and full account . . . in indelible characters in a book, that the recollection of them may not in any way be lost to posterity or any future ages."[80]

Were history and hagiography different genres for Matthew? It seems clear that Matthew saw hagiography differently. He lavished more attention on the illustrations of his saints' Lives than he did for the histories and incorporated elements from the genres of romance and epic.[81] It may be that Matthew perceived hagiography not as pure chronicle or record, but as a medium endowed with the power of persuasion—persuasion not only in the spiritual sense of conversion to faith but also persuasion used to win influence and power in court and kingdom. Perhaps it is not coincidental that the equivalent of the lawyer for the plaintiff was called the narrator during the thirteenth century.[82] Matthew makes a case for sanctity by telling the stories of saints, with the intent to persuade his audience as jury.

Matthew's persuasion operates on a number of levels. The first is marshaling of evidence. Matthew cites many documents, including charters, papal bulls and decrees, and he makes much of the presentation, reading, and authenticity of such documents in his stories and illustrations. Documents assume specific sizes and proportions, use a specialized calligraphy and, of course, are marked with seals in order to assert their authenticity with visual means as well as with legal language and signatures.[83] In both the chronicles and the saints' Lives, Matthew is careful to capture in his illustrations the proportions and "look" of legal documents (see fig. 147). Suzanne Lewis has even suggested that Matthew's script sometimes mimics the calligraphy of papal documents.[84]

Furthermore, in the Life of Edward, when an important document arrives on the scene, Matthew notes that it is read and heard.[85] This might lead the modern reader to assume that Edward was illiterate, but the Life seems to imply otherwise.[86] Rather, as Clanchy argues, it was a legal commonplace to make a record by "hearing and seeing," a quintessentially public act. Witnesses heard the words and saw the visual icon of transfer—often an object such as a knife, a branch, or a sod of earth.[87] Clanchy argues that as written records became more widely accepted, hearing and seeing was replaced by reading and hearing, as in Matthew's verbal formula.

But Matthew, as Clanchy says in another context, "treats writing as a visual skill inseparable from pictorial values,"[88] so it is not surprising that Matthew is reluctant to give up the visual signs of record making. He seems especially fond of what he calls "the testimony of a great many seals,"[89] some of which he carefully records in drawings.[90] Even the *signa* that appear in the margins of his chronicles may be considered in this light: empty purses signal a discussion of an incident of moneylending and usury;[91] two hands clasping and a ring stand for the record of a marriage.[92]

Indeed, the much discussed line in Edward's Life that notes the use of miniatures "so that what the ear hears the eyes should see"[93] may refer as much or more to this sort of strategy of authentication as to the fact that the exemplar of the text was meant to be read aloud and was illustrated. The line appears as part of a prayer to Edward in which Matthew (as the author) promises to preserve the saint's memory. The concept is very close to the medieval legal notion of hearing and seeing, which involved a performance as a means to impress witnesses with a memory of the event. To corroborate the authenticity of a document, witnesses would both listen to the proceedings and see a display of a *signum*. Matthew makes use of this approach in order to memorialize the saint, but has converted the terse and iconic forms of legal visual evidence into an expanded and rich visual narrative of testimony and "factual" detail.

One telling example of this concern for persuasion through authentication is Matthew's emphasis on place, an element that is essential even today in a legal document. It is true that hagiographers have always sprinkled their narratives with place names, but these often seem almost random, intended to create the effect of authenticity rather than constituting precise information. By modern standards, Matthew's information is sometimes just as imprecise, but he takes great care to elaborate it. His maps in the *Chronica* are justly famous, and he dedicates a number of oversize pages to itineraries from London to Apulia (with further directions on to Jerusalem).[94] In similar fashion, in his hagiographic narratives he goes into great detail about traveling, trips, and distances and chooses to illustrate a great number of such expeditions.[95]

One particular example of the depiction of a short trip is remarkable for its attempt at precision. In the Life of Edward, St. Peter appears miraculously and dedicates the newly reconstructed abbey of Westminster. A fisherman gives Peter a ride across the River Thames in his boat, and during the ride they catch a salmon.[96] Peter instructs the fisherman to explain what has happened and to give the salmon to the bishop of London, cutting short the bishop's journey to the church so that Peter himself can perform the dedication. In the illustration of the event, we see on the left the catch and on the right the gift of the salmon (planked, as if this were a gourmet gift-shop delivery, fig. 143).[97] Between the two scenes is a visual divider, a towerlike building with a flag marked "lame bee" (Lambeth). Matthew adds a peculiar little notation at the bottom of the left side: two diminutive buildings with some wavy lines between them. Both the *titulus* on the divider building and the little *signum* are Matthew's attempts to give us more information than is contained in the text. The bishop of London resided at Lambeth, and in the shorthand notation

Figure 143. Peter catches a salmon; the testimony of the fisherman, *La Estoire de Seint Aedward le Rei,* London or Westminster, 1250. Cambridge, University Library, MS Ee 3.59, fol. 18v. (Reproduced by permission of the Syndics of Cambridge University Library)

below, Matthew is giving us an itinerary between Westminster and Lambeth, just as he represented itineraries on his maps. With this notation, he informs us that the usual route from one to another is across the river. Furthermore, he tries to convey a sense of movement in the fishing scene, showing us that the catch is made while the boat is moving. Such an attempt to include supplementary, sensory data in an illustration is not unique to this instance; rather it is typical of Matthew's narrative and adds to its ability to persuade.

To strengthen his persuasive effects, Matthew also evokes other senses such as smell and hearing. The most striking example of such a sense-oriented illustration is a depiction of the rediscovery of the relics of Alban in the Dublin manuscript. The scene moves beyond the hagiography of the saint into the later history of his abbey—here, the invention of St. Alban by the pious and good king Offa. Acting on the instructions of a dream-vision, the king directs an excavation and the relics are discovered (fig. 144).[98] In his miniature, Matthew adds a few written captions, as opposed to labels or *tituli,* an element that is rare in this manuscript but has in-

Figure 144. Offa discovers Alban's relics, *Passions of Alban (Albinus) and Amphibalus*,
Matthew Paris at St. Albans, 1240 or later. Dublin, Trinity College Library, MS 177, fol. 59r.
(Reproduced by permission of the Board of Trinity College Dublin)

teresting precedents in English manuscript illustration.[99] One monk pronounces
"redolet" (it smells), and another opens his mouth to sing "te deum laudamus." Both
speech acts must be understood in terms of their hagiographic context.

The first editor of the text, observing that the monk who pronounces "redolet"
is touching his nose, read the utterance to mean "it smells bad." On the contrary,
according to both the hagiographic *topos* familiar to the faithful since the early Christian period and the connotation of *redoleo,* the sweet smell of relics discovered upon
excavation is a sure sign of sanctity.

The other caption, "te deum laudamus," represents the incipit of the hymn of
thanksgiving, the singing of which is a customary auditory marker of miracles
or the exposure of relics (note also the open mouth and swelling throat of the
singing monk).[100] Matthew also depicts the singing of this hymn in miracles
worked by the relics of Edward the Confessor and in other miracles in Edward's
vita.[101] By immersing the viewer in sound, sight, and smell through aural, visual,

Figure 145. The translation of Alban's relics, *Passions of Alban (Albinus) and Amphibalus,*
Matthew Paris at St. Albans, 1240 or later. Dublin, Trinity College Library, MS 177, fol. 61 v.
(Reproduced by permission of the Board of Trinity College Dublin)

and olfactory signs, Matthew is, in effect, offering conclusive evidence about the
relics' authenticity.

Other examples sustain and develop such effects. Soon after the invention, in a
scene depicting the martyr's elevation, Matthew again evokes the sense of smell
with the prominent depiction of a swinging censer and suggests a spoken testimony
with the caption: "hic est vere martir" (figs. 145 and 146). In contrast, Matthew depicts the *absence* of sound in a miniature of the Life of Edward (fig. 147). In the text
he specifies that a document is read silently. In order to convey this peculiar silence,
he turns the pictured readers' backs to us.[102] Finally, these sorts of "you are there"
effects of sound and smell are paralleled with the persistent use in the *tituli* of the
phrase, "Ci veit." This phrase recurs often in the text describing Alban's conversion.
It refers to the vividness of Alban's own witness and his visions of Christianity, but
it also reaches out to include the viewer of the miniatures—"Here see."[103]

A final episode confirms Matthew's purposeful use of the senses and concludes

THE END OF THE MONASTIC TRADITION

Figure 146. The elevation of Alban's relics, *Passions of Alban (Albinus) and Amphibalus*,
Matthew Paris at St. Albans, 1240 or later. Dublin, Trinity College Library, MS 177, fol. 61r.
(Reproduced by permission of the Board of Trinity College Dublin)

the illustration of the Dublin manuscript with a flourish of reader involvement (figs.
148 and 149). After Offa has discovered the relics of Alban, built the monastery, and
endowed it, he goes to Rome to obtain the pope's confirmation of the charter. In the
last scenes of the manuscript we see the virtuous Offa, just disembarked from his return voyage, leaving his horse in the care of a groom and then hastening to present
his charter to the abbot (his pious actions are an admonition to any royal viewer). At
the far right, a little man energetically rings the monastery's bells in celebration. The
vivid sense of motion conveyed in the figure makes the bells almost audible. Indeed,
Matthew wants us not only to hear the bells but also to respond to them. Bells play
an important role in the *Chronica majora* on two occasions. They are rung to call the
people to witness a legal proceeding, and they are silenced by the great papal inter-
diction of England, only to be rung upon its lifting. In both cases, the bells call the

Figure 147. The pope grants the English bishops a charter, *La Estoire de Seint Aedward le Rei*,
London or Westminster, 1250. Cambridge, University Library, MS Ee 3.59, fol. 14v.
(Reproduced by permission of the Syndics of Cambridge University Library)

people together in powerful corporate assembly, and Matthew renders these bells as
signa, silenced or ringing in the margins of his history manuscripts.[104]

The presentation of a foundation charter to a monastery is an equally important
legal and historical event. As Clanchy has observed, the act of granting a charter
would have been witnessed by the local populace,[105] and the charter of an important monastic foundation would mark the inception of a powerful religious community. In fact, the Anglo-Norman *titulus* to this scene states that the king "made
a present of his purchase at the high altar in the sight of his people." However, despite the expectations that these traditions and text engender, Matthew's illustration is remarkably devoid of people, excepting the two nobles next to the king's
horse. The lack of a pictured crowd, assembly, or community is especially striking
if one compares the charter miniature with the elevation miniature a few folios earlier. That miniature includes an impressive line of processing bishops, each one care-

Figure 148. Offa arrives at St. Albans, *Passions of Alban (Albinus) and Amphibalus,* Matthew Paris at St. Albans, 1240 or later. Dublin, Trinity College Library, MS 177, fol. 62v. (Reproduced by permission of the Board of Trinity College Dublin)

fully labeled (see fig. 145). We know that these same bishops in fact served as witnesses to the charter because their names are recorded below the depiction of Offa's presentation.[106]

The stark contrast suggests that Matthew left out the witnessing bishops and populace for a specific reason. Just as Clanchy argues that contemporary legal documents were shifting their emphasis from the living memory of witnesses to the potential of the written document to witness for all futurity, it would seem that Matthew wanted to draw attention to potential *reading* witnesses to this scene. He does so simply by eliminating pictured witnesses. The strategy forces the readers of the manuscript to become the required witnesses of not only the pious actions of the good king, but also, and more important, the authenticity and truth of the document. Hence, both charter and saint's Life are validated—not "you *were* there," but "we *are* there."[107] Finally, if Matthew is the advocate for the plaintiff, we become the court. Matthew intends that we be fully convinced not only of the sanctity of

Figure 149. The charter is presented to St. Albans and the bells are rung, *Passions of Alban (Albinus) and Amphibalus,* Matthew Paris at St. Albans, 1240 or later. Dublin, Trinity College Library, MS 177, fol. 63r. (Reproduced by permission of the Board of Trinity College Dublin)

Alban but also of the saint's prestige and of the prestige of his resting place, the monastery of St. Albans.

MATTHEW'S THEMATIC INNOVATIONS

As a hagiographer in the thirteenth century, Matthew did what hagiographers, especially pictorial hagiographers, have always done—he renewed the Life of the saint in terms of contemporary concerns. Rather than focus on emotional reactions aroused by a martyr's tortures as did an older form of hagiography, he develops a narrative that allows the viewer to imitate Alban's devotional spirituality and, like a university master of theology, explicates the deeper symbolic meaning of his miracles. In a further updating, unlike the narratives of the early martyrs, this narrative includes miracles that fail to convert all witnesses. Rather than the stunned and instantly converted viewers of early martyr miracles, the presence of hard-hearted viewers, unimpressed with evidence of the divine, reminds Matthew's audience of the obduracy of heretics and unbelievers. Such ineffectual viewing is the opposite of proper Christian vision, which, as Matthew shows, is a protracted experience, prepared by learning and prayer, and accomplished with faith.

Other variations that Matthew introduces into his martyr's story establish Alban's power and prestige. In contrast to unworldly early medieval martyrs, Alban is a perfected reflection of his courtly audience. Matthew takes pains to represent Alban and his convert Aracle as pinnacles of chivalric virtue. Alban and Aracle have the fine manners of the chivalric nobility. They are saints that the nobility can emulate.

Finally, in taking advantage of contemporary developments in conceptions of authentication and witnessing, Matthew proves himself a narrator of unusual force and creativity. He expertly "works" his audience, incorporating rhetorical structures of authority and evidence to reassure and persuade, and in so doing transforms these holy martyrs not into historical figures but rather into powerful patrons of contemporary sanctity.

Matthew Paris may not be a typical hagiographer of the thirteenth century. Few hagiographers can write text and draw illustrations, and fewer still have Matthew's creativity and commitment. His work, however, sheds considerable light on the changes in late medieval hagiography. At the same time, these changes reveal what an essential foundation earlier pictorial hagiography supplied: it is the bedrock upon which Matthew's innovations rise. Matthew can "build" an efficacious image of sanctity only because he so perfectly commands the genre.

EPILOGUE

Narrative Innovation

૩૭

Ending this study with Matthew Paris implies that his innovations are remarkable. His stories, however, appear at a time when the narrative arts are flourishing—in poetry, song, and even in sermons—and it is essential to consider developments in other media in order to assess Matthew's creative contribution. In particular, frescoes and stained glass are important loci of narrative innovation and will require close examination. Even before assessing these media, however, Matthew's work should be situated in relation to the primary concern of this study, that is, the working of the genre of pictorial hagiography.

GENRE AND INNOVATION IN HAGIOGRAPHY

In assessing the ways in which Matthew's storytelling relies on the norms and working of genre, it will be useful to review our findings concerning pictorial hagiography and its "types."

The understanding of genre that this study develops is intimately engaged with narrative effects and audience reaction. Little is formulaic or obvious about the medieval reception of saints' Lives. Types mix, expectations are reversed, and genders exchange goals and virtues. Notwithstanding this unpredictability, reading the Lives as a genre not only makes them understandable but discloses an unexpected richness of meaning.

One striking characteristic of hagiographic texts and pictures is their quality of intertextuality and interpictoriality. A reader's or viewer's understanding of saintly

Lives was and is informed by many different texts and their visual representation. It is by no means surprising but nonetheless significant that the Bible proves to be very important in supplying both metaphors and paradigms of action. Wise Virgins dominate the Lives of female martyrs. "Hastening" to a "heavenly home" motivates the stories of monks. The paired actions of preaching and teaching (Christ's injunction to the Apostles), structures the Lives of bishops, and the humble enactment of charity for widows and orphans finds an important place in the Lives of kings. Even a tone or voice might be borrowed from biblical texts: one virgin's Life reads like a variant of the Song of Songs, and any martyr's Life is reminiscent of the prayerful discourse of the Psalms. In addition to such biblical texts many other texts, from liturgies to the Benedictine Rule to the *Psychomachia* of Prudentius, shape the narrative of Lives, lending emphases and literary structures as well as details.

Finally, however, the most important shaping force for hagiographic narratives remains other hagiographic narratives. In making meaning, saints' Lives function as a genre with many shared qualities and structures. Although Gregory of Tours claims a sameness in the *"Life* of the Saints," that sameness does not consist of the literal repetition of Lives but in their realization of a common goal—the renewal of Christ's Life through new narratives. Instead of sameness, the genre of hagiography produces a "horizon of expectation" that it both works with and against. Indeed, every new text and picture relies both on convention for intelligibility and on innovation for renewed effect.

Thus, rather than using fixed lists of virtues or required scenes, hagiographers look for new effects in a relatively predictable environment. Like the working of miracles, the impact of hagiographic narrative relies upon some element of the unexpected in order to achieve the desired end of inducing compunction and compassion in the viewer. If martyrs' Lives become too repetitious or predictable, they no longer move the viewer. Virgins' Lives depend upon eliciting a pity for the destruction of physical beauty in order to drive home the message that true beauty is divine.

In contrast, confessors' Lives are less dependent on effects of pity and more insistent on structuring a hierarchy within which the viewer might find a place. The Lives of bishops project an "image of power" not merely through the frontal and ceremonial pose of the bishop but through a narrative insistence upon hierarchy and the power of the unified Church and its liturgy. Insofar as the power of the liturgy is depicted as glorious, viewers are persuaded to believe that their place in it can be glorious as well. Bishops become a perfected image of their office.

Similarly, Lives of monks and abbots reveal the perfection that obedience and attendance to the details of a structured Life can achieve. Monks' Lives, however, emphasize the variability of hagiographic narrative, emphatically replacing standardized scenes with *topoi* that show infinite adjustments to particular surroundings. In the end, particularly in the case of abbots, a monastic holy Life is one marked by grace not by rule alone. The audience of such Lives, often monks themselves, might not achieve sanctity but might be led through imitation of the Lives to a perfection of spirit and a joy in community. Lay viewers might perceive the perfected power of a patron and come to trust in God's care for their sustenance.

The Lives of kings further explore the role of orders and offices in lay society. In particular, the question of the right use of power is appraised and given narrative expression. Because such Lives are often addressed to kings themselves, they structure an admonitory narrative that insists upon the ecclesiastical values delimiting kingship: among others, consultation with bishops, respect for ecclesiastical property, royal charity, and royal mercy. To the extent that they speak to monks and pilgrims, royal Lives also insist on the power of both the living and the dead king to make miracles and protect his people.

In contrast, queens seem to follow monastic and occasionally episcopal narrative models in preference to those of kings. No matter what the model, however, a queen's Life is clearly circumscribed in terms of her potential exercise of mundane power. This was not true for other sorts of confessors and is surely an effect of gender. In the Life of Radegund, the queen's spiritual power is particularly grounded in her body—her right hand makes miracles, and her touch conveys both a sense of motherly care and the ability to heal. The intimacy of touch creates a warmth and an emotive quality that, once more, actively directs the viewer's response, as did the effects of compunction induced by martyrs' Lives.

Finally, Matthew Paris's telling of Alban's *vita* knits together many of the themes and issues of earlier saints' types but also works many new narrative strategies. Alban testifies as a martyr, exercises episcopal prestige, even practices monastic virtues. His cult is renewed and celebrated by an exemplary king. However, he is also imbued with chivalric virtue and enjoys the veneration of a chivalric follower. Matthew makes use of intertextuality and specific interpictoriality but also exploits new strategies of storytelling with an almost cinematic sense of action and detail.

Of special interest is Matthew's use of the "frame" in his narrative, because it is explicitly linked to generic norms and the creation of readerly expectations by the text. Two examples of rhetorical frames in Lives were examined in earlier chapters.

The frame in the Life of Romanus sets a discourse of active moral example within another discourse of explication (which, however, also contains action), expressed first in text but amplified by an imaginative artist. In the frame used in the pictorial Life of Lucy, pictures structure a reading of the Life that insists upon a proper use of the senses in apprehending the texts *and* pictures. Finally, the frame employed in the Life of Alban encompasses or even exceeds both these approaches. By demonstrating the power that sight can have in vivifying faith, the Life of Alban invests the process of viewing narrative with a decisive importance. The frame claims a sort of semiotic perfection of the cross, which throughout the narrative controls teaching, dogma, and devotion. In turn, the frame encloses and sets in motion a narrative, full of action, that seeks to rediscover that perfection.

Against this background, it is particularly clear that Matthew's hagiography reflects many of the new ideas of the thirteenth-century cult of saints as well. He creates a representation of chivalric sanctity and strengthens the themes of devotion and authentication in saints' Lives. These same themes are reflected in the contemporary *Dialogue on Miracles* by the Cistercian abbot Caesarius of Heisterbach. Like Gregory the Great's project, the *Dialogues,* with which he taught his household (and the Christian world) how to venerate the saints, Caesarius's project was a teaching device for novices, imitative of the *Dialogues* but with new miracles.[1] Caesarius mirrors the form of Gregory's text and includes audience reaction, but he brings the project into the modern world in much the same way as did Matthew. In this sense, Matthew must be seen as participating in a larger hagiographic trend, even if his expression is unique.

OTHER POSSIBILITIES
IN LATER MEDIEVAL HAGIOGRAPHY

In ending with the thirteenth century, I purposefully selected the hagiography of Matthew Paris as a focus of attention. Needless to say, looking at his manuscripts is just one of several possibilities for examining how the hagiographic genre and types developed during that century and later. Given that hagiography is rarely marked as the product of individual "genius," and is so often an anonymous endeavor, perhaps it would have been more appropriate to look to less distinctive products of the thirteenth century. Many other illustrated manuscripts might have served as appropriate subjects and would have resulted in somewhat different assessments of the relationship between innovation and genre. Nevertheless, most show a purposeful "updating" of norms. For example, the 1250 Life of Denis (Paris, Bibliothèque nationale, MS n.a. fr. 1098), in a long series of twenty-one miniatures comprising fifty-two scenes celebrates a monastic patron with the intention of teaching an audience of noble pilgrims about the saint.[2] Like Matthew's hagiography, there is a mixture of languages: the text is in French and captions are in Latin. Alternatively, the thirteenth-century Eligius Roll of Noyon depicts the conventional miracles of a bishop saint but characterizes them as contemporaneous events.[3] The artist does so by borrowing some of Matthew Paris's tricks and compositions.[4] The inclusion of an almost *cinéma vérité* depiction of the saint's funeral attended by ranks of mourners, both clergy and laity, with a full range of emotions and a remarkable quality of detail, brings the saint's death directly into the life of the viewer.

Other hagiographic projects of the later Middle Ages, the fourteenth and fifteenth centuries, also build upon earlier hagiography and push the boundaries of the genre to create powerful new narratives and even new types—such as the mystic, usually a woman.[5] These manuscripts present tempting subjects for further study.

The fourteenth-century pictorial Lives of Louis, which we were able to examine all too briefly above, expand the possibilities of royal sanctity.[6] They exhibit a new vision of pious action in life through charity and a new idea of holy war. The fifteenth-century German Life of Hildegard from the monastery of Kempten creates a unique picture of posthumous royal care through miracles. Unlike Queen Radegund, Hildegard, who was said to be a wife of Charlemagne, appears in royal regalia along with her son Louis the Pious, dressed in similar raiment, in depictions of miracle after miracle at the abbey she reputedly founded.[7]

Even the Life of an apostolic bishop could be made to serve decidedly political and civic ends, as Charlotte Lacaze has shown. Multiple fourteenth-century copies of, again, the Life of St. Denis were made at the monastery's behest in order to curry favor at court. The famous manuscript in Paris (Bibliothèque nationale MS. fr. 2090–2092) with its "bridges" and depictions of trades sets Denis' story in the contemporary city of Paris, represented as a vision of Paradise, dominated by peace, prosperity, and good government.[8]

The fourteenth-century Lives of Hedwig and Benoite and the fifteenth-century manuscript of Colette turn from overtly political concerns to spiritual ones and explore new areas of women's visions. The 1312 manuscript of the Life of Benoite was made for Heluis d'Escoufflans, a nun of the abbey of Sainte-Benoite d'Origny with royal connections. St. Benoite is an extraordinary example of a virgin saint who seems to preach and baptize like a bishop and must have served as an unequaled patron for her monastery.[9] Hedwig, on the other hand, was born to sanctity. She was part of the "dynasty of saints" that also produced Elisabeth of Hungary—one of the first miniatures in the manuscript of her Life (dated 1353, J. Paul Getty Museum, 83.MN.126, Ludwig XI 7) depicts her saintly genealogy.[10] Like that of Elisabeth, but with even more detail, Hedwig's Life shows an imitable life of charity and self-deprivation. Hedwig also models means of devotion, especially the use of art to visualize and pray. Alternatively, the Life of the reforming Poor Clare, Colette, is filled with extraordinary and beautiful miniatures of visions, some of which she experienced as tortures.[11] In her suffering she reiterates narrative conventions of virgins' Lives, but in her historical life she was a powerful figure and the founder of many monasteries; Margaret of York, the patron for whom the manuscript was made, must have found Colette a compelling model. Of course, there are also many late medieval manuscripts like the tiny illustrated examples of the Life of Margaret in Princeton, that although not gorgeous objects, clearly represent the category of manuscripts made for private possession.[12]

The Getty manuscript (MS 26) of the Life of the Italian brothers Aimus and Vermondus of Meda, virtually identical to another illustrated manuscript of the same Life, more resembles an illustrated miracle collection than a *vita*.[13] However, in the very few miniatures dedicated to their living sanctity, the brothers act as exemplary laymen. They go out to hunt, get chased up a tree by savage and murderous boars, and in exchange for the Virgin's miraculous intercession on their behalf, found a church where they are eventually interred. In their many miracles, during which they are depicted as beautiful, gentle, noble, and well mannered, they seem to act as the special patrons of the lay nobility of their region.

Of course, other illustrated Lives seem less concerned with innovation and more involved in simply telling stories that were important for particular audiences. In a copy of the Lives of Geneviève and Magloire of the first quarter of the fourteenth century made for the library of Charles V and thus intended to be read by the Parisian court (Paris, Bibliothèque nationale, MS fr. 13508), small illustrations inserted in the columns follow the texts of the many miracle accounts. Geneviève is, of course, the patron saint of Paris, having saved the city from the Huns. The relics of the Irish monastic saint Magloire were housed in a monastery dedicated to him in Paris.[14]

I have mentioned only a few of the many manuscripts dedicated to saints' Lives that continue to enrich the tradition described in this book. Looking more carefully at the generic and innovative qualities of the narrative of each would be a tempting avenue to follow in both the continuation and expansion of the principles of this study.

But beyond the medieval heritage, I would contend that issues of genre and modeling in hagiography continue even today. On 9 June 1997, the *New York Times* reported:

> At the Mass today, [Pope John Paul II] used the canonization of Poland's revered Queen Jadwiga, the 14th-century founder of a royal dynasty, to call on Poles to rejoice in their heritage. But there was also a hint to Poland's current political leaders to heed her example. "Undertaking great works in the national and international sphere, she desired nothing for herself," he said, citing the queen's life as an example of how religious faith and culture can strengthen each other.

Perhaps using a fourteenth-century queen as a model for post-communist democratic male leaders seems an extreme mixing of subgenres. However, we have seen something remarkably similar in the fashion in which St. Louis develops his sanctity through the exercise of feminine royal virtues. Thus, the hagiographic project continues—qualities persist, yet in that very persistence they set the stage for change. Ultimately, Matthew's hagiography is just one particularly interesting example within the normal working of the hagiographic genre.

PICTORIAL NARRATIVE OF THE LATER MIDDLE AGES: INNOVATION AND OTHER MEDIA

But Matthew's narrative cannot be assessed only in terms of hagiography in manuscripts. His innovations must also be situated within the larger picture of the development of later medieval narrative. The question of whether Matthew was himself responsible for these innovations at a time when the narrative arts were burgeoning in many forms is a difficult one. Given the better preservation of documents, and narratives in other media in the later Middle Ages, there may no longer be any justification in confining an investigation to manuscripts alone (although at least one scholar argues that late medieval manuscripts are more suited than ever to the exploitation of visual narrative).[15] In particular, claims have been made for the primacy of stained glass and fresco as uniquely fruitful venues of narrative invention. Have these media eclipsed manuscripts as arenas of innovation?

I have characterized Matthew's work as in every way fuller and more expressive than earlier narrative because it is cinematic and insistently active, calls upon expressive gesture and emotion, and is concerned with setting and the details of life. Furthermore, the narratives are emphatically longer than those of earlier Lives. Dogmatic, still images that called upon the viewer to reflect and recall analogous images and ideas have been left almost entirely behind, and the viewer is caught up in the rush and complexity of a unique narrative. Multiple thematic elements weave in and out of the story and comments are made (literally) in asides. Nevertheless, there is also a strong sense of organization. The narrative is arranged into clearly differentiated sequences and punctuated with oppositional structures. Authentication and witnessing are primary concerns. Can we find these same qualities in narratives in other media?[16]

In Italy, as Hans Belting argues, two new narrative modes surfaced in the thirteenth and fourteenth centuries in frescoes. One, represented by Giotto's Life of Christ in Padua, has a new "psychological interpretation and stresses the expression of moods and personalities."[17] This surely surpasses anything Matthew attempts, but it is hardly typical of the thirteenth century. Giotto's achievement was not fully exploited until much later in the history of art. Belting's second narrative mode, represented by the Life of Francis in the upper church at Assisi, is, on the other hand, very like Matthew Paris's, albeit in a general sense. It is filled with evidential detail and topographical specificity as well as action that resembles that of a "painted movie."[18] Is it a coincidence that the second mode should be found in a saint's Life and especially in the Life of Francis? As I noted at the outset of chapter 9, very early in its history, Franciscan spirituality found a special place for art as both authentication of sanctity and as a form of public preaching. Following this trend, the cycle of Francis at Assisi became a canonical narrative in a way unlike that of any other saint. Dieter Blume has argued that sketches of the Assisi cycle were used to reproduce the Life in at least four other monasteries.[19] My contention that hagiography is a primary field for the exploration of narrative possibilities is supported by this evidence. More clearly addressing the question at hand, it may be said that Matthew's narrative innovations are paralleled, although not surpassed (except perhaps by Giotto), in thirteenth-century fresco painting.

Nevertheless, fresco does present a unique opportunity for a more public form of narrative. In a study centered on watercolor copies of lost trecento narrative frescoes of Margaret of Cortona, Joanna Cannon and André Vauchez argue for the prestige of visual witness.[20] The copies were made as evidence for canonization procedures for the saint. Cannon effectively compares the frescoes to two extant versions of Margaret's Life—on a painted panel and in a series of reliefs from her tomb—and distinguishes subtle variations in intention and reception. One remarkable fresco depicts Cardinal Orsini visiting Cortona, authenticating various miracles *in situ*. This fresco thus doubly "witnesses," for the miracles and simultaneously for the validity of art as "witness." Cannon argues that the frescoes and other art work that decorated Margaret's shrine promoted a particular interest in the saint as a civic figure appealing to a lay audience, but she also notes that while the frescoes closest to the tomb in the nave have labels in the vernacular, those closer to the altar have Latin labels. These narrative subtleties recall those of Matthew Paris (although we should remember that Matthew composed the texts himself; apparently trecento artists had to have them translated in order to illustrate them).[21]

Furthermore, from the evidence presented by Cannon and Vauchez, it is clear that the centrality of imagery and art that is so marked in the cult of Francis of Assisi is not unique among Italian cults of saints. Indeed, Cannon offers evidence of a remarkable originality and vigor in the promotion of saints' cults by means of art in Italy during the fourteenth century. Both in the case of Margaret of Cortona and in the other cults, images were used extensively as evidence, portraits, and cult substitutions for a visible body. Nevertheless, the claim is also made that Margaret's shrine is exceptional—second only to that of Francis in the range and ambition of its artistic embellishment. Because of the interaction of the many public media used to promote the cult of the saint, the evidence from Cortona does not so much argue for the particular effectiveness of fresco in regard to narrative effects, but rather demonstrates the potential impact of a more public art at a somewhat later date.[22]

Finally, stained glass has been similarly praised for its public storytelling. It has often been called a superbly effective "Bible of the illiterate." Given the propensity during the thirteenth century for complex narrative effects, how clearly did these stories communicate? Were they the source of narrative innovations that thereafter passed to other media? Some scholars have made peremptory claims about the significance of stained glass for the history of narrative in the Middle Ages.

Surely, the medium of stained glass did experience an explosion of pictorial narrative during the thirteenth century. Even if the phenomenon is relatively short lived and confined almost exclusively to that century alone, the volume of narrative produced during the short period is very impressive. The cathedral of Chartres contained 185 figurative windows, and the Sainte Chapelle had narrative windows with as many as 205 scenes. Can these numbers argue that "the medium of stained glass itself . . . took on the challenge of the extended sequence almost as an experiment and in so doing brought the whole genre of narrative painting a great step further"?[23]

With this question in mind, Wolfgang Kemp has made an attempt to characterize the narratives of stained glass in the thirteenth century, and his characterizations hold many similarities and some important differences to what we have found in the work of Matthew Paris.[24] Kemp has also sought to trace the origins of these elements. He emphasizes the role of the *jongleur* in opening narrative to daily life and secular entertainment, and in providing a recognizable codification of gesture available for use in artistic representation. He finds a habit of typological thought that not only allows narratives to express relationships between the Old and New Testaments but also to use typological structure to include secular elements and other sorts of oppositional elements into signifying structures. These are not confined to occasional oppositions but extend so far that they clearly organize the entire narrative. They take remarkable advantage of the visual possibilities of seeing all-at-once that are unique to pictorial narrative and stained glass.

Similarly, Émile Mâle has argued that, in the Good Samaritan window at Sens, the main theme is depicted in the four central lozenges, rising vertically through the window. Circling this core, a typological narrative from Genesis is retold.[25] It is precisely the schematic order of the window that makes the typology "readable." Kemp accepts this arrangement as paradigmatic but shows that in other examples typological elaboration is expanded for reasons of narrative impetus or pleasure so that the theology is no longer legible and apparent.

Kemp particularly focuses on the thirteenth-century sermon as an element that influenced or paralleled the structure of stained glass windows. He argues that these sermons were both more open to their audience than those of earlier centuries and marked with carefully constructed mnemonic divisions and subdivisions. Such structures also occur in poetry, music, architecture, and philosophy.[26] He credits this "powerfully evoked . . . spatial order" as a parallel to what he sees as the most innovative element in stained glass—its geometric structure.

It is here, at the question of visual structure, that Matthew and the tradition of manuscript hagiography part company with the narratives of stained glass as described by Kemp. If indeed the geometric schemata of the windows are their most distinctive feature, and "*divisio* can be a carrier of meaning,"[27] then stained glass has a much more structured approach to story than does anything we have seen in manuscripts.[28]

Madeline Caviness, however, describes a somewhat different view of narratives in stained glass. Like Kemp, she emphasizes contemporary literary and oral traditions. Although in a summary of subjects, she gives a prominent place to hagiography, she concludes that Old Testament, New Testament, and hagiographic stories all finally tell of "heroes" of "popular romance."[29] Furthermore, she argues for a divergence from written text and suggests that the narratives have a quality of recitation.[30] On the other hand, directly opposed to Kemp's approach is her skepticism about the organizational clarity and narrative abilities of stained glass. She emphasizes developmental change and variability over principles of order,[31] and asserts that programs can be "incoherent."[32]

What needs to be kept in mind in reading both glass and hagiography is that medieval narrative pictures are more than "mere illustrations" and cannot be adequately summed up in verbal titles or fairly assessed according to modern logic. In that way, rather than marking a story as a "failure" as both Kemp and Caviness ultimately do, medieval comments about narrative confusion could be used to assess reception and modes of reading. For example, in a mid-thirteenth-century sermon on the Good Samaritan by Eudes de Châteauroux, the French cardinal relates a story:

> "A man was going down from Jerusalem to Jericho, and he fell among thieves." Whenever I reach this place, I am reminded of when I was a boy and used to look at a window in which this parable or story was depicted and as I had no idea what it all meant, a young man came up to me, a layman I did not know, and told me: These paintings made the clerics and the priests very confused, because if the priest and the layman are compared here, it appears that the priests have no pity for the poor and the suffering, whereas the laity have a great deal. And then he expounded the gospel story to me.[33]

This anecdote is rich with possibilities. It makes a compelling argument for the striking quality of images and the way that they become linked in memory with ideas and words. It also seems to argue that stories can have different receptions with different audiences, here lay or cleric (although we must remember a cleric is speaking). That a boy "had no idea" of the meaning does not imply that the narrative failed, but rather demonstrates that in addition to being read, the story had other meaning (at least to the *adult* Eudes), dependent on context. In this sermon explicating the Good Samaritan story, the adult Eudes is making an exemplum of his own childish need to understand and goes on to find that "this story was fulfilled in . . . Francis, who was no cleric but a layman." He concludes that the Good Samaritan's inn was symbolic of the Franciscan order.[34] Whether or not Eude's adult theologizing has anything to do with the original meaning of the stained glass is open to question. Nevertheless, the passage shows both that viewers read windows and narratives in personal ways, and that "typological" and schematic structures could be read intertextually.

Thus, glass narratives are perhaps not as different from those in hagiographic manuscripts as they may have at first appeared.[35] Systematic order does not seem to be as important an element as some stained glass scholars have argued. And finally, it may be granted that, in some sense, hagiographic narratives antedate glass narratives.[36]

One unique innovation in glass, however, might lie in the use of secondary narratives and themes. While manuscript illustrations usually closely follow accompanying texts, windows are free from textual constraint.[37] Glass could take advantage of a new sensibility such as that apparent in the Good Samaritan windows, where reference to secular entertainments and monetary exchange is intrinsic to the story.[38] Furthermore, when hagiographic material is involved, although narratives often conform to genre qualities—as in the episcopal *topoi* evident in the window of St. Lubin at Chartres[39]—many times fresh subjects are chosen and explored in novel ways. Windows with the stories of Julian the hospitaller and Eustache, in particular, reveal an innovative attention to lay concerns.

In the end, the question of whether Matthew was an innovator or merely part of a larger cultural development cannot be fully resolved. However, although Matthew works somewhat later than the earliest of achievements in stained glass, it is clear that his narratives are not specifically derivative of narrative in glass. His work, although the source of certain compelling narrative devices, and particularly cogent and complex in its effects,[40] is not unusual in any particular for the thirteenth century. Ultimately, we must conclude that Matthew was one of many creative storytellers of the later Middle Ages.

Stained glass, however, *is* singled out among media in a contemporary recognition of narrative effectiveness that is notable for what it says about the ultimate goals of religious pictorial narrative. In the early thirteenth-century, Pierre de Roissy described the glass of Chartres as "divine writings . . . [that] throw the light of the true sun, that is to say the light of God, into the interior of churches, that is, into the hearts of the faithful by filling them with light."[41] With these comments, Roissy emphatically returns us to certain themes that were important at the outset of this study. He unequivocally equates the visual and the written and does not differentiate pictures from writing in the ability of narratives to teach. More importantly, despite the grandeur of his light metaphor and the particular aptness of his description for glass, the idea of knowledge gaining special access to the heart through the eyes is remarkable for its familiarity. Gregory the Great, of course, described precisely the same trajectory of the perception of the divine *through* sight to memory, faith, and final portrayal on the heart. Throughout this study, the conversion of the heart through narrative "writings" and light or sight has been put forward as the essence of effective narrative.

The title of this book, of course, was derived from those same comments by Gregory about "pictured imagery." As leader of the Western Church, Pope Gregory's larger project was to edify the faithful, whether through biblical commentary, or the Lives of saints. As a visual thinker, when it served his purposes, Gregory never disdained using imagery, real or metaphorical. Following Gregory's lead, I have argued for the effectiveness of visual narratives in achieving the edification of the faithful. Saints' stories, both textual and pictorial, are an inherently serious endeavor meant to do the hard work of hagiography, that is, to change the heart of the viewer. Pictorial hagiography is especially useful to these ends, employing devices such as empathy and compunction and strategies such as opening an entry for viewer, while taking advantage of the striking effect of seeing-all-at-once. Nevertheless, for Gregory the final effect was necessarily interior. The aim of hagiography was not to be found in any creation of the hagiographer, pictorial or textual, but in inducing a movement beyond words and images—in creating an effect on the soul. If pictorial hagiography is finally successful, it leaves lines, colors, and words behind and rises to more rarefied images, pictures that might, ultimately, be "revolved in the mind" and "portrayed on the heart."

APPENDIX

List of Manuscripts Cited

This list is intended to give a general picture of the hagiographic *libelli* as discussed in this book in as concise a fashion as possible. It is first of all based on Wormald's list in "Some Illustrated Manuscripts of the Lives of the Saints," which was expanded and formalized in appendices in Carrasco, "Some Illustrations," and Svoboda, "Illustration of the Life of St. Omer." For bibliography on individual manuscripts, consult the text and notes (by way of the index under the saint's name). Texts are in Latin unless otherwise noted. Folios and pages in boldface type indicate the location of illustrated narrative. These entries represent all the *libelli* known to me from c. 900 to 1200, with the addition of the later Matthew Paris manuscripts. The few examples predating 1200 that do not receive extensive treatment in the book are mentioned, for the sake of completeness, in notes to this appendix.

PASSION OF **AGATHA** (d. 251)

Nine folios

Paris, Bibliothèque nationale, MS lat. 5594
France, late tenth/early eleventh century
(fragment), single column, twenty-three lines
19.5 × 15.6 cm

Contents

The contents are of various dates and were bound together after the Middle Ages. This fragment consists of a gathering with a leaf sewn to the end.

67–72	*Passio* of Agatha
67–70	Thirteen scenes in seven miniatures across bottom of pages, spaces left for others
72–75	Ambrose, letter with passions of Vitalis, Protasius, and Gervasius
75–75v	Beginning of a second letter

PASSIONS OF **ALBAN** (ALBINUS) and **AMPHIBALUS** (both d. third century)

Dublin, Trinity College Library, MS 177
Matthew Paris at St. Albans, c. 1240 or later
75 folios + 2, double column, 39 lines
24 × 16.2 cm

Contents

LIFE OF **AMAND** (d. 679/684)[1]

Valenciennes, Bibliothèque municipale, MS 502
Saint-Amand at Elnone (Saint-Amand-les-Eaux), c. 1050–1100
143 folios, single column, 25 lines
23.8 × 17.5 cm

Contents

PASSION OF **AMPHIBALUS**

See above, sub nom. **Alban**

LIFE OF **AUBIN** (ALBINUS) (d. 550)

Paris, Bibliothèque nationale, MS n.a. lat. 1390
Saint-Aubin, Angers, late eleventh century
Seven folios (fragment), no text
29.5 × 20.5 cm

Contents

LIVES OF **BENEDICT** (d. 547), **MAURUS** (d. 584), and **SCHOLASTICA** (d. 547) [the latter unillustrated] LECTIONARY[2]

Vatican, Biblioteca apostolica, MS Vat. lat. 1202
Monte Cassino, c. 1070
261 folios, double column, 21 lines
37 × 25.5 cm

Contents

LIFE OF **CUTHBERT** OF LINDISFARNE AND DURHAM (d. 687)[3]

Oxford, University College Library, MS 165
Durham Cathedral Priory, c. 1100–20
203 pages, single column, 24 lines
19.7 × 12.2 cm

Contents

PASSION OF **EDMUND**, KING AND MARTYR (d. 869)

New York, The Pierpont Morgan Library, MS M. 736
Bury St. Edmunds, c. 1130
100 folios, single column, 32 lines
27.3 × 18.4 cm

Contents

LIFE OF **EDWARD THE CONFESSOR** (d. 1066)

Cambridge, University Library, MS Ee 3.59
London or Westminster, 1250
37 folios, double or triple columns, 44 lines
28 × 19.2 cm

Contents

Matthew Paris, *La Estoire de Seint Aedward le Rei*
Sixty-four tinted drawings spanning the top of the page, many half-width.

LIFE OF **GUTHLAC** (d. 714)

London, British Library, Harley Roll Y.6
Crowland, c. 1210
16 × 28.5 cm

Contents

The manuscript consists of a parchment roll with eighteen outline drawings in contiguous medallions. There may have been as many as three others on a missing first sheet of vellum. There is no text.

PASSIONS OF **KILIAN** OF WÜRZBURG (d. 689) and **MARGARET** OF ANTIOCH (fourth century)

Hannover, Niedersächsische Landesbibliothek, MS I 189
Fulda, c. 970
38 folios, single column, 18 lines
20.6 × 15 cm

Contents

LIFE OF **LIUDGER** OF MÜNSTER (d. 809)

Berlin, Staatsbibliothek Preußischer Kulturbesitz, Cod. lat. theol.
fol. 323
Werden, c. 1100
33 folios, single column, 33 lines
90 × 24 cm (originally with ivory cover [Probianus diptych])

Contents

PASSION OF **LUCY** (d. 304)

Berlin, Staatliche Museen, Preußischer Kulturbesitz, Kupferstichkabinett, 78 A 4
Monastery of St. Vincent, Metz, c. 1130
67 folios, single column
22.4 × 15 cm

Contents

PASSION OF **MARGARET** OF ANTIOCH

See above, sub nom. **Kilian**

LIFE OF **MARTIN OF TOURS** (d. 397)

Tours, Bibliothèque municipale, MS 1018
Tours, c. 1100
217 folios, single column, 15 lines
21 × 14.7 cm

Contents

LIFE OF **MAURUS** OF GLANFEUIL (d. 584)

[Vatican MS: See above, sub nom. **Benedict**]
Troyes, Bibliothèque municipale, MS 2273
Saint-Maur-des-Fossés, c. 1050–1100

125 folios, single column, 30 lines
28.1 × 19.3 cm

Contents

LIFE OF **OMER** (AUDOMARUS) (d. 667)

Bibliothèque de l'Agglomération de Saint-Omer, MS 698
For the canons of Saint-Omer, third quarter of the eleventh century
67 folios, single column, 20–22 lines
31.6 × 20.8 cm

Contents (various dates)

AUTHENTIQUE, OR PASSION, OF **QUENTIN** (QUINTINUS) (d. 303)

Saint-Quentin, manuscrit de l'Église paroissiale déposé à la
Bibliothèque municipale de Saint-Quentin
Saint-Quentin, c. 1050–1100
91 folios (paginated), single column, 22 lines
28 × 17.6 cm cropped

Contents

Twenty surviving miniatures interspersed in text with two nine-
teenth-century watercolor copies of lost minatures (47, 49)

LIFE OF **RADEGUND** OF POITIERS (d. 587)

Poitiers, Médiathèque François-Mitterrand, MS 250
Sainte-Croix, Poitiers, c. 1050–1100
79 folios, double columns, 25 lines
28.2 × 21.8 cm

Contents (various dates)

<table>
<tbody>
<tr><td>44–47</td><td>Gregory of Tours, De Gloria Confessorum 106 (burial of Radegund); Historia Francorum, VI:21 (death of Disciola)</td></tr>
<tr><td>47v–73</td><td>Homilies and Gospel readings</td></tr>
<tr><td>73v–79</td><td>Letter by Radegund to bishops of France, spurious charters</td></tr>
</tbody>
</table>

PASSION OF **ROMANUS** OF ANTIOCH
(d. 303) [*Peristephanon* X, part of Prudentius's *Opera*]

Bern, Burgerbibliothek Cod. 264
Reichenau (?), c. 900
289 pages (145 folios), single column, 30 lines
27.5 × 21 cm

Contents (portions missing, some paper leaves interfoliated)

<table>
<tbody>
<tr><td>2</td><td>Life of Prudentius</td></tr>
<tr><td>3–4</td><td>Preface</td></tr>
<tr><td>5–34</td><td>Cathemerinon I–XI</td></tr>
<tr><td>39–56</td><td>Peristephanon V:539–XI:240</td></tr>
<tr><td>61–96</td><td>Psychomachia to verse 283 and 521–640</td></tr>
<tr><td></td><td>Illustrations throughout</td></tr>
<tr><td>99–149</td><td>Peristephanon XI:241–XIII, XII, IV, XIV, III, VI, VII, IX, and X</td></tr>
<tr><td>119–121</td><td>Peristepanon IX, Passion of Cassian, four narrative scenes in three miniatures</td></tr>
<tr><td>131–149</td><td>Peristephanon X, Passion of Romanus, twenty narrative scenes in twelve miniatures</td></tr>
<tr><td>149–150</td><td>Epilogue</td></tr>
<tr><td>151–159</td><td>Dittochaeon</td></tr>
<tr><td>160–198</td><td>Apotheosis</td></tr>
<tr><td>199–233</td><td>Hamartigenia</td></tr>
<tr><td>236–289</td><td>Contra Symmachum</td></tr>
<tr><td>289</td><td>Subscriptio</td></tr>
</tbody>
</table>

PASSION OF **WANDRILLE** (WANDRE-GISILUS) OF FONTENELLE (d. 663)

Bibliothèque de l'Agglomération de Saint-Omer, MS 764
Saint-Bertin (?), end of tenth century
96 folios, single column, 20 lines
26.1 × 17.9 cm

Contents (various dates)

LIFE OF **WENCESLAUS** (d. 929/935)

Wolfenbüttel, Herzog August Bibliothek, Cod. Guelf. II.2
Augusteus 4.
Bohemia (Prague?), before 1006
109 folios, single column, 20 lines
22.5 × 18 cm

Contents (various dates; mostly twelfth–fourteenth century)

ABBREVIATIONS AND FREQUENTLY CITED BIBLIOGRAPHY

AASS	*Acta Sanctorum quotquot toto orbe coluntur, vel a catholicis scriptoribus celebrantur quae ex latinis et graecis. . . . ,* 71 vols. Paris, 1863–1940.
Auban	A. R. Harden, ed. *La Vie de seint Auban.* Anglo-Norman Texts 19. Oxford, 1968.
BHG	F. Halkin. *Bibliotheca hagiographica graeca.* Subsidia hagiographica 8a, 3rd. ed. 1957.
BHL	[A. Poncelet]. *Bibliotheca hagiographica latina antiquae et mediae aetatis.* Subsidia hagiographica 6 Brussels, 1898–1901; reprint 1949. *Supplementum.* Subsidia hagiographica 12. Brussels, 1911.
Bibliotheca	*Bibliotheca sanctorum.* ed. Biblioteca apostolica Vaticana. 12 vols. Rome, 1961–69.
Dialogues	O. J. Zimmerman, trans. *Gregory the Great: Dialogues.* The Fathers of the Church: A New Translation. New York, 1959.
Estoire	Kathryn Young Wallace, ed. *La Estoire de seint Aedward le Rei.* Anglo-Norman Text Society 41. London, 1983.
Gerald	Gerard Sitwell, ed. and trans. *The Life of St. Gerald of Aurillac by St. Odo.* New York, 1958.
Glory of the Confessors	Raymond Van Dam, trans. *Gregory of Tours: Glory of the Confessors.* Philadelphia, 1988.
Glory of the Martyrs	Raymond Van Dam, trans. *Gregory of Tours: Glory of the Martyrs.* Philadelphia, 1989.
Life of the Fathers	Edward James, trans. *Gregory of Tours: Life of the Fathers.* Liverpool, 1986.
LCI	*Lexikon der christlichen Ikonographie.* ed. Engelbert Kirschbaum and Wolfgang Braunfels. Vols 1–4: *Allgemeine Ikonographie.* Vols. 5–8: *Ikonographie der Heiligen.* Rome, 1968–76.
MGH	Monumenta Germaniae Historica. Hannover, 1826– (multipart series).

MGH *Diplomata*	Monumenta Germaniae Historica: *Diplomata Regum et Imperatorum Germaniae.* ed. T. Sickel. Hannover, 1879–1975.
MGH *Leges*	Monumenta Germaniae Historica: *Leges Nationum Germanicarum.* ed. K. Zeumer. Hannover, 1907–78.
MGH *Scriptores*	Monumenta Germaniae Historica: *Scriptores Rerum Langobardicum et Italicarum Rerum Langobardicum saec. VI–IX.* ed. G. Waitz. Hannover, 1878.
PG	*Patrologiae cursus completus, Series graeca,* ed. J.-P. Migne, 161 vols. in 166 pts. Paris, 1857–66.
PL	*Patrologiae cursus completus, Series latina,* ed. J.-P. Migne, 221 vols. in 222 pts. Paris, 1844–80.
Prudentius	H. J. Thomson, trans. *Prudentius.* Loeb Classical Library. 2 vols. London, 1949.
Rule	T. Fry, ed. *The Rule of Saint Benedict: In Latin and English with Notes.* Collegeville, Minn., 1981
Sacramentarium	G. Richter and A. Schönfelder, eds. *Sacramentarium Fuldense, Saeculi X Cod Theol 231 der K. Universitätsbibliothek zu Göttingen.* Quellen and Abhandlungen zur Geschichte der Abtei und der Diözese Fulda 9. Fulda, 1912.

NOTES

INTRODUCTION

1. Schrade, *Vita des heiligen Liudger und ihre Bilder,* 10–12. The child who shuns childish games is a saintly commonplace that also appears in the Life of Cuthbert. Colgrave, *Two Lives of St. Cuthbert,* 154–59; see also the miniature in Cambridge University Library MS 165, p. 8.

2. The rescue of Liudger's mother from drowning in a well is the first miniature of the cycle. Both her sons became bishops. Schrade, *Vita des heiligen Liudger,* 6–10. For another mother cast as Ecclesia, see chapter 3.

3. Queen Mathilda was thus interested in the letters of the Life of her mother—Saint Margaret of Scotland. Clanchy, *From Memory to Written Record,* 215.

4. Here the saint, Cassian, is a teacher, and his secular and trivial writing and teaching yield to the salvific writing and teaching of his body. Roberts, *Poetry and the Cult of the Martyrs,* 145.

5. The metaphor is taken even further—the passage reads:

> Christ is the book of life, sealed with seven seals . . . wherein lies . . . salvation, life and resurrection for us, the book which the apostles carried like a crown through the whole world, with great glory of miracles. . . . The author of this book was Christ Himself, because He suffered of His own will. The small and black letters of it were written on the parchment as it were of His own body, by the bruising blows of the scourge; the red letters and capitals by the piercing of the nails; and the full stops and commas by the pricking of the thorns. Well had that parchment been polished beforehand by many a blow, marked by buffeting and spitting, and lined with the reed. (Caesarius of Heisterbach, *Dialogue on Miracles,* II:35 [book 7, chap. 35])

Like that of *puer senex*, the image of the body as text (which Kathryn Smith is studying) is a *topos*. See Curtius, *European Literature and the Middle Ages,* 302–47; Jager, "The Book of the Heart"; and Rubin, *Corpus Christi,* 306–8.

6. I. Ševčenko, "Illuminators of the Menologium of Basil II," 272.

7. See Mango, *Art of the Byzantine Empire,* 37–39.

8. See the valuable (albeit somewhat dated) annotated bibliography in Wilson, ed., *Saints and Their Cults;* the listings of works-in-progress published by the Hagiography Society run by Sherry Reames of the English Department of the University of Wisconsin at Madison; and Web pages maintained by Thomas Head (http://orb.rhodes.edu/encyclop/religion/hagiography/hagindex.html) and Paul Halsall (http://www.fordham.edu/halsall/sbook.html). Useful resources on Eastern saints include the Dumbarton Oaks Hagiography Database (see http://www.doaks.org/DOHD.html) and the Byzantine Saints' Lives in Translation series, edited by Alice-Mary Talbot and published by Dumbarton Oaks.

9. Suzanne Lewis's ideas about indeterminacy and semantic gaps in visual narrative are of great relevance to my interpretations here. See her *Rhetoric of Power in the Bayeux Tapestry,* 2, 32.

10. Vitz, *Medieval Narrative,* 141.

11. Henry Maguire briefly addresses the issue in his *Icons of Their Bodies,* 194, 196–97. For studies of textual narrative and audience, see Heffernan, *Sacred Biography;* Vitz, *Medieval Narrative;* and André Vauchez's comments in his *Sainthood in the Later Middle Ages,* 141, 532.

12. "Pictorial hagiography," a term I introduced in my "Picturing the Text: Narrative in the Life of the Saints," and now generally accepted among art historians, includes all forms of visual representations of saints and implies the purposeful construction of these images rather than any act of "mere illustration."

13. An exception might be St. Wilgefortis, a bearded female saint, whose strange demeanor is often said to have resulted from a misidentified image of Christ crucified. See Farmer, *The Oxford Dictionary of Saints,* 437.

14. André Vauchez (*Sainthood in the Later Middle Ages*) focuses on "new" saints, as does Michael Goodich (*Vita Perfecta*) and most historians. Despite these authors' fascinating and worthwhile analyses of such new saints, one must not forget that it was established saints who dominated cult practice.

15. For legendaries, see Philippart, *Les Légendiers latins,* Coens, *Recueil d'études bollandiennes;* for All Saints' images, "Allerheiligenbild," in *LCI* I, 101–3.

16. See Head, *Hagiography and the Cult of the Saints,* 121.

17. For Litanies, see Coens, *Anciennes litanies.*

18. Richter and Schönfelder, *Sacramentarium Fuldense,* fol. 111r; and for All Saints' images, "Allerheiligenbild," in *LCI* I, 101–3. One of the earliest All Saints' images has been taken to represent the Litany: Deshman, "Anglo-Saxon Art after Alfred," 179.

19. Svoboda, "The Illustration of the Life of St. Omer," 156–61. The hymn appears in *Repertorium Hymnologicum,* II, Louvain, 1897, no. 12701. Svoboda points out (217 n. 187) that Omer's feast was originally celebrated on November 1—All Saints' Day.

20. Although new saintly types prevailed after the thirteenth century, even later medieval audiences continued to be exposed to older saints in liturgical readings. André Vauchez (in *Sainthood*) considers saints by types but uses types of more historical (or even juridical) importance—for example, clerical and lay, mendicant, or mystic.

21. This reality is, of course, a consequence of several factors, including (among others) the

survival or destruction of particular manuscripts or other objects and the likelihood that certain saintly types reflect monastic patronage. See p. 129.

22. For discussions of hagiography from an art historical perspective, see the bibliography for works by (among others) Barbara Abou-el-Haj, Jonathan Alexander, Paul Binski, Magdalena Carrasco, Cynthia Hahn, Rosemary Svoboda, and Francis Wormald.

23. Kemp, *Narratives of Gothic Stained Glass;* Manhes-Deremble, *Les Vitraux.*

24. Here I am using the word *context* as something of a shorthand for a number of issues. I am well aware that the context is no more secure than any other construction of meaning. See Bal and Bryson, "Semiotics and Art History."

25. Although it does not explore narrative per se, Barbara Abou-el-Haj's work generally problematizes the circumstances of the production of saints' Lives. See especially, her *Medieval Cult of Saints.* For discussions of similar issues, see also Hahn, *Peregrinatio et Natio;* Kelly, "Forgery, Invention, and Propaganda"; and Carrasco, "Spirituality and Historicity" and "Spirituality in Context." For an exploration of how a narrative might argue the needs of a particular audience, see Hahn, "Golden Altar."

26. I do not agree with some aspects of her reading. For example, in her discussion of the Golden Altar of Sant'Ambrogio in Milan (11–12), Abou-el-Haj implies that a dispute between the canons and the monks at the church should color our reading of the object. That dispute, however, can only represent the "afterlife" of the altar, since it occurred after the altar was created. She also mentions competition with the cult of Augustine at Pavia, or that of Gervasius and Protasius in Ravenna. The translation of the body of Augustine to Pavia may indeed figure as one aspect in a complex competition by cities for episcopal prestige. See Hahn, "Narrative on the Golden Altar."

27. Certainly cost and beauty could equally well work as bludgeons, but perhaps the most compelling argument about the use of many of these objects concerns their pictorial expression of "conviction (ideology, not propaganda)" (Abou-el-Haj, *The Medieval Cult of Saints,* 27). In this sense, the eleventh- and twelfth-century manuscripts support episcopal strength (Abou-el-Haj's study disregards tenth-century virgins and martyrs and focuses predominantly on episcopal saints; see ibid., 28). In representing saintly bishops, especially using the "image of power" (ibid., 98–104), these objects construct a picture of social hierarchy and might that seems incontrovertible (although I am reluctant to see it as "destructive power," as does Abou-el-Haj, [ibid., 99]). This schema does not always function smoothly in considering particulars. With the notable exception of St. Omer (see Svoboda, "Life of St. Omer"), most of the bodies of holy bishops were held not by cathedrals but by monasteries. Episcopal might was the linchpin of ecclesiastical power during the high Middle Ages, so as a general rule, these Lives produce an unrelenting image of strength. For more nuanced accounts of how this power might serve episcopal interests, see Carrasco, "Spirituality and Historicity"; Hahn, "Golden Altar"; or Hahn, "Interpictoriality on the Limoges Chasses of Stephen, Martial and Valerie." I would like to have seen "ideology," as expressed by the pictures, more fully and specifically explored in Abou-el-Haj's book; the concept remains somewhat schematic in her treatment.

28. Only while making final changes to this manuscript was I able to read Mary Carruthers's

insightful new book, *The Craft of Thought: Meditation, Rhetoric, and the Making of Images, 400–1200,* Cambridge Studies in Medieval Literature 34 (1998). Much of what she writes there works in tandem with my own arguments.

CHAPTER 1

1. This historical overview is by no means intended as a survey of the history of hagiography. For a more complete treatment see Hippolyte Delehaye's *Legends of the Saints* (and other works by the same author), as well as the *Subsidia Hagiographica* of the Société des Bollandistes. Recent studies include Patrick Geary, *Furta Sacra,* Thomas Head, *Hagiography,* and André Vauchez, *Sainthood,* and, taking a more literary perspective, Alison Goddard Elliott, *Roads to Paradise.* Head is also planning a general survey of hagiography. Noble and Head, *Soldiers of Christ,* is an excellent and quite short general essay with translated primary sources. For the specific manuscripts that will be considered in this study, see the appendix.

2. Both also serve as primary documents for the modern understanding of medieval sanctity, in their narrative as well as their editorial asides.

3. Gregory of Tours does not seem to have known of Gregory the Great, Chadwick, "Gregory of Tours and Gregory the Great," 38–49. However, Adalbert de Vogüé ("Grégoire le Grand, lecteur de Grégoire de Tours?" 225–33) suggests that he did. Joan Petersen (*Dialogues,* 66) argues that they shared the *Gesta Martyrum* as a source. Raymond van Dam (*Leadership,* 228) repeats a legend in which they converse.

4. The project, according to Gregory also included the books of miracles of Julian and Martin. See Van Dam, introduction to *Glory of the Martyrs,* 4–5. I will cite this translation as well as Van Dam's *Glory of the Confessors,* and James's *Life of the Fathers.* The Latin may be found in Krusch, *Gregorii episcopi Turonensis Miracula.*

5. For the *Dialogues,* I use the translation by O. J. Zimmerman. For discussions of Gregory's thought, see Dagens, *Saint Grégoire le Grand;* Evans, *The Thought of Gregory the Great;* McCready, *Signs of Sanctity;* Petersen, *Dialogues;* and Straw, *Gregory the Great* and the bibliographies cited in these works. For the Latin, an introduction, and a French translation, see Adalbert de Vogüé, in the series *Sources chrétiennes* 251.

6. Victricius is quoted and discussed in Kemp, *Canonization and Authority,* 3–5; and Brown, *Cult of the Saints, passim;* and for the text: Herval, *Origines chrétiennes,* and *PL* 20:443 ff.

7. The continuing importance of Augustine in the Middle Ages goes without saying. For Gregory and the *Dialogues,* see Crépin, "L'Importance de la pensée de Grégoire le Grand"; Petersen, *Dialogues,* 191; and even Clark, *Pseudo-Gregorian Dialogues.*

8. For Gregory of Tours, see Brown, *Cult of Saints,* and Van Dam, *Saints and Their Miracles.* Even a writer as unpretentious as the author of the Life of Foi was familiar with both Gregories: Sheingorn, *Book of Sainte Foy,* 25. See also Caesarius of Heisterbach, *Dialogue on Miracles,* which takes its title and its form from Gregory the Great. Caesarius's work is also very dependent on Augustine.

9. *De pignoribus sanctorum,* in *PL* 156:613 ff.

10. *Liber miraculorum s. Fidis.* For a translation, see Sheingorn, *Book of Sainte Foy.* A new edition by Luca Robertini has just appeared.

11. E. Gordon Whatley has made similar comments discussing the cult of relics and has singled out Thierry of Echternach's *Flores epitaphium sanctorum* (early twelfth century) as the "first theological treatise in about seven hundred years devoted solely to saints' relics." However he goes on to comment that Thierry is not a "landmark theologian but rather an apologist," *Saint of London,* 45.

12. See Kemp, *Canonization;* and Vauchez, *Sainthood.* Thomas Head's forthcoming work on trial by fire centers on these same problems of discriminating true from false.

13. See Chazelles, "Pictures," and pp. 48–49.

14. For a discussion of the *Dialogues* taken as a popular text, see McCready, *Signs of Sanctity,* 47 ff. For a medieval condemnation of excesses in the cult of saints see Guibert of Nogent's *De pignoribus sanctorum,* in *PL* 156:613 ff.

15. See, among other works, Brown's *Cult of the Saints* and Hamburger's *Rothschild Canticles.*

16. See Brown, "Images as a Substitute for Writing." I would like to thank the author for graciously allowing me to read this article in typescript before publication.

17. For Gregory the Great, see Chazelles, "Pictures," 138 ff; and Duggan, "Was Art Really the Book?" 227–51. In the case of John of Damascus, I am referring to a text used by the Second Nicaean Council (*De imag. orat.* III [*PG* 94:337 ff.] cited in Mango, *Art of the Byzantine Empire,* 171–72). John distinguished levels of *imago* descending from the Trinity to the memory of miracles and good deeds, which may include the literature of the scripture and saints' Lives as well as physical images. For an English translation, see Mango, *Art of the Byzantine Empire,* 171–72. The *Libri Carolini,* a Carolingian statement on images, seems to prefer narrative cycles. The second book, *capitulum XXII,* emphasizes that God is spirit and that sensible things do not represent him; the derivation of the virtues of the saints from Christ may only be recognized by spiritual eyes and ears. "Ad contemplandum itaque Christum, qui est *Dei virtus* et *Dei sapientia* sive ad intuendas virtutes, quae ab eo in sanctis eius derivatae sunt, non corporeus nobis visus" (*Libri Carolini,* 81); *Imagines* must lift the viewer to the original in Christ, but they may do so by reminding him of the deeds of the saints: "gestarum rerum possit reminisci" (*Libri Carolini,* 81).

18. Celia Chazelle reminds us that *sancti* can mean holy things, "Pictures," 150. Historians such as Jean-Claude Schmitt ("L'Occident, Nicée II et les images du VIIIe siècle," 271–301) have explored more widely with the same result; see especially a letter of Pope Nicholas I, quoted at p. 281. This article puts image theory into its various polemical contexts.

19. In his ninth-century biographies of the bishops of Ravenna, Agnellus explained his biography of an early bishop of whom there was no written record: "And if any among you should wonder how I was able to create the likeness I have drawn, you should know that a picture taught me." Agnellus cites as authority Ambrose's similar activity, noted in the *Passion* of Gervasius and Protasius. *Agnelli Liber Pontificalis,* 297. For Basil the Great and John of Ephesus, see Vikan, "Ruminations on Edible Icons," 57 and 58 n. 37.

20. Camille, "Seeing and Reading," 26–49.

21. The term *Passio,* or Passion, designating the Life of a martyr, will not be consistently employed here because of the ubiquitous mixing of types, that is, "martyr" with "confessor."

22. The *Bibliotheca Hagiographica Latina* and *Bibliotheca Hagiographica Graeca* published by the Bollandistes list the versions of a given saint's *vita* (in approximately chronological order and designated by *BHL* or *BHG* numbers).

23. Lucy (discussed below in chapter 2) is a good example. She is most famous for the loss of her eyes, but early Lives make no mention of the torture.

24. See, for example, Kemp, *Canonization and Authority;* and Vauchez, *Sainthood.*

25. Kemp, *Canonization and Authority,* 1.

26. Kemp, *Canonization and Authority,* 29.

27. Heinzelmann, *Translationsberichte.*

28. Ward, *Miracles and the Medieval Mind.*

29. *Civ. Dei,* 22, 8.

30. Vauchez, *Sainthood,* 496 n. 43.

31. Vauchez, *Sainthood,* 490–93.

32. So called by Arcoid, canon of St. Paul's in London, in his Miracles of St. Erkenwald: Whatley, *Saint of London,* 79.

33. Gregory the Great, *Dialogues,* I:12, 51–52. For miracles revealing the saint, see *Dialogues,* I: prol. 9, p. 6.

34. Vauchez, *Sainthood,* 499.

35. Hahn, "Seeing and Believing."

36. Kemp, *Canonization and Authority,* 5.

37. Head, *Hagiography,* chap. 4; Reinberg, "Praying to Saints."

38. McCulloh, "Cult of Relics."

39. Kemp, *Canonization and Authority,* 6.

40. Guibert of Nogent, *Memoirs,* I:1, quoted in Benton, *Self and Society,* 124–25.

41. See Hahn, "Voices of the Saints"; and Hahn, "Golden Altar."

42. Coens, "Anciennes litanies."

43. See Sheingorn, *"Te Deum* Altarpiece."

44. Dubois, *Martyrologies.*

45. For example, Perdrizet, *Calendrier parisien.*

46. Dix, *Shape of the Liturgy, passim.* See Sherry Reames's forthcoming analysis of a saint's office in a Consortium for the Teaching of the Middle Ages (TEAMS) volume from the Medieval Institute publications on medieval liturgy to be published by Western Michigan University.

47. See Peter Brown's discussion of the famous invention by Ambrose of the relics of Gervasius and Protasius: *Cult of Saints,* 36–37.

48. For dedications: Delehaye, "Loca sanctorum." For ex-votos: Freedberg, *Power of Images,* 136–60.

49. Toynbee and Ward-Perkins, *Shrine of St. Peter.*

50. The following list does not purport to be complete and largely depends upon Nancy Ševčenko's admirable work at gathering the material, presented in her dissertation, "St. Nicholas,"

The published version (*The Life of Saint Nicholas*) does not contain as much background material. See also Grabar, *Martyrium*, 39–104.

51. Images of Saints Crispin, Crispinian, and Benedicta arrested and martyred are preserved in Ss Giovanni e Paolo: Kaftal, *Iconography of the Saints*, II, fig. 359–60; Prudentius describes pictures of martyrdom in his *Peristephanon:* Ševčenko, "St. Nicholas," 14; Hahn, "Seeing and Believing," 7–9.

52. Ševčenko, "St. Nicholas," 16.

53. Mango, *Art of the Byzantine Empire*, 37–39.

54. Speyer, "Euphemia-Rede."

55. Sauvel, "Saint-Martin," 153–79, and Kessler, "Pictorial Narrative," 75–91.

56. See discussion in Hahn, "Seeing and Believing."

57. Grüneison, *Sainte Marie Antique*, pls. 141–42; Grabar, *Martyrium*, 100 ff.

58. Kaftal, *Iconography of the Saints*, II, figs. 452–53.

59. Ševčenko, "St. Nicholas," 22.

60. *Drogo-Sakramentar*, 91 r.

61. Hahn, *Passio Kyliani*, 78–81; see also Appleby, "Holy Relic and Holy Image."

62. Bern, Burgerbibliothek, Cod. 264: Homburger, *Handschriften der Bibliothek Bern*, pls. 42–60. XLII–LX, Taf. 9 and 10.

63. Goldschmidt, *Elfenbeinskulpturen*, I, nr. 57, 31–32, Taf. 23.

64. Harris, "Arca of San Millán."

65. For Anno, see Legner, *Monumenta Annonis*, 61–64 and 188–91; For Albinus, Hadelin, Heribert, and Remaclus, see *Rhein und Maas*, I: K2, G4, H 17, and G10–10a. For Anno, Albinus, and Heribert, see *Ornamenta Ecclesia*, II: F90, E 80, and E91.

66. Volbach, "Gli smalti."

67. Walichiego, *Drzwi Gnieznienskie;* and Goldschmidt, *Bronzetüren*.

68. Wormald, "Some Illustrated Manuscripts." A few, such as the Hannover manuscript of Kilian and Margaret, contain two saints.

69. Abou-el-Haj, *Cult of the Saints*.

70. Wormald, "Some Illustrated Manuscripts."

71. Bischoff, "Uber Gefaltene Handschriften."

72. Abou-e-Haj, *Medieval Cult*, 8; Rudolph, *Things of Greater Importance*.

73. Hamburger, "Visual and Visionary"; Chazelle, "Pictures"; and Appleby, "Sight."

74. Wormald, "Some Illustrated Manuscripts"; and Head, *Hagiography and the Cult of Saints*, 129.

75. Head, "Relics," *Dictionary of the Middle Ages*, X, 296–99; and Hermann-Mascard, *Reliques des saints*.

76. Kemp cites Carolingian concerns about such profit from shrines: *Canonization and Authority*, 39.

77. See, for example, comments on the cult of Marsus: Honselmann, "Gedanken sächsischer Theologen," 38–43.

78. Head, *Hagiography and the Cult of Saints*, chap. 3.

79. The notes include drawings, one of which bears a remarkable resemblance to the Margaret frontispiece of Hannover N.L. MS I 189: Schnitzler, "Frühottonisches Fuldaer Kunstwerk."

80. For Agatha, see Carrasco, "Early Illustrated Manuscript"; for Romanus, see Hahn, "Speaking Without Tongues." The Bern manuscript of the *Opera* of Prudentius includes an illustrated Life of Cassian. However, the Life consists of only three scenes in two illustrations, presented as a vision of Prudentius at the shrine of the saint.

81. The Wandrille *libellus* may have been made at Saint-Omer and is preserved there, Bibliothèque municipale, MS 764. See Deschamps, "Notice sur un manuscript"; and Porcher, *L'Enluminure française,* 12–13, fig. 9.

82. Honselmann, "Gedanken sächsischer Theologen," 38–43.

83. Dienemann, *Kult des heiligen Kilian.*

84. Hamburger, "The Use of Images."

85. Such translations were noted in Delehaye, "Martyrs d'Egypte," and argued by Philippart, *Légendiers latins,* 32.

86. Roberts, *Poetry and the Cult of the Martyrs.*

87. Brown, "Relics and Social Status in the Age of Gregory of Tours," in *Society and the Holy,* 222–50.

88. The Morgan manuscript of Edmund's Life corresponds closely in style to the *Albani Psalter,* and it is thought that the artists who worked at both monasteries were laymen. For bibliography and a discussion of the program of the manuscript, see Hahn, "Peregrinatio et Natio."

89. Abou-el-Haj concentrates on these examples in her *Cult of Saints.* A twelfth-century illustrated *Dialogues* in Brussels (Bibliothèque royale, 9916–9917) is exceptional. Though not, strictly speaking, a *libellus,* it contains (as its book 2) a lengthy illustrated Life of Benedict. Made for the monastery of Saint-Laurent-de-Liège, it must have been intended for reading and meditation rather than for the promotion of a patron saint. Gaspar-Lyna, *Principaux manuscrits,* 78 ff.

90. *Dialogues,* II:16, 81.

91. Hahn, "Peregrinatio et Natio," 125; and Head, "I Vow Myself to Be Your Servant," 222–24.

92. Genicot, "Discordiae concordantium." One other aspect of this contrast is interesting. Gregory is concerned with establishing the validity of the powers of a living confessor as opposed to those of a dead martyr. He is concerned with the here and now. While it is significant that the miracles occur in Italy, he is more concerned with the now—that is, that saints can exist outside the era of martyrs.

93. Abou-el-Haj, "Bury St. Edmund." Abou-el-Haj's sweeping introduction, *Cult of Saints,* at times makes the production of *libelli* and other objects correspond more precisely to political struggles than may be justified. She also leaves out earlier saints' Lives, claiming that the Life of Amand is the "first" (36).

94. Kelly, "Forgery, Invention, and Propaganda."

95. Svoboda, "Life of St. Omer."

96. Carrasco, "Spirituality in Context."

97. Abou-el-Haj, "Audiences" and *Cult of Saints;* in the latter, Abou-el-Haj ultimately disparages any potential power of the images as monastic "fantasies" (59) that need the support of "real economic and political clout" (60).

98. Optimistic about the powers of images, I class these sorts of documents together. Abou-el-Haj values cartularies over illustrated manuscripts, claiming that illustrated *libelli* are a "largely failed enterprise." *Cult of Saints,* 105. In some cases it is clear that the cartulary is given less attention than the saint's cult: Sheingorn, *Book of Sainte Foy,* 25.

99. Brown, *Cult of the Saints,* Van Dam, *Leadership.* I am grateful to Thomas Head for clarifying some of these ideas.

100. Abou-el-Haj, *Cult of Saints.*

101. Kelly, "Forgery, Invention, and Propaganda," 3.

102. Similarly, the monastery of St. Albans possessed the cross that was a relic of Alban, spattered with his blood, and pictured in his *libellus.* See p. 291. The reliquary of Martial depicts the staff given the saint by Peter and preserved in Limoges. See *L'Oeuvre de Limoges,* 109–11.

103. See Esther Cohen, "In the Name of God and Profit."

104. James, *La Estoire,* 29.

105. Bibliothèque nationale, MS n.a. fr. 1098: DeLisle, "Notice"; Omont, *Vie et Histoire de St. Denys;* and, for the text, Liebman, *Étude sur la vie en prose de Saint Denis.*

106. Maria Theresa of Austria called for the relics at the birth of her child, as did the Dauphin's wife, Delphinum, in 1682: AASS, 5 July, 29C–D.

107. Sumption, *Pilgrimage,* 291.

108. These virtues were first adumbrated in the Lives of holy Ottonian bishops. See Jaeger, *Origins of Courtliness.*

109. Hahn, "Proper Behavior."

110. Lacaze, *Vie de St. Denis.*

111. Lacaze, *Vie de St. Denis,* 57–85.

CHAPTER 2

1. Thomas Heffernan's *Sacred Biography* from its very title seems to fall into this error. The book is otherwise a useful introduction to questions of textual narrative in hagiography.

2. Nichols, *Romanesque Signs,* 5.

3. The quoted phrase is Thomas Head's, from discussion, and represents the trend in recent historical studies on hagiography toward considering how saints' Lives construct sanctity.

4. McCready develops a similar idea in his discussion of the facticity of the *Dialogues. Signs of Sanctity,* 165. Thomas Head (in *Hagiography and the Cult of Saints,* 103), notes that hagiographers found their task to be that of representing an ideal and quotes Adrevald of Fleury: "[Lives] are placed in our hearts through the recitation of their story, so that they are restored to presence in our mind's eyes as if through some mirror." *Vita s. Maximini* I c. 2; see also p. 130 (again quoting Adrevald): "[Aimo] also composed a *sermo* in praise of . . . Benedict. . . . He produced a most precious pearl of signs [*signa,* that is miracles], so that this man should be regarded as equal in virtue to the attesting patriarchs," *Vita Gauzlini* c. 2. Raymond Van Dam develops a similar idea from Constantius's comments on the Life of Germanus, whose author seeks glory of the saint

visible through a few "adequate" stories that will represent the saint's divine powers: *Leadership and Community*, 145.

5. Talbot, ed., "Willibald's 'Life of Boniface,'" 29.

6. I have discussed this sort of attempt at metadiscourse in medieval narrative in general in "Purification, Sacred Action, and the Vision of God."

7. Nichols, *Romanesque Signs,* 120.

8. Augustine, *De Doctrina Christiana,* IV:4, 6 and *passim.* Thomas Heffernan (*Sacred Biography,* 8), argues that Augustine insisted on sufficient eloquence to persuade. He also notes that in *De Mendacio* (*PL* 40:508), Augustine articulates a preference for the acts of saints over the explication of theology: 4.

9. McCready discusses rhetorical manipulation in saints' Lives, *Signs of Sanctity,* 162–75. See also Cameron, *Christianity and the Rhetoric of Empire,* 141–54.

10. Guibert of Nogent, *On Saints and Their Relics,* bk. 1, trans. Thomas Head in *Medieval Hagiography,* 406–7. The Latin appears in *PL* 156:621.

11. Colgrave, ed., *The Earliest Life of Gregory the Great,* 128–33. The Life was written c. 700.

12. Jauss, "Levels of Identification," and *Aesthetic Experience,* 97–104. William Ryding also compares Aristotle's theories to medieval poetics in *Structure in Medieval Narrative,* 9–12.

13. The full passage, which Jean Doignon has likened to effects of compunction, appears in the *Moralia in Job*:

> Sometimes, even if the lashes of the whip seem to have stopped outside, God inflicts wounds on the inside, striking the hardness of our heart by the desire that he gives for him. But, by striking, he cures, because in piercing us with the dart, he makes us fear, he returns us to the sense of the right. Our hearts are not healthy when they are not wounded by the love of God, when they are not realizing the misery of their exile, when they do not let themselves sympathize, even in the lightest way, with their neighbor's weakness. When they are wounded, on the contrary, the purpose is to heal because god strikes insensitive hearts with the darts of his love and renders them sensible with the fire of his love. This is why the Spouse of the Song of Songs says "I am wounded by love." The soul, in fact, when it was unhealthy and it was sleeping in the blind security of the exile here below, did not see the Lord and did not try to see him. But if it is struck by the darts of his love, it is wounded in its most intimate place by a feeling of affection, it burns with a desire of contemplation and, in an astonishing manner, its wound gives it life. Whereas before it was plunged into a health where it was dead, now it warms up, it pants, and henceforth desires to see the one it fled. Thus it is the shock undergone that brings it back to health, because the fever of love brings it back toward the security of an interior peace. (*Moralia* 6.25.42, quoted and translated into French in Doignon, "Blessure d'affliction," p. 203)

Although here Gregory is not specifically concerned with narrative, we get a clear idea of the process of the conversion of compunction. See pp. 48–49.

14. Here Jauss cites Rabanus Maurus, *PL* 112:331.

15. Jauss, "Levels of Identification," 295–96.

16. Caesarius of Heisterbach, *Dialogue on Miracles,* xv.

17. By this I mean the sort of analysis promulgated by the school of Vladimir Propp, not a more general meaning of the word *structuralist.* Evelyn Vitz criticizes such narratological approaches in *Medieval Narrative,* 1–10. For a discussion of Abou-el-Haj's "core scenes," which are similar in some ways to this sort of structuralism, see p. 173 and note 4.

18. *Glory of the Martyrs,* 87, recounts the story of a martyr who got no respect without a *vita.* See also Brown, "Relics and Social Status," 222–50.

19. Jauss, *Toward an Aesthetic,* 105. Jauss's definition of genre is thus distinguished from the limiting one articulated by van Uytfanghe in "L'Hagiographie"—an interesting argument, but one based on altogether different issues and assumptions. For a discussion of medieval genres and commentaries on the Song of Songs as a genre, see Matter, *The Voice of My Beloved,* chap. 1.

20. Jauss, *Toward an Aesthetic of Reception,* 101, 103.

21. On this point Jauss reassures us that "The history of art [literature and art] is distinguished from other spheres of historical reality by the fact that in it the formation of the immortal is not only visibly carried out through the production of works, but also through reception, by its constant reenactment of the enduring features of works that long since have been committed to the past." Jauss, *Toward an Aesthetic of Reception,* 75.

22. McKitterick, "Charles the Bald and His Library," 28–47, esp. 36; also, idem, "The Palace School of Charles the Bald," 385 ff, quoted in part in the epigraph to chap. 3.

23. Hrotsvitha of Gandersheim, "Dulcitia," in *Plays of Hrotsvit.*

24. Head, *Hagiography and the Cult of the Saints,* 225.

25. Bayless, *Parody in the Middle Ages.* See also Walsh, "Martin of Tours," 308–12, and John Bellairs's wonderful comic "dossier" on "St. Fidgeta," in *Saint Fidgeta and Other Parodies* (New York, 1966).

26. Weinstein and Bell, *Saints and Society,* 97–99, 220–38.

27. Bynum, *Holy Feast.*

28. See Hahn, "Absent No Longer."

29. Especially Bonaventure's version of the Life as in Habig, *St. Francis.*

30. See, for example, *Life of the Fathers,* 27; see also Poulin, *L'Idéal de sainteté,* 119–25.

31. *Life of the Fathers,* 28.

32. Prudentius uses the metaphor effectively in the Life of Romanus (*Peristephanon* X); see also *Life of the Fathers,* 29, 35.

33. "While others are imitating vain things and building with stones which will not make them happy, you desire to be taught with the true words of edification." Meyer, ed., *Palladius: The Lausiac History,* 21 and n. 10.

34. Evans, *Thought of Gregory the Great,* 141; Straw, *Perfection in Imperfection,* 66–89.

35. One example is in Ruotger's tenth-century Life of Bruno: "honorabilis pulchritudo et ornatus domus Domini." Philippart, "Le Saint comme parure," 128.

36. Head, *Hagiography and the Cult of the Saints,* 60. See also Deshman, "The Imagery of the Living Ecclesia"; and Carrasco, "The Construction of Sanctity."

37. Straw, *Perfection in Imperfection,* 71.

38. *Dialogues,* I: prol., 3–4.

39. *Dialogues,* I:1, 6; III:31, 168.

40. *Dialogues,* I:7, 30.

41. Bamberg Staatsbibliothek, MSC. Bibl. 22: Bayerische Staatsbibliothek München, *Bayerns Kirche,* 46, Taf. III. For a similar idea of spiral development in deepening repetition, see Elliott, *Roads to Paradise,* 62. This miniature is a frontispiece to the Song of Songs on fol. 4v of an Ottonian glossed manuscript of the Songs of Songs, Proverbs, and Daniel. The figures may represent the young women as souls, the "perfect men" of the Church who will announce the truth of God, and, of course, Ecclesia as the spouse of Christ, all set into a context of the sacramental life of the Church. The most significant commentators of the Song of Songs include Gregory the Great, *PL* 79: 477; and Bede, *PL* 91:1065–1236. See Matter, *Voice of My Beloved;* and Davy, *Guillaume de Saint-Thierry, passim* and 39.

42. *Dialogues,* III:35, 176; III:37, 185.

43. The discussion appears in the context of a translation of relics: Petrus Damianus *Sermones* 2, cited by Pelikan, *The Christian Tradition,* 181.

44. *Dialogues,* III:22, 154.

45. *Dialogues,* I:1, 6.

46. The practicality and explicative nature of narrative was recommended by Augustine: "If the hearers need teaching, the matter treated of must be made fully known by means of narrative." *On Christian Doctrine,* IV:4, 6; Charles Jones (*Saints' Lives,* 217 n. 59), cites this passage and notes that the form of narrative used is the saint's Life. Michael Goodich (*Vita perfecta,* 64) paraphrases Gregory's *Moralia* as stating, "hagiography is defined as religion teaching by example."

47. Even today, when the average "enlightened" person considers the phenomenon of medieval saints to have been a sort of hoax pulled off by the Church, or worse yet, a popular delusion and continuation of the idolatry of pagan gods, I notice that many Catholic students, filled with the stories of the saints as children, are fascinated by how it is that the stories once held such narrative power.

48. Van Uytfanghe ("Scepticisme doctrinale") interprets Peter's questions as a sort of embodiment of contemporary skepticism. More typically, Joan Petersen (*Dialogues,* 21) argues that the form helped to meld stories of uneven length. See also Evans, *Thought of Gregory the Great,* 14; and McCready, *Signs of Sanctity,* 84, 173, both of whom comment only briefly on Peter's function. McCready notes the obviously rhetorical quality that the choice of a dialogue form entails. Caesarius of Heisterbach explicitly mentions Gregory and implicitly approves of his form by using it himself: *Dialogues on Miracles,* II:29 (bk. 7, chap. 29).

49. Hope and fear—*Dialogues,* III:7, 123; delight—*Dialogues,* III:22, 154, IV:3, 192; eagerness—*Dialogues,* II:7, 70; pleasure—*Dialogues,* III:23, 156; awe—*Dialogues,* III:13, 130, 169; wonder—*Dialogues,* III:32, 169; astonishment—*Dialogues,* II:35, 106, III:15, 142, III:31, 169. He expresses marvel (*Dialogues,* I:6, 28, III:37, 183) and amazement (*Dialogues,* III:19, 150).

50. *Dialogues,* I:12, 52, III:17, 148.

51. Poulin, "Les Saints dans la vie religieuse," 64–74: "le saint mérovingien ou carolingien est

inimitable. Inimitable parce qu'il détient déjà toute perfection dès sa naissance; il n'effectue aucun progrès" (71).

52. *Dialogues*, III:1, 115.

53. *Dialogues*, III:34, 173 ff. Herbert Kessler demonstrates that some theologians thought that the visual more readily moved its audience to compunction than did text. See his "Diction in the 'Bibles of the Illiterate.'"

54. *Dialogues*, IV:57, 268.

55. See Jauss, *Aesthetic of Reception;* Iser, *The Act of Reading;* and specifically for saints' Lives, Heffernan, *Sacred Biography.*

56. Jauss, *Toward an Aesthetic,* 80.

57. Buettner discusses the applicability of Cerquiglini's theory of variance (*In Praise of the Variant,* 36–37 and *passim*) to pictorial narratives. "[Cerquiglini] argues that the repetition and variation of a limited number of narrative units are at the core of medieval literary aesthetics, a principle he calls variance . . . a representational system that runs parallel to the text," and that results in what Buettner sees in imagery as "self-referential articulation, based on the similarity, repetition, and contrast of pictorial signs." *Boccaccio's 'Des Cleres et Nobles Femmes,'* 57–58.

58. The first term is Victor Turner's: *Image and Pilgrimage.* The latter term appears in Jauss, *Toward an Aesthetic,* 81. One could also use Stephen Nichols's "anagogic structures": *Romanesque Signs,* 100.

59. *Romanesque Signs,* 100–101.

60. *Dialogues*, II:8, 72–73.

61. Joan Peterson's consideration of these analogies in her discussion of typology in the *Dialogues* (*The Dialogues of Gregory the Great,* 25–55) tends to overlook their narrative function.

62. In a similar vein, Victricius of Rouen likened the community of the saints to the Trinity: see Kemp, *Canonization and Authority,* 3–5.

63. McCready, *Signs of Sanctity,* 243–55.

64. *Dialogues*, II:8, 72–73.

65. Petersen, *The Dialogues of Gregory the Great,* 131.

66. Zimdars-Swartz, "Confluence of Imagery," 331, citing *In Ezechielem,* 1, 6, 9, *PL* 76:832–33.

67. Lewis, *Reading Images,* 51.

68. Gregory the Great, however, argued that even one repetition is a marker of meaning "Non enim vacat a mysterio quod iteratur in facto." *Hom in Evan* 2.24.5, *PL* 76:1186–87, cited in Mc-Cready, *Signs of Sanctity,* 247.

69. Gaiffier, "La Lecture des Actes."

70. Van Dam, *Leadership,* 236, quoting the *Glory of the Martyrs,* 63.

71. Gaiffier, "Les 'Doublets.'"

72. Curtius, *European Literature,* 79–105.

73. Leopold Genicot ("Discordiae concordantium," 65–75) points out the importance of even a minor change in a *topos* in a saint's Life. Among narrative theorists, Cirquiglini marks a similar argument; see *In Praise of the Variant,* 36–37. See also a discussion of Michael Riffaterre in Tompkins, *Reader-Response Criticism,* xiii and 37 ff.

74. For *topoi* in hagiographic texts, see, among others, Kleinberg, *Prophets in Their Own Country,* 54; Kreuger, *Symeon the Holy Fool;* and Rampolla, "A Mirror of Sanctity."

75. Evans, "Episodes in Analysis."

76. Pizarro, *Rhetoric of the Scene.* See also Jauss, *Aesthetic Experience,* 99–100.

77. See Hahn, "Picturing the Text," and pp. 142–53.

78. For contrast as a rhetorical device in Byzantium, see Henry Maguire's argument in *Art and Eloquence,* 45, that through the use of *antithesis* the tortures of the saints are made to produce joy in the viewer or reader; and see also idem, "The Art of Comparing," 88–103; and most recently *Icons of Their Bodies,* 156.

79. It is, in general, difficult to publish such a complete analysis. For something close to what I think can be done in analyzing narratives see Hahn, *Passio Kyliani,* chaps. 2–5.

80. See also Rapp, "Figures of Female Sanctity," 313.

81. *Dialogues,* III:37, 183.

82. Hahn, "Picturing the Text," 5.

83. Bynum, *Holy Feast,* 278; Geary, *Furta Sacra;* Vitz, *Medieval Narrative,* 141.

84. Evans, *The Thought of Gregory the Great,* 78; here Gregory is referring to scripture.

85. *Dialogues,* I:5, 23. Gregory subsequently refers to Luke 16:15: "What is highly esteemed among men is an abomination in God's sight."

86. Maraval, "Fonction pédagogique," 385–86. The healing miracles use purposefully absurd means in order to demonstrate to rationalistic skeptics the role of grace in healing.

87. *Dialogues,* I:4, 19.

88. Vitz, *Medieval Narrative,* 141.

89. See pp. 69 and 83. See also Lewis, *Reading Images,* 26, who notes that the *vita* of John frames his apocalyptic visions, giving them authority as well as intimacy, and provides a human intermediary for their divine truths.

90. See Hahn, "Absent No Longer," and pp. 287–94.

91. See Hahn, "Speaking Without Tongues."

92. Vance, "Chaucer's Pardoner," 738 ff; and Hahn, "Purification, Sacred Action, and the Vision of God."

93. Grabar, "History of Art, History of Literature."

94. See Hahn, "Peregrinatio et Natio."

95. The effect is often called "discourse time"; see Martin, *Recent Theories of Narrative.* This is not time as a theological construct, although ultimately the two might be connected in a unified cultural theory of time. See Ricoeur, *Time and Narrative,* vol. 1.

96. These kinds of conventions are discussed in the colloquium on ancient and early Christian narrative published in *The American Journal of Archaeology* 61 (1957), 43 ff; and in Ringbom, "Some Pictorial Conventions."

97. For example, Winter, "After the Battle Is Over: The *Stele of the Vultures* and the Beginning of Historical Narrative in the Art of the Ancient Near East," and other essays in Studies in the History of Art 16 (*Pictorial Narrative in Antiquity and the Middle Ages,* edited by Herbert Leon Kessler and Marianna Shreve Simpson [Washington, 1985]).

98. *Rise of Pictorial Narrative,* 14–16.

99. Magdalena Carrasco ("The Construction of Sanctity") argues that this same device creates a saintly effect of "simultaneity and permanence" or, in some cases prophecy, rather than any effect of the passage of time.

100. *Moralia in Job,* 27.20.41, cited by Evans, *The Thought of Gregory the Great,* 59.

101. Gregory, "How Do We Interpret Images?" 310–30; and Barlow, "What Does the Brain See?" 5–25.

102. Summers, "Conditions and Conventions," 208.

103. Barthes, "Structural Analysis of Narratives," 89.

104. White, "Value of Narrativity," 1.

105. Grover Zinn ("Sound, Silence and Word") summarizes comments by Gillet, Dagens, and others.

106. Chazelles, "Pictures"; and Duggan, "Was Art Really the 'Book of the Illiterate'?"

107. Kessler, "Pictorial Narrative and Church Mission."

108. The translations are those of Herbert Kessler, "Pictorial Narrative," 75–76. Gregory the Great, *Registrum Epistolarum,* Letters IX: 209 and XI:10. See also Chazelles, "Pictures"; and Duggan, "Was Art Really the 'Book of the Illiterate'?"

109. Kessler, "Pictorial Narrative," 75 and n. 9, 89. In the note, Kessler traces the emotive value of images to Horace and also Christian writers. He does note that the emotive "may have been important."

110. *Pastoral Care,* 81 (II:10). This passage discusses the correction of sin, but Gregory's aside on images is not any less interesting for that. In fact, immediately after, he gives a visual example of a "teacher" revealing "vision" to "mundane hearts" (83). *Pastoral Care* was required reading for bishops in the Carolingian era as established at various councils. MGH *Concilia,* ed. A. Werminghoff (Berlin, 1906): Reims of 813, p. 255; Mainz of 813, p. 259; Tours of 813, p. 287, cited by Markus, "Gregory the Great's *Rector,*" 137. The text is repeated in the *Moralia in Job,* 26.6.65.

111. Chazelle, "Pictures," 141.

112. The thought is reflected as well in "mirrors for princes," in which kings are advised to look while they are being read to. Brigitte Buettner characterizes this looking as an active engagement, versus the passive quality of listening. See her *Boccaccio's 'Des Cleres et Nobles Femmes,'* 24.

113. Suzanne Lewis also discusses this effect (*Reading Images,* 51), which she implies depends on the device in literary contexts with episodic narrative, but I believe that there is a good possibility that the pictorial arts originated the strategy.

114. The engraved heart is a common Christian metaphor for truth: Vance, *Signals,* 8. See also Jager, "Book of the Heart"; and Curtius, *European Literature,* 302–47. The figure is less often compared to the impact of the visual: Gregory of Tours felt it appropriate to make an association between the *tabulis cordis* and the *tabulis visibilibus* of an icon of Christ: *Glory of the Martyrs,* 40; Photios in his sermon on the *Theotokos* in Hagia Sophia argued even more explicitly that "Just as speech is transmitted through hearing, so a form is imprinted on the tablets of the soul through the sight . . . and conveys knowledge. . . . The memory is most effective when acting through the sight." The translation is that of Robin Cormack, *Writing in Gold,* 150.

115. Carruthers, *Book of Memory*.

116. Elsner, *Art and the Roman Viewer*, 97 ff.

117. Philostratus, *Life of Apollonius of Tyana*, quoted in Elsner, *Art and the Roman Viewer*, 26.

118. Longinus, *De Sublimitate*, 15:1, quoted in Elsner, *Art and the Roman Viewer*, 26.

119. For material that is more explicitly about image use than anything in the early medieval West but is much like the implications of Gregory's comments as I interpret them, see the discussion of the mosaics at Sinai in Elsner's *Art and the Roman Viewer*, chap. 3. Much of this is reminiscent of Jauss's treatment of the exemplary as discussed above, pp. 31–32.

120. Esrock, *Reader's Eye*, 93–97.

121. Esrock, *Reader's Eye*, 103, 139, and 115–18. These factors—emotion and bizarreness—also take a very prominent place in memory theories of the past. See Yates, *Art of Memory*, and Carruthers, *Book of Memory*.

122. Esrock, *Reader's Eye*, 92.

123. Pizarro, *Rhetoric of the Scene*, esp. 48–50.

124. Nie, "Iconic Alchemy," 159. De Nie compares the work of the contemporary theologian and psychologist Eugen Drewerman to sixth-century miracles.

125. Esrock, *Reader's Eye*.

126. *Agnelli Liber Pontificalis Ecclesiae Ravennatis*, xviiii, 32 (MGH, *Scriptores Rerum Langobardicarum*, 297), quoted in Jones, *Saints' Lives*, 63.

127. Thomson, ed., *Prudentius*, II, *Peristephanon*, IX, 223. Roberts, *Poetry and the Cult*, 131–48.

128. Roberts, *Poetry and the Cult*, 145.

129. Bern Burgerbibliothek Cod. 264, p. 121. See Stettiner, *Die illustrierten Prudentius handschriften*, Taf. 160. The story of Cassian—martyred by being stabbed to death with the pens of his resentful, pagan students—should give pause to any teacher.

130. Roberts, *Poetry and the Cult*, 139, quoting *Sermones post Maurinos reperti*, 14.3, ed. G. Morin, 1.67.24–26.

131. Roberts, *Poetry and the Cult*, 134–35.

132. Schmitt, "L'Occident, Nicée II et les images du VIIIe siècle," 287, quoting *PL* 142:1306C.

133. Schmitt's entire article reveals a similar elegance of thought and expression. However, because Schmitt does not consider Gregory's comments in the *Moralia* and in the *Pastoral Care*, he sees Gerald as innovative in a way that I do not. Gregory's comments resemble those of an earlier pope. In a sermon on Good Friday, Leo said of the Passion: "I think that this narrative must have come to cling to your hearts in such a way that the Gospel reading has become a vision for all of you who hear it." *PL* 54:380B. The translation is Peter Brown's, "Images as a Substitute for Writing."

134. Kessler, "Diction in the 'Bibles of the Illiterate.'" Grover Zinn ("Sound, Silence, and Word") although arguing for aural elements of perceiving the divine, concedes the importance of the visual for Gregory.

135. *Sermons . . . by S. Augustine*, II, 541–42 (Sermon 76, on John V). Gregory wrote something similar in *Moralia* 36.12.17–18, cited by Markus, *Signs and Meanings*, 68. Markus emphasizes that Gregory sees the evidence of God in creation as wholly apparent.

136. *Dialogues,* IV:7, 200.

137. *Dialogues,* IV:7, 201. The remark is that of Benedict, watching the soul of Germanus, bishop of Capua, rise into heaven.

138. For purified sight and mind in Augustine see Hahn, "Purification," 72.

139. Walsh, ed., *Letters of St. Paulinus,* II, Letter 30, 119. I am grateful to Eugene Vance for directing my attention to this text and its significance in a talk he delivered at the College Art Association meetings of 1998, to be published in a collection edited by Alice Christ.

140. *Letters of St. Paulinus,* II, Letter 30, 122.

141. *Letters of St. Paulinus,* II, Letter 30, 123–24.

142. This and the remainder of the quotations from Paulinus, unless otherwise noted, are from *Letters of St. Paulinus,* II, Letter 32, 136–37.

143. *Letters of St. Paulinus,* II, Letter 30, 122.

144. Georgia Frank's 1994 Harvard dissertation ("The Memory of the Eyes: Pilgrimage to Desert Ascetics in the Christian East during the Fourth and Fifth Centuries") treats this material.

145. Elsewhere, Paulinus recommends prayer with vision (*Letters of St. Paulinus,* II, Letter 31, 126), and other more didactic experiences of vision: "for peasant people, not devoid of religion but not able to read." *Carmen,* 27, 512–96, quoted in Goldschmidt, *Paulinus' Churches,* 61–65.

146. Evans, *Thought of Gregory the Great,* 44–45, 49, and 104; and McCready, *Signs of Sanctity,* 84, 246.

147. Schmitt, *La Raison des Gestes;* Pizarro, *Rhetoric of the Scene,* 109–69.

148. Brooke, *Scripta Leonis,* 19, 122–23.

149. For a similar approach to the image of John in Apocalypse manuscripts, see Lewis, *Reading Images,* 34.

150. Trexler, *Christian at Prayer,* 25–26.

151. Davidson, "Visual Arts and Drama," 45–59, citing Trexler, *Christian at Prayer,* 126 n. 37, and see p. 56.

152. In this quotation from the epilogue to his book (slightly paraphrased by Trexler), the thirteenth-century Ottobeuren scribe makes Peter the Chanter into something of a Miss Manners of the holy. Trexler, *Christian at Prayer,* 118.

153. See Hahn, "Interpictoriality."

CHAPTER 3

1. Liddell-Scott, *Greek-English Lexicon,* 1082.

2. Delehaye, *Passions des martyrs.*

3. Hahn, "Speaking Without Tongues."

4. The volume contains the *opera* of Prudentius; of these works, only the *Psychomachia,* the Life of Cassian, and the Life of Romanus are illustrated. Illuminated initials also occur. Homburger, *Handschriften der Bibliothek Bern,* 136–58; and Beer, "Stil und Herkunft des Berner Prudentius-Codex 264."

5. Roberts, *Poetry and the Cult of Martyrs*, 9.

6. The phrases are common but in this case are taken from the Life of Margaret: Mombritius, *Sanctuarium*, 191.

7. *Glory of the Martyrs*, 12.

8. Hahn, "Speaking Without Tongues."

9. *Prudentius*, 233: *Peristephanon*, X, ll. 56–57.

10. The king is the emperor Galerius. All the figures are dressed in contemporary dress, and Romanus is tonsured, as most clerics of his stature would have been in the tenth century.

11. Mackie, "New Light."

12. See Hahn, "Speaking Without Tongues."

13. *Prudentius*, 269, 271, 273.

14. The sign of the cross was largely protective in nature. Dölger, *Sphragis*.

15. *Glory of the Martyrs*, 20, 23, 29, 35–36, 51, 54, 73, 77, 81, 124, 130; *Glory of the Confessors*, 63–64; and Head, *Hagiography and the Cult of Saints*, 156.

16. Hahn, *Passio Kyliani*, 91.

17. Scarry, *Body in Pain*, 4.

18. *Glory of the Martyrs*, 24, 44. "Why do you seek to understand the mysteries, when you cannot enter the hidden sources of Light? Be stunned into silence then." Fortunatus, *Vita Martini*, 358.

19. See Hahn, "Purification."

20. *Prudentius*, 283; compared to similar examples in Hahn, *Passio Kyliani*, 107.

21. *Prudentius*, 273.

22. *Prudentius*, 267.

23. See Hahn, "Speaking Without Tongues," 176–80.

24. Pickering, *Literature and Art*, 238–41.

25. Hahn, *Passio Kyliani*, 108–9.

26. *Prudentius*, 265.

27. Silvestre, "Aperçu sur les commentaires carolingiens de Prudence."

28. Head, *Hagiography and the Cult of Saints*, 268–69.

29. Hahn, *Passio Kyliani*, 109.

30. Hahn, *Passio Kyliani*, 120.

31. Hahn, *Passio Kyliani*, 112–13.

32. Athanasius, *Life of Anthony*, 17, chap. 3.

33. In a paper written for my seminar at the University of Michigan, Bessette argued that the body was aggrandized in this way in the narrative in part because of its effectiveness to the community as a relic. David Areford also did an insightful paper on the *libellus* in a seminar at Florida State University.

34. Bessette compares this figure to tormentors at the crucifixion represented in the Theodore and Barbarini Psalters and reproduced in Schiller, *Iconography*, II, pls. 298–99.

35. See *Prudentius*, 266–67.

36. Brown discusses the "emotional inversion of suffering"—tortures into benefits for believers—in *Cult of the Saints*, 84.

37. Tertullian, trans. C. Dodgson, *Apologetic and Practical Treatises*, 152.

38. Hahn, *Passio Kyliani*, 117–18.

39. Hahn, *Passio Kyliani*, 111–15.

40. Hahn, *Passio Kyliani*, 116–18.

41. Gregory makes these comments in frustration, in reference to people who do not believe despite witnessing miracles. He calls them heretics. The miracle in this instance involved a baptismal font that filled miraculously with water: *Glory of the Martyrs*, 44.

42. *Life of the Fathers*, 29.

43. *Prudentius*, 276 and 278, ll. 726–35, 277 and 279.

44. *Prudentius*, 276–77, l. 700.

45. A similar image of a martyr from whom flows the fountain of life (or more literally in this case the four rivers of Paradise) can be seen in an early Christian (sixth century) silver reliquary from Carthage now in the Vatican: Buschhausen, *Die spätrömischen Metallscrinia*, I, 242–43, Taf. 48–49.

46. Images of court proceedings are reproduced in Grabar, *Christian Iconography*, fig. 146.

47. *Life of the Fathers*, 27.

48. Brown, *Cult of the Saints;* Thomas Head has further substantiated the importance of the clergy in saints' cults with material from the Carolingian Orleanais: *Hagiography and the Cult of the Saints.*

49. Hahn, *Passio Kyliani*, chap. 5.

50. Hahn, "Speaking Without Tongues."

51. Scarry argues that torture "deconstructs" and destroys speech in a sort of reversal process. *Body in Pain*, 20.

52. See Scarry, *Body in Pain*, 4.

53. Cobham Brewer, *A Dictionary of Miracles*, 292–93. The examples are chiefly bishops.

54. *Prudentius*, 303.

55. *Prudentius*, 303.

56. Compare Hahn, *Passio Kyliani*, 90, fig. 35.

57. Schmitt, *Raison des gestes*, 37–40.

58. Musurillo, *Acts of the Christian Martyrs*, 3.

59. Musurillo, *Acts of the Christian Martyrs*, 13.

60. Brown, *Cult of the Saints*, chap. 3. See pp. 112–22 for a further discussion of this idea.

61. Scarry, *Body in Pain*, 28, 56.

62. See my discussion of this gesture and its relationship to preaching (Matt. 28:19) in "Picturing the Text," 12–20.

63. Trexler, *Christian at Prayer*, 48.

64. Polycarp's prayer for the community: Musurillo, *Acts of the Christian Martyrs*, 7 and 9; his private prayer: ibid., 7; and his liturgical prayer: ibid., 13.

65. Scarry, *Body in Pain*, 16 and 17.

CHAPTER 4

1. Luce Irigaray, *This Sex Which Is Not One,* trans. Catherine Porter (Ithaca, N.Y., 1985), 24, 26; cited by Burns, *Bodytalk,* 179.

2. I take this polarity from Burns, *Bodytalk,* 76.

3. Cazelles, *Lady as Saint,* 48–49. In fact, the "intactness" that Cazelles uses as a euphemism for sexual virginity applies to the entire virgin body. She may be tortured and cut but as in the Life of Agatha, she is restored, even before death, to her true inviolate body.

4. Brundage, "Prostitution," 832; and Robertson, "Medieval Medical Views," 147. See also Elliott's discussion of Cassian's six levels of abstinence: at level 4, the celibate overcomes arousal at the sight of a woman. *Fallen Bodies,* 16.

5. Bynum, *Holy Feast.*

6. This notion of virginal woman as symbol may be true throughout the Middle Ages but has been argued as based on specific developments calling for chastity in the eleventh and twelfth centuries: "Women's absence from competitive space had the advantage of allowing for an un-gendered definition of man"; and "Among monks safely segregated from women, perhaps the safest way to restore the gender system was to play both roles and, by implication, deny the need for women in any capacity." McNamara, "Herrenfrage," 5 and 20.

7. Robertson, "Corporeality"; and Cazelles, *Lady as Saint,* 34, 38.

8. Easton, "Saint Agatha."

9. Gravdal, *Ravishing Maidens.*

10. A similar critique appears in Bynum, "Body of Christ," 85.

11. Boeckler, *Stuttgarter Passionale;* Michon, *Grand Passionaire de Weissenau;* and Bucher, *Pamplona Bibles.*

12. As is the case with Weinstein and Bell's survey (*Saints and Society*), the survey is only as good as the classification system. I classed half-nude as "nude." Sometimes gestures are difficult to determine: I generally considered prayer to be represented by two hands turned out symmetrically. One hand turned out was considered a gesture of witness or humility. What of figures who hold a book in one hand? This was a judgment call and at times was classed as a praying figure. I counted multiple martyrs as single examples unless there were two genders, then one tally was put in each category. Nevertheless, the numbers are too small and I have been too selective to consider this survey statistically valid.

13. Blessing may usually stand for the liturgical gesture of the sign of the cross. See Hahn, "Voices of the Saints."

14. Michon, *Grand Passionaire de Weissenau,* pl. 101. St. Gertrude heals a blind woman with a blessing gesture.

15. Weinstein and Bell, *Saints and Society,* 220–21. Two of our examples may have been illustrated before 1000, the year with which Weinstein and Bell began their survey, but not by a significant amount. The authors describe an important change in numbers in the thirteenth century, but none of the *libelli* of women considered here date that late.

16. Wogan-Browne, "Saints' Lives and the Female Reader"; and Cazelles, *Lady as Saint,* 15, 73. The role of women as patrons should be noted as well: see McCash, *Cultural Patronage of Medieval Women,* 176, 178, 229, 237.

17. Women follow heretics and "spin" to changing doctrines, according to Jerome. The critique of Thecla is a good early example of the condemnation of an expanded female role. See Van Dam, *Leadership and Community,* 74, 101. It takes careful study to differentiate new roles for women that have appeared in saints' Lives. See Corbet, *Saints Ottoniens,* 236–40, and *passim.*

18. This list appears in a version of the Life of Margaret. Weitzmann-Fiedler, "Zur Illustration der Margareten Legenden." A similar but expanded list appears in Cazelles, *Lady as Saint,* 73. Such lists also seem to have occurred in Byzantium; see Rapp, "Figures of Female Sanctity," 330, noting that "narrators align their female saints with female prototypes," 329. Aldhelm in *De Virginitate* gives a catalogue of virgins, including Agatha, Agnes, Cecilia, Eugenia, Eulalia, Eustochium, Lucy, and Thecla. Schulenburg, *Forgetful,* 133.

19. Robertson, "Corporeality," 273; Sheingorn, "The Wise Mother."

20. J. Dünninger, "Vierzehn Nothelfer," *LCI* 8:546–50.

21. Calmet, *Histoire de Lorraine,* II, 96.

22. In the responses and antiphons: Calmet, *Histoire de Lorraine,* I, xxvi. See also Agostino Amore, "Lucia," *Bibliotheca sanctorum,* VIII, 247–52. Bishop Thierry of Metz (d. 984) was given the relics by Otto I. Indeed, Thierry obtained a number of relics at this moment: Dupré-Theseider, "Grande rapina." Venetian claims date either to 1038 or 1204 and involve relics brought from Constantinople. The elaborate reliquary was commissioned by the abbot of St. Vincent upon his return from pilgrimage to Jerusalem and the Holy Land. It was dedicated by bishop Poppo of Metz on 14 April 1093. Beaugrand, *Lucie,* 51. During that period, St. Vincent's abbot was first among the abbots of Metz, privileged to serve in the bishop's place if he were absent. Calmet, *Histoire de Lorraine,* II, 98. The Latin texts are gathered in *Gallia Christiana* (Paris, 1715–1865), XIII, 919. For the manuscript: Wescher, *Beschreibendes Verzeichnis,* 8–10; Milde, "Manuscrit en l'honneur de sainte Lucie"; Brandis, *Zimelien,* 95–96; and Prochno, *Das Schreiber- und Dedikationsbild,* II. The Marburg Index includes two illustrations—the Wise Virgins, and Lucy before Paschasius.

23. The Life of Agatha is bound with a collection of saints' Lives of uncertain provenance: Carrasco, "Early Illustrated Manuscript." The Life of Margaret is contained in a manuscript that includes a number of prayers containing words with feminine endings. Hahn, *Passio Kyliani,* 30–31. The textual Lives of Margaret and Agatha are discussed in detail by Karen Winstead in the context of narratives of virgin martyrs in monasteries. *Virgin Martyrs,* 12–14, and 19–63.

24. Weinstein and Bell, *Saints and Society,* 220, 222–23.

25. Bynum, *Holy Feast.*

26. For an example, see Weitzmann, *The Icon,* pl. 34.

27. See Hahn, "Speaking Without Tongues," and Schmitt, "L'Occident."

28. The *vita* is usually given a date of fifth to sixth century. The text (*BHL* 4992) is printed in Beaugrand, *Lucie,* 61–64. For the liturgy, see Baudot-Chaussin, *Vies des saints,* XII, 408.

29. Manitius, *Geschichte der lateinischen Literatur,* III, 332–50. For the verse Life, see Dümmler, "Sigebert von Gembloux *Passio Sanctae Luciae Virginis.*" I have not been able to find a full published version of the sermon, although Gaetani, *Vitae Sanctorum Siculorum,* I, 98–102 (cited by Milde, "Manuscrit en l'honneur de sainte Lucie," 476 n. 27), may contain it. It would appear that some scholars refer to this sermon as a Life of Lucy. See also *BHL* 4999, although most of the

publications listed only publish part of the sermon. Smits van Waesberghe ("Neue Kompositionen," as cited by Milde, 475) argued that the hymns and sequences are by Sigebert. That would leave the antiphon of uncertain authorship. Schmidt-Chazan, "La chronique de Sigebert de Gembloux," 1–26, discusses Sigebert's importance as the author of a chronicle.

30. Schulenburg, *Forgetful,* 34, citing Alcuin's Lives of Willibrod.

31. For Denis see Delisle, "Notice sur un livre"; for Alban, see chapter 9.

32. Lucy is said to have cured many women during the translation of the body, and the word *gravidas,* which could be taken to mean *pregnant,* is rubbed on fol. 23r.

33. The name of the abbot who died in 1119 is uncertain; Arnulfus(?), Ranulfus(?): *Gallia Christiana* XIII, 919. It is interesting to note that the earliest vernacular French Life, that of the virgin martyr Eulalie, was written as a sequence by and for the monks of Saint-Amand: Cazelles, *Lady as Saint,* 27, 313–14.

34. Lucy has a vision and pronounces that at this moment Diocletian has retired and Maxentius has descended from the throne. However, these two events occurred in 305 and 310 respectively, therefore not simultaneously as the saint had claimed. Baudot-Chaussin, *Vies des saints,* 411.

35. The text in the manuscript (fol. 56v) reads: Virgines sequntur agnum quocunque ierit. sine macula enim sunt ante thronam dei. Si agnes ubique est sequaces etiam eius ubique esse credendum est in omnia potente omnia possunt.

36. Lucy's right hand is positioned as if to grasp something in front of her chest. Perhaps the artist wanted to add the palm in green and forgot to finish this detail.

37. On fol. 29r we read: "gemmata colla fulva monilia. aulea regum. rara tapetia; a fronte margarita pendens . . . structura lecti staret eburnea . . ." Dümmler, "Sigebert," 28.

38. Hahn, *Passio Kyliani,* 102–3, esp. fig. 44 (Boulogne-sur-Mer, Bibliothèque municipale, MS 107, fol. 87v [Mary enthroned with virgins]).

39. Von Simson, *Sacred Fortress,* 100–2, pl. 43.

40. Liturgy can be narrative if narrative is considered to be movement or development rather than any sort of story tied to real time. See Sinding-Larsen, "Some Observations on Liturgical Imagery," 206.

41. Baudot-Chaussin, *Vies des saints,* XII, 408.

42. I am grateful to Hans Mueller for help with this translation.

43. *Bibliotheca Sanctorum,* VIII, 253. Swedes celebrate her feast day on the shortest day of the year, which once fell on Lucy's feast day, 13 December, as a festival of light; see Farmer, *The Oxford Dictionary of Saints,* 270.

44. I illustrate only the Wise Virgins. The two images are almost identical. However, an illustration of the Foolish Virgins can be found in *Zimelien,* 125. The visual formulation is very similar to that of the Wise Virgins page except that there are no pedestals, the Virgins hold empty jars turned downward, and they show grief. Two of the Virgins do not wear crowns, but all are dressed in court costume. The inscriptions read: (in mandorla frame) Vigilate itaq[ue] quia nescitis diem neq[ue] horam; (in a scroll held by Christ) am dico vobis nescio vos; (next to Christ's head) Sponsus; (above the Virgins' heads) D[omi]ne D[omi]ne Aperi Nobi[s].

45. H. Sachs, "Jungfrauen, Kluge und Törichte," *LCI* 3:462.

46. Origen was the first to make the association. Augustine seems to rely on Origen for his formulation and the latter's becomes the standard throughout the Middle Ages. Rahner, "Le Début d'une doctrine des cinq sens spirituels," esp. 144 n. 238; and idem, "La Doctrine des 'sens spirituel,'" 263. It is interesting to compare the treatment of the senses in a more practical discussion in the *Ancrene Wisse*. See Wogan-Browne, "Chaste Bodies," 27, 29, and 34.

47. Augustine, Sermon 93, *PL* 38:573–80 and Schaff, *Saint Augustine*. See also: Sermon 76, PL 39:1892–95.

48. Augustine, Epistola 140, *PL* 33:572, cap. 31, cited by Rahner, "Le Début d'une doctrine des cinq sens spirituels," 125.

49. William of Saint-Thierry, *Golden Epistle*, 52, as cited by Solterer, "Seeing, Hearing," 130. Karen Winstead also notes that the *Ancrene Wisse* recommends reading as good prayer: *Virgin Martyrs*, 39.

50. Perhaps clearest in Augustine's discussion in Epistola 140, *PL* 33:572, cap. 31–34, esp. 31, cited by Rahner, "Le Début d'une doctrine des cinq sens spirituels," 125.

51. The Passional is at the Bibliotheca Bodmeriana in Geneva, cod. 127. The text appears on fol. 1v; see Michon, *Grand Passionnaire de Weissenau*, 28 and 184. See also Augustine, *De diversis quaestionibus octoginta tribus, PL* 40:45–46.

52. Hahn, "Vision."

53. William of Saint-Thierry, *Golden Epistle*, 53 (after Bernard).

54. Trexler, *Christian at Prayer*, prostrate prayer: 40; humiliation: 48; and copulation: 36.

55. As Caroline Bynum has shown, later medieval women found spiritual value in bleeding as Christ had bled. "Body of Christ," 102.

56. Beaugrand, *Lucie,* LXII.

57. The bowls hold blue cones, but since bread was at times represented in this conical shape, one must surmise that the colorist has used his imagination.

58. Boeckler, *Stuttgarter Passionale,* St. Verena, pl. 137 (mismarked as 138).

59. Bynum, *Holy Feast,* 73–112.

60. Miles, "Virgin's One Bare Breast."

61. "Hacc lavat ulceribus putrentes." fol. 34v; Dümmler, "Sigebert von Gembloux *Passio Sanctae Luciae Virginis*," 31. On fol. 16v, Sigebert mentions the cures of virgins by the relics.

62. Wolfthal, "A Hue and a Cry," 42.

63. The gesture appears in a number of saints' Lives from Europe to Byzantium (see Hahn, *Passio Kyliani*, fig. 34—Menologium of Basil II; and Margaret's Life in the Hannover manuscript). A similar gesture of drapery clasping appears on the *Ara Pacis Augustae* and may indicate the origin of the gesture in the ancient world. Torelli, *Typology and Structure,* pl. II.23.

64. Gravdal, *Ravishing Maidens.*

65. See Elliott's discussion of Cassian's six levels of abstinence to be achieved by a monk. Level 3 involves overcoming arousal by sight. *Fallen Bodies,* 16.

66. Cazelles, *Lady as Saint,* 49; quoting Tertullian, *Ante-Nicene Fathers,* 4:28, 34.

67. Garnier, *Langage de l'image,* II, 89–91, states that beard-pulling can be a sign of perplexity or anger. Here it would seem to signify sensuality.

68. "Fidem coronat. perfidiam abdicat," fol. 48v; Dümmler, "Sigebert von Gembloux *Passio Sanctae Luciae Virginis,*" 39. On the St. Petersburg reliquary of St. Valerie, a chiastic structure similar to that used in the Life of Lucy is used to express a similar reversal. See Hahn, "Valerie's Gift."

69. Stanbury, "Feminist Masterplots," discusses a similarly powerful look in the *Pearl* and contrasts its effect to Freudian and Lacanian theories of the gaze.

70. The phrase "eyes of faith" is Jerome's, describing Paula in the Holy Land. However, most discussions of Christian vision argue that faith precedes true vision. Jerome, *Epistola,* 108.10.2.

71. The Byzantine, Theodore Bestos, regretted descriptions of Euphemia's breast and navel "before priestly men." Rapp, "Figures of Female Sanctity," 325.

72. Agatha's full condemnation of Quintian is: Quintian "Impie, crudelis et dire tyranne, non es confusus amputare in faemina, quod ipse in matre suxisti? Sed ego habeo mamillas integras intus in anima mea ex quibus nutrio omnes sensus meos, quas ab infantia Christo Domino consecravi." AASS, 5 Feb., 616F. Her claim to whole and internal breasts that nourish her senses is a particularly interesting element.

73. See the previous note. On the medieval view of breasts and bodies see Miles, "Virgin's One Bare Breast," and Bynum, "Body of Christ." Nevertheless, I am arguing that the breast can be both sexual and nutritive. Bynum seems to insist on replacing one with the other.

74. For a brief note about homosexuality among another group of women—nuns—see Schulenburg, *Forgetful,* 353.

75. Anson, "Female Transvestite," 1–32, argues for a similar presentation and transformation of monastic desire through narrative.

76. After her first torture, a whipping of her breasts, the prefect opines, "Oh, what beauty you have lost!" He is then angered by her refusal to comply and orders further torture. "Truly the executioners acceded and macerated her body. Now the impious prefect covered his face. On account of the flowing out of blood he could not look at her. Similarly, the others could not either." The Latin is quoted in Hahn *Passio Kyliani,* 301, 302. Cazelles (*Lady as Saint,* 19) briefly alludes to similar imbedded effects in Gautier of Coinci's *Life of Saint Christina,* presumably ll. 1600–16, 148.

77. William of Saint-Thierry, *Golden Epistle,* 52.

78. Cazelles, *Lady as Saint,* 28, 50, 58. Cazelles makes much of this quality (although it is also often a characteristic of male saints), as an element of women's suffering of "forced visibility," 50. She presents a dialectic of female visibility and silence over against male invisibility and speech. This may be truer of the later Lives she deals with, which have a somewhat sensationalist cast.

79. The translation is that of Damrosch in *"Non Alia sed Aliter,"* 189.

80. See chapter 1. Theologians continued to express suspicion of such use of the senses and the affective: Bynum, "Body of Christ," 88.

81. Harrison, *Beauty and Revelation in the Thought of Saint Augustine,* 138. Augustine refers to Wisdom as a beautiful woman, ibid., 197.

82. Augustine, *Confessions,* 10:6; and *Sermons on Selected Lessons,* II, 541–42 (Sermon 76, on John V).

83. *Le Livre de l'expérience des vrais fidèles,* para. 167, 382–84, cited by Bynum, "Body of Christ," 91. Such an explicit discussion is not to be expected in the earlier Middle Ages but realizes a tendency that is already present.

84. Harrison, *Beauty and Revelation in the Thought of Saint Augustine,* 237, quoting Psalm 32, ii, 6.

85. Bynum, "Body of Christ," 101. Although, as Bynum notes, at times Mary becomes priest— a role not granted to early medieval virgin saints.

86. *Sacramentarium,* Taf. 41.

87. Bynum, "Women Mystics and Eucharistic Devotion."

88. See no. 20 in the catalogue of the exhibit, *L'Oeuvre de Limoges,* 116–18, and the bibliography cited there. The most important discussion is Gauthier, "La Légende de sainte Valérie."

89. "Miracula Sancta Valeriae," 278–84; Bollandist Society, *Catalogus Codicum Hagiographicorum . . . Bibliotheca Nationali Parisiensi,* I, 41–44; I, 196–98; II, 401–403; II, 2–5.

90. The fourth scene, on the upper left, not discussed here, shows the conversion of the duke to Christianity.

91. Cephalophores are usually male, and the miracle generally refers in some way to the saint's place of burial. Coens, "Nouvelles Recherches sur un thème hagiographique: La Céphalophore," and Colledge, "Cephalologie." Here, the carrying of the head becomes an offering. See Hahn, "Valerie's Gift."

92. The events of Lucy's Life are situated in Catania, as the first illumination makes clear by depicting and labeling the city walls (see fig. 33). There is a sense of geographic specificity on the St. Petersburg Valerie reliquary in the elaborate representation of the stones of the city walls; at the time of the manufacture of the reliquary, there were two such walls, defending the ducal and the cathedral portions of the city, respectively. Bernadette Barrière, "Le Limousin et Limoges au temps de l'émail champlevé," Taburet-Delahaye Boehm, *L'Oeuvre de Limoges,* p. 23.

93. For such *sancti,* see Hahn, *Passio Kyliani,* 61.

94. Again this is a typical quality of saints. Its most vivid illustration appears in the Utrecht Psalter in the illustration of Psalm 115 (116), which describes "saints" who make offerings of praise and which was interpreted by Augustine and others to represent the bodily sacrifice of the saints, here shown martyred, for the Church. Hahn, *Passio Kyliani,* 116–17. Valerie's executioner was said to be named Hotarius. See the discussion of the sacrifice motif in Hahn, "Valerie's Gift."

95. Ignatius of Antioch, Letter to the Romans 4:1, uses a metaphor of himself as the host: "I am like wheat to be ground by the teeth of the lions to be made into bread, a pure offering." Lake, *Apostolic Fathers,* I, 231. Other saints' Lives use similar metaphors. I would like to thank Maureen Tilley for drawing this one to my attention.

96. See note 6 above.

97. In Byzantium as well, virgin's Lives were especially recommended to women. They seem to have been perceived by men as ideals. Women seem to have read Lives of both men and women. Rapp, "Figures of Female Sanctity," 315, 321, 326–27.

98. A hauntingly similar story of a young woman committing herself to virginity and distributing her goods to the poor appears in a Tamil Buddhist text. Richman, "The Portrayal of

a Female Renouncer in a Tamil Buddhist Text"; and Bynum's introduction, 1–22 in *Gender and Religion*.

99. See the theological discussions cited by Bynum, "Body of Christ," 98.

100. This may at times have occurred against their will. See the fascinating play of theological interpretation and female reality in the stories of Eloise and Abelard as in Cazelles, *Lady as Saint*, 76–80.

101. Coakley, "Friars, Sanctity, and Gender," 98, 104–5.

102. Schaff, *Saint Augustine*, 401. The senses are also discussed: 402.

CHAPTER 5

1. K. J. Leyser described the effect in the sacrality of kings: "We know of it mainly through literary sources, liturgical texts, . . . and the visual arts. How this sacrality acted in society and what its functions were are [central] questions [that despite the constancy of their depiction in material and literary culture, show an] infinite malleability in action." *Rule and Conflict*, 81–82.

2. Barbara Abou-el-Haj, *Cult of the Saints*, treats these men almost exclusively.

3. Michel Sot shows the historical interdependence of the types in "La Fonction du couple saint évêque/saint moine."

4. L. Traube, ed., MGH: *Poetae Latini Aevi Carolini* (Berlin, 1906), III:204–7, vv. 139–40.

5. *Glory of the Confessors*, 78.

6. Raymond Van Dam, in *Leadership*, discusses the gradual melding of Christian ideology and Roman administrative and social structures. This joining was not contemporaneously realized in all parts of Europe. Gregory of Tours's comments, although not universally representative, will serve adequately in this discussion.

7. Leyser, *Rule and Conflict*, 79.

8. *Glory of the Confessors*, 94 and 83. The marking of a boundary is accomplished with the shroud from the tomb of Remigius of Reims. The boundary prevents the plague from attacking the city.

9. *Glory of the Confessors*, 73; and *Life of the Fathers*, 43. In the latter story, a man later recognized as a saint, Quintianus, is forced out of town after he moves the relics of the local patron. See also Raymond van Dam's discussion of Priscillian's treatment by Bishop Hydatius as an example of a bishop jealous of his prerogatives of leadership: *Leadership*, 101 ff.

10. For an argument about such pictorial defenses, see Abou-el-Haj, "Bury St. Edmunds Abbey."

11. Van Dam has shown that through the "time" of the liturgy, the clergy provided a powerful unifying and controlling system to their people: *Leadership*, 277–300.

12. *Life of the Fathers*, 27.

13. Brown, *Cult of the Saints*, 126. The cult of Martin is treated in Van Dam, *Leadership*, esp. chaps. 9–13.

14. *Glory of the Confessors*, 23, 43, 76, 94, 104; *Glory of the Martyrs*, 33, 54, 83–84.

15. She is also buried in Martial's tomb, just as Gervasius and Protasius were buried in Ambrose's tomb. See Hahn, "Golden Altar."

16. Hahn, *Passio Kyliani*. See also Mainfränkische Museum Würzburg, *Kilian*.

17. There are, of course, important differences between bishops from southern and northern Gaul and from Germanic lands that should be carefully considered in studying any specific bishop. I focus here on commonalities.

18. Carrasco, "Notes on the Iconography."

19. The scene of Kilian preaching may represent an election by popular acclamation: see Hahn, *Passio Kyliani*, 51.

20. For a more detailed discussion of the Life of Kilian and this scene, see Hahn, *Passio Kyliani*, 47. The liturgy is found in Vogel-Elze, *Pontifical romano-germanique*, Ordos 63, 65, and 66.

21. Abou-el-Haj, in *Cult of the Saints*, 95–98, summarizes her earlier article, "Consecration and Investiture."

22. The involvement of the king did not begin, at least in Gaul, until the sixth century: Van Dam, *Leadership*, 206.

23. See Abou-el-Haj, *Cult of Saints*, figs. 29–33. As André Vauchez notes, German episcopal Lives of the tenth and eleventh centuries were more political in nature: *Sainthood*, 289. Heribert represents the zenith of such political involvement—he is represented with the emperor three times on his reliquary: *Ornamenta Ecclesiae*, II, 318, 319, 321.

24. See the illustrations of Heribert, reproduced in Abou-el-Haj, *Cult of Saints*, figs. 12–13.

25. Hahn, "Golden Altar."

26. Quentin also sets out with companions in illustrations of his Life. See the manuscript of his Life (Bibliothèque municipale de Saint-Quentin), p. 9. Such apostolic references are common in bishop's Lives: Beaujard, "Cités, évêques et martyrs en Gaule," 183–86.

27. See Sulpicius Severus, "Life of Martin," sections 7, 11.

28. Initially Martial's apostolic mission was emphatically denied, only to later be accepted as a matter of course: Landes, *Relics, Apocalypse and the Deceits of History*.

29. Hahn, *Passio Kyliani*, 149–51.

30. See Hahn, *Passio Kyliani*, 149–51, for the "discordant audience."

31. Hahn, "Picturing the Text," 16.

32. The Life of Arnulf appears in a historiated initial in the Drogo Sacramentary. See the facsimile: *Drogo-Sakramentar*, fol. 91r.

33. The translation is that of Abou-el-Haj, *Medieval Cult of Saints*, 190–91. She compares this scene to the later version of the Life of Amand and concludes that the liturgical gesture was controversial on the evidence of its omission. I would argue that the change follows larger narratival trends in saints' Lives that eschew such dogmatic images.

34. Abou-el-Haj, *Medieval Cult of the Saints*, 99–100.

35. The issue is discussed from the perspective of art history by Thomas Dale, "Inventing a Sacred Past," and from a historical perspective by Richard Landes, *Relics, Apocalypse and the Deceits of History*. Thomas Head weaves together both artistic and historical evidence in "Art and Artifice."

36. I have discussed this sequence extensively in "Picturing the Text."

37. McLaughlin, "The Word Eclipsed?" 107.

38. John Chrysostom, *De Sacerdotio* IV:4, in *PG* 48:681.

39. Not surprisingly, the altar of Ambrose is similarly dominated by such liturgical imagery (see fig. 52). Abou-el-Haj has listed a thorough assortment of other examples of this "image of power," including a miniature in a Boulogne-sur-Mer collection of saints' Lives that depicts St. Bertin surmounted by an image of Christ as the sacrificial lamb and the words of the Agnus Dei, the prayer of sanctification for the host. Perhaps the clearest example of the intent of this liturgical gesture in a single image, the Boulogne-sur-Mer frontispiece serves as the perfect frontispiece for and summary of a bishop's Life: Abou-el-Haj, *Cult of the Saints,* 99–100, and fig. 176. Cf. the liturgical gesture of Quentin's torture with nails (pp. 76–77, pl. 2).

40. Van Dam argues for charisma of bishops as a product of societal need for a leader: *Leadership,* 95.

41. Quentin, an apostle to Gaul and contemporary of Denis, escapes from prison in order to preach and baptize (although the last was performed through an intermediary, since Quentin was not a priest). See the manuscript of his Life (Bibliothèque municipale de Saint-Quentin), pp. 20 and 23.

42. Hahn, *Passio Kyliani,* 56–57.

43. It is interesting that this baptism of the community contains no women. Contrast the examples containing images of women in the Life of Boniface in the Fulda sacramentaries (*Sacramentarium Fuldense,* Taf. 28–29) and in the Life of Quentin, p. 23. Perhaps the symbolism of "priest and king" seemed inappropriate to women.

44. Compare the baptism in the Life of Omer, in which a three-month-old infant (the child of a politically important figure) gives the correct responses to the baptismal *ordo.* Svoboda, "Illustrations to the Life of St. Omer," 140–45.

45. "Ubi sanctus audomarus adrovaldum baptizat quem de errore gentilitatis praedicando convertit."

46. Abou-el-Haj, *Cult of Saints,* fig. 38. Other such depictions of donations do not represent conversion so much as imperial or royal support of missionary work—Charlemagne's grant to Liudger (ibid., fig. 34); Pepin's grant to Hadelin (ibid., fig. 37); Sigebert's grant to Remaclus (ibid., fig. 36); and Theodebert's grant to Maur (ibid., fig. 35). Liudger, for example, immediately sets out to "convert" the formerly pagan site to a Christian building (ibid., 39). Of course, the depictions also serve to visually document and affirm such donations, some of which were eventually contested.

47. A good apostolic precedent for this can be seen in München, Bayerische Staatsbibliothek, Clm 13074, a collection of the Lives of the Apostles. On the frontispiece for the Life of Matthew, there are four scenes: Matthew building, baptizing the king of the Ethiopians, veiling the king's daughter, and martyrdom. The first three all represent the "building" of the Church. *Ornamenta ecclesiae,* B 19, 184–85. This same notion of building has been observed in Lives, especially that of Willibald's Life of Boniface: Leonardi, "Modelli agiografici," 513.

48. *Vita vel actus beati Desiderii episcopi Cadurcensis,* chap. 25, MGH *Scriptores,* 4:582. Translated and cited by William Dieboldt in a talk in April 1996 at the Metropolitan Museum of Art, New York.

49. Abou-el-Haj includes a thorough discussion of building in her *Cult of the Saints,* 41–42, 77–83; most saint's Lives, however, do not illustrate recognizable buildings.

50. Episcopal building projects might also have been undertaken by wealthy bishops in order to deflect criticism. Brown, *Cult of the Saints,* 40 n. 82. See also Vauchez, *Sainthood,* 289–90.

51. The idea may be most clearly stated in a comment about an abbess: "Thus indeed in accord with the Apostle's instruction, Rusticula, as a wise builder, laid her foundation; she built on earth what afterwards she found in heaven, because those saints whom she venerated with such love on earth prepared celestial habitations for her in paradise through their intercession." Here the specially gendered role of caring for saints' shrines comes into play. Schulenburg, *Forgetful,* 84, quoting and translating MGH *Scriptores,* 4:343. Regarding women's care for saintly bodies, see Hahn, *Passio Kyliani,* 60.

52. Abou-el-Haj, "Bury St. Edmunds Abbey"; Gaiffier, "Revendications"; and Little, "Spiritual Sanctions."

53. Van Dam, *Leadership,* chap. 12.

54. Van Dam, *Leadership,* 265, gives one assessment why these illnesses are prominent among those at the shrine.

55. Sulpicius Severus, "Life of Martin," sections 7, 11; and *Dialogues,* II:32, p. 101. Cf. Acts 9:36–41, and 20:9–10.

56. Curing of paralytics in Omer: fol. 29v; Albinus: fol. 28v (discussed in Abou-el-Haj, *Cult of the Saints,* 111, 109).

57. Schrade, *Liudger,* 21. Freise, *Vita Sancti Liudgeri* includes a facsimile of this manuscript. Unfortunately, I have not been able to consult it.

58. Brown, *Cult of the Saints,* 106.

59. Brown, *Cult of the Saints,* 112.

60. Van Dam, *Leadership,* 61.

61. See Hahn, *Passio Kyliani,* 64.

62. See Hahn, "Voices of the Saints."

63. The full passage (quoted in McKitterick, *Carolingian Reforms,* 63) reads: "Quia tanta est sanctitatis sacri ministerii ut salva altioris mysterii intelligentia, etiam per prophetam Dominus prohibuerit, ne cum sanctis vestimentis sacerdos procedat ad populum, sed intra sancta illa dimittat ad eum a colloquio divino rediens."

64. *Glory of the Confessors,* 27, 84, 89 (wine); 20, 26 (oil).

65. Carrasco, "Notes on the Iconography," 338.

66. Fol. 24v: Abou-el-Haj, *Cult of the Saints,* 191–93.

67. Schrade, *Liudger,* 22–24.

68. Gregory of Tours quotes Prudentius's *Cathemerinon* 6:133–36: *Glory of the Martyrs,* 133.

69. See Hahn, "Voices of the Saints."

70. *Life of the Fathers,* 106, cited by Brown, *Cult of the Saints,* 107.

71. More examples may be found in *Glory of the Confessors,* 68, 80, 87.

72. Carrasco, "Spirituality," 6. The representation does not correspond to the text of the Life of Martin at all. In chapter 8:2, Martin comes upon a group of people mourning the suicide of

a slave. Martin insists that everyone leave the room and then lies on the dead body, gradually reviving it. "Soon life began to return to the features of the dead man, as his still languid eyes were lifted to look into the face of Martin. Forcing himself slowly to rise and grasping the hand of the blessed man, he stood up." "Life of Martin," 114. For the Latin text and a French translation, see Fontaine, *Sulpice*, 270–71. This textual version of the miracle would preclude Martin making any gesture at all, because the slave grasps his hand; nor does it mention the sign of the cross. The representation of the gesture in the miniature is nonetheless true to the spirit of the text, for the Life makes frequent mention of Martin using it. Jacques Fontaine (*Sulpice*, 528, 726, 744–45, 1170–71), argues for the importance and power of the sign as a standard or weapon.

73. M. Tony Sauvel compares the scene to the dead rising from their graves in "Miracles," 170.

74. This resurrection and the one immediately preceding it were adduced by Martin's hagiographers as evidence of the saint's apostolicity. Amand and Liudger also resurrect the dead—in fact, both save hanged men, a *topos;* Gaiffier, "Pendu sauvé."

75. Constable, "Interpretation of Mary and Martha."

76. This is a description of the never sainted Egbert of Trier, born and bred to power, but still said to have a modest core: *Inventio et miracula s. Celsi:* AASS, 3 Feb., 397, cited by Head, "Art and Artifice," 70. Head also provides a fascinating description of Egbert's use of art in the service of his episcopal power.

77. Sulpicius, *Life of Martin,* 10, quoted in Noble and Head, *Soldiers of Christ,* 13.

78. Noble and Head, *Soldiers of Christ,* 14.

79. This may derive from the bishop's assumption of the Roman magistrate's position: Scheibelreiter, "Frühfränkische Episkopat," 142–43. See also Vauchez, *Sainthood,* 294.

80. Both episodes are described in *Glory of the Confessors,* 67

81. Svoboda, "Illustrations to the Life of St. Omer," 309–10.

82. Gaiffier, "Pendu sauvé," and *Life of the Fathers,* 68.

83. Discussed and illustrated in Abou-el-Haj, "Bury St. Edmunds Abbey."

84. Compare to St. Severus, who "flourishes like a palm tree" in heaven. *Glory of the Confessors,* 60.

85. Brown, *Cult of the Saints,* 36–37.

86. Cuthbert literally reaches out from his grave to heal a paralytic. See British Library, Yates Thompson MS 26, fol. 83r, reproduced in Abou-el-Haj, *Cult of Saints,* fig. 123.

87. See my description of the hierarchy of the senses as an avenue of empathy in Ambrose's Life: Hahn, "Golden Altar."

88. Abou-el-Haj, "Feudal Conflicts."

89. Vauchez, *Sainthood,* 305–10.

CHAPTER 6

1. Goodich, *Vita Perfecta,* 128 and 131.

2. Albertson, ed., Felix's "Life of St. Guthlac," prologue, 169.

3. Albertson, ed., Felix's "Life of St. Guthlac," 165. For the last scene and the scrolls that represent gifts to the abbey of Crowland, see Kelly, "Forgery, Invention, and Propaganda."

4. In her dissertation and subsequent book, Barbara Abou-el-Haj assembled a list of common scenes occurring in the Lives of saints, many of whom were monks. She generated a table in which each illustrated saint's Life is summed up as it were by a series of *x*'s in the appropriate boxes. Abou-el-Haj, *Cult of Saints,* 154–55. She focuses on "core scenes" of the monastic or religious experience, to which she argues other scenes were added to create various Lives.

5. See Abou el-Haj, *Cult of Saints,* 37–40.

6. Warner, *The Guthlac Roll,* 1–20; Kelly, "Forgery, Invention and Propaganda." For the presumed text for the roll, see the translation by Albertson of Felix's "Life of St. Guthlac," chap. 20, 178. For the roll's commissioning by Crowland Abbey, see Morgan, *Early Gothic Manuscripts,* no. 22; Kelly, "Forgery, Invention, and Propaganda."

7. Kelly, "Forgery, Invention, and Propaganda." Although it has also been suggested that the object is a design for a stained glass window or other object, the roll seems too finished for this use. It was not perhaps used long in any capacity, for unrelated sketches of a somewhat later date appear on the reverse.

8. Berlin, Staatsbibliothek Preussischer Kulturbesitz, MS theol. lat. fol. 323: Schrade, *Die Vita Heiligen Liudger.*

9. The Rule of Benedict did not encourage oblation: see Fry, ed., *The Rule of Saint Benedict,* esp. chaps. 58–59, which treat admittance to the order. However, Benedict himself accepted oblates, including Maurus. Wickstrom, "Life of St. Benedict," 36.

10. Goldschmidt, *Die Bronzetüren.*

11. The manuscript made for Abbot Desiderius is a lectionary that includes readings and illustrations from the Lives of Benedict and Maurus, Benedict's foremost pupil. Benedict was believed to be buried at Monte Cassino. The pictures are arranged as multipart, full-page illustrations with *tituli.* See Brenk, *Das Lektionar,* Mayo, "The Illustrations," Wickstrom, "Text and Image," and idem, "Life of St. Benedict."

12. *Dialogues,* II:1.

13. From the missal of Robert of Jumièges, cited by Constable, "Ceremonies and Symbolism," 813.

14. Gaiffier, "Miracles bibliques," 50–61. Almost all the literature on illustrated saints' Lives (beginning with Wormald, "Some Illustrated Manuscripts," 248–68) makes this point.

15. Albertson, ed., Felix's "Life of St. Guthlac."

16. See Kelly, "Forgery, Invention, and Propaganda," where all the scenes are illustrated and discussed.

17. Dubler, *Das Bild des heiligen Benedikt;* and the facsimile edition of Vat. lat. 1202: *Codex Benedictus,* ed. Meyvaert, which includes the lives of Benedict, Maurus, and Scholastica with commentary by Penelope Mayo. Beat Brenk, *Das Lektionar,* provides a commentary on the manuscript, as does an earlier facsimile: Inguanez and Avery, *Miniature cassinese.* The c. 1160 manuscript from Saint-Laurent-de-Liège, commissioned by a monk as a gift (Brussels, Bibliothèque royale MS 9916–17), contains all four books of the *Dialogues,* but book 2 has the largest number of il-

lustrations. It is thus clearly not a *libellus*. The Vatican and Brussels manuscripts seem unrelated in respect to their illustrations. The Brussels manuscript contains most of the same miracle scenes but does not have the same emphasis on the teaching and building scenes. See Gaspar-Lyna, *Principaux manuscrits,* 78 ff. This manuscript deserves closer scrutiny.

18. Particularly, Tours, Bibliothèque municipale, MS 1018. See Kessler, "Pictorial Narrative."

19. See Kauffmann, *Romanesque Manuscripts,* no. 26; and Baker, "Medieval Illustrations."

20. Svoboda, "Life of St. Omer."

21. Morel-Payen, *Les plus beaux manuscrits,* 52–58.

22. Fry, ed., *Rule of Saint Benedict,* prologue. Wickstrom emphasizes the Passion quality of the end of Maurus's Life, "Text and Image," 71–75.

23. *Dialogues,* II:7.

24. Mayo, "Illustrations," 48–49.

25. Timothy Verdon offers an interesting discussion in the introduction to *Monasticism and the Arts,* 10. Here, he interprets a painting of the same subject by Fra Filippo Lippi, comparing it to a passage on obedience from the Rule and framing the message of the painting in community— that "we 'save' our brothers or sisters through service prompted by the obedience of faith."

26. Pächt, *Rise of Pictorial Narrative,* 14–16.

27. Pächt also maintains that this device is not intended to combine two originally separate scenes (as some scholars have argued) but rather to incorporate "the element of time . . . in the pictorial rendering." *Rise of Pictorial Narrative,* 15. For the temporal aspect of narrative, see pp. 36 and 46–47.

28. See the use of this quotation by Verdon in his introduction to *Monasticism and the Arts* in note 25 above. John Wickstrom, who wrote a paper on the Vatican Life of Maurus in my Michigan seminar (now published as "Text and Image"), expanded my original understanding of this passage.

29. Mayo, "Illustrations," 66. I have amended "returns" (*recurrit*) to read, more literally, "runs back."

30. Albertson, ed., "Felix's 'Life of St. Guthlac,'" 214.

31. See Wickstrom. "Text and Image," fig. 2. For the Troyes manuscript (Bibliothèque municipale, MS 2273), see Morel-Payen, *Les plus beaux manuscrits,* 52–58.

32. See: Baker, "Medieval Illustrations of Bede's 'Life of St. Cuthbert.'" Pächt, *Rise of Pictorial Narrative,* 15. The text is that of Bede and may be found in Colgrave, *Two Lives of Saint Cuthbert,* chap. 12, 194–97. Obedience comes into play in this scene in two ways. First, the boy follows the saint's command and "runs." Second, the boy fails to carry out the spirit of the saint's request and must return a portion of the fish to the eagle as the bird's rightful share. I am not suggesting that the Life of Cuthbert copies that of Benedict but that this composition has been created to suit the illustration of obedience by two different artists.

33. Colgrave, *Two Lives of Saint Cuthbert,* chap. 36, 266–71.

34. Abou-el-Haj, *Cult of Saints,* 197.

35. Saint-Omer MS 698, fols. 10r and v. See Svoboda, "The Illustrations of the Life of St. Omer," 291–92.

36. "[A]gain he tells teachers: Whoever listens to you, listens to me (Luke 10:16)." Rule, 5:6.

37. Other examples in Vat. lat. 1202 illustrate the Rule, as well as the principle of obedience. One episode has a monk accept a handkerchief from a woman. Benedict knows without being told and reprimands the monk for accepting a personal gift (fol. 52v). Another episode concerns a monk who wants to leave the monastery; he obtains Benedict's approval but is terrorized by a dragon outside the monastery (fol. 62r).

38. The Cuthbert miracles that are related to food or drink in some way are as follows: p. 20: Cuthbert's horse discovers a loaf and some meat in a barn; 26: Cuthbert entertains an angel at Ripon; 38: Cuthbert, cut off by a storm, finds three pieces of dolphin's flesh; 41: the eagle brings a fish (as above); 61: Cuthbert drives away birds eating a crop; 89: a reeve is cured by eating bread blessed by Cuthbert; 94: at a meal, Cuthbert sees the soul of a man carried to heaven; 97: Cuthbert tastes water and gives it the flavor of wine; 98: two monks who disobey Cuthbert's order to eat a goose are imprisoned by a storm (as above); 135: King Alfred gives food to a pilgrim and is rewarded by Cuthbert.

39. Fol. 43v: *Dialogues,* II:12.

40. Fol. 127v. The caption reads: "Behold the Rule. Follow it. Take the weight and the measure, and go forth," Mayo-Meyvaert, "Illustrations," 82.

41. Wickstrom, "Text and Image," 63–65.

42. *Rule of Saint Benedict,* ed. Fry, 424. The metaphor of sacramental sharing also appears in the Old Testament. Compare Zach. 14:20–21, which describes the use of holy vessels.

43. The scene appears on the doors of Sta. Sabina in Rome. See *LCI* 2:205.

44. Folio 18r. Penelope Mayo makes this observation in "Illustrations," 62. *Dialogues,* II:1.

45. Schapiro, "The Religious Meaning of the Ruthwell Cross," 236. See also Meyvaert, "A New Perspective," 135–31.

46. *Dialogues,* II:28–29.

47. Albertson, ed., "Felix's 'Life of St. Guthlac,'" 168.

48. For Amand: fol. 13v in Valenciennes, Bibliothèque municipale MS 502, discussed in Abou-el-Haj, *Cult of the Saints,* 176–77 (where the image is associated with apostolic "fishers of men"), and illustrated at fig. 151. For Liudger: fol. 14v in the Berlin MS and Schrade, *Vita des heiligen Liudger,* 24–25.

49. Colgrave, *Two Lives of Saint Cuthbert,* chap. 37, 276–77.

50. Athanasius, *Life of Anthony,* 75, chap. 13.

51. Colgrave, *Two Lives of Saint Cuthbert,* chap 16, 211. The scene seems to be one of perfect accord. However, one monk is barefoot, perhaps representing the more severe Irish monasticism that the Rule replaced (p. 50).

52. See also the death of Benedict (fig. 94) and Courcelle's "La Vision cosmique." Compare Benedict's death to those of Aubin, Liudger, Maurus, and Omer, which are communal but also sometimes dominated by the ecclesiastical hierarchy, in the form of bishops. See illustrations in Abou-el-Haj, *Cult of the Saints,* figs. 80, 82, 85, and 87. Jacques Dalarun, "La Mort des saints fondateurs," gives bibliography for liturgies and describes the significance of death. He notes instances of monks dying during the liturgy. Like Maurus, Dominic died in the presence of twelve companions (p. 199).

53. Such images are not common in monastic Lives until later depictions of Franciscan life.

Although the Vision at Arles depicts Francis as dominant over the other monks, the intent is to show that he was with them in spirit in their meeting in chapter. See Goffen, *Spirituality in Conflict,* 33, 42–43, 48, and 70–71.

54. *Dialogues,* II:2. The point is not that the notion of lust is unrelated to women (see Vat. lat. 1202, fol. 36r with nude, lascivious women), but rather that Gregory represents lust as essentially a battle of self-control.

55. *Dialogues,* II:3.

56. Alternately, Felix could be said to be modeling Guthlac on the Antonine ideal that also inspired the Rule: Kurtz, "From St. Antony to St. Guthlac," 103–46.

57. Roundel 8, in exposing the saint's bare legs while he is held upside down, may imply his helplessness in the face of such temptation. See also the discussion of nude legs in relation to temptation in Wickstrom, "Life of St. Benedict," 55.

58. "Felix's 'Life of St. Guthlac,'" ed. Albertson, chap. 36, 195.

59. Kelly, "Forgery, Invention, and Propaganda," 3.

60. Colgrave, *Two Lives of Saint Cuthbert,* chap. 10, 188–91.

61. Kelly, "Forgery, Invention, and Propaganda," 9, scene 5. These architectural structures may also refer to contemporary Crowland and the legal issues of ownership.

62. See University College MS 165, p. 67 (Cuthbert); see Colgrave, *Two Lives of Saint Cuthbert,* chap. 22, 228–31; Vat. lat. 1202, fol. 36r (Benedict). Anthony is similarly described as leaning out a window: Athanasius, *Life of Anthony,* 66, II.12. Radegund is repeatedly shown in this fashion.

63. See McLaughlin, *Consorting with Saints.*

64. In some cases, this change appears to be documented in historical texts. See Paxton, "Liturgy and Healing."

65. The abbot's Life is also exemplary of the Rule, for according to the Rule, "anyone who wishes to know more about his [Benedict's] life and character can discover in his Rule exactly what he was like as abbot, for his life could not have differed from his teaching." *Dialogues,* II:36. See Wickstrom, "Life of St. Benedict."

66. Svoboda, "Illustrations of the Life of St. Omer," 124–28. Svoboda is struck by the resemblance of this scene to a dedication picture.

67. See Wickstrom, "Text and Image."

68. Strictly speaking, Benedict returns to the eremitic life almost immediately because of the sins of this first group of monks. However, in the miniatures of the Vatican manuscript, Benedict's return to his cave is not pictured and from this point forward, the saint's actions are characterized as those of an abbot or leader. See *Dialogues,* II:3.

69. Mayo-Meyvaert, "Illustrations," 64. See Wickstrom's treatment of the same scene in Maurus's Life, "Text and Image," 55–57. He notes the first appearance of Maurus's halo in this scene.

70. The facsimile of the Vatican codex mistranslates this phrase as "Fathers [of the Church]." Mayo-Meyvaert, "Illustrations," 64. I believe that the phrase refers instead to the Fathers of monasticism and the desert Fathers.

71. See Wickstrom, "Text and Image," 57.

72. *Dialogues,* II:4.

73. Although Wickstrom argued this in his seminar paper, he does not emphasize the point in the published version of the paper.

74. Radegund refused the office, but her demeanor and actions are decidedly those of an abbess.

75. See Von Daum Tholl, "Life According to the Rule."

76. Abou-el-Haj, *Cult of the Saints,* fig. 39—Liudger. Benedict builds Monte Cassino, first purging it of demons; fig. 150—Amand builds churches and monasteries; fig. 41—Cuthbert builds his hermitage. See also Carrasco, "First Life of Cuthbert," for a discussion of the possible meaning of building as monastic renewal.

77. *Dialogues,* II:8–11, pp. 74–77. The quotation appears on p. 74. See also Mayo-Meyvaert, "Illustrations," 67–69, fols. 39v–40r; 73, fol. 57r (supervision of building by means of a vision).

78. Mayo-Meyvaert, "Illustrations," 83, fol. 132v. The fall and miracle supposedly occurred at Vercelli.

79. Exod. 17:9–13. See the discussion of this scene in medieval art in Schapiro, *Word and Pictures,* 17–36.

80. In the sacramentary of Ivrea, the liturgy of a burial is described in a remarkable cycle of ten miniatures. In these illustrations, a female mourner is very prominent. Here, in the burial of a rich man, others wash the body, but the woman (perhaps the wife of the deceased, or perhaps a mourner) plays a highly emotive role in the process of burial. Schmitt, *Raison des gestes,* 211–24.

81. From the Life of Maurus, AASS 1:1039–50, section 17, as cited by Wickstrom, "Text and Image," 69.

82. The Life of Scholastica, Benedict's sainted sister and the first Benedictine nun, is copied in the Vatican manuscript but is not illustrated.

83. Goffen, *Spirituality in Conflict,* xvi; and see Diket, "An Exemplary Life," which argues for a pictorialization of the monastic life. For Brother John, see p. 56.

84. Bonaventure, "Sermones 4 de S. Francisci," trans. Doyle, *The Disciple and the Master,* 87; cited by Goffen, *Spirituality in Conflict,* 67.

85. Wickstrom notes the likeness of this image and the corresponding image in the Life of Maurus to a ladder: Wickstrom, "Text and Image," 68–70, figs. 8 and 9; *Dialogues,* II:37. See also Wickstrom, "Life of St. Benedict," 58–65, 73 n. 75.

CHAPTER 7

1. Nelson, "Lord's Anointed," 158.

2. Folz, *Saints rois,* 21, 113. See also Vauchez, *Sainthood,* 164, 361.

3. Robert Folz (*Saints rois,* 23–115), discusses all of the saintly Christian kings up to the thirteenth century, balancing historical truth against hagiographic construction. See also Ridyard, *Royal Saints,* 236.

4. This is K. Gorski's theory. See Ridyard's discussion. *Royal Saints,* 248.

5. Cheney, *Cult of Kingship;* and Rollason, "Cults of Murdered Royal Saints."

6. Graus, *Volk, Herrscher und Heiliger,* 393, 427–33.

7. Ridyard, *Royal Saints,* 77.

8. Duby, *Three Orders,* 92–108. See Hahn, "Peregrinatio et Natio," 129. Percy Ernst Schramm (*English Coronation,* 18), explicitly links Dunstan's new ideas on kingship to a reform of "order, rules, and obedience" in monastic life.

9. Head, *Hagiography,* 241–55. That Dunstan should appear in this legend is interesting. He was an important early codifier of monarchic theory, Schramm, *English Coronation,* 18–20.

10. James Campbell (*Bede's Reges and Principes,* 11–12), emphasizes the importance of the economy of horses in early medieval kingship. The oxcart that was customary for the Merovingians became a ludicrous image for the Carolingians: Geary, *Before France and Germany,* 224.

11. Sitwell, "Gerald of Aurillac." Chapter numbers cited hereafter and in the text refer to the original edition; the text is reprinted in Noble and Head, *Soldiers,* 293–362. See also Poulin, *L'Idéal de sainteté,* 81–98, and Iogna-Prat, "Hagiographie dans le Cluny de l'an mil."

12. Jaeger, *Origins of Courtliness.*

13. Head and Landes, *Peace of God.*

14. Garnier, *Langage d'image,* II, 250.

15. Three miracles involving fishes occur in the Life of Gerald: *Gerald,* II:29–30. The pilgrimage miracle is recounted in II:19.

16. The saintly Sigebert, a seventh-century East Anglian prince, precedes Gerald in this folly by entering into battle armed only with a rod: he was massacred, according to Bede. Folz, *Saints rois,* 48.

17. AASS, 5 July, 266D.

18. AASS, 5 July, 266D.

19. Duby, *The Knight,* 124.

20. Duby, *The Knight,* 31.

21. Although it may be the purely happenstance result of the circumstances of survival that two of the extant royal narratives are English, England seems to have been the center of the medieval development of ideas of royal sanctity. It was the home both of many of the sainted kings and of many of the most influential hagiographic texts on the subject. Folz gives a good overall picture: *Saints rois, passim.*

22. Most discussion of the Morgan manuscript has centered on its style and date. Pächt, Wormald, and Dodwell attribute the Morgan manuscript to the Alexis Master of the Albani Psalter (*St. Albans Psalter,* 167) and also mention his workshop (ibid., 118). Most scholars since have assigned the Morgan manuscript to the workshop of the Alexis Master: Bateman, "Pembroke 120 and Morgan 736," and McLachlan, *The Scriptorium of Bury St. Edmunds,* which reproduces the Morgan manuscript in full. McLachlan finds the script hand of the Morgan manuscript in a group of manuscripts from the abbey and on that basis concludes that the illuminations, which are not typical of Bury St. Edmunds, were executed by a visiting artist who first worked at St. Albans. See McLachlan Parker, "A Twelfth-Century Cycle of Drawings," and eadem, "The Scriptorium of Bury St. Edmunds."

The date of the manuscript has also been disputed. R. M. Thomson has dated it to 1124/25 based on his understanding of the reasons for the inclusion of two letters in the first gathering of the book: "Early Romanesque Book Illumination"; and idem, "A Twelfth-Century Letter." However, C. M. Kauffmann does not agree that these letters can reliably date the manuscript and gives a date of c. 1130 (*Romanesque Manuscripts,* 74). In a more recent publication, Thomson seems to have allowed more chronological leeway in his dating of the manuscript, now giving a date of c. 1124/25 but adding "no later than c. 1130"; see *Manuscripts from St. Albans Abbey,* 26. For a general discussion of Edmund, see Ridyard, *Royal Saints,* 211–33.

23. The initials are by a different artist and interpret the scenes differently. For example, Edmund kills Sweyn in the full-page miniatures with a spear; in the initials, he uses a sword. McLachlan, *Scriptorium,* 102, fig. 54. This seems neither supplemental nor coordinated at all; it is merely different.

24. Schnitzler, *Rheinische Schatzkammer,* I, 19–21; Folz, *Souvenir;* and Brown and Cothren, "The Twelfth-Century Crusading Window of the Abbey of St.-Denis."

25. The royal virtue of courtesy that Binski notes (*Westminster Abbey,* 61–62), is best understood in a fully hagiographic context, as in Hahn, "Proper Behavior."

26. Lewis (*Art of Matthew Paris,* 36–42) discusses the evidence. Matthew Paris was the major exception, and he is the hagiographer at issue here.

27. Raynaud, "Pouvoir royal," in *Images et Pouvoirs.*

28. Folz, *Saints rois,* 142–48.

29. Although Edmund's dominion was limited to East Anglia, this prehistory seems to grant him a larger territorial authority. It is notable that both later Anglo-Saxon and post-Conquest coronations style the king "regnum Anglorum vel Saxonum." Schramm, *English Coronation,* 28. Edmund is probably represented as king of all England in these post-Conquest illustrations.

30. See brief discussion in Binski, *Westminster Abbey,* 52. It is uncertain whether the Life of Edward was illustrated by Matthew Paris. See pp. 284–85.

31. Careful observation will reveal that the horses are even contrasted in this picture—the powerful charger of the evil king has nailed hooves; the gentle horse of the queen does not. This detail is typical of the illustration of Matthew Paris and appears as well in the Life of Alban. See p. 392 n. 24.

32. For the Hours of Jeanne d'Evreux, see Holladay, "Education of Jeanne d'Evreux," and Chung-Apley, "The Illustrated *Vie et miracles de Saint Louis.*" For the Hours of Jeanne de Navarre, see Thomas, "L'iconographie de Saint Louis."

33. Chung-Apley, "The Illustrated *Vie et miracles de Saint Louis.*"

34. This is discussed by Tania Mertzman in her master's thesis, "The Office of Saint Louis in the Book of Hours of Jeanne de Navarre," 1992, on file at Strozier Library, Florida State University.

35. The best Latin edition of Abbo's *passio* is M. Winterbottom, *Three Lives of English Saints* (Toronto, 1972); here I quote Hervey's English translation, *Corolla Sancti Eadmundi.*

36. Schramm, *English Coronation,* 62–63.

37. Schramm, *English Coronation,* 39–45.

38. Schramm, *English Coronation,* 27–28.

39. Hervey, *Corolla Sancti Eadmundi,* 14–15.

40. Schramm, *English Coronation,* 9, 36.

41. Schramm, *English Coronation*, 15.

42. Schramm, *English Coronation*, 131–33, 137.

43. Schramm, *English Coronation*, 134–36.

44. Schramm, *English Coronation*, 25, 34.

45. Raynaud, "Pouvoir royal," 104.

46. Hahn, *Passio Kyliani*, 56.

47. This may be the significance of the tiny circlet in the baby's hand in plate 5. King Edgar holds a similar circlet in the first miniature. James (*Estoire*) identifies it as the ring that plays a prominent role in the later narrative. See pp. 249–50.

48. Oil was never actually poured from a vial. Binski, *Westminster Abbey*, 127.

49. See Binski's comments: *Westminster Abbey*, 126–32.

50. Matthew Paris knew of such ceremonies firsthand as a witness: Lewis, *Art of Matthew Paris*, 4.

51. Binski, *Westminster Abbey*, fig. 171. Binski notes that the rod is exchanged for the scepter (*Westminster Abbey*, 127). The manuscripts are even closer than their association with Westminster Abbey would imply because they both owe some element of their creative origin to Matthew Paris.

52. As part of the coronation ritual, the king was expected to perform a vigil and meditation in Westminster Abbey on the night before the coronation. See Binski, *Westminster Abbey*, 130. In the *Estoire*, Edward performs the vigil after he learns he has been chosen as king in a vision but before receiving official confirmation (fol. 8r). On the other ceremonials of coronation, see Nelson, "The Lord's Anointed."

53. Hunting figures occur in the illustrations of the Life of Edmund. Hunters blowing horns appear in the first miniature of a series that recounts the finding of Edmund's head; their quarry—a wolf—is reprieved because he protects the saint's head between his paws (see fig. 111).

54. The coronation ceremony is depicted in elaborately illustrated French manuals. Hedeman, *Royal Image*, 112–13; and idem, "Copies in Context."

55. Hahn, "Peregrinatio et Natio," 120–24.

56. Hervey, *Corolla Sancti Eadmundi*, 16–17.

57. The statement is quoted in Cheney, *Cult of Kingship*, 256–57, where it is attributed to the Anglo-Norman saint Dunstan. Here, with widows and orphans, is the first inclusion of *peregrinus*, the Latin word for both stranger and pilgrim. The phrase "widows and orphans" occurs repeatedly in the literature on the duties of the king. For examples, see Dickinson, "The Medieval Conception of Kingship," 320–22, citing Carolingian, Ottonian, and twelfth-century sources in support of this "ecclesiastical-patriarchal conception."

58. Labande-Mailfert, "Pauvreté," 139–63, and Mollat, *The Poor in the Middle Ages*. See also Claussen, "'Peregrinatio' and 'Peregrini,'" and Hahn, "Peregrinatio et Natio."

59. It is literally claimed by Westminster Abbey as a miracle of two of its patrons—Peter and Edward. Barlow notes that this and other miracles are added to a core of healing miracles that occur in the court, "The Vita Aedwardi," 385–97.

60. Holladay, "Education of Jeanne d'Evreux."

61. Jane Chung-Apley makes this argument in "The Illustrated *Vie et miracles de Saint Louis*." See also Le Goff, "Saint Louis."

62. Abou-el-Haj, "Bury St. Edmunds Abbey," 8–13.

63. These retribution miracles are typical in the Lives of monastic patrons protecting their monasteries. See Abou-el-Haj, "Bury St. Edmunds Abbey," 8–13.

64. Hahn, "Proper Behavior," 246. Edward himself claimed Edmund as his "kinsman" in two separate writs: Barlow, *Edward the Confessor*, 257; Ridyard, *Royal Saints*, 225.

65. Osbert wrote a Life of Edward and a Life of Ethelbert of East Anglia (Folz, *Saints rois*, 30, 96), as well as miracles of Edmund (Hahn, "Natio et Peregrinatio," 132).

66. Similarities, especially to the Life of Edward, include prominent images of coronation (Alexander's includes the anointing) and the king's frequent reception of messengers. Raynaud, "Pouvoir royal." Although some ecclesiastics condemned Alexander for *superbia*, Matthew saw fit to include him in his history; a portrait of Alexander appears in the *Chronica majora* (Cambridge, Corpus Christi College 26, p. 24), Lewis, *Art of Matthew Paris*, 137–38.

67. Raynaud, "Pouvoir royal," 114. Violence does occur in the *Estoire* with the representations of the conquest of England by William of Normandy.

68. The later medieval patron of England was the "personification of the ideals of Christian chivalry": Farmer, *Saints*, 177. George, after defeating the dragon, would take no reward but asked the king to "maintain churches, honor priests, and show compassion to the poor" (177). For Charlemagne, see pp. 235–36. For further discussion of saintly chivalry, see pp. 302–6.

69. The illustration of the battle alludes to the Massacre of the Innocents. Earlier in the cycle, Edmund's ancestors are described fighting valiantly like contemporary knights. See Hahn, "Peregrinatio et Natio," 129–30.

70. Campbell, *Bede's Reges and Principes*, 12.

71. St. Stephen of Hungary recommends the power of prayer to conquer enemies in his *Libellus de institutione morum* of c. 1015, Folz, *Saints rois*, 150–51.

72. Binski, *Westminster Abbey*, 57, 146.

73. The different versions of the Life record different responses. The *Estoire* specifies that Edward "smiles as if in a trance" (l. 1291).

74. Reynaud, "Pouvoir royal," 104.

75. Holladay, "Education of Jeanne d'Evreux," and Thomas, "L'Iconographie de St. Louis."

76. The battle of Damietta is recounted in the Saint-Pathus manuscript: chap. 13, p. 199. See Chung-Apley, "The Illustrated *Vie et miracles de Saint Louis*."

77. Binski attributes this observation to Kauffmann, *Westminster Abbey*, 118 n. 191. The miniature depicts a hunt, an activity equated with violence. Louis's prayers neutralize that violence.

78. Saints do, however, appear in battle in posthumous miracles, as does Aubin in the Paris manuscript (fol. 7v), an armed warrior who appears to defend Aubin's people from the Normans, or the more famous example of St. James appearing in battles against the Muslims as "Matamoros." Edmund's killing of Sweyn occurs after the saint's death.

79. Folz, "Naissance et manifestations d'un culte royal," 227.

80. The many scenes of consultation have an additional significance in the *Estoire*. They ex-

hibit not only the consultation with clerical advisers but the just and open court held by the king. Like Alexander, Edward is an ideal chivalric and feudal prince, surrounded by his barons. Raynaud, "Pouvoir royal," 114. In this respect the Life may allude to the king's peacemaking abilities: he keeps his barons happy and in this way ensures peace. Frank Barlow has correlated the vision miracles in the Life with the succession of courts typically held by the English king: Christmas at Gloucester, Easter at Winchester (or in this case Westminster), and Whitsuntide at Westminster. "Vita Aedwardi," 385–97.

81. Marrow, "Circumdederunt me canes multi."

82. Crowns in this era were not worn lightly. They were assumed only in liturgical ceremonies conducted by the clergy. Schramm, *English Coronation,* 31, 42, 56.

83. The robe as insignia of office is discussed in Schramm, *English Coronation,*134–35.

84. Francis Wormald ("Some Illustrated Manuscripts," 248–68), was the first to note this similarity.

85. Mollat, *The Poor in the Middle Ages.* The forest, associated with uncivilized wilderness, is the natural habitat of the barbaric Danes, who are characterized as wild animals. It is also, however, the domain of the wolf—in a sense the European king of beasts. In this respect it is significant that is it a wolf that recognizes Edmund as his lord, protects him, and follows him. But as Aelfric (as opposed to Abbo) makes clear, the wolf escorts the body only as far as the boundary of his "kingdom": "the wolf followed forth with the head until they came to the town, as if he were tame, and then turned back again unto the wood" (*Aelfric's Lives,* ll. 161–3). Miniature 22 (fol. 17v). The recognition of sanctity by animals is a *topos* in saints' Lives, for example, those of Cuthbert and Francis.

86. Abou-el-Haj, "Bury St. Edmunds Abbey," 6–7, pl. 3.

87. Hervey, *Corolla Sancti Eadmundi,* 54–55. The sequence of images also emphasizes the incorruption of the body of Edmund, a somewhat unusual status shared by Edmund with another saintly body, that of Cuthbert, one of the most powerful of all England. Incorruption is a significant mark of the holy and also implies a pure life of chastity. See Folz, "Naissance et manifestations d'un culte royal," 230.

88. It does not seem to be coincidence that other saintly heads are associated with royalty and state. Hervey, *Corolla Sancti Eadmundi,* 17, 29, 43, 43, 41, and 45. Arnold, *Memorials,* 54. The particular motif of the speaking head recurs often in the context of kingship. In Celtic mythology the disembodied head of King Brân foretells the future and protects his kingdom. See Colledge and Marler, "Céphalogie," 421, who note that the Celts use the same word (*pen*), for both head and chief, as did Latin-speaking peoples. Denis, the patron saint and apostle of France, was famous not only for his disembodied talking head but also for carrying that head to the site that became the royal necropolis. Parallels between the lives of Denis and Edmund have already been noted by Antonia Gransden, who argues that Edmund's hagiographer Abbo, as a Frenchman, was familiar with the Life of St. Denis and aware of its importance to French royalty and that he used Denis as a model in composing the Life of the Anglo-Saxon royal saint. Gransden, "Legends and Traditions," 6. A twelfth-century poem specifically compares Edmund to Denis and Demetrius (of Greece), "each the glory of his own people," Hervey, *Corolla Sancti Eadmundi,*

166–67. The association did not end there: an eleventh-century abbot of Bury St. Edmunds, Baldwin, was originally a monk of Saint-Denis; a series of twelfth-century capitals in the crypt of Saint-Denis depicts the life of Edmund, with a focus on Edmund's martyrdom, the discovery of his head and miracles of the relics. See Blum, "The Saint Benedict Cycle," 74; and a forthcoming study of Saint-Denis and these capitals by Jan van der Meulen, which he kindly allowed me to read. Furthermore, an altar of Denis was consecrated at Bury St. Edmunds by Abbot Anselm to replace a parish church dedicated to that saint: Williamson, *Letters of Osbert of Clare*, 197. These connections indicate that in the developing discourse on sacral kingship, England and France shared the symbols of *caput* and *membra Christi*.

89. Hervey, *Corolla Sancti Eadmundi*, 40–41.

90. Bloch, *The Royal Touch*.

91. The king's touch is represented in a miracle on fol. 21v.

92. Binski, *Westminster Abbey*, 55.

93. Although Charlemagne is not considered a saint by today's Church, he received canonization (by an anti-pope) in 1165 and was an important royal and saintly precedent: Vauchez, *Sainthood*, 166.

94. For example, in the circle of the Confessor, Cnut went to Rome in 1027, and Duke Robert of Normandy went to Jerusalem in 1034. Barlow, *Edward the Confessor*, 38 and 40. André Vauchez associates such pilgrimages in the later Middle Ages with the laity: *Sainthood*, 511–12.

95. The miniature was painted before the shrine was completed and therefore does not represent the finished structure. Binski, *Westminster Abbey*, 59.

96. Binski, *Westminster Abbey*, 50, 66; Barlow, *Edward the Confessor*, 269, 282.

97. A Byzantine imperial crown of the same period with *pendulia* is illustrated in Evans and Wixom, *The Glory of Byzantium*, 187.

98. Goodwin, *The Abbey of St. Edmundsbury*, 7. Goodwin cites evidence from William of Malmesbury: "Even kings, who are masters of others, think it is an honor to be his servants, and are accustomed to send him their royal crowns, which they are glad to redeem at a high price, if they wish to wear them." Hervey, trans., *Corolla Sancti Eadmundi*, 111–13. Even if Bury St. Edmunds never became the coronation site, this ritual ransoming of the crown seems to imply that Edmund must give his blessing in order for the "crown" (that is, the power conferred by it) to be effective.

99. Binski, *Westminster Abbey*, 122, 134.

100. Milde, *Mittelalterliche Handschriften der Herzog August Bibliothek*, 64–73, discusses the Wenceslaus *vita* in Wolfenbüttel, Herzog August Bibliothek, Cod. Guelf. 11.2 Augusteus quarto, fols. 18v–37, esp. 18v, the coronation. The text is by Bishop Gumpold of Mantua (d. 985), and the manuscript can be dated before 1006. The other significant scene represents the saint's martyrdom.

101. I argue (in "Peregrinatio et Natio") that Edmund was the king of a "pilgrim people," and the notion of a unity between king and people is an important element of the notion of kingship. See Nelson, "Lord's Anointed," 146–49, and esp. 164, where Nelson notes that Charles the Bald was crowned by Hincmar of Reims, and the people joined him as "citizens of heaven."

102. See Hahn, "Peregrinatio et Natio."

CHAPTER 8

1. "Chlothild," in McNamara et al., *Sainted Women*, 1, 41. In a remarkable passage, women are ranked according to their degree of sanctity: Virgins produce fruit a hundredfold. Widows only produced sixtyfold and wives thirtyfold. McNamara traces the imagery to the New Testament by way of Jerome.

2. Clare of Assisi even compares the body to a cloister: Wood, "Perceptions of Holiness," 321.

3. Gäbe, "Radegundis: *Sancta, Regina, Ancilla;* Corbet, *Saints ottoniens,* 236; Gracco, "La Sainteté féminine du haut Moyen Age," 396–417; and McNamara, *"Imitatio Helena."*

4. Schulenburg, "Strict Active Enclosure," 73–78; and Skinner, "Benedictine Life for Women."

5. Magdalena Carrasco argues that the manuscript was made at the monastery rather than by the cathedral canons of Poitiers. She also contends that a number of miniatures make reference to relics of Radegund. Carrasco, "Spirituality in Context," 416, 430.

6. Smith also argues for a distinctive episodic narrative structure in the Lives of female confessors (see "The Problem of Female Sanctity," 20–21). Given that most pictorial hagiography has an episodic character to it, however, I find no gender distinction here. Suzanne Wemple ("Female Spirituality") also argues that these Lives offer spiritual models.

7. "Balthild," in McNamara et al., *Sainted Women*, 18, 277.

8. McNamara et al., *Sainted Women*, 38–40, 60–65, 264–68; McNamara, "Need to Give"; and especially, McNamara, *"Imitatio Helenae."*

9. McNamara, "Living Sermons," 20–21.

10. Corbet argues the hagiographic type of the sainted queen dates earlier than that of the confessor-king: see his *Saints ottoniens,* 240.

11. Corbet, *Saints ottoniens,* 109, 131, 135.

12. Corbet, *Saints ottoniens,* 238. The only illustration of this *topos* of which I am aware does not appear in a queen's Life, but in the *vita* of the son of a distinguished queen: St. Louis's mother, Blanche de Castile figures prominently in his hagiography, illustrated in both the Hours of Jeanne de Navarre and the illustrated Life by Guillaume de Saint-Pathus (Paris, Bibliothèque nationale MS fr. 5716). See Thomas, "L'iconographie de St. Louis," 211.

13. Corbet, *Saints ottoniens,* 102.

14. Corbet, *Saints ottoniens,* 88. See also Brennan, "Deathless Marriage," 77.

15. "Radegund," in *Sainted Women,* II:14, 91; Nelson, "Lord's Anointed," 171.

16. Corbet, *Saints ottoniens,* 98 and 236.

17. McNamara, "Living Sermons," 27; but Schulenburg ("Strict Active Enclosure") argues that claustration was stricter.

18. Ridyard, *Royal Saints,* 82 ff.

19. McNamara, "Living Sermons," 32–33.

20. McNamara, "Living Sermons."

21. Bloch, "Medieval Misogyny," 12–14.

22. "Saint Elizabeth," in Jacobus de Voragine, *Golden Legend,* 302–18, esp. 304, 308, 309.

23. McNamara et al., *Sainted Women,* "Chlothild," 5, 43; 7, 44; "Radegund," I:9, 74; I:13, 75;

I:13–14, 76; II:4, 88, "Balthild," 8, 272. Corbet notes that the greatest mark of humility of a royal saint is the giving of royal symbols of power to the Church. He cites Otto II's gift of his mantle to the shrine of St. Martin at Tours and notes that such gifts already appear in the Life of Balthild. Corbet, *Saints ottoniens*, 98, 236. Cristiani also mentions this gesture, "La Sainteté féminine du haut Moyen Age," 403. See also Coon, *Sacred Fictions*, 37–42, 53, 132.

24. "Radegund," in *Sainted Women*, I:30, 83; "Chlothild," 12, 48; Julia Smith ("Problem of Female Sanctity," 20) cites a number of examples of "handiwork," especially embroidery, in saints' Lives. A lost miniature from the Life of Radegund represented the saint at her spindle: see Ginot, "Le Manuscrit de Ste. Radegonde."

25. "Radegund," in *Sainted Women*, I:17, 77; see also Constable, "Interpretation of Mary and Martha."

26. Carrasco, "Spirituality in Context."

27. "Radegund," in *Sainted Women*, I:2, 71. This behavior, especially Radegund's reluctance to participate in games, is reminiscent of Cuthbert's childhood behavior, which foretold his episcopal dignity: *Two Lives of Saint Cuthbert*, III:65.

28. "Radegund," in *Sainted Women*, I:2, 71. E. Ginot was the first to note that Radegund was sweeping the dust from the sanctuary: "Le Manuscrit de Ste. Radegonde."

29. Wolfthal, "A Hue and a Cry," 42.

30. "Radegund," in *Sainted Women*, I:5, 73. A similar but gender-reversed image appears in Guillaume de Saint-Pathus's Life of Louis on p. 232. Chung-Apley, "The Illustrated *Vie et miracles de Saint Louis*," 49, fig. 23.

31. Historians are profuse in their condemnation of Clothar, but the illustrator as well as both hagiographers refuse to criticize him openly.

32. "Radegund," in *Sainted Women*, I:12, 75.

33. "Radegund," in *Sainted Women*, I:13, 75.

34. In fourteen representations of Radegund that follow, ten show her in the golden veil, 35v, 39r, and 41r are the exceptions. Only the last, which represents perhaps her most significant miracle—a resurrection—shows her in a gold dress. The first two images of the saint as a girl also show a gold veil. See Fortunatus's discussion of virginity as suited to regal attributes in his *De Virginitate*: Brennan, "Deathless Marriage," 82–83.

35. "Radegund," in *Sainted Women*, I:17, 77; I:19, 78. The first episode mentions that she "girded" herself with a cloth, which seems to appear in the miniature; the second episode specifically mentions foot-washing.

36. Fortunatus does follow this event immediately with mention of miracles before Radegund retires to her monastery. "Radegund," in *Sainted Women*, I:20, 78.

37. "Radegund," in *Sainted Women*, I:21, 79.

38. For a discussion of the motif of ascension into prison, see pp. 73–77. Claustration is specifically characterized as a tomb in some contexts: Schulenburg, "Strict Active Enclosure," 60–61; Carrasco, "Spirituality in Context," 420 and 423; and (discussing Fortunatus's treatment of claustration) Brennan, "Deathless Marriage," 87, 93.

39. MacCormack, *Art and Ceremony*.

40. Madgalena Carrasco, "Images of Enclosure in the Lives of Medieval Women Saints," talk presented at the Sewanee Annual Medieval Colloquium, University of the South, April 1993.

41. "Radegund," in *Sainted Women*, II:5, 89.

42. "Radegund," in *Sainted Women*, I:25, 81.

43. This is Baudonivia's characterization: "Radegund," in *Sainted Women*, II:18, 100.

44. "Radegund," in *Sainted Women*, I:26, 81.

45. The gesture on fol. 34r is reminiscent of anointing. Radegund uses her thumb to heal a blind woman. On fols. 34v, 35r, and 37r she makes gestures of blessing to accomplish various acts of healing, primarily exorcisms. On fol. 39r she appears in a dream and seems to pour oil over a woman in a tub in a simulacrum of baptism.

46. "Radegund," in *Sainted Women*, II:15, 97. It would be interesting to see whether the pictures that may have illustrated the missing text of the Life by Baudonivia in the Poitiers manuscripts differed from those of Fortunatus as much as the text does. Baudonivia portrays Radegund as a peacemaker and a founder worthy of emulation in order to defend the abbey from disruptions after Radegund's death: Brennan, "Deathless Marriage," 96.

47. "Radegund," in *Sainted Women*, I:36, 84.

48. Perfection of the senses reaches a high point in Benedict's vision of the death and ascension of Germanus. See Hahn, "Vision."

49. "Radegund," in *Sainted Women*, I:37, 84–85.

50. "Radegund," in *Sainted Women*, I:37, 85.

51. See Hahn, "Voices of the Saints," for a discussion of the powers of the bishop's right hand.

52. "Radegund," in *Sainted Women*, I:38, 85.

53. Steinberg, *Sexuality*, 1–5, and 110–16, and Bynum's rebuttal in "Body of Christ."

54. Michon, *Grand Passionaire*, pls. 101 and 102.

55. "Gertrude," in *Sainted Women*, miracula 5, 231.

56. Indeed, Steinberg also associates the gesture with the care of children, although he calls the gesture "patronizing." *Sexuality*, 111.

57. Athanasius, *Life of Anthony*, 81, chap. 14.

58. "Gertrude," in *Sainted Women*, miracula 2, 229.

59. The death itself is not represented, presumably because it would show the body that no longer was resident at Sainte-Croix.

60. "Radegund," in *Sainted Women*, II:20, 101. The vision is described in Baudonivia's Life of Radegund, which has been cut out of the Poitiers manuscripts after the introductory author portrait. A memorable vision from an early medieval nun's Life is Aldegundis's vision of Amand's death: see p. 132 and plate 3.

61. On these objects, see the studies by Erika Dinkler-von Schubert listed in the bibliography. Anja Petrakopoulas ("Sanctity and Motherhood," 270) suggests that Elisabeth may have intentionally modeled herself upon Radegund.

62. Dinkler-von Schubert, *Schrein der Hl. Elisabeth*, 89. Dinkler-von Schubert argues that much of the shrine's imagery is based on canonization documents rather than on the *Golden Legend*, which she associates with unsubstantiated miracles. However, even in the *Golden Legend*, Elisa-

beth's story is relatively unadorned with the miraculous. See Jacobus de Voragine, *Golden Legend*, 302–18.

63. There is early evidence (1232) that this love was celebrated in vernacular song: Dinkler-von Schubert, *Schrein der Hl. Elisabeth,* 99.

64. The analogies are noted by Dinkler-von Schubert, *Schrein der Hl. Elisabeth,* 96.

65. In documents concerning Elisabeth's life, this washing of the feet is specifically referred to as a *mandatum:* Dinkler-von Schubert, *Schrein der Hl. Elisabeth,* 94. Dinkler-von Schubert notes that both Radegund and Elisabeth wash the right leg of the beggars and use chalicelike wash-tubs. She would therefore also refer the ceremony to the Mass.

66. Dinkler-von Schubert, *Schrein der Hl. Elisabeth,* 89–93. Dinkler-von Schubert argues that the scenes are included to represent the Seven Acts of Mercy, imagery especially apparent in the windows.

67. Goodich, *Vita Perfecta;* Holladay discusses Elisabeth's relationship to the Acts of Mercy and provides bibliography. Holladay, "The Education of Jeanne d'Evreux," 592–93.

68. Baudot-Chaussin, *Vies des Saints,* XI, 666, and Vauchez, *Laity,* 176. In these respects, the depiction of Elisabeth should be compared with paintings of Clare of Assisi. Wood, "Perceptions of Holiness." However, in the dossal for Santa Chiara, because Clare was cloistered, there are no representations of good works, only miracles.

69. Chung-Apley, "The Illustrated *Vie et miracles de Saint Louis.*"

70. Holladay, "The Education of Jeanne d'Evreux." See also Kauffmann, "The Image of St. Louis."

71. Corbet, *Saints ottoniens;* Petrakopoulas, "Sanctity and Motherhood."

72. "Balthild," in *Sainted Women,* 264–78.

73. Nie, "Consciousness Fecund through God," 146. Abbots sometimes take on these virtues, but they are not to my knowledge represented in pictorial hagiography. One particularly motherly *topos* is noted by Cristiani—the cure of a nun by an abbess with a vial of milk, "La Sainteté féminine du haut Moyen Age," 433.

74. *Historiarum Libri X,* 9, 38, cited by de Nie, "Consciousness Fecund through God," 140.

CHAPTER 9

1. Jauss, *Toward an Aesthetic,* 28.

2. Vauchez, *Sainthood,* 232, and chap. 13.

3. Vaughan, *Matthew Paris,* 138.

4. Vauchez, *Sainthood,* 86 n. 8, 236, 237, 240, 242; and Goffen, *Spirituality in Conflict,* 13 and 24.

5. Vauchez, *Sainthood,* 449, 451 (see also 366).

6. The quotation from Salimbene criticizing secular clergy in competition with the mendicant orders ("aliquis ymago ad modum sancti alicubi debet depingi . . .") is cited in Vauchez, *Sainthood,* 86 n. 6.

7. See also Hahn, "Absent No Longer," 168–71.

8. To name only a few: Ahl, "Benozzo Gozzoli's Cycle"; Goffen, *Spirituality in Conflict;* Frugoni, "St. Francis"; Wood, *Women, Art, and Spirituality;* Wolff, "Heilige Franziskus."

9. Lewis, *Art of Matthew Paris,* and Vaughn, *Matthew Paris.*

10. Lewis, *Art of Matthew Paris,* 64–66, 315, 319.

11. Lewis, *Art of Matthew Paris,* 64–66.

12. Lewis, *Art of Matthew Paris,* 14.

13. Lewis, *Art of Matthew Paris,* 4.

14. The three main volumes are Cambridge, Corpus Christi MS 26 and 16, and British Library MS Roy. 14.C. VII. Lewis, *Art of Matthew Paris,* 9. Matthew also produced a series of abbreviated histories.

15. Morgan, *Gothic,* I, 130–33.

16. Lewis, *Art of Matthew Paris,* 433–37.

17. Although Matthew calls his saints' Lives *romances,* the term may simply be a reference to the Romance language. I am thinking here rather of his *Vitae Offarum,* a fictitious history that reads like a romance. *Vitae Offarum,* ed. Wats.

18. See below, note 27 for a description of Matthew's ingenious approach to manuscript construction. See also Lewis, *Art of Matthew Paris,* 43, 66–71, for Matthew's use of *signa* to help mark his history texts.

19. The *Vitae Offarum,* is included in the first folios of British Library MS Cotton Nero D. I.

20. Morgan, "Matthew Paris."

21. M. R. James is usually credited with establishing the fact that Matthew wrote the text of the Lives of Edward and Alban, *La Estoire,* 17–28. Richard Vaughan confirmed it: *Matthew Paris,* 169–81. The editors of the texts concerned have all agreed on Matthew. Wallace, *Estoire,* 983; Harden, *Auban;* Meyer, *Thomas;* and Baker, "Edmond."

22. Vaughan, *Matthew Paris,* 19.

23. Matthew's hagiographic innovation can be compared to earlier line drawings, such as the Guthlac or Eloi Rolls, in only the most general way. Matthew's work has the sense of a continuous and interconnected narrative and is marked by a distinctive page format and unusual narrative devices. See pp. 286–87.

24. For boats, see the discussion of travel, n. 95 below. The horses have a distinctive arch to their necks, peculiarly swollen heads, and tiny muzzles, as well identical dispositions of the legs. Certain details of the drawings correspond as well, of which one is particularly striking. Nigel Morgan, arguing that Matthew was not responsible for the drawings in the Lives of Edward or Thomas, notes that in those manuscripts nails are almost always visible protruding from the horses' shoes, a detail also noted by James. (See Morgan, *Gothic,* I, 49.) Morgan asserts that these elements do not appear in the Matthew's Life, but in fact they do—in the depiction of war horses (fols. 41r, 45r). Without going into tedious further detail, which could include comparisons of hats, saddle-buttons, costumes, and the blue wavy lines that indicate heaven, I think this sort of example can stand as evidence that, at the least, Matthew's modelbooks must have been accessible to the artists of the Lives of Edward and Thomas, and not the contrary. However, Morgan (in "Matthew Paris") argues on codicological grounds that the Life of Thomas predates any of

Matthew's hagiographic work and that therefore any innovation should be attributed to anonymous London *scriptoria*. Nonetheless, the best comparisons to the Becket MS in this generally cogent article seem to cluster around the year 1250, after or contemporary with the Alban manuscript. And, of course, that is not even taking into account the possibility of an artist working in an archaic style and format, as indeed Matthew himself does.

25. I believe Matthew worked from a model that, although detailed, was sketchy enough to be open to misunderstandings. A number of such misunderstandings occur, for example, in the Life of Edward, where two different feet protrude from the same robe (Cambridge, University Library, MS Ee 3.59, fol. 25v). But the mistake that is least ambiguous in leaving evidence of its generation occurs in the miracle of the carpenter in the same Life (*Estoire*, ll. 2898–3018). A carpenter working in the woods falls asleep and awakens to find that he has lost his sight. After twenty years of blindness, he is cured by Edward, who makes him guardian of the palace of Westminster. This story appears in the context of a series of miracle stories recounting Edward's miraculous acts of healing the blind using water in which he washed his hands. The carpenter's story is composed of three scenes with two *tituli* on pp. 41 (sc. 1 and 2) and 42 (sc. 3). On p. 42, a second story begins immediately next to scene 3, involving four blind men. I would argue that the artists of the Life of Edward did not read the text of the *vita* carefully and assumed that the sketch they saw in their model represented a separate healing incident in which the recipient was made the guardian of Westminster (as the rather ambiguous *titulus* states). I say this because the "carpenter" has suddenly experienced a radical social upgrade from the rank of guardian to that of chamberlain, as his long costume and distinctive "pageboy" coiffure on fol. 23v (sc. 3) reveals. Often, in the miracle stories, a chamberlain is instrumental in convincing the humble king to perform healing miracles, so it is even possible that the artist has made an attempt to make scene 3 in effect scene 1 of the next but immediately adjacent miracle—Edward does seem to point back from this next miracle toward scene 3. Commentators on the Life have consistently been confused by scene 3: James simply calls it "Edward throned" (*La Estoire*, 53). In either case, the artist copying Matthew's sketches does not seem to have understood that this is the last episode of the carpenter's story.

26. The flyleaf of the Dublin manuscript records a series of short verses on saints to be included in a manuscript for the countess of Winchester: James, *La Estoire*, 29.

27. One of Matthew's sketches survives—a scrap of vellum contains heraldic devices with color notes (perhaps sketched at some court gathering) used to create fols. 171r and v of the *Liber Additamentorum*, and bound into the same book as fol. 200r. One of the sketches is even sideways on the sheet.

Furthermore, there is clear evidence in the Dublin manuscript that Matthew worked out his program very carefully. In marginal notes in his own hand at the bottom of some folios, he briefly indicated the contents of the miniatures. Most of these notes are illegible because they are trimmed, leaving only the ascenders of the letters. However, in the few cases where they are legible, although they clearly refer to the miniatures, they do not necessarily correspond exactly. For example, on fol. 61v the marginal note seems to read "Processio Rex et suis. Abbas," yet the abbot is not represented with the king; rather, we see bishops and an archbishop. (I read the last word as *abbas,* in comparison with that word on the bottom of fol. 60v, which refers to the appointment of the abbot of St. Alban by Offa.)

The first such note that I was able to read appears on fol. 42v. It reads quite clearly (with abbreviations expanded) "lupus et aquila." Others that are clearly legible appear on 43v: "lamentatio"; 51r: "papa cum suis Sci Germanus Sci Lupus"; and 61r: "monachi [feretrum adorent?]" Others that I am not able not to decipher or am unsure of appear on fols. 41 v: "occisae?——"; 47v (where it may help identify the missing miniature); 53v: "episcopi.——"; 54r: "——albani ——auxilium——"; 57r: totally illegible; 60r: totally illegible; 60v "——abbas"; and 62r. Other marginal notes at the bottom of the pages (such as that on 51r and 62v) seem to refer to Matthew's construction of the texts in the manuscript; the former reads: "xlii pagine de passio[ne] incipit inventio." Quire markings in red in Matthew's hand (typical of his manuscripts) appear on fols. 29v, 30v, 31v, 33v, and 56v. (I understand that Patricia Quinn who was responsible for the recent rebinding of the Alban manuscript intended to publish a study on these marginal notes, but I have not been able to locate it.)

The sort of planning and subsequent change indicated by these notes suggest the intermediary of a preparatory model in which compositions were conceived. In the Alban manuscript, given the care with which the miniatures are detailed and the fact that they are executed in a linear technique with transparent wash, which makes mistakes almost impossible to correct, the intermediary of preparatory sketches seems likely. I argued something similar for the *Estoire* manuscript above and would also argue the same for the *Vitae Offarum,* which was completed by a Gothic artist with many details reminiscent of Matthew's work (in particular, the representation of boats).

28. Paul Binski argues for Matthew's responsibility for the design of the miniatures in "Reflections," and "Abbot Berkyng's Tapestry." In the latter, he argues for a Westminster recension for the Life of Edward, which does not match the *Estoire.*

29. See Meyer, *Thomas,* and Baker, "Edmond."

30. Lewis discusses the dating controversy in *Art of Matthew Paris,* 387.

31. Here I refer to the Life of Edmund, which was dedicated to Isabel de Warenne, countess of Arundel: See Morgan, *Gothic,* I, 132; and the *Estoire,* the text of which was dedicated to Eleanor of Provence. Paul Binski (in "Reflections") argues that the copy in Cambridge was created for Eleanor of Castile. If so, this would be an English parallel to the French royal ladies' devotion to the Life of Louis.

32. Lewis, *Art of Matthew Paris,* 10.

33. Belting, "New Role of Narrative," 152–53.

34. Lewis, *Reading Images,* 38. See also Hahn, "Visio Dei," and "Absent No Longer."

35. On folio 56v, the last page of the gatherings that include the *Vie,* a designation IIII appears in red. Matthew Paris customarily numbered his gatherings in red in this fashion, on the verso of the last page. See Lewis, *Art of Matthew Paris,* 443, 498 n. 230, and 500 n. 52. In this position this numbering could only indicate that the *Vie* was once a unit, separate from the preceding materials.

36. McCulloch, "Saints Alban and Amphibalus," 785.

37. Although the manuscript has now been rebound in proper order, at the time that the pages were foliated, certain portions were out of order.

38. The material is clearly manipulated to correspond to the texts. The charter material begins on fol. 63r, breaking into the text on the invention of Alban. On this page is the image of Offa presenting the charter, confirmed by the pope, to the monastery. The text of the invention resumes at a certain "sign," as Matthew is careful to note in the margin. And indeed it does.

39. On two separate occasions I have written about the first four illustrations of the Alban Life. There was little overlap in those two discussions, a circumstance that I would argue indicates the richness of the narrative: Hahn, "Absent No Longer," and Hahn, "Visio Dei."

40. Vauchez, Sainthood, 530.

41. Kruger, Dreaming, and see Hahn, "Visio Dei."

42. McCulloch, "Saints Alban and Amphibalus," 780.

43. The one other example of the cross with corpus in the Life of Alban also concerns a conversion: fol. 41r—Amphibalus baptizes the new converts.

44. The window is used in a similar way in English illustrations of the Apocalypse, which depict St. John peering into a divinely revealed vision or prophecy that he then records. The window in these illustrations serves the same function as it does in the Life of Alban, separating the earthly from the heavenly, as well as directing the gaze and making the vision manifest. See Lewis, Reading Images, 6–10.

45. The window is not visible, it may be obscured in the binding. Compare to what may be a "copy" (Paris, Bibliothèque nationale MS 403, fol. 1), in which pagans peer through a window at St. John baptizing. See Kemp, Narratives of Gothic Stained Glass, fig. 52.

46. Matthew may be unwilling to completely deny the power of the Christian deed even for pagans. The Saracen who witnesses and reports to the governor may be the unnamed and self-proclaimed pagan narrator of the account, who in the end is also converted (as suggested by McCulloch, "Saints Alban and Amphibalus," 776). This same narrative unit of baptism and pagan witnessing is repeated in St. John's Life in the Apocalypse manuscript, Paris, Bibliothèque nationale, MS. 43, fol. 1r (illustrated in Kemp, Narratives of Gothic Stained Glass, fig. 52). I would argue this is Matthew's influence.

47. Vaughan, Chronicles, 218–19.

48. Baker, "Edmond," 380–81, ll. 1996–1220. For the chronicle illustration, see Lewis, Art of Matthew Paris, pl. 10.

49. Lewis, Reading Images, 207.

50. Vauchez, Sainthood, 527, 529.

51. The narrative introduces other themes here: fol. 36v does not carry a miniature, but 37r addresses the conversion of Aracle. The next opening concludes Alban's Passion.

52. Fol. 45r. Amphibalus continued to preach while his persecutors removed his bowels.

53. Matthew shows himself praying before an image of the Virgin. Lewis, Art of Matthew Paris, fig. 2.

54. See, for example, Camille's discussion in Gothic Idol, pt. 1.

55. The Life is elaborated in Latin in versions of Gildas, Bede, Geoffrey of Monmouth, William

of St. Albans and a verse Life of Ralph of Dunstable. McCulloch, "Saints Alban and Amphibalus," 764–67.

56. The passion of Aracle begins at l. 800 and concludes at 1013.

57. AASS, 4 June, 147–59, esp. 153 F, which refers to a *miles.*

58. *Auban,* 26. Part of the poem about Aracle is headed: "Ci cumence la passiun Seint Aracle" (title after l. 935).

59. *Auban,* ll. 805–25, esp. 806. For a discussion of the ceremony of the dubbing to knighthood, see Kean, *Chivalry,* 64–82, and esp. figs. 13–15.

60. *Auban,* l. 981; also 936 and 970.

61. *Auban,* ll. 994–95.

62. *Auban,* titles ll. 109–12.

63. Painter, *Chivalry,* 153.

64. The knight is generally said to be beautiful: North, "Ideal Knight," 122–25.

65. Matthew labels a defeated leader "effeminate" in his *Chronica majora:* Vaughan, *Chronicles,* 97.

66. In the chronicles, the four-lobed flower appears on the cloak of Edmund Ironside: CCC Ms. 26, 160 [fol. 80 v.] (Lewis, *Art of Matthew Paris,* pl. III). However, it would appear that Matthew did not think of this motif as Edmund's identifying arms, because in the Life of Edward in the Cambridge manuscript, fol. 4v, a different motif appears. Of course in the latter case, the motif could have been changed or even added to Matthew's sketches by the copyist of the Cambridge manuscript.

67. Lewis, *Art of Matthew Paris,* 120.

68. *Auban,* titles, l. 97.

69. Kean, *Chivalry,* 102–24; Jaeger, *Courtliness,* xii, 228.

70. Gerould, "King Arthur and Politics."

71. *Auban,* l. 23.

72. *Auban,* titles, ll. 251–53.

73. *Estoire,* ll. 1544–50. The representation of a monk in the illustration confirms the text's indication of Verolanum's status.

74. *Auban,* ll. 676–86.

75. *Auban,* ll. 21.

76. Vauchez, *Sainthood,* 498.

77. Clanchy, *From Memory to Written Record,* 7.

78. Abou-el-Haj (*Cult of the Saints,* 88–90 and 40–41), discusses groups of witness appended to the Life of Amand, as well as images of charters and grants of land.

79. Lewis, *Art of Matthew Paris,* 9, 45, and *passim.*

80. Matthew Paris, *English History,* II, 139.

81. Hahn, "Proper Behavior."

82. Clanchy, *From Memory to Written Record,* 221.

83. The point was argued by Thomas G. Waldman, "Hugh 'of Amiens,' Archbishop of Rouen, 1130–1164," at the Charles Homer Haskins Society Conference, Houston, Texas, November 1989.

84. Lewis (*Art of Matthew Paris,* 35) notes that the ascenders have a lobe that can be likened to the twelfth-century "papal knot" of the chancery.

85. *Estoire,* l. 1838: "Le veie e oie." Other variants are l. 834: "ot——e etent"; and l. 3450: "en ecscrit e en memoire."

86. For example, Edward requires that a document be written in both Latin and French: *Estoire,* l. 2348.

87. Clanchy, *From Memory to Written Record,* 203–4.

88. Clanchy, *From Memory to Written Record,* 230.

89. Matthew Paris, *English History,* trans. J. A. Giles, 2 vols. (London 1852–54), II, 137.

90. Lewis, *Art of Matthew Paris;* see entry on "seals" in index, 550.

91. Lewis, *Art of Matthew Paris,* 248, fig. 157; the purses are pictured in CCC 16, fol. 95r.

92. Lewis, *Art of Matthew Paris,* 256, fig. 162 shows the clasped right hands (the *iunctio dextrarum*—the legal sign of marriage since antiquity), of Frederick II and Isabella surmounted by a crown and ring from CCC 16, fol. 94 v. A similar sign also appears on fol. 96r (marriage of Henry III and Eleanor of Provence); a ring appears only in British Library MS Roy. 14.C. VII, fol. 106v (marriage of Hubert de Burgh to Margaret).

93. *Estoire,* l. 3966.

94. Lewis, *Art of Matthew Paris,* devotes a chapter to "Matthew's Cartography," 321–76.

95. The monk could almost be accused of being a mental gyrovage; he is fascinated with traveling. Indeed in the Life of Alban, any excuse is adequate for the introduction of a travel scene. Seven remain, and at least one other existed: Montague James proposes that a scene of Offa traveling to Rome was one of the scenes removed on the missing folio between fols. 61 and 62. See his *Illustrations to the Life of St. Alban,* 35. As a result, there are an extraordinary number of illustrations of the two foremost medieval means of travel: boats and horses. Each of these is distinctively represented by Matthew. In fact a naval scholar has devoted a study to the boats in the Life of Edward that establishes just how unusual those boats are: Brindley, "Ships." (Brindley focuses on the mike or crutch and the bowsprit in the Cambridge manuscript.) The inclusion of the distinctive tiller-man in the Lives of Edward, Thomas, and Alban, as well as in the Chronicles, suggests that he is an element of maritime reality that Matthew himself observed and illustrated in his distinctive, reductive visual form. Similarly, distinctive boats appear in an Apocalypse in Moscow (Morgan, *Gothic,* II, fig. 172) and another in Oxford (ibid., fig. 165), but these are later and therefore must, I believe, derive from Matthew.

96. *Estoire,* ll. 2076–265.

97. *Estoire,* Wallace in her commentary (158), notes that this legend is the basis for a traditional tithe of salmon.

98. *Auban,* titles, ll. 385–96.

99. Michael Camille has discussed the speech-act written out in the Pembroke Gospel depiction of the Unprepared Wedding Guest in terms of its representation of the "present and direct voice," of which picture and script are ultimately only degraded signs. See his "Seeing and Reading," 31–32. I would contend that Matthew's use here of speech acts are also only signs, not of the voice but of a more general reality and authenticity, what I refer to as the "you

are there" effect but which should have, perhaps, a more metaphysical name such as "truth" or "sanctity."

100. Finucane, *Miracles and Pilgrims,* 156, describes the Te Deum as the appropriate liturgical response to a miracle in discussion of primarily twelfth- and thirteenth-century English miracle cults. Sumption, *Pilgrimage,* 39, notes the "spontaneous" singing of the Te Deum at the 1162 exposure of the relics of Genevieve. The Te Deum is primarily a hymn of thanksgiving: Steiner and Caldwell, "Te Deum," 641–44.

101. The singing of the Te Deum is noted in the *Estoire* in l. 2008 and pictured as a speech-act caption in the appropriate picture on p. 29. A Te Deum is also mentioned in l. 3930 at the death of the king and his entry into heaven but is not illustrated until p. 55 in a scene of miracles at the tomb (where the text would seem to indicate a Deo Gratias: l. 4062).

102. *Estoire,* l. 1646.

103. *Auban,* tituli, ll. 9, 13, 77; the verb *voir* also appears frequently in the Life, especially during the conversion sequence of the text: ll. 6, 12, 15, 22, 30, 188, 201, 364, and 415.

104. Lewis, *Art of Matthew Paris,* figs. 104, CCC 16 fol. 27v (bell silenced by the Interdict); and fig. 105, B. L. Roy. 14.C. VII, fol. 94r (the Interdict lifted and the bells rung).

105. Clanchy, *From Memory to Written Record,* 297.

106. The charters are copied on fols. 63r–66r of the Dublin manuscript. The episcopal witnesses are: Humbertus archepiscopus, Ceolwulphus ep. and Unwona ep. on fol. 64r, with repetitions on fols. 63v, 64v, and 65r. The copy of the charter on this page breaks into the text of the narrative of Alban's invention.

107. This manipulation of time and reality through script and picture is much more than Michael Camille's depiction of "direct voice" (see n. 99 above); rather it is an attempt to approach a lasting truth.

EPILOGUE

1. Caesarius of Heisterbach, *Dialogue on Miracles,* II, 29.

2. DeLisle, "Notice sur un livre," 11.

3. Photos from the Branner collection at Oxford and the Musée Carnavalet, Paris, are on file at the Getty Photo Archive, Los Angeles.

4. The more striking elements in common are prominence of bells, the bishop's many journeys, and the carrying of a cripple very like the episode in the Life of Edward the Confessor.

5. Peter Dinzelbacher lists only a few figures in the twelfth century but many in the thirteenth: "Nascita e funzione," 495.

6. See bibliography in Holladay, "Education of Jeanne d'Evreux."

7. Christies sale of June 29, 1994, no. 36, with twenty-seven full-page miniatures.

8. Lacaze, "Vie de St. Denis," 126–38.

9. Berlin, Kupferstichkabinett, 78 B 16: Wescher, *Beschreibendes Verzeichnis.*

10. Braunfels, *Hedwigs-Codex.*

11. Corstanje et al., *Vita Sanctae Coletae.*

12. Princeton University Art Museum Inv. 52–56 and 52–57. Discussed in Weitzmann-Fiedler, "Margareten Legenden."

13. The other copy is in the Trivulzio collection in Milan. See Bologna, *Leggende Lombarde,* a facsimile of the manuscript.

14. Baudot-Chaussin, *Vie des saints,* X, 823–25.

15. Suzanne Lewis argues that there has been a shift in reading "from an oral tradition to a visual orientation." *Reading Images,* 3. I believe that many of the innovations of the Apocalypse narrative and that the "new and more powerful interpretive role of its illustrations" (ibid., 3 and 37–39) were inspired by Matthew rather than vice versa.

16. Lewis's "indeterminacy" may well be a quality of all narratives: *Rhetoric of Power,* 2, 131, and *passim.* The work of Matthew Paris bears some resemblance to the Bayeux Tapestry in its use of *topoi,* and particularly reversed and strip narrative, but the tapestry represents other secular genres (epic, encomium, fable) of which it is nearly a unique example. See ibid., chap. 2.

17. Belting, "New Role of Narrative," 152.

18. Belting, "New Role of Narrative," 152–53.

19. Blume, *Wandmalerei,* 37 ff.

20. "The visual—whether extant or recorded, whether a work of art, a procession, or the body of a saint—is an essential primary source for the historian." Cannon and Vauchez, *Margherita,* 8.

21. Cannon cites a document that demonstrates the extraordinary care that was taken to acquaint artists with the texts of saints' Lives, that is, a contract that specifies the commissioning of a translation of the Life of Sabinus in order that Pietro Lorenzetti might paint it: *Margherita,* 153.

22. The issues of narrative storytelling could be further developed in this case by additional correlation of text quoted from the Life and dossier of Margaret with the visual narrative. For example, Cannon quotes a *lauda* that was sung to Margaret's honor in the fourteenth century in conjunction with the panel painting of her Life, because it mentions one of the scenes—Margaret's temptation by the devil. However, one line of that *lauda* could further serve as a precise description of the repeated representations of Margaret in virtually the same position of prayer in seven of nine scenes of the panel: she defeated the devil before he could begin to deceive her, because she would not engage him; "he found her motionless in prayer" (*Margherita,* 170). Her lack of motion implies her unassailability, her steadfastness, and even her likeness to other legendary virgins such as Lucy, who was herself an "immovable mountain."

Often the contemporary miracle texts that Cannon cites evoke a sense of intervention occurring "just in time." Instead of highlighting this element, Cannon chooses to praise the artists' observational powers, noting the tearing and catching of the sail in the wind in the image of the rescue at sea and comparing it to the still-swinging severed rope of the cradle in the image of the rescue and resuscitation of a fallen infant. These could be pure artistic invention, but they could also be visual signifiers of the immediacy of the saint's care and succor. Along with contemporary buildings and costume, this immediacy seems to place Margaret in the real world of "this very moment"—a vision of the saint as superhero, swooping in to save endangered lives from the "jaws of death" (171).

23. Kemp, *Narratives of Gothic Stained Glass*, 6, 28.

24. Kemp, *Narratives of Gothic Stained Glass*.

25. Mâle, *Gothic Image*, 196.

26. Here Kemp finds that philosophy is the least like the other arts he mentions. Although he does not cite Erwin Panofsky's *Gothic Art and Scholasticism*, his comment is surely an allusion to Panofsky's argument.

27. Kemp, *Narratives of Gothic Stained Glass*, 157.

28. Kemp fails to convince his reader of the precise meaning of such divisions and schemata beyond typological implications. He rejects meanings that other scholars have proposed, yet clings to an insistence on the importance of the geometric divisions of the windows. Finally, on the last page of his book, he both praises the "mastery of systematic order" of the narratives and writes: "As narrative (not as framework), it reveals clear proportions throughout, and . . . systematic . . . sequences." Kemp, *Narratives of Gothic Stained Glass*, 226.

29. Caviness, "Biblical Stories," 147.

30. Caviness, "Biblical Stories," 124.

31. Caviness notes significant differences between Saint-Denis and Chartres. Caviness, "Biblical Stories," 109, 147.

32. Caviness, "Biblical Stories," 117.

33. Kemp, *Narratives of Gothic Stained Glass*, 72 and n. 65. Kemp argues that the window in question is the "failed" Bourges example, but it could equally well be the "successful" Sens window. Most troubling in Kemp's argument remains his proclivity to describe windows using only numbered schemata and titles and to divide stained glass narratives among successes and failures according to the approach that he has proposed. Kemp, *Narratives of Gothic Stained Glass*, 70, 73. If so many narratives fail according to a system of reading, perhaps it is the system that is faulty, not the narratives.

34. Kemp, *Narratives of Gothic Stained Glass*, 81.

35. See the analysis of the Lubin window by Manhes-Deremble, "Saint Lubin."

36. Kemp, *Narratives of Gothic Stained Glass*, 110, 125.

37. Kemp calls the use of secondary narratives and tangents in stained glass "an older more truncated form of the same stylistic tendency" that was only later developed in manuscripts and texts. Kemp, *Narratives of Gothic Stained Glass*, 113.

38. Kemp, *Narratives of Gothic Stained Glass*, passim.

39. Manhes-Deremble, "Saint Lubin," and *Vitraux narratifs*.

40. In particular, I would argue that Matthew is responsible for the motif of the witness who peers through a window. Kemp briefly discusses some of Matthew's innovations in the context of the contributions of the "sermo humilis," which he finally condemns as overwrought. Kemp, *Narratives of Gothic Stained Glass*, 112–14. It is a hagiographic "frame" of the Life of John that initiates an illustrated Apocalypse manuscript (Paris, Bibliothèque nationale MS fr. 403). These illustrations of the Life of John are clearly conceived in the narrative style originated by Matthew. Details as diverse as pagans peering though windows to witness a baptism, the precise depiction of nautical details, and an abbreviated piece of narrative continuing the story along with the

viewer's interest to the right and out of the scene precisely resemble elements in Matthew's narrative of the Life of Alban. Compare Kemp's figure 52 (lower register) to figs 131–32; figure 53 (lower register) to images of ships in Matthew's work; and fig. 54 (lower register) to fig. 132.

41. From the *Manuale de mysteriis ecclesiae:* Manhes-Deremble, *Vitraux,* 22–26, cited and translated by Pastan and Shepard, "Torture of Saint George," 12.

APPENDIX

1. For this entry, see Abou-el-Haj, *Medieval Cult of Saints,* 156–63, especially for descriptions of MSS 500 and 501, with Lives of Amand, which are considered only briefly above.

2. An additional manuscript of the Life of Benedict, Brussels, Bibliothèque royale, MS 9916–9917, c. 1160, illustrating book 2 of Gregory's *Dialogues* (as well as some miniatures for the other books), has no apparent relationship to a developed cult and cannot be properly called a *libellus.* See Gaspar-Lyna, *Principaux manuscrits,* 78 ff.

3. A late twelfth-century illustrated luxury copy of Bede's Life is in the British Library, Yates Thompson MS 26. See Baker, "Medieval Illustrations."

BIBLIOGRAPHY

Abou-el-Haj, Barbara. "The Audiences for the Medieval Cult of Saints." *Gesta* 30 (1991): 3–15.

———. "Bury St. Edmunds Abbey between 1070 and 1124: A History of Property, Privilege and Monastic Art Production." *Art History* 6 (1983): 1–30.

———. "Feudal Conflicts and the Image of Power at the Monastery of St. Amand D'Elnone." *Kritische Berichte* 13 (1985): 5–29.

———. *The Medieval Cult of Saints: Formations and Transformations.* Cambridge, 1994.

Acher, Jean. "Sur un livre relatif à Saint-Denis et à son monastère." *Revue des langues romanes* 58 (1915): 137–44.

Ahl, Diane Cole. "Benozzo Gozzoli's Cycle of the Life of Saint Francis in Montefalco: Hagiography and Homily." In *Saints: Studies in Hagiography,* edited by Sandro Sticca, 191–214. Medieval and Renaissance Texts and Studies 141. Binghamton, N.Y., 1996.

Albertson, Clinton. "Felix's 'Life of St. Guthlac.'" In *Anglo-Saxon Saints and Heroes,* edited and translated by Clifton Albertson, 165–219. New York, 1967.

Alexander, Jonathan J. G. *Medieval Illuminators and Their Methods of Work.* New Haven, 1993.

Anson, John S. "The Female Transvestite in Early Monasticism: The Origin and Development of a Motif." *Viator* 5 (1974): 1–32.

Appleby, David F. "Holy Relic and Holy Image: Saint's Relics in the Western Controversy over Images in the Eighth and Ninth Centuries." *Word and Image* 8 (1992): 333–43.

———. "Sight and Church Reform in the Thought of Jonas of Orleans." *Viator* 27 (1996): 11–33.

Arnold, Thomas. *Memorials of St. Edmund's Abbey.* Rolls Series 96. Vol. 1. London, 1890.

Athanasius. *The Life of St. Anthony the Great.* Willits, Calif., n.d.

Atkinson, Robert. *Vie de Seint Auban.* London, 1876.

Augustine. *Sermons on Selected Lessons of the New Testament by S. Augustine, Bishop of Hippo.* Oxford, 1845.

Bähr, Ingeborg. *Saint Denis und seine Vita im Spiegel der Bildüberlieferung der französischen Kunst des Mittelalters.* Worms, 1984.

Baker, A. T. "La Vie de saint Edmond." *Romania* 55 (1929): 332–81.

Baker, Malcolm. "Medieval Illustrations of Bede's 'Life of St. Cuthbert.'" *Journal of the Warburg and Courtauld Institutes* 41 (1978): 16–49.

Bal, Mieke, and Norman Bryson. "Semiotics and Art History." *Art Bulletin* 73 (1991): 174–208.

Barlow, Frank. *Edward the Confessor.* Berkeley, 1970.

———, ed. *The Life of King Edward Who Rests at Westminster.* 2d ed. Oxford, 1992.

———. "The Vita Aedwardi (Book II): The Seven Sleepers: Some Further Evidence and Reflections." *Speculum* 40 (1965): 385–97.

Barlow, Horace. "What Does the Brain See? How Does it Understand?" In *Images and Understanding: Thoughts About Images, Ideas About Understanding,* edited by H. Barlow, C. Blakemore, and M. Weston-Smith, 5–25. Cambridge, 1990.

Barthes, Roland. "Introduction to the Structural Analysis of Narratives." In *Image—Music—Text,* translated by S. Heath, 79–124. New York, 1977.

Bastgen, Hubertus, ed. *Libri Carolini.* MGH, *Legum,* Sectio iii, Concilia, Tom. II, Supplementum. Hannover, 1924.

Bateman, Katherine R. "Pembroke 120 and Morgan 736: A Reexamination of the St. Albans–Bury St. Edmunds Manuscript Dilemma." *Gesta* 17 (1978): 19–35.

Baudot, J. L., L. Chaussin, et al. *Vies des saints et des bienheureux selon l'ordre du calendrier, avec l'histoire des fêtes.* 13 vols. Paris, 1935–59.

Bayerische Staatsbibliothek München. *Bayerns Kirche im Mittelalter: Handschriften und Urkunden.* Munich, 1960.

Bayless, Martha. *Parody in the Middle Ages: The Latin Tradition.* Ann Arbor, 1996.

Beaugrand, Augustine. *Sainte Lucie.* Paris, 1882.

Beaujard, Brigitte. "Cités, évêques et martyrs en Gaule à la fin de l'époque romaine." In *Les Fonctions des saints dans le monde occidental (IIIe–XIIIe siècle),* 175–91. Collection de l'École française de Rome 149. Rome, 1991.

Beer, Ellen J. "Überlegungen zu Stil und Herkunft des Berner Prudentius-Codex 264." In *Florilegium Sangallense: Festschrift für Johannes Duft zum 65. Geburtstag,* edited by O. P. Clavadetscher, H. Maurer, and S. Sonderegger, 15–57. St. Gall, 1980.

Bélanger, Rodrigue. "Anthropologie et parole de Dieu dans le commentaire de Grégoire le Grand sur le Cantiques des Cantiques." In *Grégoire le Grand: Chantilly, Centre culturel les Fontaines, 15–19 septembre 1982,* edited by J. Fontaine, R. Gillet, and S. Pellistrandi, 245–54. Paris, 1986.

Belting, Hans. "The New Role of Narrative in Public Painting of the Trecento: *Historia* and Allegory." In *Pictorial Narrative in Antiquity and the Middle Ages,* edited by Herbert L. Kessler and Marianna Shreve Simpson, 151–68. Studies in the History of Art 16. Washington, 1985.

Benton, John F. *Self and Society in Medieval France: The Memoirs of Abbot Guibert of Nogent (1064–c. 1125).* New York, 1984 (orig. Toronto, 1970).

Bernard of Angers. *Liber miraculorum s. Fidei.* Edited by A. Bouillet. Paris, 1897.

Bibliotheca sanctorum. Rome, 1961–69.

Bibliothèque nationale. *Drogo-Sakramentar, Ms. Lat. 9428, Bibliothèque Nationale.* Codices Selecti Phototypice Impressi, 49. 2 vols. Paris and Graz, 1974.

Binski, Paul. "Abbot Berkyng's Tapestries and Matthew Paris' Life of St. Edward the Confessor." *Archaeologia* 109 (1991): 85–100.

———. "Reflections on *La Estoire de Seint Aedward le Rei*: Hagiography and Kingship in Thirteenth-Century England." *Journal of Medieval History* 16 (1990): 333–50.

———. *Westminster Abbey and the Plantagenets*. New Haven, 1995.

Bischoff, Bernhard. "Über gefaltene Handschriften vornehmlich hagiographischen Inhalts." In *Mittelalterliche Studien: Ausgewählte Aufsätze zur Schriftskunde und Literaturgeschichte*, I: 93–100. Stuttgart, 1966.

Blaauw, Sible de. *Cultus et decor: Liturgia e architettura nella Roma tardoantica e medievale: Basilica Salvatoris, Sanctae Mariae, Sancti Petri*. Studi e testi 355–56. Vatican City, 1994.

Bloch, Marc. *The Royal Touch: Sacred Monarchy and Scrofula in England and France*. London, 1973.

Bloch, R. Howard. "Medieval Misogyny: Woman as Riot." *Representations* 20 (1987): 1–24.

Blum, Pamela Z. "The Saint Benedict Cycle on the Capitals of the Crypt at Saint-Denis." *Gesta* 20 (1981): 73–87.

Blume, Dieter. *Wandmalerei als Ordenspropaganda: Bildprogramme im Chorbereich franziskanischer Konvente Italiens bis zur Mitte des 14. Jahrhunderts*. Worms, 1983.

Boeckler, Albert. *Das Stuttgarter Passionale*. Augsburg, 1923.

Boesch Gajano, Sofia. "Uso e abuso del miracolo nella cultura altomedioevale." In *Les Fonctions des saints dans le monde occidental (IIIe–XIIIe siècle)*, 109–22. Collection de l'École française de Rome 149. Rome, 1991.

Bohm, Lennart. *La vie de Ste. Geneviève de Paris, poème religieux*. Uppsala, 1955.

Bollandist Society, ed. *Catalogus Codicum Hagiographicorum Latinorum Antiquiorum saeculo XVI qui asservantur in Bibliotheca Nationali Parisiensi*. Vol. I. Brussels, 1889.

Bologna, Giulia. *Leggende Lombarde: Aimo e Vermondo di Meda. Il Codice Trivulziano 509*. 2 vols. Milan, 1982.

Bonaventure, Saint. *Opera Omnia*. Florence, 1901.

Braga, Gabriella. "*Moralia in Job*: Epitomi dei secoli VII–X e loro evoluzione." In *Grégoire le Grand: Chantilly, Centre culturel les Fontaines, 15–19 septembre 1982*, edited by J. Fontaine, R. Gillet, and S. Pellistrandi, 561–68. Paris, 1986.

Brandis, Tilo, ed. *Zimelien: Abendländische Handschriften des Mittelalters aus den Sammlungen der Stiftung Preussischer Kulturbesitz Berlin*. Wiesbaden, 1975.

Branner, Robert. "The Saint-Quentin Rotulus." *Scriptorium* 21 (1967): 252–60.

Braunfels, Wolfgang, et al., eds. *Der Hedwigs-Codex von 1353*. Berlin, 1972.

Brenk, Beat. *Das Lektionar des Desiderius von Montecassino: Ein Meisterwerk italienischer Buchmalerei des 11. Jahrhunderts*. Zurich, 1987.

Brennan, Brian. "Deathless Marriage and Spiritual Fecundity in Venantius Fortunatus's *De Virginitate*." *Traditio* 51 (1996): 73–97.

Brindley, H. H. "Ships in the Cambridge Life of the Confessor." *Proceedings of the Cambridge Antiquarian Society* 18 (1913/14): 67–75.

Brooke, Rosalind B., ed. *Scripta Leonis Rufini et Angeli sociorum S. Francisci: The Writings of Leo, Rufino, and Angelo, Companions of St. Francis*. Oxford, 1970.

Brown, Elizabeth A. R., and Michael Cothren. "The Twelfth-Century Crusading Window of the Abbey of Saint Denis: *Praeteritorum Enim Recordatio Futurorum Est Exhibito.*" *Journal of the Warburg and Courtauld Institutes* 49 (1986): 1–40.

Brown, Peter. *The Body and Society: Men, Women, and Sexual Renunciation in Early Christianity.* New York, 1988.

———. *The Cult of the Saints: Its Rise and Function in Latin Christianity.* Haskell Lectures on History of Religions 2. Chicago, 1981.

———. "Images as a Substitute for Writing." In *East and West: Modes of Communication,* edited by Evangelos Chrysos and Ian Wood, 15–34. London, 1999.

———. "Relics and Social Status in the Age of Gregory of Tours." In *Society and the Holy in Late Antiquity,* 222–50. Berkeley, 1982.

———. *Society and the Holy in Late Antiquity.* Berkeley, 1982.

Brundage, James A. "Prostitution in Medieval Canon Law." *Signs* 1 (1976): 825–45.

Bucher, François. *The Pamplona Bibles.* New Haven, 1970.

Buettner, Brigitte. *Boccaccio's 'Des Cleres et Nobles Femmes.'* Seattle and London, 1996.

Burns, E. Jane. *Bodytalk: When Women Speak in Old French Literature.* Philadelphia, 1993.

Buschhausen, Helmut. *Die spätrömischen Metallscrinia und frühchristlichen Reliquiare.* Wiener byzantinische Studien 9. Vienna, 1971.

Bynum, Caroline Walker. "The Body of Christ in the Later Middle Ages: A Reply to Leo Steinberg." In *Fragmentation and Redemption: Essays on Gender and the Human Body in Medieval Religion,* 79–118. New York, 1992.

———. *Fragmentation and Redemption: Essays on Gender and the Human Body in Medieval Religion.* New York, 1992.

———. *Holy Feast and Holy Fast: The Religious Significance of Food to Medieval Women.* Berkeley, 1987.

———. "Women Mystics and Eucharistic Devotion in the Thirteenth Century." In *Fragmentation and Redemption: Essays on Gender and the Human Body in Medieval Religion,* 119–50. New York, 1992.

Caesarius of Heisterbach. *The Dialogue on Miracles.* 2 vols. London, 1929.

Calmet, R. P. *Histoire de Lorraine.* Nancy, 1748 (reprint Paris, 1973).

Cameron, Averil. *Christianity and the Rhetoric of Empire.* Berkeley, 1991.

Camille, Michael. *The Gothic Idol: Ideology and Image-Making in Medieval Art.* Cambridge, 1989.

———. "Seeing and Reading: Some Visual Implications of Medieval Literacy and Illiteracy." *Art History* 8 (1985): 26–49.

Campbell, James. *Bede's Reges and Principes.* Newcastle upon Tyne, 1979.

Cannon, Joanna, and André Vauchez. *Margherita of Cortona and the Lorenzetti: Sienese Art and the Cult of a Holy Woman in Medieval Tuscany.* University Park, Pa., 1998.

Carrasco, Magdalena. "The Construction of Sanctity: Pictorial Hagiography and Monastic Reform in the First Illustrated Life of St. Cuthbert (Oxford, University College Ms. 165)." *Studies in Iconography* 21 (2000): 47–89.

———. "An Early Illustrated Manuscript of the Passion of St. Agatha (Paris, Bibl. Nat. Ms. Lat. 5594)." *Gesta* 24 (1985): 19–32.

———. "Notes on the Iconography of the Romanesque Illustrated Manuscript of the Life of St. Albinus of Angers." *Zeitschrift für Kunstgeschichte* 47 (1984): 333–48.

———. "Some Illustrations of the Life of St. Aubin (Albinus) of Angers (Paris, Bibliothèque nationale, Ms. n.a.l. 1390) and Related Works." Ph.D. dissertation, Yale University, New Haven, 1980.

———. "Spirituality and Historicity in Pictorial Hagiography: Two Miracles by St. Albinus of Angers." *Art History* 12 (1989): 1–21.

———. "Spirituality in Context: The Romanesque Illustrated Life of St. Radegund of Poitiers (Poitiers, Bibl. Mun. Ms. 250)." *Art Bulletin* 72 (1990): 414–35.

Carruthers, Mary. *The Book of Memory: A Study of Memory in Medieval Culture.* Cambridge, 1990.

Cassidy, Brendan, ed. *The Ruthwell Cross.* Princeton, 1992.

Caviness, Madeline H. "Biblical Stories in Windows: Were They Bibles for the Poor?" In *The Bible in the Middle Ages: Its Influence on Literature and Art,* edited by Bernard S. Levy, 103–47. Binghampton, N.Y., 1992.

Cazelles, Brigitte. *The Lady as Saint: A Collection of French Hagiographic Romances of the Thirteenth Century.* Philadelphia, 1991.

Cerquiglini, Bernard. *In Praise of the Variant: A Critical History of Philology.* Translated by Betsy Wing. Baltimore, 1999.

Chadwick, W. Owen. "Gregory of Tours and Gregory the Great." *Journal of Theological Studies* 50 (1949): 38–49.

Chazelle, Celia. "Memory, Instruction, Worship: 'Gregory's' Influence on Early Medieval Doctrines of the Artistic Image." In *Gregory the Great: A Symposium,* edited by John Cavadini, 181–215. Notre Dame, Ind., 1995.

———. "Pictures, Books, and the Illiterate: Pope Gregory I's Letters to Serenus of Marseilles." *Word and Image* 6 (1990): 138–53.

Cheney, William A. *The Cult of Kingship in Anglo-Saxon England: The Transition from Paganism to Christianity.* Berkeley, 1970.

Chung-Apley, Jane Geein. "The Illustrated *Vie et miracles de Saint Louis of Guillaume de Saint-Pathus* (Paris, B.N., MS fr. 5716)." Ph.D. dissertation, University of Michigan, Ann Arbor, 1998.

Clanchy, Michael T. *From Memory to Written Record: England 1066–1307.* London, 1979.

Clark, Francis. *The Pseudo-Gregorian Dialogues.* Vol. 2. Leiden, 1987.

Claussen, M. A. "'Peregrinatio' and 'Peregrini' in Augustine's 'City of God.'" *Traditio* 46 (1991): 33–75.

Coakley, John. "Friars, Sanctity, and Gender: Mendicant Encounters with Saints, 1250–1325." In *Medieval Masculinities: Regarding Men in the Middle Ages,* edited by Clare A. Lees, 91–110. Minneapolis, 1994.

Cobham Brewer, E. *A Dictionary of Miracles.* Detroit, 1966 (reprint of 1884 edition).

Coens, Maurice. "Anciennes litanies des saints." In *Recueil d'Études Bollandiennes,* Part II. Subsidia hagiographica 37. Brussels, 1963.

———. "Nouvelles Recherches sur un thème hagiographique: La Céphalophore." In *Recueil d'Études Bollandiennes,* 9–31. Subsidia hagiographica, 37. Brussels: Société des Bollandistes, 1963.

Cohen, Esther. "In the Name of God and Profit: The Pilgrimage Industry in Southern France in the Late Middle Ages." Ph.D. dissertation, Brown University, 1976.

Cohen, Jeffrey Jerome, and Bonnie Wheeler, eds. *Becoming Male in the Middle Ages*. The New Middle Ages 4. New York, 1997.

Colgrave, Bertram, ed. *The Earliest Life of Gregory the Great*. Lawrence, Kans., 1968.

———. *Felix's Life of Saint Guthlac*. Cambridge, 1956.

———, ed. *Two Lives of Saint Cuthbert*. Cambridge, 1940.

Colledge, Edmund. "'Cephalologie': A Recurring Theme in Classical and Mediaeval Lore." *Traditio* 37 (1981): 411–26.

Cologne, Schnütgen-Museum. *Rhein und Maas: Kunst und Kultur 800–1400*. Vol. 2. Cologne, 1972–1973.

Constable, Giles. "The Ceremonies and Symbolism of Entering Religious Life and Taking the Monastic Habit, from the Fourth to the Twelfth Century." In *Segni e riti nella chiesa altomedievale occidentale*, 771–834. Settimane di studio del Centro italiano di studi sull'alto medioevo 33. Spoleto, 1987.

———. "The Ideal of the Imitation of Christ." In *Three Studies in Medieval Religious and Social Thought,* 143–248. Cambridge, 1995.

———. "The Interpretation of Mary and Martha." In *Three Studies in Medieval Religious and Social Thought,* 1–142. Cambridge, 1995.

———. "The Orders of Society." In *Three Studies in Medieval Religious and Social Thought,* 249–360. Cambridge, 1995.

Coon, Lynda L. *Sacred Fictions: Holy Women and Hagiography in Late Antiquity*. Philadelphia, 1997.

Corbet, Patrick. *Les Saints Ottoniens: Sainteté dynastique, sainteté royale et sainteté féminine autour de l'an mil*. Sigmaringen, 1986.

Corblet, J. *L'Hagiographie du diocèse d'Amiens*. Vol. 3. Paris, 1873.

Cormack, Robin S. *Writing in Gold: Byzantine Society and Its Icons*. London, 1985.

Corstanje, C. van, Y. Cazaux, J. Decavele, and A. Derolez. *Vita Sanctae Coletae (1381–1477)*. Tielt and Leiden, 1982.

Courcelle, Pierre. "La Vision cosmique de saint Benoît." *Revues des Études Augustiniennes* 13 (1967): 97–117.

Crépin, André. "L'Importance de la pensée de Grégoire le Grand dans la politique culturelle d'Alfred, roi de Wessex (871–899)." In *Grégoire le Grand: Chantilly, Centre culturel les Fontaines, 15–19 septembre 1982,* edited by J. Fontaine, R. Gillet, and S. Pellistrandi, 579–86. Paris, 1986.

Cristiani, Marta. "La sainteté féminine du haut moyen âge." In *Les Fonctions des saints dans le monde occidental (IIIe–XIIIe siècle),* 385–434. Collection de l'École française de Rome 149. Rome, 1991.

Curtius, Ernst Robert. *European Literature and the Latin Middle Ages*. New York, 1963 (orig. ed. 1953).

Dagens, C. *Saint Grégoire le Grand: Culture et expérience chrétiennes*. Paris, 1977.

Dalarun, Jacques. "La Mort des saints fondateurs: De Martin à François." In *Les Fonctions des saints dans le monde occidental (IIIe–XIIIe siècle),* 193–215. Collection de l'École française de Rome 149. Rome, 1991.

Dale, Thomas. "Inventing a Sacred Past: Pictorial Narratives of St. Mark the Evangelist in Aquileia and Venice c. 1000–1300." *Dumbarton Oaks Papers* 48 (1994):53–104

Damrosch, David. *"Non Alia Sed Aliter:* The Hermeneutics of Gender in Bernard of Clairvaux." In *Images of Sainthood in Medieval Europe,* edited by Renate Blumenfeld-Kosinski and Timea Szell, 181–95. Ithaca, N.Y., 1991.

Davidson, C. "The Visual Arts and Drama, with Special Emphasis on the Lazarus Plays." In *Le Théâtre au moyen âge,* edited by G. Muller, 45–59. Paris, 1981.

Davis, H., ed. *Gregory the Great: Pastoral Care (Regula Pastoralis).* Westminster, Md., 1955.

Davy, M.-M., ed. *Guillaume de Saint-Thierry: Commentaire sur le Cantique des Cantiques.* Bibliothèque des textes philosophiques. Paris, 1958.

Delehaye, Hippolyte. *The Legends of the Saints.* Translated by V. M. Crawford. London, 1907.

———. "Loca Sanctorum." *Analecta Bollandiana* 48 (1930): 5–64.

———. "Martyr et Confesseur." *Analecta Bollandiana* 39 (1921): 20–49.

———. "Martyrs d'Egypte." *Analecta Bollandiana* 40 (1922): 5–154, 299–364.

———. *Les Passions des martyrs et les genres littéraires.* Subsidia Hagiographica 13b. Brussels, 1921.

———. "Sanctus." *Analecta Bollandiana* 28 (1909): 145–200.

Delisle, Leopold. "Notice sur un livre à peintures exécuté en 1250 dans l'abbaye de Saint-Denis." *Mémoires de l'Institut. Académie des Inscriptions et Belles Lettres* 38 (1877): 444–76.

Deschamps, Louis. "Notice sur un manuscrit de la Bibliothèque de Saint-Omer." *Mémoires de la Société des antiquaires de la Morinie (Saint-Omer)* 5 (1839–40): 173–209.

Deshman, Robert. "Anglo-Saxon Art after Alfred." *Art Bulletin* 56 (1974): 176–200.

———. "The Imagery of the Living Ecclesia and the English Monastic Reform." In *Sources of Anglo-Saxon Culture,* edited by Paul E. Szarmach, 261–82. Kalamazoo, Mich., 1986.

Dickinson, John. "The Medieval Conception of Kingship as Developed in the Policratius of John of Salisbury." *Speculum* 1 (1926): 308–37.

Dienemann, Joachim. *Der Kult des heiligen Kilian im 8. und 9. Jahrhundert: Beiträge zur geistigen und politischen Entwicklung der Karolingerzeit.* Quellen und Forschungen zur Geschichte des Bistums und Hochstifts Würzburg 10. Würzburg, 1955.

Diket, Read Montgomery. "An Exemplary Life: Spinello Aretino's Cycle of Saint Benedict in Context." *Athanor* 11 (1992): 22–31.

Dinkler-von Schubert, Erika. *Der Elisabethschrein zu Marburg.* Marburger Reihe 4. Marburg, 1974.

———. *Der Schrein der Hl. Elisabeth zu Marburg: Studien zur Schrein-Ikonographie.* Marburg, 1964.

Dinzelbacher, Peter. "Nascita e funzione della santità mistica alla fine del medioevo centrale." In *Les Fonctions des saints dans le monde occidental (IIIe–XIIIe siècle),* 489–506. Collection de l'École française de Rome 149. Rome, 1991.

Dix, Gregory. *The Shape of the Liturgy.* 2d ed. London, 1945.

Dodgson, C., ed. *Tertullian: I. Apologetic and Practical Treatises.* Library of Fathers of the Holy Catholic Church Anterior to the Division of East and West. Oxford, 1842.

Dods, M., ed. *Augustine: On Christian Doctrine.* The Works of Aurelius Augustinus, 9. Edinburgh, 1873.

Doignon, Jean. " 'Blessure d'affliction' et 'blessure d'amour' (Moralia, 6, 25, 42): Une Jonction de thèmes de la spiritualité patristique de Cyprien à Augustin." In *Grégoire le Grand: Chantilly, Centre culturel les Fontaines, 15–19 septembre 1982,* edited by J. Fontaine, R. Gillet, and S. Pellistrandi, 297–303. Paris, 1986.

Dölger, Franz Josef. *Sphragis: Eine altchristliche Taufbezeichnung in ihren Bezeihungen zur profanen und religiösen Kultur des Altertums.* Studien zur Geschichte und Kultur des Altertums 5. Bd. Heft 3/4. Paderborn, 1911.

Doyle, Eric, ed. *The Disciple and the Master: St. Bonaventure's Sermons on St. Francis of Assisi.* Chicago, 1983.

Dubler, Elisabeth. *Das Bild des heiligen Benedikt bis zum Ausgang des Mittelalters.* Munich, 1966.

Dubois, Jacques. *Les Martyrologes du moyen âge latin.* Typologie des sources du moyen âge occidental 26. Turnhout, 1978.

Duby, Georges. *The Knight, The Lady and the Priest: The Making of Modern Marriage in Medieval France.* Translated by B. Bray. Chicago, 1984.

———. *The Three Orders: Feudal Society Imagined.* Translated by A. Goldhammer. Chicago, 1980.

Duggan, Lawrence G. "Was Art Really the 'Book of the Illiterate'?" *Word and Image* 5 (1989): 227–51.

Dümmler, E. "Sigebert von Gembloux Passio Sanctae Luciae Virginis und Passio Sanctorum Thebeorum." *Abhandlungen der königlichen Akademie der Wissenschaften in Berlin, philosophische-historische Klasse* I (1893): 1–43.

Dupré-Theseider, E. "La 'grande rapina dei corpi santi' dall'Italia al Tempo di Ottone I." In *Festschrift Percy Ernst Schramm,* I: 420–32. Wiesbaden, 1964.

Duval, Yvette. "Sanctorum sepulchris sociari." In *Les Fonctions des saints dans le monde occidental (IIIe–XIIIe siècle),* 333–51. Collection de l'École française de Rome 149. Rome, 1991.

Easton, Martha. "Saint Agatha and the Sanctification of Sexual Violence." *Studies in Iconography* 16 (1994): 83–118.

Elliott, Alison Goddard. *Roads to Paradise: Reading the Lives of the Early Saints.* Hanover, N.H., 1987.

Elliott, Dyan. *Fallen Bodies: Pollution, Sexuality, and Demonology in the Middle Ages.* Philadelphia, 1999.

Elsner, Jaś. *Art and the Roman Viewer: The Transformation of Art from the Pagan World to Christianity.* Cambridge, 1995.

Esrock, Ellen J. *The Reader's Eye: Visual Imaging as Reader Response.* Baltimore, 1994.

Evans, Gillian Rosemary. *The Thought of Gregory the Great.* Cambridge, 1986.

Evans, Helen C., and William D. Wixom, eds. *The Glory of Byzantium: Art and Culture of the Middle Byzantine Era, A.D. 843–1261.* New York, 1997.

Evans, Jonathan D. "Episodes in Analysis of Medieval Narrative." *Style* 20 (1986): 126–41.

Farmer, David Hugh. *The Oxford Dictionary of Saints.* 2d ed. Oxford, 1987.

Farmer, Sharon. "Softening the Hearts of Men: Women, Embodiment, and Persuasion in the Thirteenth Century." In *Embodied Love,* edited by P. M. Cooey, S. Farmer, and M. E. Ross, 115–34. San Francisco, 1987.

Favreau, Robert, ed. *La Vie de sainte Radegonde par Fortunat: Poitiers, Bibliothèque municipale manuscrit 250.* Paris, 1995.

Ferré, M.-J., and L. Baudry, eds. *Le Livre de l'expérience des vrais fidèles: Texte latin publié d'après le manuscrit d'Assise.* Paris, 1927.

Finucane, Ronald C. *Miracles and Pilgrims: Popular Beliefs in Medieval England.* London, 1977.

Folz, Robert. "Naissance et manifestations d'un culte royal: Saint Edmond, roi d'Est-Anglie." In *Geschichtsschreiben und geistiges Leben im Mittelalter: Festschrift für Heinz Löwe zum 65. Geburtstag,* edited by K. Hauck and H. Mordek. Cologne, 1978.

———. *Les saints rois du Moyen Age en Occident (VIe–XIIIe siècles).* Subsidia Hagiographica 68. Brussels, 1984.

———. *Le Souvenir et la Légende de Charlemagne.* Paris, 1950.

Fontaine, Jacques, ed. *Sulpice Sévère: Vie de Saint Martin.* Sources chrétiennes 133. 3 vols. Paris, 1967.

Fortunatus, Venantius. *Vita Martini.* MGH *Auctorum antiquissimorum,* edited by F. Leo. Vol. 4. Berlin, 1877–1919.

Freedberg, David. *The Power of Images.* Chicago, 1989.

Freise, Eckhard, ed. *Vita Sancti Liudgeri: Staatsbibliothek zu Berlin Preussischer Kulturgesitz, Ms. theol. lat. fol. 323.* Codices Selecti, 95. Graz, 1994.

Frugoni, Chiara. "Saint Francis: A Saint in Progress." In *Saints: Studies in Hagiography,* edited by Sandro Sticca, 161–90. Medieval and Renaissance Texts and Studies 141. Binghamton, N.Y., 1996.

Fry, T., ed. *The Rule of Saint Benedict: In Latin and English with Notes.* Collegeville, Minn., 1981.

Gäbe, Sabine. "Radegundis: *sancta, regina, ancilla.* Zum Heiligkeitsideal der Radegundisviten von Fortunat und Baudonivia." *Francia* 16 (1989): 1–30.

Gaetani, Ottavio. *Vitae Sanctorum Siculorum.* Palermo, 1657.

Gaiffier, Baudouin de. "Les 'doublets' en hagiographie latine." *Analecta Bollandiana* 96 (1978): 261–69.

———. "La Lecture des Actes des martyrs dans la prière liturgique en Occident." *Analecta Bollandiana* 72 (1954): 134–66.

———. "Miracles bibliques et vies des saints." In *Études critiques d'hagiographie et d'iconologie,* 50–61. Subsidia Hagiographica 43. Brussels, 1967.

———. "Les revendications de biens dans quelques documents hagiographiques du XIe siècle." *Analecta Bollandiana* 50 (1932): 123–38.

———. "Un thème hagiographique: Le Pendu miraculeusement sauvé." In *Études critiques d'hagiographie et d'iconologie,* 194–226. Subsidia Hagiographica 43. Brussels, 1967.

Garnier, François. *Le Langage de l'image au moyen âge: Grammaire des gestes.* 2 vols. Paris, 1982.

Gaspar, C., and F. Lyna. *Les Principaux Manuscrits à peintures de la Bibliothèque royale de Belgique.* 2 vols. Brussels, 1984.

Gauthier, Marie-Madeleine S. "La Légende de sainte Valérie et les émaux champlevés de Limoges." *Bulletin de la Société archéologique et historique du Limousin* 86 (1955): 35–80.

Geary, Patrick J. *Before France and Germany: The Creation and Transformation of the Merovingian World.* New York, 1988.

———. *Furta Sacra: Thefts of Relics in the Central Middle Ages.* Princeton, 1978.

————. "Saints, Scholars, and Society: The Elusive Goal." In *Saints: Studies in Hagiography,* edited by Sandro Sticca, 1–22. Medieval and Renaissance Texts and Studies 141. Binghamton, N.Y., 1996.

Genicot, Leopold. "'Discordiae concordantium': Sur l'intérêt des textes hagiographiques." *Académie royale de Belgique. Bulletin de la classe des lettres et des sciences morales et politiques* 51 (1965): 65–75.

Gerould, G. H. "King Arthur and Politics." *Speculum* 2 (1927): 33–51.

Ginot, E. "Le Manuscrit de Ste. Radegonde de Poitiers et ses peintures du XIe siècle." *Bulletin de la Société Française de Reproduction de Manuscrits à Peintures, années 1914–20* (1920): 9–80.

Goffen, Rona. *Spirituality in Conflict: Saint Francis and Giotto's Bardi Chapel.* University Park, Pa., 1988.

Goldschmidt. *Die Elfenbeinskulpturen aus der Zeit der karolingischen und sächsischen Kaiser VIII.–XI. Jahrhundert.* Vol. I. Berlin, 1969 (reprint).

Goldschmidt, Adolf, and R. Hamann. *Die Bronzetüren von Nowgorod und Gnesen.* 2 vols. Marburg, 1932.

Goldschmidt, Rudolf C., ed. *Paulinus' Churches at Nola.* Amsterdam, 1940.

Goodich, Michael. *Vita Perfecta: The Ideal of Sainthood in the Thirteenth Century.* Monographien zur Geschichte des Mittelalters 25. Stuttgart, 1982.

Goodwin, A. *The Abbey of St. Edmundsbury.* 2d ed. Oxford, 1931.

Gorski, K. "La Naissance des états et le 'roi saint': Problème de l'idéologie féodale." In *L'Europe aux IXe–XIe siècles aux origines des états nationaux,* edited by T. Manteuffel and A. Gieysztor, 425–32. Warsaw, 1968.

Grabar, André. *Christian Iconography.* Bollingen Series. Princeton, 1961.

————. *Martyrium. Recherches sur le culte des reliques et l'art chrétien antique.* 2 vols. Paris, 1946.

Grabar, Oleg. "History of Art and History of Literature: Some Random Thoughts." *New Literary History* 3 (1972): 559–68.

Gransden, Antonia. "The Legends and Traditions Concerning the Origins of the Abbey of Bury St. Edmunds." *English Historical Review* 100 (1985): 1–24.

Graus, František. *Volk, Herrscher und Heiliger im Reich der Merowinger: Studien zur Hagiographie der Merowingerzeit.* Prague, 1965.

Gravdal, Kathryn. *Ravishing Maidens: Writing Rape in Medieval French Literature and Law.* Philadelphia, 1991.

Gregory, Richard. "How Do We Interpret Images?" In *Images and Understanding: Thoughts about Images, Ideas about Understanding,* edited by H. Barlow, C. Blakemore, and M. Weston-Smith, 310–30. Cambridge, 1990.

Grüneison, Wladimir De. *Sainte Marie Antique.* Rome, 1911.

Habig, M. A., ed. *St. Francis of Assisi. Writings and Early Biographies.* Chicago, 1983.

Hahn, Cynthia. "Absent No Longer. The Saint and the Sign in Late Medieval Pictorial Hagiography." In *Hagiographie und Kunst: Der Heiligenkult in Schrift, Bild und Architektur,* edited by Gottfried Kerscher, 152–75. Berlin, 1993.

————. "Icon and Narrative in the Berlin Life of St. Lucy (Kupferstichkabinett MS78A4)." In *The*

Sacred Image East and West, edited by Robert Ousterhout and Leslie Brubaker, 72–90. Illinois Byzantine Studies 4. Urbana and Chicago, 1995.

―――. "Interpictoriality in the Limoges Chasses of Stephen, Martial, and Valerie." In *Image and Belief: Studies in Celebration of the Eightieth Anniversary of the Index of Christian Art,* edited by Colum Hourihane, 109–24. Princeton, 1999.

―――. "Narrative on the Golden Altar of Sant' Ambrogio: Presentation and Reception." *Dumbarton Oaks Papers* 53 (1999): 167–87.

―――. *Passio Kiliani. Ps. Theotimus, Passio Margaretae. Orationes. Vollständige Faksimile-Ausgabe . . . des Codex Ms I 189 . . . Niedersächsischen Landesbibliothek Hannover.* Codices Selecti, 83*. Graz, 1988.

―――. "Peregrinatio et Natio: The Illustrated Life of Edmund, King and Martyr." *Gesta* 30 (1991): 119–39.

―――. "Picturing the Text: Narrative in the Life of the Saints." *Art History* 13 (1990): 1–32.

―――. "Proper Behaviour for Knights and Kings: The Hagiography of Matthew Paris, Monk of St. Albans." *Charles Homer Haskins Society Journal* 2 (1990): 237–48.

―――. "Purification, Sacred Action, and the Vision of God: Viewing Medieval Narratives." *Word and Image* 5 (1989): 71–84.

―――. "Seeing and Believing: The Construction of Sanctity in Early-Medieval Saints' Shrines." *Speculum* 72 (1997): 1079–1106.

―――. "Speaking Without Tongues: The Martyr Romanus and Augustine's Theory of Language in Illustrations of Bern Burgerbibliothek Codex 264." In *Images of Sainthood in Medieval Europe,* edited by Renate Blumenfeld-Kosinski and Timea Szell, 161–80. Ithaca, N.Y., 1991.

―――. "Valerie's Gift: A Narrative Enamel Chasse from Limoges." In *Reading Medieval Images,* edited by Elizabeth Sears and Thelma Thomas. Ann Arbor, in press.

―――. "Visio Dei: Changes in Medieval Visuality." In *Visuality Before and Beyond the Renaissance: Seeing as Others Saw,* edited by Robert Nelson, 169–96. Cambridge, 2000.

―――. "The Voices of the Saints: Speaking Reliquaries." *Gesta* 36 (1997): 20–31.

Hamburger, Jeffrey F. *The Rothschild Canticles: Art and Mysticism in Flanders and the Rhineland Circa 1300.* New Haven, 1990.

―――. "The Use of Images in the Pastoral Care of Nuns: The Case of Heinrich Suso and the Dominicans." *Art Bulletin* 71 (1989): 20–46.

―――. "The Visual and the Visionary: The Image in Late Medieval Monastic Devotions." *Viator* 20 (1989): 161–82.

Hanning, Robert. *The Individual in Twelfth-Century Romance.* New Haven, 1977.

Harden, A. R., ed. *La Vie de seint Auban.* Anglo-Norman Texts 19. Oxford, 1968.

Harris, Julie. "The Arca of San Millán de la Cogolla and Its Ivories." Ph.D. dissertation, University of Pittsburgh, 1989.

Harrison, Carol. *Beauty and Revelation in the Thought of Saint Augustine.* Oxford, 1992.

Head, Thomas. "Art and Artifice in Ottonian Trier." *Gesta* 36 (1997): 65–82.

―――. *Hagiography and the Cult of the Saints: The Diocese of Orléans.* Cambridge, 1990.

———. "I Vow Myself to Be Your Servant: An Eleventh-Century Pilgrim, His Chronicler and His Saint." *Historical Reflections/Réflexions Historiques* 11 (1984): 215–51.

———. *Medieval Hagiography: An Anthology*. New York, 2000.

———. Head, Thomas, and Richard Landes, eds. *The Peace of God: Social Violence and Religious Response in France around the Year 1000*. Ithaca, N.Y., 1992.

Hedeman, Anne D. "Copies in Context: The Coronation of Charles V in His Grandes Chroniques de France." In *Coronations,* edited by János M. Bak, 72–87. Berkeley, 1990.

———. *The Royal Image: Illustrations of the Grandes Chroniques de France, 1274–1422*. Berkeley, 1991.

Heffernan, Thomas. *Sacred Biography: Saints and Their Biographers in the Middle Ages*. Oxford, 1988.

Heinzelmann, Martin. *Translationsberichte und andere Quellen des Reliquienkultes*. Typologie des sources du moyen âge occidental 33. Turnhout, 1979.

Hermann-Mascard, Nicole. *Les Reliques des saints: Formation coutumière d'un droit*. Paris, 1975.

Herval, René. *Origines chrétiennes de la IIe Lyonnaise gallo-romaine à la Normandie ducale (IVe–XIe siècles): Avec le texte complet et la traduction du "De laude sanctorum" de saint Victrice (396)*. Paris, 1966.

Hervey, F. *Corolla Sancti Eadmundi. The Garland of St. Edmund King and Martyr*. London, 1907.

Holder-Egger, O., ed. *Agnelli Liber Pontificalis Ecclesiae Ravennatis*. MGH *Scriptores Rerum Langobardicarum et italicarum*, edited by G. Waitz. Hannover, 1878 (reprint 1964).

Holladay, Joan. "The Education of Jeanne d'Evreux: Personal Piety and Dynastic Salvation in Her Book of Hours at the Cloisters." *Art History* 17 (1994): 585–611.

Holman, Sheri. *A Stolen Tongue*. New York, 1997.

Homburger, Otto. *Die illustrierten Handschriften der Bibliothek Bern: Die vorkarolingischen und karolingischen Handschriften*. Bern, 1962.

Honselmann, K. "Gedanken sächsischer Theologen des 9. Jahrhunderts über der Heiligenverehrung." *Westfalen* 40 (1962): 38–43.

Hrotsvitha. *The Plays of Hrotsvit of Gandersheim*. New York, 1989.

Hughes, Andrew. "Literary Transformation in Post-Carolingian Saints' Offices: Using all the Evidence." In *Saints: Studies in Hagiography,* edited by Sandro Sticca, 23–50. Medieval and Renaissance Texts and Studies 141. Binghamton, N.Y., 1996.

Inguanez, D. M., and M. Avery. *Miniature Cassinese del Secolo XI illustranti la Vita di S. Benedetto. Cod. vat. lat. 1202*. Monte Cassino, 1934.

Iogna-Prat, Dominique. "Hagiographie, théologie et théocratie dans le Cluny de l'an mil." In *Les Fonctions des saints dans le monde occidental (IIIe–XIIIe siècle),* 241–57. Collection de l'École française de Rome 149. Rome, 1991.

Iser, Wolfgang. *The Act of Reading: A Theory of Aesthetic Response*. Baltimore, 1978.

Jacobus de Voragine. *The Golden Legend: Readings on the Saints*. 2 vols. Princeton, 1993.

Jaeger, C. Stephen. *The Origins of Courtliness: Civilizing Trends and the Formation of Courtly Ideals*. Philadelphia, 1985.

Jager, Eric. "The Book of the Heart: Reading and Writing the Medieval Subject." *Speculum* 71 (1996): 1–26.

Jakobs, F., and F. A. Ukert. *Beiträge zur ältern Literatur oder Merkwürdigkeiten der Herzoglichen öffentlichen Bibliothek zu Gotha*. Heft 3 (= Vol. II, Heft 1). Leipzig, 1836.

James, Edward. *Gregory of Tours: Life of the Fathers.* Vol. I. Liverpool, 1985.

James, Montague Rhode, ed. *La Estoire de Seint Aedward le Rei.* Oxford, 1920.

Jauss, Hans Robert. *Aesthetic Experience and Literary Hermeneutics.* Minneapolis, 1982.

———. "Levels of Identification of Hero and Audience." *New Literary History* 5 (1973–74): 283–317.

———. *Toward an Aesthetic of Reception.* Minneapolis, 1982.

Jones, Charles Williams. *Saints' Lives and Chronicles in Early England.* Ithaca, N.Y., 1947.

Jounel, Pierre. "Le culte de Saint Grégoire le Grand." In *Grégoire le Grand: Chantilly, Centre culturel les Fontaines, 15–19 septembre 1982,* edited by J. Fontaine, R. Gillet, and S. Pellistrandi, 671–80. Paris, 1986.

Kaftal, George. *The Iconography of the Saints in Italian Painting from Its Beginnings to the Early XVth Century.* 4 vols. Florence, 1952–85.

Kauffmann, Claus Michael. *Romanesque Manuscripts, 1066–1190.* A Survey of Manuscripts Illuminated in the British Isles, 3. London, 1975.

Kauffmann, Martin. "The Image of St. Louis." In *Kings and Kingship in Medieval Europe,* edited by Anne J. Duggan, 265–86. London, 1993.

Kean, Maurice. *Chivalry.* New Haven, 1984.

Kelly, Kimberly. "Forgery, Invention and Propaganda: Factors behind the Production of the Guthlac Roll." *Athanor* 8 (1989): 1–13.

Kemp, Eric Waldram. *Canonization and Authority in the Western Church.* London, 1948.

Kemp, Wolfgang. *The Narratives of Gothic Stained Glass.* Cambridge, 1997 (German ed., 1987).

Kessler, Herbert Leon. "Diction in the 'Bibles of the Illiterate.'" In *World Art: Themes of Unity in Diversity. Acts of the XXVth International Congress of the History of Art,* edited by I. Lavin, 297–308. University Park, Pa., 1989.

———. "Pictorial Narrative and Church Mission in Sixth-Century Gaul." In *Pictorial Narrative in Antiquity and the Middle Ages,* edited by Herbert Leon Kessler and Marianna Shreve Simpson, 75–91. Studies in the History of Art 16. Washington, 1985.

Kirschbaum, Engelbert, ed. *Lexikon der Christlichen Ikonographie.* 8 vols. Rome, 1968–76.

Kleinberg, Aviad M. *Prophets in Their Own Country: Living Saints and the Making of Sainthood in the Later Middle Ages.* Chicago, 1992.

Kreuger, Derek. *Symeon the Holy Fool: Leontius' Life and the Late Antique City.* Transformations of the Classical Heritage 25. Berkeley, 1996.

Kruger, Steven F. *Dreaming in the Middle Ages.* Cambridge, 1992.

Krusch, B., ed. *Gregorii episcopi Turonensis Miracula et Opera Minora.* MGH, *Scriptores Rerum Merovingicarum,* I. Vol. part II., 1885 (reprint 1969).

Kupfer, Marcia. *Romanesque Wall Painting in Central France: The Politics of Narrative.* New Haven, 1993.

Kurtz, Benjamin P. "From St. Antony to St. Guthlac." *University of California Publications in Modern Philology* 12 (1926): 103–46.

Labande-Mailfert, Jacqueline. "Pauvreté et paix dans l'iconographie romane XIe–XIIe siècle." In *Études d'iconographie romane et d'histoire de l'art,* 139–63. Poitiers, 1982.

Lacaze, Charlotte. *The "Vie de St. Denis" Manuscript (Paris, Bibliothèque nationale, Ms. fr. 2090–2092)*. Outstanding Dissertations in the Fine Arts. New York and London, 1979.

Lake, K., ed. *Apostolic Fathers*. Loeb Classical Library. London, 1924–25.

Landes, Richard. *Relics, Apocalypse and the Deceits of History: Ademar of Chabannes (989–1034)*. Cambridge, Mass., 1995.

Lavin, Marilyn Aronberg. *The Place of Narrative: Mural Decoration in Italian Churches, 431–1600*. Chicago, 1990.

Leclercq, Jean. *L'Idée de la royauté du Christ au moyen âge*. Paris, 1959.

———. "Solitude and Solidarity: Medieval Women Recluses." In *Peace Weavers: Medieval Religious Women*, edited by John A. Nichols and Lilian Thomas Shank, 67–84. Kalamazoo, Mich., 1987.

Legner, Anton, ed. *Monumenta Annonis. Köln und Siegburg, Weltbild und Kunst im hohen Mittelalter*. Vol. 2. Cologne, 1975.

———, ed. *Ornamenta Ecclesiae: Kunst und Künstler der Romanik (Katalog zur Ausstellung des Schnütgen-Museums in der Josef-Haubrich-Kunsthalle*. 3 vols. Cologne, 1985.

Le Goff, Jacques. "La Sainteté de saint Louis: Sa Place dans la typologie et l'évolution chronologique des rois saints." In *Les Fonctions des saints dans le monde occidental (IIIe–XIIIe siècle)*, 285–93. Collection de l'École française de Rome 149. Rome, 1991.

Leonardi, Claudio. "Modelli agiografici nel secolo VIII: da Beda a Ugeburga." In *Les Fonctions des saints dans le monde occidental (IIIe–XIIIe siècle)*, 521–25. Collection de l'École française de Rome 149. Rome, 1991.

Lewis, Suzanne. *The Art of Matthew Paris in the Chronica Majora*. Berkeley, 1987.

———. *Reading Images: Narrative Discourse and Reception in the Thirteenth-Century Illuminated Apocalypse*. Cambridge, 1995.

———. *The Rhetoric of Power in the Bayeux Tapestry*. Cambridge Studies in New Art History and Criticism, edited by Norman Bryson. Cambridge, 1999.

Leyser, Karl J. *Rule and Conflict in Early Medieval Society: Ottonian Saxony*. Bloomington, Ind., 1979.

Liddell, Henry, and Robert Scott. *A Greek-English Lexicon*. Oxford, 1968.

Liebman, Charles. *Étude sur la vie en prose de Saint Denis*. Geneva, N.Y., 1942.

Little, Lester. "Spiritual Sanctions in Wales." In *Images of Sainthood in Medieval Europe*, edited by Renate Blumenfeld-Kosinski and Timea Szell, 67–80. Ithaca, N.Y., 1991.

Löffler, K. *Schwäbische Buchmalerei in romanischer Zeit*. Augsburg, 1928.

MacCormack, Sabine. *Art and Ceremony in Late Antiquity*. Berkeley, 1981.

Mackie, Gillian. "New Light on the So-Called Saint Lawrence Panel at the Mausoleum of Galla Placidia, Ravenna." *Gesta* 29 (1990): 54–60.

Maguire, Henry. *Art and Eloquence in Byzantium*. Princeton, 1981.

———. "The Art of Comparing in Byzantium." *Art Bulletin* 70 (1988): 88–103.

———. *The Icons of Their Bodies: Saints and Their Images in Byzantium*. Princeton, 1996.

———. "Truth and Convention in Byzantine Descriptions of Art Works." *Dumbarton Oaks Papers* 28 (1974): 114–40.

Mainfränkische Museum Würzburg. *Kilian: Mönch aus Irland—aller Franken Patron, 689–1989.* Würzburg, 1989.

Malamud, Martha. *A Poetics of Transformation: Prudentius and Classical Mythology.* Ithaca, N.Y., 1989.

Mâle, Émile. *The Gothic Image: Religious Art in France of the Thirteenth Century.* New York, 1958.

Mango, Cyril. *The Art of the Byzantine Empire, 312–1453.* Sources and Documents in the History of Art 3. Englewood Cliffs, N.J., 1972.

Manhes-Deremble, Collette. "Saint Lubin: Mutation d'un thème du temps carolingien au vitrail de Chartres." In *Les Fonctions des saints dans le monde occidental (IIIe–XIIIe siècle),* 295–316. Collection de l'École française de Rome 149. Rome, 1991.

———. *Les Vitraux narratifs de la cathédrale de Chartres: Études iconographiques.* Corpus vitrearum France, Serie études 2. Paris, 1993.

Manitius, M. *Geschichte der lateinischen Literatur des Mittelalters.* Munich, 1931.

Maraval, Pierre. "Fonction pédagogique de la littérature hagiographique d'un lieu de pèlerinage: L'Exemple des Miracles de Cyr et Jean." In *Hagiographie cultures et sociétés, IVe–IXe siècles: Actes du Colloque organisé à Nanterre et à Paris (2–5 mai 1979),* 385–86. Paris, 1981.

Markus, Robert A. "Gregory the Great's *Rector* and His Genesis." In *Grégoire le Grand: Chantilly, Centre culturel les Fontaines, 15–19 septembre 1982,* edited by J. Fontaine, R. Gillet, and S. Pellistrandi, 137–46. Paris, 1986.

Markus, R. A. *Signs and Meanings: World and Text in Ancient Christianity.* Liverpool, 1996.

Marrow, James. "'Circumdederunt me canes multi': Christ's tormentors in Northern European Art of the Late Middle Ages and Early Renaissance." *Art Bulletin* 59 (1977): 167–81.

———. *Passion Iconography in Northern European Art of the Late Middle Ages and Early Renaissance: A Study of the Transformation of Sacred Metaphor into Descriptive Narrative.* Kortrijk, Belgium, 1979.

Martin, Wallace. *Recent Theories of Narrative.* Ithaca, N.Y., 1986.

Matter, E. Ann. *The Voice of My Beloved: The Song of Songs in Western Medieval Christianity.* Philadelphia, 1990.

Matthew Paris. *English History.* 2 vols. London, 1852–54.

Mayo, Penelope, and Paul Meyvaert. "The Illustrations, Captions and Full-Page Initials of the Codex Benedictus." In *The Codex Benedictus. Vat. Lat. 1202,* edited by Paul Meyvaert, 59–91. New York and Zurich, 1982.

McCash, June Hall. "The Cultural Patronage of Medieval Women: An Overview." In *The Cultural Patronage of Medieval Women,* edited by June Hall McCash, 1–49. Athens, Ga., 1996.

McCready, William D. *Signs of Sanctity: Miracles in the Thought of Gregory the Great.* Toronto, 1989.

McCulloch, Florence. "Saints Alban and Amphibalus in the Works of Matthew Paris: Dublin, Trinity College MS 177." *Speculum* 56 (1981): 761–85.

McCulloh, John M. "The Cult of Relics in the Letters and 'Dialogues' of Pope Gregory the Great." *Traditio* 32 (1976): 145–84.

McKitterick, Rosamund. "Charles the Bald (823–877) and His Library: The Patronage of Learning." *English Historical Review* 95 (1980): 28–47.

———. *The Frankish Church and Carolingian Reforms, 789–895.* Studies in History. London, 1977.

———. "The Palace School of Charles the Bald." In *Charles the Bald: Court and Kingdom, Papers*

Based on a Colloquium Held in London in April, 1979, edited by M. Gibson and J. Nelson, Oxford, 1979.

McLachlan Parker, Elizabeth. "The Scriptorium of Bury St. Edmunds in the Third and Fourth Decades of the Twelfth Century." *Medieval Studies* 40 (1978): 328–48.

——. *The Scriptorium of Bury St. Edmunds in the Twelfth Century.* New York, 1986.

——. "A Twelfth-Century Cycle of Drawings from Bury St. Edmunds Abbey." *Proceedings of the Suffolk Institute of Archaeology* 31 (1969): 263–302.

McLaughlin, Megan. *Consorting with Saints: Prayer for the Dead in Early Medieval France.* Ithaca, N.Y., 1994.

McLaughlin, R. Emmet. "The Word Eclipsed? Preaching in the Early Middle Ages." *Traditio* 46 (1991): 77–122.

McNamara, Jo Ann. "The Herrenfrage: The Restructuring of the Gender System, 1050–1150." In *Medieval Masculinities: Regarding Men in the Middle Ages,* edited by Clare A. Lees, 3–30. Minneapolis, 1994.

——. "Imitatio Helenae: Sainthood as an Attribute of Queenship." In *Saints: Studies in Hagiography,* edited by Sandro Sticca, 51–80. Medieval and Renaissance Texts and Studies 141. Binghamton, N.Y., 1996.

——. "Living Sermons: Consecrated Women and the Conversion of Gaul." In *Peace Weavers: Medieval Religious Women,* edited by John A. Nichols and Lilian Thomas Shank, 19–38. Kalamazoo, Mich., 1987.

——. "Muffled Voices: The Lives of Consecrated Women in the Fourth Century." In *Distant Echoes: Medieval Religious Women,* edited by John A. Nichols and Lilian Thomas Shank, 11–30. Kalamazoo, Mich., 1984.

——. "The Need to Give: Suffering and Female Sanctity in the Middle Ages." In *Images of Sainthood in Medieval Europe,* edited by Renate Blumenfeld-Kosinski and Timea Szell, 199–221. Ithaca, N.Y., 1991.

McNamara, Jo Ann, John E. Halborg, and E. Gordon Whatley, eds. *Sainted Women of the Dark Ages.* Durham, N.C., 1992.

Meyer, Paul, ed. *Fragment d'une Vie de Saint Thomas de Cantorbéry.* Paris, 1885.

Meyer, R. T., ed. *Palladius. The Lausiac History.* Ancient Christian Writers 34. Westminster, Md., 1965.

Meyvaert, Paul. "A New Perspective on the Ruthwell Cross: Ecclesia and Vita Monastica." In *The Ruthwell Cross,* edited by Brendan Cassidy, 95–166. Princeton, N.J., 1992.

Michon, Solange. *Le Grand Passionnaire enluminé de Weissenau et son scriptorium autour de 1200.* Geneva, 1990.

Milde, W. "Jean Baptiste Maugérard et le manuscrit en l'honneur de sainte Lucie de Sigebert de Gembloux." In *Histoire sociale, sensibilités collectives et mentalités: Mélanges Robert Mandrou,* 469–80. Paris, 1985.

——, ed. *Mittelalterliche Handschriften der Herzog August Bibliothek.* Frankfurt am Main, 1972.

Miles, Margaret R. "The Virgin's One Bare Breast." In *The Expanding Discourse: Feminism and Art History,* edited by Norma Broude and Mary D. Garrard, 27–38. New York, 1992.

"Miracula Sancta Valeriae." *Analecta Bollandiana* 8 (1889): 278–84.

Mollat, Michel. *The Poor in the Middle Ages.* New Haven, 1978.

Mombritius [Mombrizio], Bonino. *Sanctuarium, Sive Vitae Sanctorum.* Paris, 1910 (original ed., Milan, c. 1477).

Monfrin, Françoise. "Voir le monde dans la lumière de Dieu: A propos de Grégoire le Grand, Dialogues II, 35." In *Les Fonctions des Saints dans le monde occidental (IIIe–XIIIe siècle),* 37–49. Collection de l'École française de Rome 149. Rome, 1991.

Morel-Payen, L. *Les plus beaux manuscrits et les plus belles reliures de la Bibliothèque de Troyes.* Troyes, 1935.

Morgan, Nigel. *Early Gothic Manuscripts, 1190–1285.* 2 vols. London, 1982.

———. "Matthew Paris, St. Albans, London, and the Leaves of the 'Life of St. Thomas Becket.'" *Burlington Magazine* 130 (1988): 85–96.

Musurillo, Herbert. *The Acts of the Christian Martyrs.* Oxford Early Christian Texts. Oxford, 1972.

Nelson, Janet L. "The Lord's Anointed and the People's Choice: Carolingian Royal Ritual." In *Rituals of Royalty: Power and Ceremonial in Traditional Societies,* edited by David Cannadine and Simon Price, 137–80. Cambridge, 1987.

Nichols, Stephen G., Jr. *Romanesque Signs: Early Medieval Narrative and Iconography.* New Haven, 1983.

Nie, Giselle de. "'Consciousness Fecund Through God': From Male Fighter to Spiritual Bride-Mother in Late Antique Female Sanctity." In *Sanctity and Motherhood: Essays on Holy Mothers in the Middle Ages,* edited by Anneke B. Mulder-Bakker, 101–64. New York, 1995.

———. "Iconic Alchemy: Imaging Miracles in Late Sixth-Century Gaul." *Studia Patristica* 33 (1997): 158–66.

Noble, Thomas F. X., and Thomas Head. *Soldiers of Christ: Saints and Saints' Lives from Late Antiquity and the Early Middle Ages.* University Park, Pa., 1995.

Norberg, D., ed. *Gregory the Great. Registrum Epistolarum.* Corpus Christianorum 140, 140A. Turnhout, 1982.

North, Sally. "The Ideal Knight as Presented in Some French Narrative Poems, c. 1090–1240: An Outline Sketch." In *The Ideals and Practice of Knighthood: Papers from the First and Second Strawberry Hill Conferences,* edited by C. Harper-Bill and R. Harvey, 116–18. Woodbridge, Suffolk, 1990.

Omont, H. *Vie et Histoire de St. Denys (Facsimile des 30 miniatures du Ms. n. a. fr. 1098).* Paris, 1905.

Pächt, Otto. *The Rise of Pictorial Narrative in Twelfth-Century England.* Oxford, 1962.

Pächt, Otto, Francis Wormald, and C. R. Dodwell. *The St Albans Psalter (The Albani Psalter).* London, 1960.

Painter, Sidney. *French Chivalry.* Baltimore, 1940.

Panofsky, Erwin. *Gothic Architecture and Scholasticism.* New York, 1957.

Pastan, Elizabeth Carson. "The Torture of Saint George Medallion from Chartres Cathedral in Princeton." *Record of the Art Museum of Princeton University* 56 (1997): 11–34.

Paxton, Frederick S. "Liturgy and Healing in an Early Medieval Saint's Cult: The Mass *In honore sancti Sigismundi* for the Cure of Fevers." *Traditio* 49 (1994): 23–44.

Pelikan, Jaroslav. *The Christian Tradition: The History of the Development of Doctrine.* III: *The Growth of Medieval Theology (600–1300).* Chicago, 1978.

Perdrizet, Paul. *Le Calendrier parisien à la fin du moyen âge d'après le Bréviaire et les livres d'heures.* Publications de la Faculté des Lettres de l'Université de Strasbourg 63. Paris, 1933.

Petersen, Joan M. *The Dialogues of Gregory the Great in Their Late Antique Cultural Background.* Toronto, 1984.

Petrakopoulos, Anja. "Sanctity and Motherhood: Elizabeth of Thuringia." In *Sanctity and Motherhood: Essays on Holy Mothers in the Middle Ages,* edited by Anneke B. Mulder-Bakker, 259–96. New York, 1995.

Philippart, Guy. *Les Légendiers latins et autres manuscrits hagiographiques.* Typologie des sources du moyen âge occidental 14–15. Turnhout, 1977.

———. "Le Saint comme parure de Dieu: Héros séducteur et patron terrestre d'après les hagiographes lotharingiens du Xe siècle." In *Les Fonctions des saints dans le monde occidental (IIIe–XIIIe siècle),* 123–42. Collection de l'École française de Rome 149. Rome 1991.

Pickering, Frederick P. *Literature and Art in the Middle Ages.* Coral Gables, Fla., 1960.

Pietri, Charles. "L'Evolution du culte des saints aux premiers siècles chrétiens: Du Témoin à l'intercesseur." In *Les Fonctions des saints dans le monde occidental (IIIe–XIIIe siècle),* 15–36. Collection de l'École française de Rome 149. Rome, 1991.

Pietri, Luce. "Culte des saints et religiosité politique dans la Gaule du Ve et du VIe siècle." In *Les Fonctions des saints dans le monde occidental (IIIe–XIIIe siècle),* 353–69. Collection de l'École française de Rome 149. Rome, 1991.

Pizarro, Joaquin Martinez. *A Rhetoric of the Scene: Dramatic Narrative in the Early Middle Ages.* Toronto, 1989.

Porcher, Jean. *L'Enluminure française.* Paris, 1954.

Postlewate, Laurie. "Vernacular Hagiography and Lay Piety: Two Old French Adaptions of the Life of Saint Margaret of Antioch." In *Saints: Studies in Hagiography,* edited by Sandro Sticca, 115–30. Medieval and Renaissance Texts and Studies 141. Binghamton, N.Y., 1996.

Poulin, Joseph-Claude. *L'Idéal de sainteté dans l'Aquitaine carolingienne d'après les sources hagiographiques (750–950).* Travaux du laboratoire d'histoire religieuse de l'Université de Laval 1. Quebec, 1975.

———. "Les Saints dans la vie religieuse au moyen âge." In *Religions populaires: Colloque international, 1970,* edited by B. Lacroix and P. Boglioni, 64–74. Quebec, 1972.

Prochno, Joachim. *Das Schreiber- und Dedikationsbild in der deutschen Buchmalerei.* Vol. 2. Leipzig, 1929.

Propp, Vladimir. *Morphology of the Folktale.* 2d ed. Austin, 1968.

Rahner, Karl. "Le Début d'une doctrine des cinq sens spirituels chez Origène." *Revue d'ascétique et de mystique* 13 (1932): 113–45.

———. "La Doctrine des 'sens spirituel' du moyen âge, en particulier chez Saint Bonaventure." *Revue d'ascétique et de mystique* 14 (1933): 263–99.

Rampolla, Mary Lynn. "'A Mirror of Sanctity': Madness as Metaphor in the *Vita Wulfstani.*" In *Saints: Studies in Hagiography,* edited by Sandro Sticca, 95–114. Medieval and Renaissance Texts and Studies 141. Binghamton, N.Y., 1996.

Rapp, Claudia. "Figures of Female Sanctity: Byzantine Edifying Manuscripts and Their Audience." *Dumbarton Oaks Papers* 50 (1996): 313–32.

Raynaud, Christiane. *Images et Pouvoirs.* Paris, 1993.

Reinberg, Virginia. "Praying to the Saints in the Late Middle Ages." In *Saints: Studies in Hagiography,* edited by Sandro Sticca, 269–82. Medieval and Renaissance Texts and Studies 141. Binghamton, N.Y., 1996.

Riché, Pierre. "Les Carolingiens en quête de sainteté." In *Les Fonctions des saints dans le monde occidental (IIIe–XIIIe siècle),* 217–24. Collection de l'École française de Rome 149. Rome, 1991.

Richman, Paula. "The Portrayal of a Female Renouncer in a Tamil Buddhist Text." In *Gender and Religion: On the Complexity of Symbols,* edited by Caroline Bynum, 143–65. Boston, 1986.

Richter, G., and A. Schönfelder, eds. *Sacramentarium Fuldense, Saeculi X Cod Theol 231 der K. Universitätsbibliothek zu Göttingen.* Quellen and Abhandlungen zur Geschichte der Abtei und der Diözese Fulda 9. Fulda, 1912.

Ricoeur, Paul. *Time and Narrative.* Vol. I. Chicago, 1984.

Ridyard, Susan. *The Royal Saints of Anglo-Saxon England. A Study of West Saxon and East Anglian Cults.* Cambridge, 1988.

Ringbom, Sixten. "Some Pictorial Conventions for the Recounting of Thoughts and Experiences in Late Medieval Art." In *Medieval Iconography and Narrative: A Symposium (Proceedings for the Fourth International Symposium Organized by the Center for the Study of Vernacular Literature in the Middle Ages),* 38–69. Odense, 1980.

Roberts, Michael J. *Poetry and the Cult of the Martyrs. The "Liber Peristephanon" of Prudentius.* Ann Arbor, 1993.

Robertson, Elizabeth. "The Corporeality of Female Sanctity in *The Life of Saint Margaret.*" In *Images of Sainthood in Medieval Europe,* edited by Renate Blumenfeld-Kosinski and Timea Szell, 268–87. Ithaca, N.Y., 1991.

———. "Medieval Medical Views of Women and Female Spirituality in the *Ancrene Wisse* and Julian of Norwich's *Showings.*" In *Feminist Approaches to the Body in Medieval Literature,* edited by Linda Lomperis and Sarah Stanbury, 142–67. Philadelphia, 1993.

Rollason, David. "The Cults of Murdered Royal Saints in Anglo-Saxon England." *Anglo-Saxon England* 11 (1983): 1–22.

———. "Relic-Cults as an Instrument of Royal Policy, c. 900–c. 1050." *Anglo-Saxon England* 15 (1986): 91–103.

Rubin, Miri. *Corpus Christi: The Eucharist in Late Medieval Culture.* Cambridge, 1991.

Rudolph, Conrad. *The Things of Greater Importance: Bernard of Clairvaux's Apologia and the Medieval Attitude Toward Art.* Philadelphia, 1990.

Ryding, William W. *Structure in Medieval Narrative.* The Hague, 1971.

Sauer, Christine. "Allerheiligenbilder in der Buchmalerei Fuldas." In *Kloster Fulda in der Welt der Karolinger und Ottonen,* edited by Gangolf Schrimpf, 365–402. Frankfurt am Main, 1996.

Sauvel, M. Tony. "Les Miracles de Saint-Martin: Recherches sur les peintures murales de Tours au Ve et au VIe siècle." *Bulletin Monumental* 114 (1956): 153–79.

Scarry, Elaine. *The Body in Pain: The Making and Unmaking of the World.* New York, 1985.

Schaff, P., ed. *Saint Augustine.* A Select Library of the Nicene and Post-Nicene Fathers 6. New York, 1888.

Schapiro, Meyer. "The Religious Meaning of the Ruthwell Cross." *Art Bulletin* 26 (1944): 232–45.

———. *Words and Pictures: On the Literal and Symbolic in the Illustration of a Text*. The Hague, 1973.

Scheibelreiter, George. "Der frühfränkische Episkopat: Bild and Wirklichkeit." *Frühmittelalterliche Studien* 17 (1983): 131–47.

Schiller, Gertrud. *Iconography of Christian Art*. 2 vols. London, 1972.

Schmidt-Chazan, M. "La chronique de Sigebert de Gembloux: Succès français d'une oeuvre lotharingienne." *Cahiers lorrains* (1990): 1–26.

Schmitt, Jean-Claude. "L'Occident, Nicée II et les images du VIIIème au XIIIème siècle." In *Nicée II, 787–1987: Douze siècles d'images religeuses,* edited by F. Boessflug and N. Lossky, 271–301. Paris, 1987.

———. *La Raison des gestes dans L'Occident médiéval*. Paris, 1990.

Schnitzler, Hermann. "Ein frühottonisches Fuldaer Kunstwerk des Essener Munsterschatzes." In *Studien zur Buchmalerei und Goldschmiedekunst des Mittelalters: Festschrift für Karl Hermann Usener zum 60. Geburtstag am 19. August 1965,* edited by Frieda Dettweiler. Marburg, 1967.

———. *Rheinische Schatzkammer: Die Romanik*. Dusseldorf, 1959.

Schrade, Hubert. *Die Vita des Heiligen Liudger und ihre Bilder*. Mitteilungen des Vereins für Geschichte und Altertumskunde Westfalens des Landesmuseums für Kunst und Kulturgeschichte des Landeskonservators von Westfalen-Lippe, Sonderheft 14. Münster, 1960.

Schramm, Percy Ernst. *A History of the English Coronation*. Oxford, 1937.

Schulenburg, Jane Tibbetts. *Forgetful of Their Sex: Female Sanctity and Society, ca. 500–1100*. Chicago, 1998.

———. "Strict Active Enclosure and Its Effects on the Female Monastic Experience (500–1100)." In *Distant Echoes: Medieval Religious Women,* edited by John A. Nichols and Lilian Thomas Shank, 51–86. Kalamazoo, Mich., 1984.

Ševčenko, Ihor. "The Illuminators of the Menologium of Basil II." *Dumbarton Oaks Papers* 16 (1962): 245–76.

Ševčenko, Nancy P. "Cycles of the Life of St. Nicholas in Byzantine Art." Ph.D. dissertation, Columbia University, New York, 1973.

———. *The Life of St. Nicholas in Byzantine Art*. Centro studi bizantini Bari, Monografie, 1. Turin, 1983.

Sheingorn, Pamela. "'And flights of angels sing thee to thy rest': The Soul's Conveyance to the Afterlife in the Middle Ages." In *Art into Life: Collected Papers from the Kresge Art Museum Medieval Symposia,* edited by Carol Fisher and Kathleen Scott, 155–82. East Lansing, Mich., 1995.

———. "The Te Deum Altarpiece and the Iconography of Praise." In *Early Tudor England: Proceedings of the 1987 Harlaxton Symposium,* edited by Daniel Williams, 171–82. Woodbridge, 1989.

———. "'The Wise Mother': The Image of St. Anne Teaching the Virgin Mary." *Gesta* 32 (1993): 69–80.

———, ed. *The Book of Sainte Foy*. Philadelphia, 1995.

Silvestre, Hubert. "Aperçu sur les commentaires carolingiens de Prudence." *Sacris Erudiri* 9 (1957): 50–74.

Sinding-Larsen, S. "Some Observations on Liturgical Imagery of the Twelfth Century." *Acta Archaeologica Institum Romanus Norvegia* 8 (1978): 193–212.

Sitwell, Gerald, ed. and trans. "Life of St. Gerald of Aurillac." In *St. Odo of Cluny: Being the Life of St. Odo of Cluny.* The Makers of Christendom. New York, 1958.

Skeat, W. W., ed. *Aelfric's Lives of the Saints.* Early English Text Society 2. London, 1900.

Skinner, Mary. "Benedictine Life for Women in Central France, 850–1100: A Feminist Revival." In *Distant Echoes: Medieval Religious Women,* edited by John A. Nichols and Lilian Thomas Shank, 87–114. Kalamazoo, Mich., 1984.

Smith, Julia M. H. "The Problem of Female Sanctity in Carolingian Europe c. 780–920." *Past and Present* 146 (1995): 3–37.

Smits van Waesberghe, J. "Neue Kompositionen des Johannes von Metz (um 975), Hucbalds von St. Amand and Sigeberts von Gembloux?" In *Speculum Musicae Artis: Festgabe für Heinrich Husmann zum 60. Geburtstag am 16. Dezember 1968,* 285–303. Munich, 1970.

Solterer, Helen. "Seeing, Hearing, Tasting Woman: Medieval Senses of Reading." *Comparative Literature* 46, no. 2 (1994): 129–45.

Sot, Michel. "La Fonction du couple saint évêque/saint moine dans la mémoire de l'Église de Reims au Xe siècle." In *Les Fonctions des saints dans le monde occidental (IIIe–XIIIe siècle),* 225–40. Collection de l'École française de Rome 149. Rome, 1991.

Speyer, W. "Die Euphemia-Rede des Asterius von Amaseia: Ein Missionschrift für gebildete Heiden." *Jahrbuch für Antike und Christentum* 14 (1971): 39–47.

van't Spijker, Ineke. "Family Ties: Mothers and Virgins in the Ninth Century." In *Sanctity and Motherhood: Essays on Holy Mothers in the Middle Ages,* edited by Anneke B. Mulder-Bakker, 165–90. New York, 1995.

Stanbury, Sarah. "Feminist Masterplots: The Gaze on the Body of *Pearl's* Dead Girl." In *Feminist Approaches to the Body in Medieval Literature,* edited by Linda Lomperis and Sarah Stanbury, 142–67. Philadelphia, 1993.

Steinberg, Leo. *The Sexuality of Christ in Renaissance Art and in Modern Oblivion.* New York, 1983.

Steiner, Ruth, and John Caldwell. "Te Deum." In *The New Grove Dictionary of Music and Musicians,* edited by S. Sadie, 18:641–44. London, 1980.

Stettiner, Richard. *Die illustrierten Prudentiushandschriften, Tafelband, Berlin 1905.* Berlin, 1905.

Straw, Carole. *Gregory the Great: Perfection in Imperfection.* Berkeley, 1988.

Strayer, Joseph R., ed. *Dictionary of the Middle Ages.* 13 vols. New York, 1982–88.

Sulpicius Severus. "Life of Martin." In *Sulpicius Severus.* Fathers of the Church. A New Translation. New York, 1949.

———. "The Life of Saint Martin of Tours." In *Soldiers of Christ: Saints and Saint's Lives from Late Antiquity and the Early Middle Ages,* edited by Thomas F. X. Noble and Thomas Head, 1–29. University Park, Pa., 1995.

Summers, David. "Conditions and Conventions: On the Disanalogy of Art and Language." In *The Language of Art History,* edited by Salim Kemal and Ivan Gaskell, 181–212. Cambridge, 1991.

Sumption, Jonathan. *Pilgrimage: An Image of Medieval Religion.* Totowa, N.J., 1975.

Svoboda, Rosemary Argent. "The Illustration of the Life of St. Omer (Saint-Omer, Bibliothèque municipale, ms. 698)." Ph.D. dissertation, University of Minnesota, 1983.

Sykes, S. W. "The Role of Story in the Christian Religion: An Hypothesis." *Journal of Literature and Theology* 1 (1987): 19–26.

Taburet-Delahaye, Elisabeth, and Barbara Drake Boehm, eds. *L'Oeuvre de Limoges: Émaux limousins du moyen âge.* Paris, 1995.

Talbot, C. H. "Willibald's 'Life of Boniface.'" In *The Anglo-Saxon Missionaries in Germany,* edited by C. H. Talbot. The Makers of Christendom. London, 1954.

Tertullian. *Apologetic and Practical Treatises.* A Library of Fathers of the Holy Catholic Church Anterior to the Division of East and West 10. Oxford, 1842.

Thomas, Marcel. "L'Iconographie de Saint Louis dans les Heures de Jeanne de Navarre." In *Septième centenaire de la mort de Saint Louis: Actes des colloques de Royaumont et de Paris (21–27 mai 1970),* 209–31. Paris, 1976.

Thomson, H. J., ed. and trans. *Prudentius.* 2 vols. Loeb Classical Library. London, 1949.

Thomson, R. M. "Early Romanesque Book Illumination in England: The Dates of the Pierpont Morgan 'Vita Sancti Edmundi' and the Bury Bible." *Viator* 2 (1971): 211–25.

———. *Manuscripts from St Albans Abbey, 1066–1235.* Woodbridge, Suffolk, 1982.

———. "A Twelfth-Century Letter from Bury St. Edmunds Abbey." *Revue Bénédictine* 82 (1972): 87–97.

Tompkins, Jane P., ed. *Reader-Response Criticism: From Formalism to Post Structuralism.* Baltimore, 1980.

Torelli, Mario. *Typology and Structure of Roman Historical Reliefs.* Ann Arbor, 1982.

Toynbee, Jocelyn, and John Ward Perkins. *The Shrine of St. Peter and the Vatican Excavations.* New York, 1958.

Trexler, Richard C. *The Christian at Prayer: An Illustrated Prayer Manual.* Medieval and Renaissance Texts and Studies. Binghamton, N.Y., 1987.

Turner, Victor, and Edith Turner. *Image and Pilgrimage in Christian Culture: Anthropological Perspectives.* New York, 1978.

Vance, Eugene. "Chaucer's Pardoner: Relics, Discourse, and Frames of Propriety." *New Literary History* 20 (1989): 738 ff.

———. *Mervelous Signals: Poetics and Sign Theory in the Middle Ages.* Lincoln, Neb., 1986.

Van Dam, Raymond. "Images of Saint Martin in Late Roman and Early Merovingian Gaul." *Viator* 19 (1988): 1–29.

———. *Leadership and Community in Late Antique Gaul.* Berkeley, 1985.

———. *Saints and Their Miracles in Late Antique Gaul.* Princeton, N.J., 1993.

———, ed. *Gregory of Tours: Glory of the Confessors.* Philadelphia, 1988.

———, ed. *Gregory of Tours: Glory of the Martyrs.* Philadelphia, 1989.

Van Uytfanghe, Marc. "L'Essor du culte des saints et la question de l'eschatologie." In *Les Fonctions des saints dans le monde occidental (IIIe–XIIIe siècle),* 91–107. Collection de l'École française de Rome 149. Rome, 1991.

———. "L'Hagiographie: Un 'genre' chrétien ou antique tardif ?" *Analecta Bollandiana* 111 (1993): 135–88.

———. "Scepticisme doctrinal au seuil du moyen âge? Les objections du diacre Pierre dans les

Dialogues de Grégoire le Grand." In *Grégoire le Grand: Chantilly, Centre culturel les Fontaines, 15–19 septembre 1982,* edited by J. Fontaine, R. Gillet, and S. Pellistrandi, 315–26. Paris, 1986.

Vauchez, André. *The Laity in the Middle Ages: Religious Beliefs and Devotional Practices.* Notre Dame, Ind., 1992.

———. *Sainthood in the Later Middle Ages.* Cambridge, 1997.

Vaughan, Richard, ed. *Chronicles of Matthew Paris: Monastic Life in the Thirteenth Century.* 2d ed. New York, 1986.

———. *Matthew Paris.* Cambridge, 1958.

Verdon, Timonthy. "Introduction." In *Monasticism and the Arts,* edited by Timonthy Verdon. Syracuse, N.Y., 1984.

Vikan, Gary. "Ruminations on Edible Icons: Originals and Copies in the Art of Byzantium." In *Retaining the Original: Multiple Originals, Copies, and Reproductions,* 47–59. Studies in the History of Art 20. Washington, 1989.

Vinge, Louise. *The Five Senses: Studies in a Literary Tradition.* Lund, 1975.

Vitz, Evelyn Birge. *Medieval Narrative and Modern Narratology: Subjects and Objects of Desire.* New York, 1989.

Vogel, Cyrille, and Reinhard Elze. *Le Pontifical romano-germanique du dixième siècle.* Studi e Testi 226–27. 3 vols. Vatican City, 1963–72.

Vogüé, Adalbert de. "De la crise aux résolutions: Les *Dialogues* comme histoire d'une âme." In *Grégoire le Grand: Chantilly, Centre culturel les Fontaines, 15–19 septembre 1982,* edited by J. Fontaine, R. Gillet, and S. Pellistrandi, 305–14. Paris, 1986.

———. "Grégoire le Grand, lecteur de Grégoire de Tours?" *Analecta Bollandiana* 94 (1949): 225–33.

Volbach, Wolfgang Fritz. "Gli smalti della Pala d'oro." In *Il Tesoro di San Marco,* edited by Hans R. Hahnloser, I:3–75. Florence, 1965.

Von Daum Tholl, Susan. "Life According to the Rule: A Monastic Modification of Mandatum Imagery in the Peterborough Psalter." *Gesta* 33 (1994): 151–58.

Von Simson, Otto. *Sacred Fortress: Byzantine Art and Statecraft in Ravenna.* Chicago, 1948.

Walickiego, Michala, ed. *Drzwi Gnieznienskie.* 3 vols. Warsaw, 1953.

Wallace, Kathryn Young, ed. *La Estoire de seint Aedward le Rei.* Anglo-Norman Text Society 41. London, 1983.

Walsh, Martin. "Martin of Tours: A Patron Saint of Medieval Comedy." In *Saints: Studies in Hagiography,* edited by Sandro Sticca, 283–316. Medieval and Renaissance Texts and Studies 141. Binghamton, N.Y., 1996.

Walsh, Patrick Gerald, ed. *Letters of St. Paulinus of Nola.* Ancient Christian Writers 36, 2 vols. New York, 1967.

Ward, Benedicta. *Harlots of the Desert: A Study of Repentance in Early Monastic Sources.* Cistercian Studies 106. Kalamazoo, Mich., 1987.

———. *Miracles and the Medieval Mind: Theory, Record and Event, 1000–1215.* Rev. ed. Philadelphia, 1987.

Warner, George. *The Guthlac Roll.* Oxford, 1928.

Wats, W. *Vitae Offarum.* London, 1639.

Watson, Carolyn J. "The Program of the Brescia Casket." *Gesta* 20 (1981): 285–86.

Webb, Diana. *Patrons and Defenders: The Saints in the Italian City States.* International Library of Historical Studies 4. New York, 1996.

Weinstein, Donald, and Rudolph M. Bell. *Saints and Society: The Two Worlds of Western Christendom, 1000–1700.* Chicago, 1982.

Weitzmann, Kurt. *The Icon: Holy Images, Sixth to Fourteenth Century.* New York, 1978.

Weitzmann-Fiedler, Josepha. "Zur Illustration der Margareten Legenden." *Münchner Jahrbuch der bildenden Kunst* 17 (1966): 17–48.

Wemple, Suzanne. "Female Spirituality and Mysticism in Frankish Monasteries: Radegund, Balthild and Aldegund." In *Peace Weavers,* edited by John A. Nichols and Lilian Thomas Shank, 39–53. Cistercian Studies Series 72. Kalamazoo, Mich., 1987.

Wescher, P. *Beschreibendes Verzeichnis der Miniaturen—Handschriften und Einzelblätter—des Kupferstichkabinetts der Staatlichen Museen.* Berlin, 1931.

Whatley, E. Gordon. *The Saint of London: The Life and Miracles of St. Erkenwald, Text and Translation.* Medieval and Renaissance Texts and Studies 58. Binghamton, N.Y., 1989.

White, Hayden. "The Value of Narrativity in the Representation of Reality." In *On Narrative,* edited by W. J. T. Mitchell, 1–25. Chicago, 1981.

Wickstrom, John B. "Gregory the Great's 'Life of St. Benedict' and the Illustrations of Abbot Desiderius II." *Studies in Iconography* 19 (1998): 31–74.

———. "Text and Image in the Making of a Holy Man: An Illustrated Life of Saint Maurus of Glanfeuil (MS Vat. Lat. 1202)." *Studies in Iconography* 16 (1994): 53–82.

William of Saint-Thierry. *The Works of William of St. Thierry.* IV. *The Golden Epistle.* Cistercian Fathers Series 12. Kalamazoo, Mich., 1976.

Williamson, E. W., ed. *The Letters of Osbert of Clare: Prior of Westminster.* London, 1929.

Wilson, Stephen, ed. *Saints and Their Cults: Studies in Religious Sociology, Folklore and History.* Cambridge, 1983.

Winstead, Karen. *Virgin Martyrs: Legends of Sainthood in Late Medieval England.* Ithaca, N.Y., 1997.

Winter, Irene J. "After the Battle Is Over: The Stele of the Vultures and the Beginning of Historical Narrative in the Art of the Ancient Near East." In *Pictorial Narrative in Antiquity and the Middle Ages,* edited by Herbert Leon Kessler and Marianna Shreve Simpson, 11–34. Studies in the History of Art 16. Washington, 1985.

Wogan-Browne, Jocelyn. "Chaste Bodies: Frames and Experiences." In *Framing Medieval Bodies,* edited by Miri Rubin and Sarah Kay, 24–42. Manchester, 1994.

———. "Saints' Lives and the Female Reader." *Forum for Modern Language Studies* 27 (1991): 314–32.

Wolff, Ruth. *Der heilige Franziskus in Schriften und Bildern des 13. Jahrhunderts.* Berlin, 1996.

Wolfthal, Diane. "'A Hue and a Cry': Medieval Rape Imagery and Its Transformation." *Art Bulletin* 75 (1993): 39–64.

Wood, Jeryldene. "Perceptions of Holiness in Thirteenth-Century Italian Painting: Clare of Assisi." *Art History* 14 (1991): 301–28.

———. *Women, Art and Spirituality: The Poor Clares of Early Modern Italy.* New York, 1996.

Wormald, Francis. "Some Illustrated Manuscripts of the Lives of the Saints." *Bulletin of the John Rylands Library* 35 (1952): 248–68.

Yates, Frances A. *The Art of Memory.* Chicago, 1966.

Zimdars-Swartz, Sandra. "A Confluence of Imagery: Exegesis and Christology According to Gregory the Great." In *Grégoire le Grand: Chantilly, Centre culturel les Fontaines, 15–19 septembre 1982,* edited by J. Fontaine, R. Gillet, and S. Pellistrandi, 327–35. Paris, 1986.

Zimmerman, O. J., trans. *Gregory the Great: Dialogues.* The Fathers of the Church: A New Translation. New York, 1959.

Zinn, Grover. "Sound, Silence and Word in the Spirituality of Gregory the Great." In *Grégoire le Grand: Chantilly, Centre culturel les Fontaines, 15–19 septembre 1982,* edited by J. Fontaine, R. Gillet, and S. Pellistrandi, 367–75. Paris, 1986.

INDEX

Page numbers in italics denote illustrations.
Buildings, libraries, and museums are listed under the name of the city.

Apostles, 23, 34, 42, 84, 142, 144, 153, 217, 235, 265, 276, 320, 374n. 47. *See also under* bishops

Aracle, Saint, 297, 298, 302–5, *304, 305,* 317

Aristotle, 31

Arnulf, Saint (bishop), 17, 134, 143, *144*

Arthur (king), 305

Asclepiades (Roman prefect), 66, 68, 83, 84, 144

Asterios of Amaseia, 3, 17

Aubin (Albinus), Saint, 18, 134, 153–54, *154,* 159, 335, 385n. 78

Augustine (bishop of Hippo), 3, 11, 14, 31, 35, 38, 51, 54, 68–69, 103–4, 122, 126, 128; as saint, 349n. 26; *City of God,* 11, 90; *Confessions,* 31; *De Doctrina Christiana,* 31; *De Mendacio,* 356n. 8

authentic, 15

Balthild, Saint (queen), 280, 389n. 23

Bamberg, Staatsbibliothek, MSC. Bibl. 22 (Song of Songs, Proverbs, and Daniel), *35, 36,* 358n. 41

baptism, 55–56, 142, 292, 305, 374n. 43, 395n. 46

Barbara, Saint, 93

Barthes, Roland, 48

Bartholomew (Apostle), 178, 197

Barulas, Saint, 45, 69–70, 73, 77–81, 83, *83, plate 1*

Basil of Caesarea, 13

Baudonivia, 257, 265, 341, 390nn. 46,60

beauty, 320; as divine perfection, 121–22, 127. *See also under* virgins

Beccelm, 197

Bede, Venerable, 233, 336; Life of Cuthbert, 177

Bell, Rudolph, 33, 93–94

Belting, Hans, 326

Benedict, Saint, 18, 24, 177, *177,* 179–81, *180, 186, 187,* 189, *190, 191,* 194–95, 200–203,

202, 205, 207, 208, 268, 274, *275,* 335, 401n. 2; death of, 32, *206*

Benoite, Saint, 323, 324

Berlin, Staatliche Museen, Kupferstichkabinett: 78A4 (Passion of Lucy), 97, 98, *102, 103, 107, 108, 110, 113–15, 118, 119, 123,* 216, 338–39; 78B16 (Life of Benoite), 323–24

Berlin, Staatsbibliothek, Cod. lat. theol. fol. 323 (Life of Liudger), *2, 154, 157, 160, 166, 174, 176, 189, 193,* 338

Bern, Burgerbibliothek, Cod. 264 (*Opera* of Prudentius), 18, 51, *51, 52, 53,* 61, 64, 68, *71, 74, 83, 342, plate 1*

Bernard of Angers, 12; *Book of Miracles of St. Faith,* 12, 29

Bernard of Clairvaux, 103; *Sermones super Cantica Canticorum,* 90, 121

Bessette, Lisa, 72

"Bible of the Illiterate," 48, 327

biblical citations, 320; Psalms 90, 70, 240; Psalms 115:13–17, 75–76; Eccl. 32:1, 225; Song of Songs 1:3, 103; Matt. 28:19, 143; Luke 2:42–52, 1; Luke 9:23, 34; Rom. 13:4, 211; Rom. 21:1, 90; I Cor. 3, 34; I Cor. 3:1–2, 79; I Cor. 3:10–14, 77; I Cor. 6:7, 228; I Cor. 12:12–14, 40; 2 Tim. 2:12, 257; 2 Tim. 4:7, 182; I Peter 2:5, 34; Rev. 16:10, 301

Binski, Paul, 217

bishops: acclamation of, 139; apostolic, 140, 141, 146–47, 170 (*see also* Apostles); and baptism, 149–50, 159; and building, 150–52, 166–67, 375n. 50; and care and building of community, 132–33, 150, 153, 156, 167; election of, 135–41; and geographic ties, 130–31, 167–68; and healing miracles, 153, 170; and healing of paralytics, 153–61; as judges, 164; and liturgy, 132, 145, 147–49; and the Mass, 156–57, 167; and mission, 139, 170; office of, 130–31, 149, 161, 320; and possession and

intercession, 15, 84–85, 87, 244, 250–51, 274; through pictures, 95

interpictoriality, 58, 127, 319, 321

intertextuality, 2, 208, 319, 321, 330

invention (*inventio*), 16, 310–12

investiture conflict, 136–38

Invicem, 33

Ivo of Chartres, 172

ivories, 18, 142–43, 174

Jacobus de Voragine, *Golden Legend*, 390n. 62

Jadwiga, Saint, 325

Jaeger, C. Stephen, 27, 211

James (Apostle), 385n. 78

Jauss, Hans Robert, 31, 33, 39, 43

Jeanne de Navarre, 218, 220, 225; Hours of, 225, 234, 388n. 12

Jeanne d'Evreux, 218, 227; Hours of, 234, 278

Jerome, Saint, 19

John, Brother (follower of Francis), 56, 87, 207

John, Saint, 250, 251, *251*, 360n. 89, 395nn. 44,46, 400n. 40

John of Damascus, 12, 35 1n. 17

John of Ephesus, 13

Joseph of Arimathea, 300

Julian the Hospitaller, Saint, 330

Juliana, Saint, 93

Julitta, Saint, 17

Kauffman, Martin, 234

Kemp, Wolfgang, 328–29

Kempten (monastery), 323

Kessler, Herbert, 48

Kilian of Würzburg, Saint, 18, 22–23, 62, 80, 133, 136–41, *137, 138, 142,* 147–50, *148,* *156, 158, 167, 168, 169, 338, plate 4*

kings: and *adventus,* 224, 265; anointing of, with chrism, 220, 222, 224; and charity, 320, 321; childhood of, 218; and chivalry,

217, 231, 236, 254, 285; and clerical advisors, 237, 253, 385n. 80; coronation of, 217, 218–24, 235, 250, 253, 384n. 52; and duties of office, 210, 225–27, 240, 246, 253, 317; and genealogy, 218; and healing miracles, 227, 249, 393n. 25; and mercy, 321; and nation, 252, 383n. 29; and power, 233, 244, 246, 252, 254, 321; and regalia, 222, 224, 240, 252, 385n. 83, 387n. 98; sacrality of, 210, 254; and taxation, 231; and violence, 231, 233, 237. *See also* knight / *miles;* queens

kings and nobles, and court, 214

kings and nobles as saints: marriage, 215; monastic qualities, 210–13; sacrifice, 210, 216

kingship, 46

"King's touch," 249

knight / *miles,* 211, 303–4; chivalry of, 303; initiation of, 303

Konrad II of Hildesheim (bishop), 276

Lacaze, Charlotte, 28, 323

Lambeth, 309–10

Landes, Richard, 141

Last Judgment, 103

Last Rite, 205

Last Supper, 188

Lawrence, Saint, 17, *63*

legendaries, 5, 92, *100*

Letaldus of Micy, 5–6, 33; *Vita s. Martini Vertavensis,* 5

Lewis, Suzanne, 40, 285, 296

libelli, 18–19, 22, 24–25, 27–28, 61, 97, 131, 214, 285, 333, 354n. 93, 355n. 98; illustrated, 19; and records of documents, 174

Liber additamentorum (Matthew Paris), 283, 307, 393n. 27

Liber Pontificalis, 17

Liber sancti Jacobi, 26

370n. 76; as burning, 70, 72, 117; figurative meaning of, 70; instruments of, 87, 88; and reversal of, 72, 74; as scraping with claws, 70, 72; as whipping, 70, 72, 79, 84, 121, 240

martyr type, mixed with confessor type, 60

Mary (Virgin), 1, 15, 99, 23, *100*, 218, 324

Mathilda, Saint (queen), 257

Matthew Paris, 26, 216, 233, 282–317, 319, 321–22, 325, 328, 330, 333, 337, 385n. 66, 392nn. 23,24, 393n. 27, 396n. 66, 397n. 95; *Chronica majora*, 303–4, 309, 313, 396n. 66; *Estoire de Seint Aedward le Rei*, 217, 218, *224* (*see also under* Cambridge); *Gesta Abbatum*, 291; *Liber additamentorum*, 283, 307; *Vie de seint Auban*, 284 (*see also under* Dublin); *Vitae Offarum*, 284, 392n. 17

Maurus, Saint, 18, 179–81, *180*, 183, 185, *187*, 192, *195*, 200–205, *202*, 208, 335, 339

McNamara, Jo Ann, 255, 257, 258

Medard of Soissons, 259, 263, 264

memory, 50, 329, 331

mendicants, 128, 278, 282, 285, 293

Menologium of Basil II, 3

Merovingian hagiography, 213, 255

Metz, St. Vincent (monastery), 93

Milan, Sant'Ambrogio, Golden Altar, 17, 139, *141, 145,* 349n. 26

Millán, Saint, 18

miracles, 14, 15, 24, 35, 77, 307, 317. *See also under* bishops; kings; narrative issues; queens; saints' Lives; *topoi*

"mirror for princes," 216, 361n. 112

Mock Elegy on a Gelded Ram (Sedulius Scottus), 130

monks: and building, 381n. 76; as caretakers for relics, 129, 252, 282; and community, 188, 192, 198, 265, 267, 378n. 25, 379nn. 51,53; death of, 199–200; and eremitic life, 174, 193–97; and food, 212, 379n. 38; initiation of, 173–

78, 199, 259, 263–64, 278; and monastic quality of Lives, 172–73, 178–79; and oblation, 174; and resistance to sins of the flesh, 194, 380nn. 54,57; and running and obedience, 182, 263, 320; and tonsure, 177, 174; and weight and measure, 186. *See also* Rule, of Saint Benedict

Monte Cassino, 177, 207

Moralia in Job (Gregory the Great), 47–48, 54

Morgan, Nigel, 392n. 24

Moses, 205, 297, 298

Munich, Bayerische Staatsbibliothek, Clm 13074 (Lives of the Apostles), 374n. 47

narrative, and genre, 317, 319, 322; breaking norms, 33; "generic dominant," 39, 42; generic expectations, 5, 32, 39, 44, 317, 322; Jauss's "horizon of expectations," 39, 57, 282, 320; versions, 35, 45

narrative, pictorial. *See* pictorial narrative

narrative audiences, 4, 30, 79, 87–88, 149, 170, 254, 313–15, 319; court, 304, 308, 317, 394n. 31; gendered, 97, 126; lay, 327; monastic 97, 104, 120, 280

narrative construction, 30, 57, 80–81, 131, 253, 256, 317, 377n. 4, 400n. 33; frames, 44–45, 51, 67, 73, 81, 104, 287, 321–22, 360n. 89, 400n. 40; incoherence, 329; juxtaposition, 42–43, 360n. 78, repetition, 40–41, 359n. 68; reversal, 43, 320; rhetoric, 31

narrative issues: authenticity, 307–9, 317, 326; context, 349n. 24; conversion through narrative, 13, 30, 32, 36, 77, 78, 89, 287, 291–92, 317, 331; didactic possibilities, 358n. 46; emotion, 30, 79, 87–88, 103, 323, 326, 361n. 109; emotional effect, 36–38, 281, 292; exempla, 31, 67, 69, 117, 126, 203; fear or terror, 32, 69; function of miracles, 14; humor, 33, 130; iconicity, 95, 171; ideology, 9, 171; "Life

narrative issues *(continued)*
of the Saints," 34, 39; reception, 5, 17, 94, 103, 301, 329, 357n. 21, 370n. 76, 397n. 99; reception as challenge to viewer, 120–21, 122, 127; selection of scenes, 46; time, 36, 46–47, 360n. 95, 361n. 99; truth, 30, 31, 32, 49, 66, 68–69, 307; verbal versus pictorial, 45–46. *See also* gesture; pictorial narrative; *topoi*

Nemo, 33

New York, Pierpont Morgan Library, MS M.736 (Passion of Edmund), 216, *218, 223, 232, 237, 238, 239, 241–43, 245,* 246, *247, 248,* 336–37, 354n. 88, 382nn. 22,23, *plate 6*

Nicetius of Lyons, Saint, 164

Nicholas I (pope), 351n. 18

Nichols, Stephen, 30, 39, 43

Nie, Gabrielle de, 50

nobles. *See* kings and nobles

Nothelfer, 93

Notker, 257

oblation, 176

Odo of Cluny, Life of Gerald of Aurillac, 209, 211–13, 227, 230

Offa (king), 287, 310, *311, 312,* 313, *315, 316,* 395n. 38, 397n. 95

Olybrius (prefect), 121

Omer (Audomarus), Saint, 6, 8, *8,* 18, *20, 21,* 25, 134–35, 150, *151,* 153, 159, 164, *165,* 167, 184, 200, *201,* 340, 349n. 27

On the Saints and Their Relics (Guibert of Nogent), 12, 36

Origen, 103

Orsini, Napoleone (cardinal), 327

Osbert of Clare, 231, 385n. 65

Oswald, Saint (king), 233

Ottonian hagiography, 133, 257, 280

Ottonian relic policy, 22–23

Oxford, University College Library, MS 165

(Life of Cuthbert), 177, 179, *181,* 184, *185, 194, 198,* 336

Pächt, Otto, *Rise of Pictorial Narrative in Twelfth-Century England,* 46, 181, 184

Padua, Arena Chapel, Life of Christ, 326

pagans, 293, 301, 303, 395n. 46; gods of, 65

Pamplona Bible, 92

Paris, Bibliothèque nationale: MS fr. 2090–2092 (fourteenth-century Life of Saint Denis), 323; MS fr. 5716 (Life of Louis by Saint-Pathus), 234, *235,* 388n. 12; MS fr. 13508 (Lives of Genevieve and Magloire), 324; MS lat. 5594 (Life of Agatha), *66, 67, 76, 116, 120,* 333; MS lat. 9428 (Drogo Sacramentary), 17, 143, *144;* MS n.a. fr. 1098 (thirteenth-century Life of St. Denis), 27, 28, 323; MS n.a. lat. 1390 (Life of Albinus), 62, 335

Paris, Musée du Louvre, Reliquary of Martial, 133, 134, *134, 135,* 140

Paris, Sainte Chapelle, 328

Paschasius (prefect), 112, 117

Passionals, 92, 126

Pastoral Care (Gregory the Great), 49

Paul, Saint, 178

Paulinus of Nola, 55, 167

Paul the Hermit, Saint, 189

Peristephanon (Prudentius), 18, 61, 70, 342

Peter, Saint (Apostle), 15, 35, 74, 123, 136, *139,* 140, *143,* 153, 170, 178, 192, 227, 249, 250–51, *251, 309, 310,* 384n. 59; tomb of, 17

Peterson, Joan, 40

Peter the Chanter, 57

Peter the Deacon (in *Dialogues*), 36–39, 43, 121, 358n. 48

phantasia, 49–50

Philostratus, *Life of Apollonius of Tyana,* 49

pictorial narrative, 327; audience, challenged, 117; burial scenes, 26; choice of representation, 48; conventions, 46–47;

conversion by means of, 55; effectiveness, 331; emotional impact, 49, 121; gestures in, 56; naturalizing action, 48; and pictorial hagiography, 348n. 12; reception, 45, 77, 79, 87, 88; religious ends, 330; scenic quality of, 50; totality effect, 47–48, 58; and "variance," 359nn. 57,73; viewer engagement, 48–49. *See also* narrative issues; saints; *topoi*

Pierre de Roissy, 330

pilgrimage, 26, 197, 212, 249, 255, 387n. 94

pilgrims, 16, 17, 26, 28, 46, 225, 233, 277

Pinnosa, Saint, 22–23

Pizarro, Joaquin, 50

Placidus (novice), 179–81, *180*, 183, 201

plagiarism, 41

Poetics (Aristotle), 31

Poitiers: Sainte-Croix (monastery), 25, 256, 259, 265, 267, 281; Sainte-Radegonde (church), 25

Poitiers, Médiathèque François-Mitterrand, MS 250, 174, 256, 259, *261, 262, 264, 266, 268, 269, 271, 273,* 341–42, 388n. 5, *plate 7*

Polycarp, Saint, 85, 87

poor, the, 227, 329

"portrayed on the heart" (imagery), 49. See also under *topoi*

prayer, 56, 57, 60, 85, 87, 92, 100, 235, 267, 270, 305; meditative, 94; prostrate, 106–9. *See also under* martyrs; saints; saints, female; saints' Lives

Primuliacum (baptistery), 55

Propp, Vladimir, 32

Prudentius, 3, 18, 23, 70, 81, 83, 84, 87; *Peristephanon,* 18, 50–51, 61, 70, 342; *Psychomachia,* 61, 156, 231, 320, 342

purification, 104, 122. *See also under* martyrs; virgins

queens: and building, 259, 270, 275; charity of, 276, 280; and conversion of spouse, 257; and costume, 258, 260, 263, 323,

389n. 34; and dynasty, 257, 280, 324; and family ties, 276; and freeing prisoners, 257, 259, 260, 270, 275; handiwork of, 258, 389n. 24; and healing miracles, 259, 265, 270; humility of, 257, 260, 276, 280, 388n. 23; and marriage, 257, 260, 277, 280; mercy of, 257, 260; power of, 263. *See also* saints, female; virgins

Quentin (Quintinus), Saint, 18, 62, 72–74, *75,* 80, 81, *82,* 84, 85, *86,* 133, 149, 341, 374n. 41, *plate 2*

Quiricus, Saint, 17

Radegund, Saint, 18, 25, 93–94, 161, 174, 179, 188, 198, 203–4, 255–57, 259–76, *261, 262, 264, 266, 269, 271, 273,* 278–81, 321, 323, 341–42, 390n. 61, *plate 7*

Ravenna, San Apollinare Nuovo, 99

reception. *See under* narrative issues; pictorial narrative

Regina, Saint, 41, 99

Reichenau, 18, 51, 61

relics, 15, 27, 28, 32, 85, 111, 236, 252, 256, 265, 267, 268, 295, 299, 310, 351n. 11, 355n. 102, 367n. 22; book as, 21; distribution of, 22; history of, 21; movement of, 167. *See also under* cross

reliquaries, 15, 18, 93, 276, 365n. 45, 367n. 22, 390n. 62; of Limoges, 24, 123–26

Remaclus, Saint, 18, 136

Remigius (Remi), Saint, 18, 222, 249, 372n. 8

Repton (abbey), 174, 195

Rictiovarus (prefect), 73

Rodolfus (monk at Metz), 97

romance texts, 28

Romanus of Antioch, Saint, 18, 22–23, 45, 61–70, *64, 68, 71,* 73–74, *74,* 77–84, *83,* 104, 144, 237, 246, 322, 342, *plate 1*; and authority to speak, 63, 81; production of speech in Life, 83; as *rhetor,* 61, 69, 81; torture of words, 70

Rome: St. Peter's, 17; San Crisogono, 181; Santa Costanza, *Traditio legis* mosaic, *139;* Santa Maria Antiqua, 17; Santa Maria in via Lata, 17; Ss. Giovanni e Paolo, 17

Rule, of Saint Benedict, 179, 182, 185–88, 192, 195, 199–200, 203–5, 207, 320, 379n. 37, 380n. 65. *See also under* monks

sacraments, 14, 74, 76–77, 124, 126, 131, 188, 191. *See under* liturgy; martyrs

St. Albans (monastery), 283, 305, 307

Saint-Bertin (Sithiu; monastery), 25, 150

Saint-Denis (monastery), 28

Sainte-Benoite d'Origny (monastery), 323

Saint-Maur-des-Fossés (monastery), 179

Saint-Omer: cathedral, Gothic tomb of saint, 21, *21;* collegiate church, 25

Saint-Omer, Bibliothèque de l'Agglomération de Saint-Omer, MS 698 (Life of Saint Omer), 8, *8,* 20, *20,* 136, *151, 165,* 179, 214, 340; MS 764 (Life of Wandrille), *215,* 342

St. Petersburg, Hermitage Museum, Valerie Reliquary, 123–26, *125*

Saint-Quentin, Manuscrit de l'Église paroissiale déposé à la Bibliothèque municipale, 62, *75, 82, 86,* 341, *plate 2*

saints: and beauty, 303; as books, 2–3, 347n. 5; cult of, 12; "dossier" of, 13–16, 19; as exempla, 213, 255, 256, 281; gender-specific qualities of, 90–93, 256–59, 279, 366n. 6, 388n. 6; Greek Lives, 23; and iconicity, 283; and imitation, 34, 54, 56–57, 89, 93, 209; and imitation of Christ, 70, 170, 178, 179, 212, 240, 244, 257, 265, 297, 298, 300; and imitation of Christ by women, 94; lay, 94, 324; Life or *vita,* 13, 97; and mortification of the body, 194, 260, 267, 324; and power, 25, 209; prayer to, 23; shrines of, 15; and signs of the body, 56–57, 282; and societal orders,

210–11; teaching function, 24; types of, 6, 9; unity of, 39; versions of Lives, 9

saints, female: as caretakers for relics, 375n. 51; catalogues of, 93, 367n. 18; cloistered, 94; family ties, 257, 279; motherly love, 281, 391n. 73; numbers of, 33, 92, 93; roles of, 93; spirituality of, 257, 268, 276; visions of, 257, 268, 274–75, 276, 323, 324, 390n. 60

saints' Lives, elements of: baptism, 42; childhood, 1, 347n. 1; food and drink as metaphor, 79, 109–12; miracles, 276, 281; miracles of resurrection, 140, 153, 268, 270, 296, 376n. 74; prayer, 56–57; preaching, 42; protection scenes, 25; violence, 209, 211–12; *virtus,* 15, 28; visions, 287

"Saracens," 298, 300, 301, 305, 395n. 46

Sauer, Christine, xii

Schmitt, Jean-Claude, 56

Scholastica, Saint, 335

scrofula, 249

Sebastian, Saint, 244

Sedulius Scottus, *Mock Elegy on a Gelded Ram,* 130

Sens, cathedral, 328

senses, 31, 103–4, 120, 309, 310–12, 362n. 134; perfected, 106, 128, 268; refinement of, 90, 91; spiritual, 103

sequences, 42–43, 326

Serenus of Marseilles, 38, 48

Sermones super Cantica Canticorum (Bernard of Clairvaux), 90

sermons, 16, 19, 319, 328–29

Seven Acts of Mercy, 227, 279, 391n. 66

Severus, 55

Sheingorn, Pamela, 29

Sigebert, Saint, 382n. 16

Sigebert of Gembloux, 97, 103, 111–12, 126, 127

"sign of the cross," 154, 159–61, 170, 204,

255, 258, 268, 375n.72. *See also* gesture:
of "blessing"

silence, 312. *See also under* martyrs

Smith, Julia, 256, 279

stained glass, 7, 319, 326, 327–31, 377n.7

Steinberg, Leo, *Sexuality of Christ in
Renaissance Art*, 270, 274

Stephen, Saint, 63

Stuttgart, Württembergische Landesbibliothek, Cod. Hist. 2.415 (Zwiefalten
Legendary), *105*

Stuttgart Passional, 92, 99, 109

stylus, as tool for drawing, 61

Suger (abbot of Saint-Denis), 19

Susanna, Saint, 93

Svoboda, Rosemary, 333

Sweyn (Danish king), 218, *220*, 231, *232, plate 5*

Synod of Arras, 54

Te Deum, 227, 311, 397nn.100,101

Tertullian, *Ad Martyres*, 73, 74

Thames, river, 309

Thecla, Saint, 71, 93, 367n.17

Thierry of Echternach, *Flores epitaphium
sanctorum*, 351n.11

Thomas à Becket, Saint, 284, 285, 392n.24

Thomas of Walsingham, 284

tituli, 62, 73, 236, 285, 287, 291, 293, 296, 301,
304, 312, 314

topoi, 1, 32, 34, 41–42, 43, 87, 100, 177; Apostolic preaching, 144; bishop leading
"blind" to "light," 55, 153–54; bishop's
reluctance to assume office, 163–64, 166;
chains fall at bishop's tomb, 164; "competitive miracles," 24–25; engraved heart,
49, 54, 55, 69, 331, 355n.4, 361n.114; faith
in God to provide, 191; fish leaps to capture, 191–92, 212, 309; hanged man saved,
164, 376n.74; knight fights without
killing, 212, 213, 214, 382n.16; *mons
immobilis,* 399n.22; mother as *Ecclesia,* 1;

protection against theft or taxation, 25;
puer senex, 1, 347n.1, 389n.27; rhinoceros,
211; saint healing with charity, 111; speaking without a tongue, 83; sweet smell of
sanctity, 311; teaching of abbot, 200–203;
vision of ascent to heaven, 274–75

torture. *See* martyrs' torture

Tours, Bibliothèque municipale, MS 1018
(Life of Martin), *162, 339*

Tours, Saint-Martin, 156; frescoes, 17, 111, *111*

Traditio legis, 136, *139*

translation (*translatio*), 14, 246

Troyes, Bibliothèque municipale, MS 2273
(Life of Maurus), 179, 183, 192, *195*, 205,
339

typological structure, 328, 329, 400n.28

typology, 39

Udalrich, Saint, 14

Unctio infirmis (Last Rite), 74, 123

Ursula, Saint, 22

Utrecht, Rijksuniversiteit, MS 32 (Utrecht
Psalter), *75*, 77, *78*

Valenciennes, Bibliothèque municipale:
MS 500 (Life of St. Amand), 401n.1; MS
501 (Life of St. Amand), 401n.1; MS 502
(Life of St. Amand), 18, *140, 146, 152*, 334,
plate 3

Valerie, Saint, 123, 124, *125*, 126, 133

Vance, Eugene, 45

Van Dam, Raymond, 62, 153

Vatican Library, Lat. 1202 (with Lives of
Benedict and Maurus), 177, *177*, 179, *180*,
183, *186, 187*, 189, *190*, 200, *202, 206, 207,
275*, 335–36, 377nn.11,17

Vauchez, André, 282, 296, 307, 327

Venice, St. Mark's, Pala d'Oro, 18

Vermondus, Saint, 324

vernacular poetry, 27, 28

Verolanum, 305

Victricius of Rouen, 11, 15, 34; *De Laude sanctorum*, 15, 59

Vie de saint Auban (Matthew Paris), 284, 286, 287

virgins: beauty of, 90; as bride of Christ, 90, 91, 101, 103, 106, 121, 124; costume of, 99; as "doubled bodies," 90, 91, 117, 126; and Eucharist, 92, 122–23, 124–26, 128; and iconicity, 95, 99, 101, 126, 128; inviolable, 91, 116; as model of sexual abstinence, 91, 366n. 4; and nudity, 91, 92, 121; perfected body of, 106, 268, 270; and purification, 90; and resistance to sexual advances, 195; and self-denial, 94; as subject of gaze, 117; threatened with prostitution, 112, 116, 120; and visions, 128, 368n. 34. *See also* martyrs, nudity; martyrs, and purification; saints, female

vision: and divine, 362n. 134; effects of, 54, 292, 294, 301, 331, 362n. 119; miraculous, 54; nature of, 49; preparation for, 104; spiritual or purified, 54–55, 294, 301, 361n. 110; and stasis and totality of sight, 47, 328, 331

visualization, 50–51, 54, 55, 58

Vita s. Martini Vertavensis (Letaldus of Micy), 5

Vitae Offarum (Matthew Paris), 284, 392n. 17

Vitalina, Saint, 132

Vitz, Evelyn, 44

Wandrille (Wandregisilus) of Fontenelle, Saint, 18, 22–23, 213–15, *215*, 233, 303, 342–43, 354n. 81

Ward, Benedicta, 29

water, as metaphor, 78–79, 249, 296–98, 301

Weinstein, Donald, 33, 93–94

Weissenau Passional, 92, 104, 204, 270–71, *272, 274*

Wenceslaus, Saint (king), 252, *253*, 343

Wendover, Roger, 283

Werden (monastery), 174

Westminster (abbey), 216, 224, 231, 250–52, 295, 309, 384n. 59, 385n. 80

White, Hayden, 29

Wickstrom, John, 201

Wilgefortis, Saint, 348n. 13

William of Saint-Thierry, *The Golden Epistle*, 103, 121

William of Trumpington (abbot of St. Albans), 291

William the Conqueror, 221

window, 287, 290, 395n. 44, 400n. 40

Wise and Foolish Virgins, 45, 101, *102, 104*, 128, 301, 320, 368n. 44

Wolfenbüttel, Herzog August Bibliothek, Cod. Guelf. II.2 Augusteus 4, 252, *253*, 343

Wormald, Francis, 19

wounds, 32, 69, 73, 74, 84, 88

Würzburg, Universitätsbibliothek, Th. q. 1a (Kiliansevangeliar), 167, *169*

DESIGN	Terry Bain
TEXT	11/15 Dante
DISPLAY	Dante Titling
COMPOSITION	Integrated Composition Systems
PRINTING AND BINDING	Friesens Corporation